PUBLICATIONS IN OPERATIONS RESEARCH SERIES
Saul I. Gass, *Editor*

FACILITIES LOCATION

MODELS & METHODS

Robert F. Love
Department of Management Science
and Information Systems
Faculty of Business
McMaster University
Hamilton, Ontario

James G. Morris
Department of Quantitative Analysis
School of Business
University of Wisconsin–Madison
Madison, Wisconsin

George O. Wesolowsky
Department of Management Science
and Information Systems
Faculty of Business
McMaster University
Hamilton, Ontario

North-Holland
New York • Amsterdam • London

230587

Elsevier Science Publishing Co., Inc.
52 Vanderbilt Avenue, New York, New York 10017

Distributors outside the United States and Canada:

Elsevier Science Publishers B.V.
P.O. Box 211, 1000 AE Amsterdam, The Netherlands

Library of Congress Cataloging-in-Publication Data
Love, Robert F.
    Facilities location.

    (Publications in operations research series; v. 7)
    Bibliography: p.
    Includes index.
    1. Industry – Location – Mathematical models.
I. Morris, J.G. (James G.)   II. Wesolowsky, George O.
III. Title.   IV. Series.
HD58.L68   1988   338.6'042'0724   86-748
ISBN 0-444-01031-9

Composition by Impressions, Inc., Madison, Wisconsin.

Current printing (last digit):
10 9 8 7 6 5 4 3 2 1

Manufactured in the United States of America

To Our Parents

Contents

Preface

Soon after arriving (in Hong Kong) in 1978, the Citibank vice president moved to a new office building. To please his office staff he followed local custom and hired a geomancer called a fung shui man to analyze the office's omens.

The fung shui man toured the office . . . (and then gave the vice president) the bad news. Great harm would befall him unless he installed an aquarium with six black fish and put his desk in an inconvenient spot near his office door. Despite his staff's concern, Mr. Russell ignored the warning.

Within days Mr. Russell developed a painful back problem . . . while in the hospital, his secretary installed the fish tank and rearranged the furniture. Today, Mr. Russell sits by the door, near the six fish. He says his health is better than ever before. Business has boomed. . . .

Fung shui, which literally means wind and water, is based on a simple concept. It holds that if buildings, furniture, roads, and other man-made objects are placed in harmony with nature, they can bring good fortune. If not, they can wreak disaster.*

Certain facility location decisions will be dictated by overriding considerations. The successful analyst recognizes situations wherein analysis based on mathematical models is of little potential benefit (see Woolsey [1986]). This book addresses the remaining cases. We have written this book to provide a cohesive account of models and methods of analysis that might support decision making when:

a. answering the question of *where* is an integral part of a study;

---

*From *The Wall Street Journal*, December 19, 1983, p. 1.

b. the harmony sought with nature can be expressed through constraints; and

c. the good fortune sought can be adequately quantified through an objective function.

This task was undertaken in response to encouragement by Saul Gass, Editor of the Publications in Operations Research Series under the auspices of the Operations Research Society of America. Our mandate was to produce a state-of-the-art book in the field of facilities location. The hallmark of operations research is the use of models. This explains our concentration on problem formulation, model construction, and solution techniques for locating objects in a rational manner.

With their optimization viewpoint, location-allocation models are of interest to many disciplines including economics, engineering, geography, and management. However, from the seventeenth century to the middle of the twentieth century location models were developed mainly by mathematicians. Moreover, until the 1960s, a decade which coincided with a great increase in the availability of digital computers, there did not exist a unified field of study called facilities location. The simultaneous introduction of computers along with an increased emphasis on using quantitative methods in most traditional fields has coincided with a veritable explosion of research and publications on the subject.

The field seems to have developed three main topic areas. The first and oldest category contains the continuous models which allow facility locations to be anywhere on the plane or subset of the plane. The second type has arisen out of modern practice and stems from the application of mathematical programming to solving location-allocation problems. These are known as discrete models; the possible locations are specified in advance and are finite in number. The third type of location models are those which utilize graph and network theory. This book is concerned only with the first two categories since we have emphasized these in our own research. The reader interested in the third type is referred to the books by Handler and Mirchandani (1979) and Larson and Odoni (1981). Finally, we omit discussion of evaluating multiple objective impacts since the book by Keeney (1980) nicely addresses this issue in the context of siting facilities.

The material in this book has its origins in graduate seminars on location-allocation organized in the late 1960s by Robert Love at the University of Wisconsin at Madison. The growth of interest in the subject in the 1970s was reflected in the first U.S. conference on facilities location being held at St. Olaf College in the summer of 1977. This event was organized by Alan Goldman and was sponsored by the National Science Foundation and the American Mathematical Association. The first international conference was organized by Michael Goodchild and the late

Jonathan Halpern in 1978 and was held at Banff, Alberta. A second conference was held at Copenhagen in the summer of 1981 and was organized by Soren Jacobsen, Jakob Krarup, Oli Madsen, and Peter Pruzan. A third international conference, organized by a steering committee chaired by Jeffrey Osleeb and Samuel Ratick, was held in 1984 in Boston, and a fourth conference was held in Belgium in 1987; it was planned by a committee chaired by François Louveaux.

In order to completely understand the material in this book the reader should have studied differential and integral calculus, linear and nonlinear programming, and should have a rudimentary knowledge of probability theory. We have attempted to augment the material where possible with practical examples, typically abstracted from actual studies. It is intended that the scope and coverage of material will be broad enough to provide material for a rigorous senior level course or graduate seminar. To this end exercises are appended to the chapters. Mathematical appendix notes contain material of interest to those readers who wish to consider derivations. The chapters have annotated bibliographies which cite recent articles, review articles, and classical articles. These connections to the research literature are intended to overcome some of the inherent bias toward our own research. Continued growth of the literature can be followed in such journals as *European Journal of Operational Research, Geographical Analysis, IIE Transactions, INFOR, International Abstracts in Operations Research, Journal of the Operational Research Society, Journal of Regional Science, Management Science, Naval Research Logistics, Operations Research, Regional Science and Urban Economics,* and *Transportation Science.*

OUTLINE OF THE BOOK

Chapter 1 contains a preview of coming attractions and introduces the basic elements of a location model. Chapter 2 elaborates on the basic single-facility model using Euclidean, rectangular, and ℓ_p distances. Chapter 3 indicates some of the variations on the basic model, that is, location on the sphere, linear facility location, and probabilistic and dynamic models. Chapter 4 considers the case of locating several new facilities when flows between facilities are known. Dual models are considered in Chapter 5. This chapter involves more analysis than most other chapters and the material is of specialized interest. Except for the preamble to Property 7.4 in Chapter 7, a knowledge of duality is not a prerequisite for reading Chapters 6 through 10.

Chapter 6 introduces location under the minimax criterion, an alternative to the minisum objectives of previous models. The location-allocation problem is treated in Chapter 7. Here the assignments of flows to the new facilities are to be determined simultaneously with the locations of those facilities. These issues are further addressed in Chapter 8 wherein the set of possible locations for the new facilities is finite. The analysis proceeds from locating a minimal number of facilities to satisfy coverage constraints to designing one-stage, and then two-stage, distribution systems. These are the aforementioned discrete models of location.

Chapter 9 is concerned with the layout of facilities with known space requirements and known interfacility flow, in order to minimize transportation costs. In Chapter 10 the foundation is established for using mathematical distance functions to model actual travel distances in location models. Though this is the final chapter, it is an important support for the basic model of Chapter 1 and the various elaborations discussed through Chapter 7.

ACKNOWLEDGMENTS

The first outline for the book was conceived during a beautiful winter week in February 1976 at the Love farm house in Southern Ontario. Since then the work has been influenced by many individuals including Paul Dowling, Zvi Drezner, Henrik Juel, Svend Kraemer, Chuin Shen, William Verdini, and Jsun Wong. We express our appreciation to the two anonymous reviewers whose suggestions led to substantial improvements over the original version of the book. We thank the many students at McMaster, Waterloo, and Wisconsin whose suggestions led to improvements on the earlier drafts that evolved into this final work. And we especially thank Kathy McCord at Wisconsin for her careful typing and cheerful manner as revisions seemed unending. We also acknowledge the continued commitment on the part of the Elsevier Science editorial staff. Finally, we thank our wives Ingrid Love, Verelene Morris, and Sharon Wesolowsky for their support, without which little would have been accomplished.

Financial assistance has been provided not only for much of the original research upon which many of the models are based but for secretarial and other support by the following sources: The Natural Science and Engineering Research Council of Canada, The Wisconsin Alumni Research Foundation, The Graduate School of The University of Wisconsin at Madison, The Engineering Research Boards of The University of Waterloo and McMaster University, the Control Data Corporation, and the Social Science and Humanities Research Council of Canada.

Chapter 1

The Nature of Facilities Location Problems

Our analysis proceeds from an operations research framework. We will be concerned with formulating facilities location problems, constructing appropriate mathematical models, and deriving methods for solving the models. The problems considered involve the central question of *where* to locate an object (or objects) called a facility. The facility will interact with a group of other objects that have fixed locations, called existing facilities. A concept of distance between the facility to be located and the existing facilities will contribute to a performance measure. This will lead to an objective function that can be used to evaluate a trial location of the facility. The choice of locations may be restricted.

Consider the location of a regional warehouse for an electrical components manufacturer. Assume yearly demand for components in each of seven cities to be served by the warehouse is as given in Table 1.1. The location coordinates in the table are in centimeters measured from the left and bottom borders of the map shown in Figure 1.1. The facility to be located is the regional warehouse, and the existing facilities are the seven cities. The interactions stem from shipments of components from the warehouse to the cities. The performance criterion might be total annual pound-miles arrived at by calculating W where:

$$W = \sum_{\text{(all cities)}} \text{(total annual shipments from warehouse to city)} \times \text{(distance from warehouse to city)}.$$

Typically, demand is assumed to be fixed and cost is assumed to be proportional to distance. Thus, to maximize profit is to minimize W.

Perhaps the facility is a storage area on a factory floor. The existing facilities would correspond to the existing departments that will use the storage. If travel is via forklift trucks, a typical performance criterion

1

Table 1.1   Yearly Electric Component Demand.

City	Location	Demand (pounds)
Minneapolis-St. Paul	(2,43)	4,100,000
La Crosse	(19,27)	365,000
Wausau	(34,42)	520,000
Madison	(37,17)	2,200,000
Green Bay	(50,36)	495,000
Milwaukee	(51,16)	1,965,000
Chicago	(52,3)	2,732,000

would be the total daily travel distance of the forklift trucks. The objective would be to locate the storage area to minimize this total daily forklift truck travel, thus reducing transportation cost and traffic congestion in the aisles of the factory. In another instance, the facility is an electronic component in a wiring circuit. The objective function relates the location of the component to the total cost of wires or other conducting material connecting the component to other elements in the wiring system. These are examples of *single-facility* location problems.

A *multi-facility* location problem arises when there are two or more facilities to be located simultaneously, each interacting with the existing facilities and with each other. An example would be the location of two or more new departments in a manufacturing plant with flows of product taking place between each of the new departments and any number of

Figure 1.1   Locations of Cities to Be Served by a Regional Warehouse.

the existing departments, as well as between the new departments themselves.

In the general multi-facility case, the amount of flow between the existing facilities and the new facilities may not be known before locations have been determined. Suppose each existing facility has some given required amount of flow, perhaps pounds of product demanded. When the locations of several new facilities are to be determined simultaneously with the allocation of flow between each new facility and the existing facilities, the problem is referred to as a *location-allocation* problem. The storage example would be a location-allocation problem if it was required to locate two new storage areas to satisfy the known storage requirements of the existing departments, and allocations of storage were to be determined as part of the analysis. The usual aim of a facilities location study is to plan for the addition of new facilities to an existing structure, to rearrange an existing layout, or to plan a completely new system. In many cases a location-allocation model is necessary.

The possible sites for the new facilities may be a *finite* set of points (see Chapter 8) in two- or three-dimensional space such as cities for warehouse location problems or offices in an office building. The models for this type of problem use actual distances between points. The new facility sites may also be *continuous* subsets of two- or three-dimensional space (see Chapter 7). Here the distances are functions of the coordinates of the points. Often the continuous set models are used to *generate* candidate sites for *selection* by the finite set models.

A continuous set model is appropriate for the large-farm water-supply problem (Exercise 7.4). The existing facilities are points of end use for the water, such as livestock barns, irrigation systems, or houses. The new facilities are the deep wells to be drilled. If a new system is to be designed, the relevant questions are: How many wells should there be? Where should they be located? Which subset of users should each well serve? An extreme design is to locate a well at each user location. In this case, piping costs are minimized but the drilling cost may be prohibitive. Another configuration is to have one large well. A single well minimizes drilling costs, but piping and pumping costs may be prohibitive. Using one well would entail solving a single-facility location problem. When two wells are considered, drilling costs are increased, but piping and pumping costs are reduced. The allocation question is thus introduced. Where should the two wells be located and to which set of users should each one be connected? If the two-well problem can be solved, then a three-well problem can be considered, and so on, until the most economical number of wells has been found.

Variants of such basic facility location problems are often encountered. One of these is the location of emergency service facilities such as ambulance bases and fire stations. Here it may be desirable to minimize the maximum distance from the new facility to any of the points serviced. These problems, called *minimax* problems, require different solution methods from the models described thus far. It may be necessary to consider the effect on optimal locations of new facilities over future periods during which the interfacility flows may change or the number or location of the fixed points may vary. Information about the future will only be "known" in the form of probabilities. Several dynamic and probabilistic location models have been developed to support the necessary analysis.

For most location models, there exists a corresponding dual model that can be solved independently to arrive at answers identical to the primal location model. As in the case of linear programming, these duals are pure in the sense that they do not incorporate any of the primal variables in their structure. The duals provide alternative computational possibilities and give useful insights into the theory of location.

The importance of location analysis has been growing rapidly over the last decade. This is due to increasing transportation costs and recent developments of management science techniques that enable optimal solutions of complex, realistic location models to be computed. Heretofore, heuristic rules were often adopted to remove the locational aspect of a study. Optimization techniques can indicate the flaws in such rules. For example, let us suppose that a warehouse is to be located that will supply two retail outlets that are located on a single route, as shown in Figure 1.2. We have chosen an arbitrary point along the route to be the origin and have given the outlet locations as $a_1 = 10$ miles, and $a_2 = 30$ miles. Suppose that to supply outlet 1 requires $w_1 = 20$ truck trips per month, whereas the monthly requirement at outlet 2 is $w_2 = 10$ truck trips. Our problem is to locate the warehouse to minimize the total truck travel distance which, in turn, yields the lowest shipping cost.

An intuitive rule that has been used in practice is the center-of-gravity method. This method computes the warehouse location x^o according to the following weighted average formula:

$$x^o = \frac{\sum_{j=1}^{n} w_j a_j}{\sum_{j=1}^{n} w_j},$$

which for the example at hand yields

$$x^o = \frac{20(10) + 10(30)}{20 + 10} = 16.67.$$

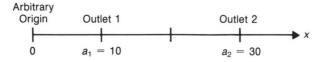

Figure 1.2 Location of Two Retail Outlets.

The total truck travel distance for this solution is $W(16.67) = 20(16.67 - 10) + 10(30 - 16.67) = 266.7$ miles. However, the optimal location, found using techniques described in Chapter 2, is $x^* = 10$, for which the total truck travel distance is $W(10) = 20(10 - 10) + 10(30 - 10) = 200$ miles. (The center-of-gravity method gives the optimal location if it is desired to minimize the sum of weights times squared distances; see Exercise 1.2).

1.1 DISTANCE MEASURES IN LOCATION PROBLEMS

A basic element in the formulation of location problems is the concept of distance. The shortest distance between two points may be a straight line, but this ideal is seldom achieved in practice. The straight-line distance between two points is an example of a relatively short distance measure. An example of a relatively long distance measure is the case of movement on plant and warehouse floors that are arranged into rectangular bays. Movement is allowed only along the aisles between the bays. Figure 1.3 illustrates two possible paths in moving from point a_1 to point a_2 in such a situation. The rectangular distance between a_1 and a_2 is given by $\ell_1(a_1,a_2) = [|0.5 - 3.25| + |1.0 - 3.0|] = 4.75$. Notice that it is not important which of the two paths is followed in moving from point a_1 to point a_2, as the rectangular distance is equal for each path.

The rectangular distance between $a_i = (a_{i1},a_{i2})$ and $a_j = (a_{j1},a_{j2})$ is given by $\ell_1(a_i,a_j) = [|a_{i1} - a_{j1}| + |a_{i2} - a_{j2}|]$. Compare this with the straight-line distance given by $\ell_2(a_i,a_j) = [(a_{i1} - a_{j1})^2 + (a_{i2} - a_{j2})^2]^{1/2}$. It can be shown that rectangular distances are always equal to or larger than the straight-line distances. In this example, the straight-line distance is $\ell_2(a_1,a_2) = [(0.5 - 3.25)^2 + (1.0 - 3.0)^2]^{1/2} = 3.4$. Rectangular distances frequently approximate those found in practice; the plant floor and city-street grid are two of the most common examples. As shown in Chapter 2, when the rectangular distance measure is adopted, the location problem quite often can be solved by back-of-the-envelope methods; however, solving straight-line distance problems usually requires a computer.

Perhaps it would seem that there are few applications for models using straight-line distances. Road travel between a pair of cities is seldom along a completely straight path. However, a good approximation of the

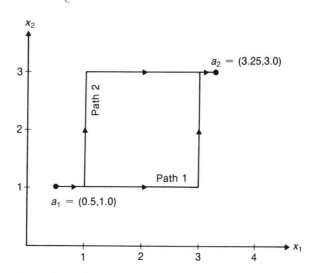

Figure 1.3   Illustration of Two Rectangular Paths Between Two Points.

average total distance between several pairs of cities in a region can often be made by using a weighted straight-line distance function. For example, within the state of Wisconsin, road distances between cities are on average about 18% larger than the straight-line distances (see Chapter 10). In the Canadian province of Ontario, they are about 30% larger, and in the U.S. as a whole, road distances between major cities are also about 18% greater than the straight-line distances. In practice, then, if we were solving a location problem in the U.S. as a whole, we could represent the distance between city i at location a_i and city j at location a_j by:

$$1.18\ell_2(a_i,a_j) = 1.18[(a_{i1} - a_{j1})^2 + (a_{i2} - a_{j2})^2]^{1/2}.$$

Rectangular and straight-line (Euclidean) distances are the special cases $p = 1$ and $p = 2$, respectively, of the ℓ_p distance between points a_i and a_j given by:

$$\ell_p(a_i,a_j) = [|a_{i1} - a_{j1}|^p + |a_{i2} - a_{j2}|^p]^{1/p}, \ 1 \leqslant p \leqslant \infty.$$

Figure 1.4 illustrates the ℓ_p distance between a_1 and a_2 of Figure 1.3 for values of p between 1 and 2. Using the ℓ_p distance function to model actual distances results in more accurate distance measures than restricting use to either of the special cases $p = 1$ or $p = 2$ alone. Techniques for empirically fitting the value of p to actual distance data are discussed in Chapter 10.

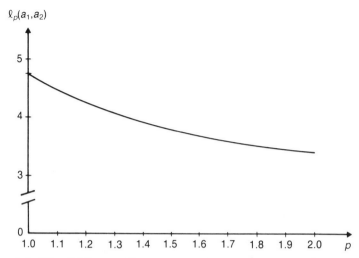

Figure 1.4 The ℓ_p Distance Between a_1 and a_2 as a Function of p.

1.2 RELEVANT COSTS

Estimating the distance between two locations on a plant floor or between two cities is a matter of using a good distance-predicting function. A second step in a location analysis is to estimate the amount of travel per unit time along the route in question in order to achieve the intended purpose. The intent is to convert these estimates into an estimated cost. If goods are to be moved along the aisles of a factory floor, then we would need to know what type of vehicle is to do the hauling. The operating cost per unit distance of the vehicle and the operator's wages per unit distance (an average vehicle speed estimate must be known) must be calculated. The question of whether to use average or marginal cost would depend on the situation. For example, if the transportation requirement of an application is small, and a vehicle and/or operator are available and underutilized, only the marginal extra cost of fuel, maintenance, and wear may be required in the calculation. In contrast, if the transportation requirements are substantial, requiring the purchase of new equipment and the hiring of extra operators, an average cost calculation may be more appropriate. The Coastal Construction Company case in Chapter 4 illustrates transportation cost calculations.

1.3 HISTORICAL PERSPECTIVE

Recorded efforts at solving location problems originated with a challenge by Fermat early in the 17th century. In his essay on maxima and minima Fermat wrote, "Let he who does not approve of my method attempt the solution of the following problem: Given three points in the plane find a fourth point such that the sum of its distances to the three given points is a minimum." Before 1640 Torricelli observed that the circles circumscribing the equilateral triangles constructed on the sides of the triangle, exterior to the triangle, intersect at the optimal point. In 1834 Heinen proved that the Torricelli property was not general; when the three points result in a triangle with one angle equal to or greater than 120°, the vertex of this angle is the minimizing point. In his *Doctrine and Application of Fluxions* (1750), Simpson generalized the problem to obtaining the point that minimizes the *weighted* sum of distances from the three given points. Weber (1909) incorporated this problem into location theory in his influential treatise on the theory of industrial location. There were two weighted material source locations and one weighted market location. An appendix by Pick treated mathematical aspects of the problem and discussed use of the Varignon frame (see Exercise 2.2) as a solution method.

The dual problem is also linked to an early history. In the *Annales de Mathmatiques Pures et Appliquées*, Vol. I (1810–11), p. 384, the problem is posed: "Given any triangle, circumscribe the largest possible equilateral triangle about it." In Vol. II (1811–12), pp. 88–93, Rochat, Vecten, Fauguier and Pilatte observe: "Thus the largest equilateral triangle circumscribing a given triangle has sides perpendicular to the lines joining the vertices of the given triangle to the point such that the sum of the distances to these vertices is a minimum. . . . One can conclude that the altitude of the largest equilateral triangle that can be circumscribed about a given triangle is equal to the sum of distances from the vertices of the given triangle to the point at which the sum of distances is a minimum." Indeed, the dual problem was stated even earlier. In *The Ladies Diary or Woman's Almanack* (1755), p. 47, a Mr. Tho. Moss requests: "In the three sides of an equiangular field stand three trees, at the distances of 10, 12 and 16 chains from one another. To find the content of the field, it being the greatest the data will admit of?" It is unlikely, however, that Mr. Moss was aware of the duality involved.

In 1857 Sylvester posed the equivalent of a location problem under the minimax criterion as he offered a one sentence problem description: "It is required to find the least circle which shall contain a given set of points in the plane." The center of the circle is the minimax location of a facility in relation to the set of points. In 1860 he gave a geometrical solution attributed to Pierce.

These early adventures could not anticipate the iterative mathematical perspective enabled by the advent of the electronic computer. This explains why almost all of the literature of facility location is quite recent. The notable exception is the paper by E. Weiszfeld, "Sur le point lequel la somme des distances de n points donnés est minimum," in the *Tôhoku Mathematics Journal* (1937), which presented an iterative procedure for locating a new facility to minimize the sum of weighted Euclidean distances to any number of existing facilities. This paper, written in French, submitted from Prague, and published in a Japanese journal in 1937, was virtually unknown until the late 1960s. For this reason the method was rediscovered by others in the late 1950s and early 1960s. The paper was 25 years ahead of the main thrust of modern facilities location research, which started to gain momentum in the early 1960s. Indeed, the single-facility location problem was described as being unsolved in *Progress in Operations Research*, Vol. II, edited by Hertz and Eddison (1964).

EXERCISES

1.1 Using a standard highway map of your locale, choose 10 pairs of cities randomly from the mileage chart. Do this by assigning each city an equal sub-interval in the (0,1) interval and reading pairs of numbers from a random number table. Then use each random number pair to choose a pair of cities. Measure the straight-line distance between the cities in each pair and, using the scale on the map, convert these distances to miles or kilometers. The actual road distance is given in the mileage chart on the map. Calculate the ratio of each actual distance to straight-line distance, and then calculate the ratio of total actual distance to total straight-line distance for the ten pairs of cities. Present your results in a table and comment on the implications for using the straight-line distance function (multiplied by a constant) to predict actual distances.

1.2 Given the problem:

$$\text{minimize } W(X) = \sum_{j=1}^{n} w_j[(x_1 - a_{j1})^2 + (x_2 - a_{j2})^2],$$

prove that the center-of-gravity location is optimal.

REFERENCE NOTES

SECTION 1.3 References to early work related to Fermat's problem and to the dual problem (including that posed by Mr. Moss) are from Kuhn (1967, 1976). Historical references for the minimax problem may be found in Elzinga and Hearn (1972a,b). Francis and Goldstein (1974) published a research bibliography containing 226 references on facilities location-allocation. In the succeeding decade, the literature increased dramatically. The bibliography by Domschke and Drexl (1985) lists some 1,800 publications on location and layout planning. Francis, McGinnis, and White (1983) and Hansen, Peeters, and Thisse (1983) provide selective literature reviews. Two early facility location texts that use an operations research framework are by Eilon, Watson-Gandy, and Christofides (1971), and Francis and White (1974).

Endre Vaszonyi Weiszfeld used his second name after immigrating to the United States during the early part of World War II. He is well known to management scientists as Andrew Vaszonyi.* He started his work while studying geometry in secondary school. An earlier paper Weiszfeld (1936) was a geometrical treatment of a four-point location problem in three-dimensional space.

*This information was given verbally to one of the authors by Professor Vaszonyi.

Chapter 2

Introduction to Single-Facility Location

This chapter treats the more common versions of the single-facility location problem. In addition to the usefulness of the models themselves, the methods of their analysis introduce many concepts and techniques that will be employed in treating the more complex models of subsequent chapters.

We will first consider location problems where both the new facility location and the existing facility locations are treated mathematically as points, and where demands and costs are known. Distances are found according to one of the distance metrics discussed in Chapter 1; for additional discussion of distances, refer to Chapter 10. All transportation costs are assumed to be proportional to distance. Finding the optimal location of the new facility is equivalent to solving the following optimization problem:

$$\underset{X}{\text{minimize }} W(X) = \sum_{j=1}^{n} w_j \ell_p(X, a_j), \qquad (2.1)$$

where

n is the number of existing facilities (or "demand points"),

w_j converts the distance between the new facility and existing facility j into cost and $w_j > 0$,

$X = (x_1, x_2)$ is the location of the new facility on the plane,

$a_j = (a_{j1}, a_{j2})$ is the location of existing facility j,

$\ell_p(X, a_j)$ is the distance between the new facility and existing facility j, and

$\ell_p(X, a_j) = (|x_1 - a_{j1}|^p + |x_2 - a_{j2}|^p)^{1/p}, \, p \geqslant 1.$

11

In the subsequent three sections, $W(X)$ is minimized for straight-line, rectangular, and general (ℓ_p) distances. What follows is a hypothetical example, created out of whole cloth, of a typical location problem.

Example 2.1   Bulk shipments of an industrial chemical arrive in 10-ton modules at a railway depot. The users of the chemical are clustered some distance from the depot and order the chemical in relatively small lots to avoid storage and inventory expenses. The supplier of the chemical is therefore considering the best location on which to construct a warehouse that would receive modules from the depot and then distribute them to the users.

Sacrificing realism for brevity, let us assume that there are only four users. Their locations and demands per year are given in Figure 2.1. Let us further assume that the cost per module per mile is $20.00 for transportation from the depot and $8.00 per ton per mile for distribution from the warehouse to the users.

Making the colossal assumption that all relevant cost structures in the system have been specified, $W(X)$ as given in problem (2.1), can now be constructed. There are five existing facilities, including the depot. The weights can be calculated as in Table 2.1. If we read the coordinates (a_{j1}, a_{j2}) of the existing facilities from Figure 2.1, and assume, for example, that $p = 1.7$, we have:

$$W(X) = 400(|x_1 - 1|^{1.7} + |x_2 - 9|^{1.7})^{1/1.7}$$
$$+ \quad 80(|x_1 - 2|^{1.7} + |x_2 - 5|^{1.7})^{1/1.7}$$
$$+ 240(|x_1 - 6|^{1.7} + |x_2 - 5|^{1.7})^{1/1.7}$$
$$+ 160(|x_1 - 7|^{1.7} + |x_2 - 10|^{1.7})^{1/1.7}$$
$$+ 220(|x_1 - 15|^{1.7} + |x_2 - 2|^{1.7})^{1/1.7}.$$

The problem is to find the location (x_1, x_2) that minimizes $W(X)$.

2.1 THE STRAIGHT-LINE DISTANCE PROBLEM

We now turn to a mathematical description of the straight-line (Euclidean) distance problem and to two of its very basic properties. To solve problem (2.1), a single new facility must be located among n existing facilities on the plane in accordance with the criterion that the sum of weighted distances be minimized. Because the straight-line distance ($p = 2$) between the new facility at (x_1, x_2) and an existing facility at (a_{j1}, a_{j2}) is:

$$\ell_2(X, a_j) = ((x_1 - a_{j1})^2 + (x_2 - a_{j2})^2)^{1/2},$$

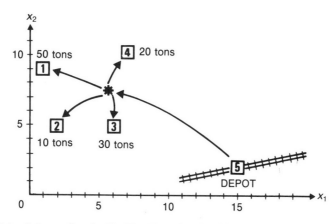

Figure 2.1   Schematic of a Facility Location Problem.

problem (2.1) becomes:

$$\text{minimize } W(X) = \sum_{j=1}^{n} w_j((x_1 - a_{j1})^2 + (x_2 - a_{j2})^2)^{1/2}. \qquad (2.2)$$
$$\phantom{\text{minimize } } X$$

   It is useful at this point in the discussion to introduce the concept of a convex function. A function $f(X)$ is said to be *convex* if the line segment between any two points, $[X^1, f(X^1)]$ and $[X^2, f(X^2)]$, on the graph of the function never lies below the graph. Formally, this means $f(X)$ is convex if

$$f[\lambda X^1 + (1 - \lambda)X^2] \leq \lambda f(X^1) + (1 - \lambda)f(X^2)$$

for all X^1 and X^2 and any $\lambda \epsilon [0,1]$. The notation X^1 and X^2 is used to denote two distinct points in the domain of f. A function $f(X)$ is said to be *strictly convex* if the above inequality holds as a strict inequality for all distinct X^1 and X^2 and any $\lambda \epsilon (0,1)$. Strict convexity of f means that the line segment lies strictly above the graph except at the two endpoints of the segment.

Table 2.1   Calculation of Weights.

j	w_j
1	$50 \times 8 = 400$
2	$10 \times 8 = 80$
3	$30 \times 8 = 240$
4	$20 \times 8 = 160$
5	$11 \times 20 = 220$

Property 2.1 [*Convexity of $w_j\ell_2(X,a_j)$*]. $w_j\ell_2(X,a_j)$ *is a convex function of X.*

The proof of convexity is given in the Appendix, mathematical note 2.1. Note that this property would not hold if the weight were negative. It can be shown (see Exercise 2.1) that the sum of convex functions is convex, and hence $W(X)$ itself is convex. This means local optima are global optima for problem (2.2), and $W(X)$ has no inflection points. With this information, we are assured that the extremal equations for $W(X)$ can produce only global optima for problem (2.2). These equations are:

$$\frac{\partial W(X)}{\partial x_k} = \sum_{j=1}^{n} \frac{w_j(x_k - a_{jk})}{\ell_2(X,a_j)} = 0 \quad \text{for } k = 1,2. \qquad (2.3)$$

One difficulty immediately presents itself. The derivatives in equation (2.3) are undefined if $\ell_2(X,a_j) = 0$. Therefore, if an optimal location for the new facility coincides with that of an existing facility, equation (2.3) cannot be used to check optimality. Fortunately, we can easily check *each* existing facility location for optimality.

Property 2.2 [*Minimum of W(X) at an existing facility location*]. $W(X)$ *is minimized at the rth existing facility location (a_{r1},a_{r2}) if, and only if:*

$$CR_r = \left[\left(\sum_{\substack{j=1 \\ \neq r}}^{n} \frac{w_j(a_{r1} - a_{j1})}{\ell_2(a_r,a_j)} \right)^2 + \left(\sum_{\substack{j=1 \\ \neq r}}^{n} \frac{w_j(a_{r2} - a_{j2})}{\ell_2(a_r,a_j)} \right)^2 \right]^{1/2} \leqslant w_r. \qquad (2.4)$$

A ready explanation for Property 2.2 is provided by the analog model in Exercise 2.2. A derivation is in the Appendix, mathematical note 2.2. There now exist many different iterative methods for finding a solution to problem (2.1). One of the oldest, as well as perhaps the simplest, follows.

In addressing the problem of minimizing $W(X)$, let us temporarily ignore the possibility that the new facility location will coincide with an existing facility location. A procedure for iterating to the optimum location can be obtained by rewriting equation (2.3) so that we have one equation for x_1 and one for x_2:

$$x_k = \frac{\displaystyle\sum_{j=1}^{n} \frac{w_j a_{jk}}{\ell_2(X,a_j)}}{\displaystyle\sum_{j=1}^{n} \frac{w_j}{\ell_2(X,a_j)}} \quad \text{for } k = 1,2. \qquad (2.5)$$

Note that x_k is not really isolated on the left-hand side in equation (2.5) because each $\ell_2(X,a_j)$ is a function of x_k. However, equation (2.5) can be used iteratively to approach (x_1^*,x_2^*), the optimum new facility location. We refer to this procedure as the Weiszfeld procedure (see Chapter 1). Let us imagine that we have just completed iteration ℓ and have obtained the location $(x_1^{(\ell)}, x_2^{(\ell)})$. We can then use equation (2.5) to find the estimate of iteration $(\ell+1)$:

$$x_k^{(\ell+1)} = \frac{\displaystyle\sum_{j=1}^{n} \frac{w_j a_{jk}}{\ell_2(X^{(\ell)}, a_j)}}{\displaystyle\sum_{j=1}^{n} \frac{w_j}{\ell_2(X^{(\ell)}, a_j)}} \quad \text{for } k = 1,2. \tag{2.6}$$

Before beginning the iterations, an initial location $(x_1^{(0)}, x_2^{(0)})$ is required. An expedient choice is the solution to the squared Euclidean distance problem, which is the same as problem (2.2) except that each distance $\ell_2(X, a_j)$ is squared. As shown in Exercise 1.2, the center-of-gravity location solves the squared Euclidean distance problem; hence, our starting point for procedure (2.6) is:

$$x_k^{(0)} = \frac{\displaystyle\sum_{j=1}^{n} w_j a_{jk}}{\displaystyle\sum_{j=1}^{n} w_j} \quad \text{for } k = 1,2. \tag{2.7}$$

The iterations will converge to an optimal location, provided that neither an iterate nor an optimal new facility location is at an existing facility location. References for convergence properties are given at the end of this chapter. Though we would expect convergence difficulties with the iterations when (x_1^*, x_2^*) coincides with an existing facility location, these difficulties do not generally materialize. When CR_r in condition (2.4) is much smaller than w_r, convergence is fairly rapid; as $\ell_2(X, a_r)$ in equation (2.5) approaches zero, computational difficulties could eventually arise. Experience shows that when condition (2.4) is near equality (whether or not it is met), convergence may be slow. It is therefore helpful to check all existing facility locations using condition (2.4) *first*. If condition (2.4) is not met, but CR_r is nearly equal to w_r at some existing facility r, iterations could be started near that point. Convergence may also be slow for certain weight structures. We are compensated by the fact that in such cases the cost "bowl" is usually shallow in the vicinity of the optimum solution.

The practical question of when to terminate the procedure can be answered by the use of a stopping criterion that employs a lower bound on the optimum value of $W(X)$. This lower bound is continually updated during the iterations. To derive this bound we need the following property.

Property 2.3 [*Dominance of the convex hull*]. *X*, an optimal solution to problem (2.1), must lie within* Ω, *the convex hull of the existing facility locations.*

The *convex hull* is defined as the smallest convex polygon that contains all the existing facility locations. A proof of Property 2.3 is the subject of Exercise 2.5b. It can be shown that the starting point defined by equation (2.7) is in the convex hull. Further, regardless of the starting point used for procedure (2.6), the next point will be in the convex hull (see Exercise 2.5a). We will now give a geometrical rationale for a stopping criterion for the Weiszfeld procedure.

To begin the discussion, recall that $W(X)$ is a convex function. This means that a plane tangent to the convex bowl-shaped graph of $W(X)$ at a given point $X^{(\ell)}$ underestimates $W(X)$ for any X. In particular, if the partial derivatives given in equation (2.3) exist, this means

$$W(X) \geqslant W(X^{(\ell)}) + \sum_{k=1}^{2} [\partial W(X^{(\ell)})/\partial x_k](x_k - x_k^{(\ell)})$$

for any X. The gradient $\nabla W(X^{(\ell)})$ is a vector with components given by the respective partial derivatives. Choosing $X = X^*$ we can write:

$$W(X^*) \geqslant W(X^{(\ell)}) + \nabla W(X^{(\ell)}) \cdot (X^* - X^{(\ell)})$$

$$(\cdot \text{ denotes scalar product})$$

$$\geqslant W(X^{(\ell)}) - |\nabla W(X^{(\ell)}) \cdot (X^* - X^{(\ell)})|$$

$$\geqslant W(X^{(\ell)}) - \|\nabla W(X^{(\ell)})\| \|X^* - X^{(\ell)}\|$$

$$(\text{since } |u \cdot v| \leqslant \|u\| \|v\|; \text{ Schwartz inequality})$$

where $\|\cdot\|$ denotes the magnitude of a vector. But X^* and $X^{(\ell)}$ are both in the convex hull Ω for $\ell \geqslant 1$. Hence $\|X^* - X^{(\ell)}\|$ cannot be greater than the straight-line distance $\sigma(X^{(\ell)})$, say, between $X^{(\ell)}$ and the point in Ω furthest away from $X^{(\ell)}$. Therefore, an upper bound on the improvement in $W(X)$ must be $\|\nabla W(X^{(\ell)})\|\sigma(X^{(\ell)})$. It is now possible to state the following property.

Property 2.4   [*Lower bound on $W(X^*)$*].

$$W(X^*) \geqslant LB^{(\ell)} = W(X^{(\ell)}) - \|\nabla W(X^{(\ell)})\|\sigma(X^{(\ell)}) \qquad (2.8)$$

where $\sigma(X^{(\ell)}) = \max_{y \in \Omega} \{\ell_2(X^{(\ell)}, y)\}$.

It is, therefore, possible to know an upper bound on further improvement in the objective function value at every iteration in the Weiszfeld procedure. A stopping criterion based on proportional suboptimality can be set using:

$$S^{(\ell)} = \frac{\|\nabla W(X^{(\ell)})\|\sigma(X^{(\ell)})}{LB^{(\ell)}}. \qquad (2.9)$$

Table 2.2 Evaluation of CR_r.

Existing Facility Location	r	CR_r	w_r
(1,1)	1	7.635	1
(1,4)	2	4.931	2
(2,2)	3	4.453	2
(4,5)	4	4.754	4

From inequality (2.8), whenever $LB^{(l)} > 0$ we have:

$$S^{(l)} \geq (W(X^{(l)}) - (W(X^*))/W(X^*).$$

Hence, if we wish to find an iterate $X^{(l)}$ with relative suboptimality bounded as $(W(X^{(l)}) - W(X^*))/W(X^*) < \epsilon$, iterations need only be continued until $S^{(l)} < \epsilon$. For example, if iterations are terminated when $S^{(l)} < 0.001$, then $W(X^{(l)})$ is within 0.1% of the minimal value $W(X^*)$. It should be mentioned that tighter lower bounds can be obtained (see the Appendix, mathematical note 2.5). This one is presented due to its geometrical simplicity.

Example 2.2 Four existing facilities are located at the points (1,1), (1,4), (2,2), and (4,5). The corresponding weights are 1, 2, 2, and 4, respectively. Values of CR_r are given in Table 2.2. Because CR_r is always greater than w_r, the optimum location of the new facility does not coincide with any of the existing facility locations. Table 2.3 shows iterations from the center-of-gravity starting point, which in this example was quite close to the optimum location. As Exercise 2.4 shows, this is not always so.

When iterations were started at (0,1000), $X^{(2)}$ was (2.557,3.669), thus demonstrating the insensitivity of the procedure to the starting point.

Table 2.3 Iterations for Example 2.2.

Iteration Number ℓ	New Facility Location	Cost	$LB^{(l)}$	$S^{(l)}$
0	(2.556,3.667)	17.646	16.407	7.55×10^{-2}
1	(2.523,3.745)	17.624	17.210	2.41×10^{-2}
2	(2.527,3.772)	17.621	17.382	1.376×10^{-2}
3	(2.536,3.785)	17.620	17.441	1.024×10^{-2}
4	(2.544,3.794)	17.619	17.481	7.934×10^{-3}
5	(2.551,3.799)	17.619	17.511	6.192×10^{-3}
6	(2.557,3.804)	17.619	17.534	4.847×10^{-3}
7	(2.560,3.807)	17.619	17.552	3.802×10^{-3}
8	(2.564,3.810)	17.619	17.566	2.987×10^{-3}
9	(2.567,3.812)	17.619	17.577	2.350×10^{-3}
10	(2.569,3.814)	17.619	17.586	1.851×10^{-3}
15	(2.576,3.818)	17.618	17.608	5.660×10^{-4}
20	(2.577,3.820)	17.618	17.615	1.742×10^{-4}
40	(2.577,3.820)	17.618	17.618	1.580×10^{-6}

Actually, as can easily be verified from a comparison of procedure (2.6) and equation (2.7), if the starting point is very far outside the convex hull, $X^{(1)}$ will be approximately the center-of-gravity solution.

2.2 THE RECTANGULAR DISTANCE PROBLEM

Rectangular distances were described in Chapter 1. In addition to being applicable in a wide variety of location problems, their use greatly simplifies many problems that are quite difficult with straight-line distances. For $p = 1$, problem (2.1) becomes:

$$\text{minimize } W(X) = \sum_{j=1}^{n} w_j(|x_1 - a_{j1}| + |x_2 - a_{j2}|). \qquad (2.10)$$

There are two properties that are useful in finding (x_1^*, x_2^*). The first will be called separability. Problem (2.10) can be rewritten:

$$\text{minimize } W(X) = W_1(x_1) + W_2(x_2) \qquad (2.11)$$

where:

$$W_1(x_1) = \sum_{j=1}^{n} w_j|x_1 - a_{j1}|,$$

$$W_2(x_2) = \sum_{j=1}^{n} w_j|x_2 - a_{j2}|.$$

Minimizing $W(X)$ is equivalent to separately finding an x_1 that minimizes $W_1(x_1)$ and an x_2 that minimizes $W_2(x_2)$. The problem now becomes:

$$\text{minimize } W_k(x_k) = \sum_{j=1}^{n} w_j|x_k - a_{jk}| \quad \text{for } k = 1,2. \qquad (2.12)$$

This problem is rather easy to solve. An analog approach is given near the end of this section (in Example 2.5) that makes the use of formulas unnecessary. However, the method of analysis that immediately follows gives mathematical conditions and relationships that will be needed in later chapters; in addition, it validates the analog approach.

We must first verify that $w_j|x_k - a_{jk}|$ is a convex function of x_k. This can be done by simply plotting the term against x_k for any $w_j > 0$ and a_{jk}. A more formal proof is the subject of Exercise 2.7. Because the sum of convex functions is convex, it follows that $W_k(x_k)$ is convex.

To facilitate analysis, a change in notation is made in problem (2.12). Let the values of a_{jk} for $j = 1,...,n$ be reordered to produce $a_{(1)k} < a_{(2)k} < a_{(3)k} < ... < a_{(n_k)k}$, and let $w_1^k,...,w_{n_k}^k$ be the corresponding positive weights.

Note that there will now be n_k coordinates, where $n_k \leq n$. The reason for this may be seen in the following example. Suppose $a_{11} = a_{31} = 4$ and $w_1 = 3$, $w_3 = 2$. We can combine the sum of terms $3|x_1 - 4| + 2|x_1 - 4|$ into the single term $5|x_1 - 4|$. We can thus create a sequence of $a_{(j)k}$'s that are strictly increasing in value. As a result, however, we may have fewer $a_{(j)k}$'s than there are a_{jk}'s.

The superscript k in w_j^k denotes ordering and consolidation in the corresponding weights. The reason is that there can now be an ordering in weights in the x_1 dimension different from that in the x_2 dimension, and we use the superscript k to distinguish these orderings.

Problem (2.12) becomes:

$$\text{minimize } W_k(x_k) = \sum_{j=1}^{n_k} w_j^k |x_k - a_{(j)k}| \quad \text{for } k = 1,2. \qquad (2.13)$$
$$x_k$$

The function $W_k(x_k)$ is now in a form convenient for calculating its derivative (see Exercise 2.8). We can write:

$$W_k'(x_k) = -\sum_{j=1}^{n_k} w_j^k \qquad \text{for } x_k < a_{(1)k} \qquad (2.14a)$$

$$W_k'(x_k) = \sum_{j=1}^{t} w_j^k - \sum_{j=t+1}^{n_k} w_j^k \qquad \text{for } a_{(t)k} < x_k < a_{(t+1)k} \qquad (2.14b)$$

$$W_k'(x_k) = \sum_{j=1}^{n_k} w_j^k \qquad \text{for } x_k > a_{(n_k)k}. \qquad (2.14c)$$

It is easy to see that the slope of $W_k(x_k)$ is made up of linear segments and changes only at points $a_{(j)k}$. To sum up, $W_k(x_k)$ is a continuous, convex, piecewise-linear function with points of discontinuity in the first derivatives occurring at the a_{jk}'s.

Before formally stating optimality conditions for minimizing $W_k(x_k)$, let us consider a numerical example to illustrate the notation and the characteristics of $W_1(x_1)$ and $W_2(x_2)$.

Example 2.3 A new facility must be located among four existing ones at $(1,1)$, $(2,4)$, $(2,3)$, and $(4,2)$. The corresponding weights are 2, 3, 1, and 2, respectively. We are about to solve the associated rectangular distance location problem graphically. Table 2.4 summarizes the data and notation. For example, with $k = 1$ in problems (2.12) and (2.13), we obtain:

$$W_1(x_1) = 2|x_1 - 1| + 3|x_1 - 2| + 1|x_1 - 2| + 2|x_1 - 4|$$

and

$$W_1(x_1) = 2|x_1 - 1| + 4|x_1 - 2| + 2|x_1 - 4|.$$

Table 2.4 Data for Example 2.3.

	Original Coordinates and Weights			Ordering in the x_1 Dimension		Ordering in the x_2 Dimension	
j	a_{j1}	a_{j2}	w_j	$a_{(j)1}$	w_j^1	$a_{(j)2}$	w_j^2
1	1	1	2	1	2	1	2
2	2	4	3	2	4	2	2
3	2	3	1	4	2	3	1
4	4	2	2			4	3

$W_1(x_1)$ and $W_2(x_2)$ are plotted in Figures 2.2(a) and 2.2(b), respectively. It is evident that $W_1(x_1)$ has a minimum value of 6 at $x_1^* = 2$, whereas the minimum value of $W_2(x_2)$ is 9 for x_2^* in the interval [2,3]. Hence, $W(X)$ has a minimum of 15 at (2,[2,3]). We can use equation (2.14) to check the slopes. For example, when $2 < x_1 < 4$, then $t = 2$ and we compute:

$$W'(x_1) = (2 + 4) - 2 = 4,$$

as can be verified in Figure 2.2(a).

Because the slope $W_k'(x_k)$ in equation (2.14) obviously increases with increasing t, the condition for a minimum to $W_k(x_k)$ to occur must be that the slope either changes from negative to positive, or changes from negative to zero at some point. In the latter case, the minimum occurs over a range of values for x_k, as in Figure 2.2(b). However, at least one point $a_{(t)k}$ must be a minimizer of $W_k(x_k)$. The following makes these claims precise.

Property 2.5 [*Conditions for a minimum to $W_k(x_k)$*]. *Suppose:*

$$\sum_{j=1}^{t-1} w_j^k - \sum_{j=t}^{n_k} w_j^k < 0 \qquad (2.15a)$$

and

$$\sum_{j=1}^{t} w_j^k - \sum_{j=t+1}^{n_k} w_j^k \geqslant 0 \qquad (2.15b)$$

are satisfied at some t^*. If condition (2.15b) is met as a strict inequality, then $x_k^* = a_{(t^*)k}$. If condition (2.15b) is met as an equality, then $x_k^* \in [a_{(t^*)k}, a_{(t^*+1).k}]$.

It is possible to express the conditions of Property 2.5 in a form more convenient for finding t^*. We can write condition (2.15a) as:

$$\sum_{j=1}^{t-1} w_j^k + \sum_{j=1}^{t-1} w_j^k - \sum_{j=1}^{n_k} w_j^k < 0,$$

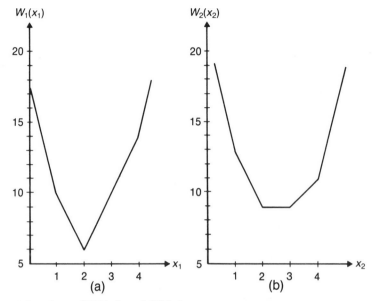

Figure 2.2 Plots of $W_1(x_1)$ and $W_2(x_2)$.

and condition (2.15b) as:

$$\sum_{j=1}^{t} w_j^k + \sum_{j=1}^{t} w_j^k - \sum_{j=1}^{t} w_j^k - \sum_{j=t+1}^{n_k} w_j^k \geqslant 0.$$

If we let:

$$C = \sum_{j=1}^{n_k} w_j^k \quad \text{for } k = 1,2,$$

then the conditions of Property 2.5 become:

$$-C + 2 \sum_{j=1}^{t-1} w_j^k < 0 \tag{2.16a}$$

$$-C + 2 \sum_{j=1}^{t} w_j^k \geqslant 0. \tag{2.16b}$$

Inequalities (2.16) now suggest a computational procedure. To $-C$ we add twice the weight of each point $a_{(t)k}$, starting from $t = 1$, until the sum first equals or exceeds zero. Note that we are merely using another expression for the slope of $W_k(x_k)$. We will then have found the optimal range or the optimal point, respectively, for x_k.

Example 2.4 We return to Example 2.3 and the data in Table 2.4 to demonstrate the use of inequalities (2.16). We first calculate:

$$C = \sum_{j=1}^{n_k} w_j^1 = 2 + 4 + 2 = 8.$$

Now, to find x_1^*, we calculate:

$$-C + 2 \sum_{j=1}^{1} w_j^1 = -8 + 4 = -4$$

$$-C + 2 \sum_{j=1}^{2} w_j^1 = -8 + 12 = 4 > 0$$

and find that condition (2.16b) is satisfied as a strict inequality. So $x_1^* = a_{(2)1} = 2$.

To find x_2^*, we calculate:

$$-C + 2 \sum_{j=1}^{1} w_j^2 = -8 + 4 = -4$$

$$-C + 2 \sum_{j=1}^{2} w_j^2 = -8 + 8 = 0$$

and find that condition (2.16b) is satisfied as an equality. So $x_2^* \epsilon [a_{(2)2}, a_{(3)2}] = [2,3]$.

But there is an easier way of solving our problem. Example 2.5 illustrates the method.

Example 2.5 We consider the same problem. Recall that there are four existing facilities at points $(1,1)$, $(2,4)$, $(2,3)$, and $(4,2)$ with weights of 2, 3, 1, and 2, respectively.

Let us imagine that the weights are "dropped" on the x_1-axis, and at the same time (in defiance of gravity) the same weights are dropped on the x_2-axis (Figure 2.3). Let us then divide the x_1-axis into two parts such that the weights are bisected. Clearly this point is at $x_1 = 2$ if we assume that weights acting on a mathematical point may be split as we wish. Similarly the weights on the x_2-axis are bisected when $2 \leqslant x_2 \leqslant 3$. As can be checked in the previous examples, these bisections produce x_1^* and x_2^*. As the reader should verify, what we have really done is to apply inequalities (2.15) or (2.16) in slightly disguised form. We can now describe the minimum to $W_k(x_k)$ as occurring at the point(s) of median weight.

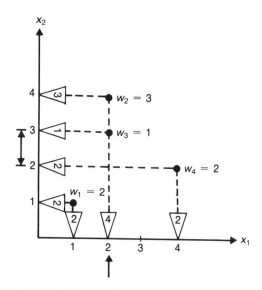

Figure 2.3 Median Weight Illustration.

2.3 THE ℓ_p DISTANCE PROBLEM

Suppose distances are modeled by the ℓ_p function. As discussed in Chapters 1 and 10, ℓ_p distances can often provide a better measure of actual travel distances than either the straight-line or rectangular distances, which, are special cases given by $p = 2$ and $p = 1$, respectively. For convenience, we repeat problem (2.1) here:

$$\underset{X}{\text{minimize }} W(X) = \sum_{j=1}^{n} w_j(|x_1 - a_{j1}|^p + |x_2 - a_{j2}|^p)^{1/p}. \qquad (2.17)$$

We first state two properties that characterize $\ell_p(X,a_j)$:

(i) $\ell_p(X,a_j)$ decreases as p increases, ie, for $X \neq a_j$, $(|x_1 - a_{j1}|^p + |x_2 - a_{j2}|^p)^{1/p} > (|x_1 - a_{j1}|^{p'} + |x_2 - a_{j2}|^{p'})^{1/p'}$, for $p < p'$,

and

(ii) as $p \to \infty$, $\ell_p(X,a_j)$ becomes the larger of $|x_1 - a_{j1}|$ and $|x_2 - a_{j2}|$.

The following property bears upon the optimization specified by problem (2.17). A proof is given in the Appendix, mathematical note 2.3.

Property 2.6 [*Convexity of $w_j\ell_p(X,a_j)$*]. $w_j\ell_p(X,a_j)$ is a convex function of X.

As each of the terms of $W(X)$ in problem (2.17) is convex, we can again use the fact that the sum of convex functions is convex to conclude that

$W(X)$ is a convex function of X. Hence, a local minimizer of $W(X)$ is also a global minimizer. As with $p = 2$, we can check to see aforehand whether the new facility would be optimally located at the site of some existing facility. The following criterion, which generalizes Property 2.2, is derived in Juel and Love (1981b).

Property 2.7 [*Minimum of W(X) at an existing facility location; ℓ_p distances*]. *W(X) is minimum at (a_{r1}, a_{r2}) if and only if:*

$$CRP_r = (|R_{r1}|^{p/(p-1)} + |R_{r2}|^{p/(p-1)})^{(p-1)/p} \leqslant w_r, \text{ for } p > 1, \quad (2.18a)$$

$$\max (|R_{r1}|, |R_{r2}|) \leqslant w_r, \text{ for } p = 1, \quad (2.18b)$$

where:

$$R_{rk} = \sum_{\substack{j=1 \\ \neq r}}^{n} \frac{w_j \, \text{sign}(a_{rk} - a_{jk})|a_{rk} - a_{jk}|^{p-1}}{(\ell_p(a_r, a_j))^{p-1}} \text{ for } k = 1,2.$$

We observe that

$$R_{rk} = \frac{\partial}{\partial x_k} \sum_{\substack{j=1 \\ \neq r}}^{n} w_j \ell_p(X, a_j)\Big|_{x_k = a_{rk}} \text{ in } (2.18a).$$

Terms on the left-hand side of inequality (2.18a) are not defined at $p = 1$. Using Property (ii) of ℓ_p distances and letting p decrease toward 1 so that $p' = p/(p-1) \to \infty$, we can easily deduce inequality (2.18b).

Example 2.6 Table 2.5 gives the parameters of the problem with $n = 5$ together with the point optimality calculations for $p = 1, 1.3, 1.5, 2$, and 5. We see that $(x_1^*, x_2^*) = (7,3)$ for $p = 1$ and $p = 1.3$; actually this point is optimal for $p \leqslant 1.385$.

It is convenient at this point to introduce a hyperbolic (see Exercise 2.11) approximation to $W(X)$ in problem (2.17). This approximation will

Table 2.5 Evaluation of CRP_r.

	Existing Facility				CRP_r		
r	Location	w_r	$p=1$	$p=1.3$	$p=1.5$	$p=2$	$p=5$
1	(1,1)	3	10.0	9.380	9.249	9.056	9.218
2	(2,6)	2	5.0	6.081	6.689	7.843	9.821
3	(4,1)	1	9.0	7.804	7.356	6.766	5.999
4	(7,3)	4	3.0	3.791	4.288	5.401	7.757
5	(8,8)	3	10.0	9.674	9.502	9.220	9.249

be especially useful in the more complex multi-facility location problem discussed in a later chapter. We replace each absolute term $|y|$ in problem (2.17) by $(y^2 + \epsilon)^{1/2}$ where ϵ is a small positive number. The approximation is always larger than the original term, but approaches the original term as $\epsilon \to 0$. Problem (2.17) is then approximated by:

$$
\begin{aligned}
\underset{X}{\text{minimize}} \; WH(X) = \sum_{j=1}^{n} & w_j(((x_1 - a_{j1})^2 + \epsilon)^{p/2} \\
& + ((x_2 - a_{j2})^2 + \epsilon)^{p/2})^{1/p}.
\end{aligned}
\tag{2.19}
$$

We first note that $WH(X)$ is strictly convex (as proved on a do-it-yourself basis in Exercise 2.12), and that all orders of derivatives are continuous at all points (as will become apparent shortly). Therefore, $WH(X)$ is a well-behaved candidate for general nonlinear descent and programming algorithms that converge to the minimizer if the function is smooth and strictly unimodal.

The question arises: If we find the location that minimizes $WH(X)$, what progress have we made in minimizing $W(X)$? We will show that we can come as close as we wish to minimizing $W(X)$ by minimizing $WH(X)$ and simply choosing small values for ϵ.

Property 2.8 [*Maximum difference between WH(X) and W(X)*].

$$
\underset{X}{\text{max}} \; \{WH(X) - W(X)\} \leq \Delta(\epsilon) = 2^{1/p} \epsilon^{1/2} (\sum_{j=1}^{n} w_j)
\tag{2.20}
$$

PROOF: It is shown in the Appendix, mathematical note 2.4, that:

$$
\begin{aligned}
(((x_1 - a_{j1})^2 + \epsilon)^{p/2} + ((x_2 - a_{j2})^2 + \epsilon)^{p/2})^{1/p} \\
- (|x_1 - a_{j1}|^p + |x_2 - a_{j2}|^p)^{1/p} \leq 2^{1/p} \epsilon^{1/2},
\end{aligned}
\tag{2.21}
$$

from which the property follows.

As the difference between $WH(X)$ and $W(X)$ never exceeds $\Delta(\epsilon)$, solving problem (2.19) will give us a solution to problem (2.17) that is at most $\Delta(\epsilon)$ from the optimum value. To see this, let X^* be a minimizer for $W(X)$ and X^{**} be the minimizer for $WH(X)$. Because $WH(X^*) - W(X^*) \leq \Delta(\epsilon)$ and $WH(X^{**}) \leq WH(X^*)$, we have $WH(X^{**}) - W(X^*) \leq \Delta(\epsilon)$. Therefore, $W(X^{**}) - W(X^*) \leq \Delta(\epsilon)$.

The Weiszfeld procedure discussed in Section 2.2 can be generalized to the ℓ_p distance case. Differentiating $WH(X)$ with respect to x_1 and x_2, setting the partial derivatives to zero, and then "isolating" x_1 and x_2 on the left-hand side (the details are requested in Exercise 2.13), we obtain:

$$
x_k^{(\ell+1)} = \frac{\displaystyle\sum_{j=1}^{n} \frac{w_j a_{jk}}{d'(X^{(\ell)},a_j)d''(x_k^{(\ell)},a_{jk})}}{\displaystyle\sum_{j=1}^{n} \frac{w_j}{d'(X^{(\ell)},a_j)d''(x_k^{(\ell)},a_{jk})}},
\tag{2.22}
$$

where

$$
d'(X,a_j) = (((x_1 - a_{j1})^2 + \epsilon)^{p/2} + ((x_2 - a_{j2})^2 + \epsilon)^{p/2})^{1-1/p}, \text{ and}
$$

$$
d''(x_k,a_{jk}) = ((x_k - a_{jk})^2 + \epsilon)^{1-p/2}.
$$

When $p = 2$ and $\epsilon = 0$, iterative procedure (2.22) is identical to procedure (2.6). Convergence is guaranteed for $1 \leqslant p \leqslant 2$, provided $\epsilon > 0$. Actually, the procedure will work well with $\epsilon = 0$. However, setting ϵ to a very small quantity (relative to the weights and computer resolution of zero) does protect one against the embarrassing possibility of dividing by zero on a computer. This occurs in procedure (2.6) when $X^{(\ell)}$ coincides with an existing facility location, or in procedure (2.22) when $x_k^{(\ell)}$ coincides with even one coordinate a_{jk} of an existing facility location. It is possible to inadvertently choose a starting point that falls in that category, or it is possible that $X^{(\ell)}$ will move too close to an existing facility location during iteration. In a slow convergence problem, a large initial value of ϵ may get us to the vicinity of an optimum solution relatively quickly. Then a smaller value can be used. However, the use of $\epsilon > 0$ is a practical necessity for Weiszfeld iterations only in the multi-facility case that is discussed in Chapter 4.

Table 2.6a   Iterations with $p = 1.5$ and $\epsilon = 0$.

Iteration Number ℓ	$x_1^{(\ell)}$	$x_2^{(\ell)}$	$WH(X)=W(X)$	$LB^{(\ell)}$	$SH^{(\ell)}=S^{(\ell)}$
0	4.846	4.000	54.849	44.350	2.37×10^{-1}
1	5.114	3.649	54.075	46.141	1.72×10^{-1}
2	5.334	3.448	53.662	47.670	1.26×10^{-1}
3	5.515	3.336	53.449	48.756	9.63×10^{-2}
4	5.665	3.273	53.319	49.486	7.74×10^{-2}
5	5.790	3.236	53.232	49.975	6.52×10^{-2}
10	6.171	3.164	53.050	51.171	3.67×10^{-2}
20	6.447	3.117	52.985	52.184	1.53×10^{-2}
30	6.542	3.098	52.975	52.585	7.42×10^{-3}
40	6.583	3.090	52.973	52.770	3.84×10^{-3}
50	6.604	3.086	52.972	52.864	2.06×10^{-3}
60	6.615	3.083	52.972	52.913	1.12×10^{-3}

Table 2.6b Iterations with $p = 1.5$ and $\epsilon = 0.01$.

Iteration Number ℓ	$\epsilon = 0.01$						
	$x_1^{(\ell)}$	$x_2^{(\ell)}$	$WH(X)$	$LBH^{(\ell)}$	$SH^{(\ell)}$	$W(X)$	$LB^{(\ell)}$
0	4.846	4.000	54.895	44.437	2.35×10^{-1}	54.849	44.350
1	5.114	3.650	54.110	46.273	1.69×10^{-1}	54.059	46.136
2	5.333	3.451	53.722	47.849	1.23×10^{-1}	53.665	47.652
3	5.513	3.341	53.516	48.975	9.27×10^{-2}	53.453	48.720
4	5.660	3.280	53.393	49.732	7.36×10^{-2}	53.324	49.431
5	5.782	3.246	53.313	50.238	6.12×10^{-2}	53.239	49.898
10	6.144	3.186	53.154	51.553	3.11×10^{-2}	53.062	50.942
20	6.370	3.154	53.112	52.667	8.45×10^{-3}	53.000	51.485
30	6.422	3.145	53.109	52.992	2.22×10^{-3}	52.992	51.556
40	6.435	3.143	53.109	53.079	5.71×10^{-4}	52.990	51.567
50	6.438	3.143	53.109	53.101	1.47×10^{-4}	52.989	51.569
60	6.439	3.142	53.109	53.107	3.76×10^{-5}	52.989	51.570

Example 2.7 Table 2.6 illustrates the iteration method [initiated using equation (2.7)] on the single-facility location problem with data given in Table 2.5. The bound $LB^{(\ell)}$ and the $S^{(\ell)}$ that were calculated are those defined in equations (2.8) and (2.9); $LBH^{(\ell)}$ and $SH^{(\ell)}$ were calculated by the same expressions, but using $WH(X)$ instead of $W(X)$. We observe that using $\epsilon = 0.01$ speeded up convergence as measured by $SH^{(\ell)}$ or by movement in $(x_1^{(\ell)}, x_2^{(\ell)})$, although using $\epsilon = 0$ gave a better value of $W(X)$ at each iteration.

EXERCISES

2.1 Consider the sum $\sum_{i=1}^{n} f_i(x_1, x_2)$, where each $f_i(x_1, x_2)$ is convex. Using the definition of convexity given in the Appendix, mathematical note 2.1, prove that the sum is also convex.

2.2 The Varignon frame is a mechanical analog for the minimization of $W(X)$ in problem (2.2). It consists of a board with holes drilled in it to correspond to fixed facility locations. A string is passed through each hole j, and the ends are tied together in a knot on top of the board. Under the board a weight is attached to each string, and the weight on string j is proportional to w_j in problem (2.2). In the absence of friction and tangled strings, the knot will come to rest at the optimum new facility location. This analog has been used in actual location studies. The analog can be analyzed in terms of forces acting to move the knot. Assume that the knot is in equilibrium. In Figure 2E.1 the weight w_4, for example, acts with a force w_4, which can be broken up into the orthogonal components w_{x4} and w_{y4}, where:

$$w_{x4} = w_4 \cos\theta_4 \text{ and } w_{y4} = w_4 \sin\theta_4.$$

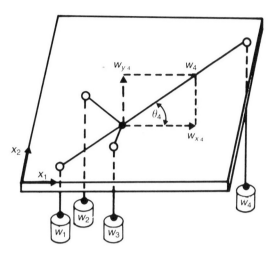

Figure 2E.1   Varignon Frame.

Note that $w_4^2 = w_{x4}^2 + w_{y4}^2$.
a. Show that:

$$\cos \theta_4 = \frac{a_{41} - x_1}{\ell_2(X, a_4)} \text{ and } \sin \theta_4 = \frac{a_{42} - x_2}{\ell_2(X, a_4)},$$

where (x_1, x_2) is the equilibrium position.
b. Show that a balance of x-direction force components and a balance of y-direction force components is, in general, equivalent to conditions (2.3).
c. Explain condition (2.4) in terms of forces. If condition (2.4) holds for point (a_{j1}, a_{j2}), what would be observed on the Varignon frame?

2.3 Show that $W(X) = \sum_{j=1}^{n} w_j (\ell_2(X, a_j))^2$ is strictly convex. (Hint: Since the second partial derivatives of W are continuous everywhere, showing strict convexity is equivalent to showing that the Hessian matrix is positive definite everywhere; see Exercise 2.12.)

2.4 Write a computer program to perform the iterations described by procedure (2.6). The program should calculate the lower bound $LB^{(t)}$ and stop when $S^{(t)}$ is below a predetermined value. Use the program to recalculate Table 2.3 for the cases where:
a. $w_2 = 10.0$, using equation (2.7) to define the starting point,
b. $w_2 = 4.9$, using equation (2.7) to define the starting point,
c. $w_2 = 4.9$, using the starting point $X^{(0)} = (0.99, 4.01)$.

2.5 a. Show that $X^{(1)}$ in procedure (2.6) will always fall in Ω, the convex hull of of the existing facility locations. (Hint: This is equivalent to showing that

$X^{(1)}$ can be written as a weighted sum of the a_j's with positive weights that sum to one.)

b. Show that X^* in problem (2.2) is in Ω. (Hint: If $X^* \neq a_j$, for any j then use conditions (2.3)).

2.6 Apply Property 2.7 to the problem in Example 2.1. Then calculate $(X^{(1)})$ based on $(X^{(0)}) = (0,0)$ using procedure (2.22) with $\epsilon = 0$.

2.7 Using the definition of convexity given in the Appendix, mathematical note 2.1, prove that $W(x) = w|x - a|$ is a convex function for any real positive w and any real a. (Hint: For any real numbers p and q, $|p + q| \leq |p| + |q|$.)

2.8 Derive equation (2.14).

2.9 A facility is to be located on a shop floor where travel is possible only along aisles that are perpendicular to each other. Deliveries will have to be made to two "demand points" located (using rectangular axes corresponding to the directions of the aisles) at $(1,1)$ and $(3,2)$. The weights for the demand points were estimated to be equal (thus taken to be 1 and 1, respectively). Problem (2.10) is to be used as the location model.

   a. On a graph showing the locations of the demand points, draw the equal-cost contour where $W(X)$, the total cost, is equal to 5. (Hint: Divide the $x_1 x_2$ plane into regions such that $W(X)$ can be described in each without using absolute values.)

   b. Plot the contour $W(X) = 3$.

   c. Plot the contour $W(X) = 1$.

2.10 Jack Smooth, an industrial sales and service representative, wants to find a new office location. His business involves several trips a week to seven factories in a large suburban area. From a travel expense diary, he has made up some averages based on several months' experience. He has marked the location of each plant on a map and, using the left and bottom borders of the map as coordinate axes, has given a location to each plant. This information is compiled in Table 2E.1. Jack Smooth's objective is to find an office location that minimizes total travel distance. He considers rectangular

Table 2E.1 Average Trips and Locations of Customers.

Customer	Average Number of Weekly Trips	Location
A	5	(5,20)
B	7	(18,8)
C	2	(22,16)
D	3	(14,17)
E	6	(7,2)
F	1	(5,15)
G	5	(12,4)

distances to be the best representations of the actual travel distances involved.

a. Solve Jack Smooth's office location problem.
b. Show that conditions (2.15) are satisfied at the optimal location.
c. Plot $W_1(x_1)$ against x_1.

2.11 a. Graph the function $y = \dfrac{a}{b} |x - x_o|$ where a and b are positive. Then overlay the graph of the hyperbola whose equation is:

$$\frac{y^2}{a^2} - \frac{(x - x_o)^2}{b^2} = 1.$$

b. Relate a to the vertical distance between the graphs at $x = x_o$.
c. Discard the lower branch of the hyperbola. Solve for y and comment on the result in relation to its use in problem (2.19) in the text.

2.12 Prove that $WH(X)$ in problem (2.19) is strictly convex. Hint: First prove that $g(x_1,x_2) = (((x_1 - a_{j1})^2 + \epsilon)^{p/2} + ((x_2 - a_{j2})^2 + \epsilon)^{p/2})^{1/p}$ is strictly convex by showing that for all $X = (x_1,x_2)$:

$$\frac{\partial^2 g(X)}{\partial x_1^2} > 0$$

and

$$\begin{vmatrix} \dfrac{\partial^2 g(X)}{\partial x_1^2} & \dfrac{\partial^2 g(X)}{\partial x_1 \partial x_2} \\[2mm] \dfrac{\partial^2 g(X)}{\partial x_2 \partial x_1} & \dfrac{\partial^2 g(X)}{\partial x_2^2} \end{vmatrix} > 0.$$

2.13 Derive iterative procedure (2.22) from the extremal conditions (partial derivatives set equal to zero) for $WH(X)$.

2.14 Consider the problem data Table 2E.1 in Exercise 2.10.
a. Check each plant location for candidacy as the optimal office location, assuming ℓ_p distances first with $p = 1$, and then with $p = 1.5$.
b. Use any available computer package for nonlinear optimization to find the optimum location for ℓ_p distances with $p = 1.1, 1.5, 2,$ and 5.
c. Write a computer program to perform the Weiszfeld iteration procedure (2.22), and repeat Exercise 2.14b.
d. Write the additional coding for the program written in Exercise 2.14c to begin by testing for optimality at the existing facility locations. Repeat Exercise 2.14b.

2.15 a. Prove that:

$$W_L(X_R^*) \geqslant W_L(X_L^*) \geqslant ((W_1(x_{1R}^*))^p + (W_2(x_{2R}^*))^p)^{1/p},$$

where:

$X_R^* = (x_{1R}^*, x_{2R}^*)$ is an optimum location for the rectangular distance problem with $W_k(x_k)$ as defined in problem (2.12); and $X_L^* = (x_{1L}^*, x_{2L}^*)$ is an optimum location for the ℓ_p distance problem with $W_L(X)$ representing $W(X)$ in problem (2.17). (Hint: Consider the Minkowski inequality stated in the Appendix, mathematical note 2.3.)
b. Apply the above result to Example 2.6 with $p = 1.3$.

REFERENCE NOTES

SECTION 2.1 The Weiszfeld procedure appeared in a paper by "Weiszfeld" (1937). It should be noted that it is one of the methods for iteratively solving nonlinear equations that appear in numerical analysis texts (eg, Dahlquist and Björck (1974), Chapter 6). Convergence properties have been discussed by, among others, Katz (1969, 1974), Kuhn (1973), and Ostresh (1978). The stopping criterion presented in this section is one of those given by Love and Yeong (1981). A somewhat tighter lower bound was given by Elzinga and Hearn (1983) and Juel (1984); Love and Dowling (1986) generalized Drezner's rectangular bound to the ℓ_p distance case.

SECTION 2.2 Some of the foundation work with rectangular distances includes that by Bindschedler and Moore (1961) and Francis (1963). The single-facility problem is closely related to the problem of finding a weighted median of a data set, as was seen in Example 2.5. Algorithms that can solve such problems in 0(n) time are available.

SECTION 2.3 The hyperbolic approximation used here is from Wesolowsky and Love (1972). Eyster, White, and Wierwille (1973) used a hyperboloid approximation procedure (HAP) to extend the original Weiszfeld procedure to both Euclidean and rectangular distances. Convergence properties including the extension to ℓ_p distances have been discussed by Morris and Verdini (1979) and Morris (1981). An acceleration of the HAP procedure is discussed by Charalambous (1985).

APPENDIX—CHAPTER 2

Mathematical Notes

2.1 *Prove* Property 2.1
$w_j((x_1 - a_{j1})^2 + (x_2 - a_{j2})^2)^{1/2}$ is convex.

PROOF: As w_j is a positive constant we can, without loss of generality, let $w_j = 1$. As a_{j1} and a_{j2} are constants, we can equivalently prove that $f(y_1, y_2) = (y_1^2 + y_2^2)^{1/2}$ is convex. This merely changes the coordinate system to one with an origin at (a_{j1}, a_{j2}). Recall that $f(y_1, y_2)$ is said to be *convex* if, given any two points, (y_1', y_2') and (y_1'', y_2''),

$$f(\lambda(y_1', y_2') + (1 - \lambda)(y_1'', y_2'')) \leqslant \lambda f(y_1', y_2') + (1 - \lambda) f(y_1'', y_2'')$$

where $0 \leqslant \lambda \leqslant 1$.

Therefore, the convexity requirement is:

$$((\lambda y_1' + (1 - \lambda)y_1'')^2 + (\lambda y_2' + (1 - \lambda)y_2'')^2)^{1/2}$$
$$\leqslant \lambda((y_1')^2 + (y_2')^2)^{1/2} + (1 - \lambda)((y_1'')^2 + (y_1'')^2)^{1/2}.$$

To show that this must be true, we turn to what is known as the triangle inequality for vectors. For two real-valued vectors $p = (p_1, p_2)$ and $q = (q_1, q_2)$,

$$((p_1 + q_1)^2 + (p_2 + q_2)^2)^{1/2} \leqslant (p_1^2 + p_2^2)^{1/2} + (q_1^2 + q_2^2)^{1/2}.$$

If we set $p_1 = \lambda y_1'$, $p_2 = \lambda y_2'$, $q_1 = (1 - \lambda)y_1''$, and $q_2 = (1 - \lambda)y_2''$,

we see that this is equivalent to our requirement.

2.2 *Prove* Property 2.2
The minimum of:

$$W(X) = \sum_{j=1}^{n} w_j((x_1 - a_{j1})^2 + (x_2 - a_{j2})^2)^{1/2}$$

occurs at a_r, if, and only if, $CR_r \leqslant w_r$.

PROOF: Consider a movement of the new facility from (x_1, x_2) a distance t to $(x_1 + td_1, x_2 + td_2)$, where $(d_1^2 + d_2^2)^{1/2} = 1$. Here d_1 and d_2 are components of a unit direction vector d. Let us find the rate of change of $W(X + td)$ with respect to t as t approaches zero when $X = a_r$:

$$\frac{dW}{dt} = \sum_{j=1}^{n} \frac{w_j((a_{r1} + td_1 - a_{j1})d_1 + (a_{r2} + td_2 - a_{j2})d_2}{((a_{r1} + td_1 - a_{j1})^2 + (a_{r2} + td_2 - a_{j2})^2)^{1/2}}$$

$$= \frac{w_r(td_1^2 + td_2^2)}{((td_1)^2 + (td_2)^2)^{1/2}}$$

$$+ d_1 \sum_{\substack{j=1 \\ \neq r}}^{n} \frac{w_j(a_{r1} + td_1 - a_{j1})}{((a_{r1} + td_1 - a_{j1})^2 + (a_{r2} + td_2 - a_{j2})^2)^{1/2}}$$

$$+ d_2 \sum_{\substack{j=1 \\ \neq r}}^{n} \frac{w_j(a_{r2} + td_2 - a_{j2})}{((a_{r1} + td_1 - a_{j1})^2 + (a_{r2} + td_2 - a_{j2})^2)^{1/2}} \cdot$$

We can write this derivative as:

$$\frac{dW}{dt} = w_r(d_1^2 + d_2^2)^{1/2} + d_1 R_1(t) + d_2 R_2(t),$$

where $R_1(t)$ and $R_2(t)$ are defined as implied above.
Therefore,

$$\frac{dW}{dt}\Big|_{t \to 0} = w_r(d_1^2 + d_2^2)^{1/2} + d_1 R_1 + d_2 R_2$$

$$= w_r + d_1 R_1 + d_2 R_2,$$

$$\text{where } R_1 = \sum_{\substack{j=1 \\ \neq r}}^{n} \frac{w_r(a_{r1} - a_{j1})}{\ell_2(a_r, a_j)}$$

$$\text{and } R_2 = \sum_{\substack{j=1 \\ \neq r}}^{n} \frac{w_r(a_{r2} - a_{j2})}{\ell_2(a_r, a_j)} \cdot$$

We can use elementary calculus *and* the condition $d_1^2 + d_2^2 = 1$ to find that the minimum of:

$$\frac{dW}{dt}\Big|_{t \to 0}$$

occurs at:

$$d_1 = -\frac{R_1}{(R_1^2 + R_2^2)^{1/2}}, \; d_2 = -\frac{R_2}{(R_1^2 + R_2^2)^{1/2}}$$

$$\text{and so min } \frac{dW}{dt}\Big|_{t \to 0} = w_r - (R_1^2 + R_2^2)^{1/2}.$$

When this derivative is positive, $W(X)$ will increase as (x_1, x_2) is moved in *any* direction from (a_{r1}, a_{r2}). Since $W(X)$ is convex, $X^* = (a_{r1}, a_{r2})$ if, and only if, $w_r \geq (R_1^2 + R_2^2)^{1/2} = CR_r$, as required.

2.3 *Prove* Property 2.6
$w_j \ell_p(X, a_j) = w_j(|x_1 - a_{j1}|^p + |x_2 - a_{j2}|^p)^{1/p}$ is convex.

PROOF: Following note 2.1 we can equivalently prove that $f(y_1, y_2) = (|y_1|^p + |y_2|^p)^{1/p}$ is convex. We will appeal to a well-known (to mathematicians, at least), inequality called the Minkowski inequality, given by:

$$(\sum_{k=1}^{K} |\alpha_k + \beta_k|^p)^{1/p} \leqslant (\sum_{k=1}^{K} |\alpha_k|^p)^{1/p} + (\sum_{k=1}^{K} |\beta_k|^p)^{1/p}$$

where $p \geqslant 1$ and α_k and β_k are real numbers.

We have $f(\lambda y_1' + (1 - \lambda)y_1'', \lambda y_2' + (1 - \lambda)y_2'')$

$$\leqslant ((|\lambda y_1'| + |(1 - \lambda)y_1''|)^p + (|\lambda y_2'|$$
$$+ |(1 - \lambda)y_2''|)^p)^{1/p} \qquad \text{(triangle inequality)}$$
$$\leqslant (|\lambda y_1'|^p + |\lambda y_2'|^p)^{1/p} + (|(1 - \lambda)y_1''|^p$$
$$+ |(1 - \lambda)y_2''|^p)^{1/p} \qquad \text{(Minkowski inequality)}$$
$$= \lambda(|y_1'|^p + |y_2'|^p)^{1/p} + (1 - \lambda)(|y_1''|^p + |y_2''|^p)^{1/p}$$
$$= \lambda f(y_1', y_2') + (1 - \lambda)f(y_1'', y_2''), \text{ as required.}$$

2.4 *Prove* $L_p(X, a_j) - \ell_p(X, a_j) \leqslant 2^{1/p} \epsilon^{1/2}$, where

$$L_p(X, a_j) = (((x_1 - a_{j1})^2 + \epsilon)^{p/2} + ((x_2 - a_{j2})^2 + \epsilon)^{p/2})^{1/p}.$$

PROOF: Let $y_1 = |x_1 - a_{j1}| \geqslant 0$, $y_2 = |x_2 - a_{j2}| \geqslant 0$ and $y_3 = \epsilon^{1/2} > 0$. Then:

$$L_p(X, a_j) = [(y_1^2 + y_3^2)^{p/2} + (y_2^2 + y_3^2)^{p/2}]^{1/p}$$
$$\leqslant [((y_1 + y_3)^2)^{p/2} + ((y_2 + y_3)^2)^{p/2}]^{1/p}$$
$$= [|y_1 + y_3|^p + |y_2 + y_3|^p]^{1/p}$$
$$\leqslant [|y_1|^p + |y_2|^p]^{1/p} + [|y_3|^p + |y_3|^p]^{1/p}$$

(Minkowski inequality; see note 2.3)

$$= [|x_1 - a_{j1}|^p + |x_2 - a_{j2}|^p]^{1/p} + [\epsilon^{p/2} + \epsilon^{p/2}]^{1/p}$$
$$= \ell_p(X, a_j) + 2^{1/p}\epsilon^{1/2}, \text{ as required.}$$

2.5 *Prove* [Rectangular bound on $W(X^*)$]. $W(X^*) \geqslant R(X^{(0)})$

$$= \min_{x_1} \sum_{j=1}^{n} w_j' |x_1 - a_{j1}| + \min_{x_2} \sum_{j=1}^{n} w_j'' |x_2 - a_{j2}|,$$

where $W(X^*)$ is defined in problem (2.2) in the text while

$$w_j' = w_j |x_1^{(l)} - a_{j1}| / \ell_2(X^{(l)}, a_j), \text{ and}$$

$$w_j'' = w_j |x_2^{(l)} - a_{j2}| / \ell_2(X^{(l)}, a_j).$$

PROOF: We may write the following inequality:

$$|x_1 - a_{j1}| \, |x_1^{(l)} - a_{j1}| + |x_2 - a_{j2}| \, |x_2^{(l)} - a_{j2}|$$

$$\leq [|x_1 - a_{j1}|^2 + |x_2 - a_{j2}|^2]^{1/2} [|x_1^{(l)} - a_{j1}|^2 + |x_2^{(l)} - a_{j2}|^2]^{1/2}$$

$$(\text{since } |u \cdot v| \leq \|u\| \, \|v\|; \text{ Schwartz inequality})$$

$$= \ell_2(X, a_j) \, \ell_2(X^{(l)}, a_j),$$

or equivalently,

$$\ell_2(X, a_j) \geq [|x_1^{(l)} - a_{j1}| / \ell_2(X^{(l)}, a_j)] |x_1 - a_{j1}|$$

$$+ [|x_2^{(l)} - a_{j2}| / \ell_2(X^{(l)}, a_j)] |x_2 - a_{j2}|.$$

Multiplying both sides by w_j, summing over j and then taking the min on both sides with respect to X yields the required result.

(Note: The bound $R(X^{(l)})$ is due to Drezner (1984). The solution $X^{(l)}$ at each iteration of the Weiszfeld procedure is used to compute the weights w_j' and w_j'' that are used in calculating $R(X^{(l)})$. While it may appear that adding another optimization problem and solving it at each iteration has increased the work required to find a lower bound, this approach has several advantages. Using techniques from Section 2.2, each part of the optimization involved in calculating $R(X^{(l)})$ can be accomplished rapidly. Also, it is not necessary to find the hull points that are used in Property 2.4.)

Chapter 3

Variations on the Single-Facility Model

This chapter introduces several of the many variations of the basic single-facility model treated in the preceding chapter. The objective remains the minimization of the sum of weighted distances. We begin with location on the surface of a sphere. Using a plane as a location surface assumes that if the location region is actually a segment of the surface of the world spheroid, this segment is small enough for the assumption to provide an adequate approximation. This assumption becomes less tenable as the scale of the location problem approaches the global. The model presented in this chapter uses exact shortest arc distances on the surface of a sphere; such distances can be used as good approximations to actual global travel distances.

The model of the preceding chapter idealized the existing facility locations as discrete points on a plane. Yet problems arise that are difficult to model by this approach. Consider, for example, the location of some facility in a large city. If each member of the population served by that facility is considered to be a separate "existing facility," then the number of existing facilities would likely be prohibitively large. (The term "existing facility" becomes inappropriate, so let us instead substitute the term "destination" in this context.)

A new facility location need not necessarily be modeled as a point in space, either. If, for example, an access way or conveyor belt is to be located, we may well describe its location as a line under the assumption that the facility is reached once the nearest point on it is reached.

In another application, a "point facility" may be called on to serve for many periods of time; during that time the parameters of the problem may change. It may be necessary to plan for the relocation of the new facility one or more times during the planning horizon.

It has also been assumed in the preceding chapter that the costs and other parameters in the model are known; an alternative often closer to the truth is that these parameters are stochastic variables. The case is analyzed wherein locations of the demand points are known only in probability.

The following sections introduce these variations to the basic single-facility location model in their simplest form. They can, of course, be adapted to the more complex models of the succeeding chapters; this has been, and is being done, in the location literature.

3.1 LOCATING A FACILITY ON A SPHERE

Suppose the existing facilities lie on a sphere. Assume that this sphere has a radius of 1.0 to simplify expressions; as will be evident, there is no loss of generality in doing this. Problem (2.1) becomes

$$\text{minimize } W(X) = \sum_{j=1}^{n} w_j A(X,a_j) \qquad (3.1)$$

where $X = (x_1,x_2)$, and x_1 and x_2 are the latitude and longitude coordinates of the facility that is to be located. $A(X,a_j)$ is the shortest distance, measured (in radians) on the surface of the sphere, between the facility at X and existing facility j at $a_j = (a_{j1},a_{j2})$. Some observations will now be made about the properties of distances, sets, and functions on the surface of the sphere.

Distances, Sets, and Functions

A plane cutting through the center of a sphere will trace a circle on the surface; this is known as a *great circle*. Examples are the equator and the Greenwich meridian. The shortest distance between any two points on a sphere must be measured along the great circle passing through them and is the shorter of the two arcs between the points. For this reason, this distance is known as the *great circle distance* or *shortest (minor) arc distance*. It is evident that the greatest possible distance between two points on the unit radius sphere is π. In this case the points are on opposite ends of a line passing through the center of the sphere and are said to be *antipodes*. As is easily visualized, when angles are measured in radians, the antipode of point X may be written $\bar{X} = (-x_1,x_2 + \pi)$.

The shortest distance between the new facility and existing facility j on a sphere with unit radius is:

$$A(X,a_j)=\cos^{-1}[\cos x_1\cos a_{j1}\cos(x_2 - a_{j2})+\sin x_1\sin a_{j1}] \qquad (3.2)$$

where a_{j1} and a_{j2} are the latitude and longitude, respectively, of the existing facility.

It will be necessary to establish the concepts of spherical circles, convex sets, and convex functions on the surface of the sphere in order to carry out the optimization required by problem (3.1). A *spherical circle* is the locus of all points with a fixed shortest arc distance from the point that is its center. Note that a spherical circle with radius π is actually the antipode of the center of the circle. A *spherical disk* is the set formed by a spherical circle and its interior.

A *convex set* on the sphere is such that every two points in the set have at least one shortest arc joining them that lies entirely within the set. For example, a hemisphere is a convex set and so is any great circle. However, a spherical disk with radius greater than $\pi/2$ is not a convex set.

Let V^λ be a point on the shortest arc between two other points $Y = (y_1, y_2)$ and $Z = (z_1, z_2)$ in some subset D of the sphere; λ is such that the distance between V^λ and Y is λ times the distance between Y and Z. Any function f is *convex* on D if:

$$f(V^\lambda) \leqslant \lambda f(Y) + (1 - \lambda) f(Z), \text{ where } 0 \leqslant \lambda \leqslant 1. \tag{3.3}$$

Property 3.1 [*Convexity of shortest arc distance*]. *The distance* $A(X, a_j)$ *is a convex function of* X *on a spherical disk with radius* $\pi/2$ *centered on point* a_j.

A proof is given in the Appendix, mathematical note 3.1. This convexity property will be important in determining when the methodology to be described can be expected to produce a global minimizer for $W(X)$. This is true because of Property 3.2.

Property 3.2 [*Unique minimum value for a convex function on a sphere*]. *A local minimizer of a convex function on a convex subset of a sphere is also a global minimizer.*

A proof is given in the Appendix, mathematical note 3.2. The following corollary is definitive (see Exercise 3.5) for problem (3.1).

Property 3.3 [*Problems for which a local minimizer is a global minimizer*]. *If all* $a_j, j = 1,...,n$ *can be covered by a spherical disk of radius* $\pi/4$, *then a local minimizer of* $W(X)$ *is also a global minimizer.*

Minimizing $W(X)$

We first investigate the extremal conditions for $W(X)$. Differentiating, we obtain:

$$\frac{\partial W(X)}{\partial x_1} = -\sum_{j=1}^{n} w_j(-\sin x_1 \cos a_{j1} \cos (x_2 - a_{j2})$$

$$+ \cos x_1 \sin a_{j1})/\sin A(X, a_j), \tag{3.4a}$$

$$\frac{\partial W(X)}{\partial x_2} = \cos x_1 \sum_{j=1}^{n} w_j \cos a_{j1} \sin (x_2 - a_{j2})/\sin A(X, a_j). \tag{3.4b}$$

These derivatives are not defined at the existing facility locations (or their antipodes) because $\sin A(X,a_j) = 0$ at $X = a_j$. However, as was done in Section 2.1 of Chapter 2, we can derive a check to see if there is a minimum at the point a_j. The difference here is that unless Property 3.3 is met, this may only be a local minimum.

Property 3.4 [*Local minimum at an existing facility location*]. *W(X) has a local minimum at a_r if, and only if:*

$$CF_r = (F_{r1}^2 + F_{r2}^2)^{1/2} \leqslant w_r \tag{3.5}$$

where:

$$F_{r1} = \sum_{\substack{j=1 \\ \neq r}}^{n} w_j(-\sin a_{r1} \cos a_{j1} \cos (a_{r2} - a_{j2})$$

$$+ \cos a_{r1} \sin a_{j1})/\sin A(a_r,a_j)$$

$$F_{r2} = \sum_{\substack{j=1 \\ \neq r}}^{n} w_j \cos a_{j1} \sin (a_{j2} - a_{r2})/\sin A(a_r,a_j).$$

The proof is given in the Appendix, mathematical note 3.3.

To find a local minimum at other than an existing facility location, set the derivatives in equation (3.4) to zero and solve to obtain:

$$\tan x_2 = \frac{\displaystyle\sum_{j=1}^{n} w_j \cos a_{j1} \sin a_{j2}/\sin A(X,a_j)}{\displaystyle\sum_{j=1}^{n} w_j \cos a_{j1} \cos a_{j2}/\sin A(X,a_j)} \tag{3.6a}$$

$$\frac{\tan x_1}{\sin x_2} = \frac{\displaystyle\sum_{j=1}^{n} w_j \sin a_{j1}/\sin A(X,a_j)}{\displaystyle\sum_{j=1}^{n} w_j \cos a_{j1} \sin a_{j2}/\sin A(X,a_j)}. \tag{3.6b}$$

This is not an explicit solution for x_1 and x_2 because these variables appear on both sides of the equations. However, as was the case for equation (2.5) of the previous chapter, these equations may be solved iteratively by a version of the Weiszfeld procedure. Essentially, if some values of x_1 and x_2 are entered on the right-hand side of equations (3.6), new and better (it is hoped) values are produced. Note that any new x_2 thus created by equation (3.6a) could also be $x_2 + \pi$. If K is the value of the right-hand side in (3.6b), then $x_1 = \tan^{-1} (K \sin x_2)$. Because $\sin (x_2 + \pi) =$

$-\sin x_2$ and $\tan(-y) = -\tan y$, the antipodes (x_1, x_2) and $(-x_1, x_2 + \pi)$ are actually produced by equations (3.6). This iterative process for some arbitrarily small positive constant ϵ can be summarized as follows.

Weiszfeld Procedure on the Sphere

Step 0 Choose a starting point $(x_1^{(0)}, x_2^{(0)})$. Set $\ell = 0$.

Step 1 Compute $X^{(\ell+1)}$ by equations (3.6) using $X^{(\ell)}$ to calculate $\sin A(X, a_j)$.

Step 2 If $|x_1^{(\ell+1)} - x_1^{(\ell)}| + |x_2^{(\ell+1)} - x_2^{(\ell)}| > \epsilon$, go to Step 1.

Step 3 Check $(x_1^{(\ell+1)}, x_2^{(\ell+1)})$ and its antipode.

Convergence of this algorithm has not been proved, but has been achieved in all computational studies so far. Unfortunately the stopping criterion stated as Property 2.4 in Chapter 2 cannot, in general, be used here because $W(X)$ is not necessarily convex. The characteristics of this procedure are very similar to those of the Weiszfeld procedure of Section 2.1. For instance, the procedure, as a rule, accomplishes the substantial part of its improvement in the objective function in the first few steps, regardless of the choice of starting point. There is one important contrast. Now convergence may be to a local maximizer and not to a minimizer. However, this need be of no practical concern because of the following easily proved property.

Property 3.5 [*Local optima at antipodes*]. *A point is a local minimizer of $W(X)$ if, and only if, its antipode is a local maximizer.*

Because we can easily keep track of the antipode at each step of the procedure, we can, in effect, always assure that convergence is to a local minimizer. Incidentally, the sum of the objective function values at antipodes is always $\pi \sum_{j=1}^{n} w_j$, and this can be used to shorten calculations.

The following general strategy is recommended. First, condition (3.5) is used to check for local minima at the existing facility locations. Property 3.3 is then used to check if a local minimum must also be a global minimum. Of course, if some point a_r is a local minimizer and Property 3.3 indicates that it is a global minimizer, then we are done. Otherwise we must choose a starting point and an "accuracy level" ϵ and carry out the iterations.

Starting points may be chosen in a variety of ways. One should choose several points if a global optimum cannot be guaranteed; they may be chosen at random or, alternatively, uniformly distributed over the surface of the sphere. Sometimes Wendell's starting point is used. It is obtained by setting $\sin A(X, a_j) = 1$ in equations (3.6), and it is analogous to the

Table 3.1 Locations, Weights, and CF_r's of Four Cities.

City	Location (degrees)	Weight	CF_r
London	(51.5,0.4)	0.12	0.19708
Bombay	(18.9,72.8)	0.03	0.16900
Manila	(14.6,121.0)	0.08	0.19263
Tokyo	(35.6,139.7)	0.10	0.14386

Table 3.2 Intercity Distances (radians).

	London	Bombay	Manila
Bombay	1.12455		
Manila	1.68040	0.80670	
Tokyo	1.49890	1.05828	0.46895

center-of-gravity starting point in the planar version of the problem. A discussion of this topic is found in Wesolowsky (1982).

Example 3.1 Table 3.1 gives the locations of four cities, their weights, and their CF_r values. Table 3.2 gives the interfacility distances divided by the radius of the sphere. Figure 3.1 shows the locations of these cities on the sphere.

As no CF_r is less than w_r, no city's location is a local minimizer. Also, because the Manila-London distance is $1.68040 > \pi/2 = 1.57080$, Prop-

Figure 3.1 Locations of Four Cities.

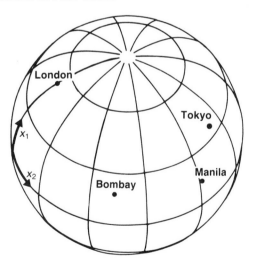

Table 3.3 Iterations for Example 3.1.

Iteration Number ℓ	$(x_1^{(\ell)}, x_2^{(\ell)})$ (degrees)	$W(X)$	$(\bar{x}_1^{(\ell)}, \bar{x}_2^{(\ell)})$ (antipode)	$W(\bar{X})$
0	(0,0)	0.53786	(0,180)	0.49887
1	(−52.641,−83.108)	0.78260	(52.641,96.892)	0.25412
2	(−47.253,−74.896)	0.78805	(47.253,105.104)	0.24868
3	(−44.077,−69.215)	0.79081	(44.077,110.785)	0.24591
4	(−42.113,−65.422)	0.79218	(42.113,114.578)	0.24454
5	(−40.906,−62.908)	0.79282	(40.906,117.092)	0.24390
10	(−39.369,−58.529)	0.79334	(39.269,121.471)	0.24338
15	(−39.123,−57.886)	0.79335	(39.123,122.114)	0.24337
20	(−39.102,−57.784)	0.79335	(39.102,122.216)	0.24337
30	(−39.098,−57.765)	0.79335	(39.098,122.235)	0.24337
40	(−39.098,−57.765)	0.79335	(39.098,122.235)	0.24337

erty 3.3 will not be able to guarantee a global minimum. Table 3.3 shows sample iterations; it is the antipode that is the minimizer in this example. Incidentally, Wendell's starting point is $(-50.925, -82.694)$. If X^* were to fall in an ocean, contour curves of $W(X)$ could be investigated (possibly using computer graphics) to obtain a constrained minimizer.

3.2 POINT AND AREA DESTINATIONS WITH RECTANGULAR DISTANCE

Suppose it is desired to locate a facility in a large U.S. city, and demand data are readily available in the form of estimates by census tracts. Demand is then only "known" to within the resolution provided by these areal units. A plausible heuristic is to treat the center of an "area destination" (one or more contiguous tracts) as a point destination weighted by the demand of that area. The weakness of this approach is that an error is introduced by the implicit assumption that the distance traveled from the facility to each destination in the area is the same as the distance from the facility to the center of the area. This error decreases as the area in question is decreased, but in the limit this decrease leads to the measurement and computation difficulties of having as many destinations as there are demand points.

To resolve this dilemma, we subdivide large populations of destinations into areas having roughly uniform demand densities per unit area. The use of point destinations along with such area destinations enables us to accurately depict even complex demand configurations.

We will consider only a rectangular distance model. General ℓ_p distances are treated by Drezner and Wesolowsky (1980a, 1980b), but the problem becomes considerably more complex to analyze. Also, for convenience, we assume *uniform* distribution of destinations over *rectan-*

gular areas. The latter assumption is not overly restrictive because the rectangular components can be used to build up more complex shapes. In both model and mode of analysis, the concept of uniformly distributed destinations is closely allied to the assumption that locations of destinations are unknown, but distributed with a uniform probability distribution over a rectangular area. This interpretation is treated later in this chapter.

Assume now that the destinations can be divided into points and into rectangular areas (with sides parallel to the coordinate axes) that have uniform distributions of destinations. Let there be t destination areas. Figure 3.2 shows rectangular area j bounded by the corners (c_{j1},c_{j2}), (d_{j1},c_{j2}), (d_{j1},d_{j2}), and (c_{j1},d_{j2}). Within the area is an infinitesimally small square area, and within that is the point (z_1,z_2). The distance between the facility at (x_1,x_2) and the point (z_1,z_2) is measured along only rectangular distance paths such as that depicted. Let u_j be the weighting constant (per unit area) that transforms distance and the area of the infinitesimally small square into cost. For example, suppose 400 people were "uniformly distributed" over two square kilometers and each demanded 30 units where each unit cost \$0.50 per kilometer to transport. The uniform distribution assumption would give us $u_j = (30)(400)(0.5)/2 = \$3000$ per kilometer of distance per square kilometer of area.

The transportation cost to area j is:

$$T_j(x_1,x_2) = u_j \int\limits_{c_{j2}}^{d_{j2}} \int\limits_{c_{j1}}^{d_{j1}} (|x_1-z_1| + |x_2-z_2|)dz_1 dz_2. \tag{3.7}$$

The problem of optimally locating a new facility among t area destinations and n point destinations can now be written:

Figure 3.2   Area Destination j.

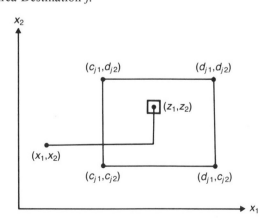

$$\underset{X}{\text{minimize}}\ WA(X) = \sum_{j=1}^{t} T_j(x_1,x_2) + \sum_{j=1}^{n} w_j(|x_1-a_{j1}| + |x_2-a_{j2}|). \quad (3.8)$$

The function $WA(X)$ has two very useful properties. It is separable in x_1 and x_2 and it is convex. These two properties are basic to finding X^*, an optimal location.

The cost term $T_j(x_1,x_2)$ can be simplified by integration. Write:

$$T_j(x_1,x_2) = T_{j1}(x_1) + T_{j2}(x_2), \quad (3.9)$$

where:

$$T_{j1}(x_1) = u_j(d_{j2} - c_{j2}) \int_{c_{j1}}^{d_{j1}} |x_1 - z_1| dz_1$$

$$T_{j2}(x_2) = u_j(d_{j1} - c_{j1}) \int_{c_{j2}}^{d_{j2}} |x_2 - z_2| dz_2.$$

For convenience, let:

$$u_{j1} = u_j(d_{j2} - c_{j2}) \text{ and } u_{j2} = u_j(d_{j1} - c_{j1}),$$

so we can write:

$$T_{jk}(x_k) = u_{jk} \int_{c_{jk}}^{d_{jk}} |x_k - z_k| dz_k, \quad (3.10)$$

and in turn:

$$WA(X) = \sum_{j=1}^{t} T_{j1}(x_1) + \sum_{j=1}^{t} T_{j2}(x_2) + W_1(x_1) + W_2(x_2) \quad (3.11)$$

where:

$$W_k(x_k) = \sum_{j=1}^{n} w_j|x_k - a_{jk}|.$$

If we now let:

$$WA_k(x_k) = \sum_{j=1}^{t} T_{jk}(x_k) + W_k(x_k), \quad (3.12)$$

it is clear that we can find (x_1^*,x_2^*) by minimizing first $WA_1(x_1)$ to obtain x_1^*, then minimizing $WA_2(x_2)$ to obtain x_2^*. To proceed, it is necessary to obtain $T_{jk}(x_k)$ in another form.

Table 3.4　The Algebraic Breakdown of $T_{jk}(x_k)$.

$x_k < c_{jk}$	$c_{jk} \leqslant x_k < d_{jk}$	$x_k \geqslant d_{jk}$
$T_{jk}(x_k)/u_{jk}$	$T_{jk}(x_k)/u_{jk}$	$T_{jk}(x_k)/u_{jk}$
$= 1/2((x_k-d_{jk})^2$	$= 1/2((x_k-d_{jk})^2$	$= -1/2((x_k-d_{jk})^2$
$-(x_k-c_{jk})^2)$	$+(x_k-c_{jk})^2)$	$-(x_k-c_{jk})^2)$
$= x_k(c_{jk}-d_{jk})$	$= x_k^2-(c_{jk}+d_{jk})x_k$	$= x_k(d_{jk}-c_{jk})$
$+ 1/2(d_{jk}^2-c_{jk}^2)$	$+ 1/2(c_{jk}^2+d_{jk}^2)$	$+ 1/2(c_{jk}^2-d_{jk}^2)$

Table 3.4 summarizes the results of integration and Figure 3.3 plots the function and its derivative. As is evident by inspection of Figure 3.3 (or formally, Exercise 3.6), $T_{jk}(x_k)$ is convex. As all terms $W_k(x_k)$ are also convex, $WA_k(x_k)$ is convex.

There is an easy way to find an optimum location. Recall that in the rectangular distance location problem with destination *points* (existing facility locations), we could find x_1^* by locating the median weight on the x_1-axis and x_2^* by locating the median weight on the x_2-axis (see Example 2.5). We can think of the areas as being composed of a *very* large number of points. The representation of an area by points can be made as accurate as desired by increasing the number of points. It would seem to follow that we again need only locate the medians of weights on the respective

Figure 3.3　$T_{jk}(x_k)$ and Its Derivative $T'_{jk}(x_k)$.

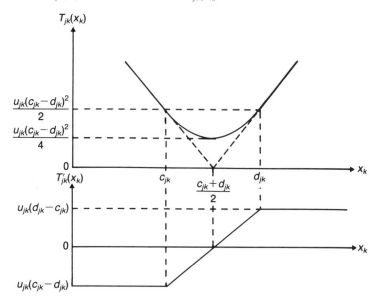

axes to find the optimal facility locations. The total weight of an area j is simply the constant u_j (which is a weight per unit area) multiplied by the size of the area. This intuition is indeed correct as can be shown using the derivatives in Figure 3.3. Exercise 3.7 requests the proof for this.

Example 3.2 Table 3.5 and Figure 3.4 present a location problem with three area destinations and two point destinations.

The calculation of $WA_k(x_k)$ and its derivatives at selected points x_k is summarized in Tables 3.6 and 3.7.

As sample calculations, we find $WA_1(x_1)$ and $WA_1'(x_1)$ at $x_1 = 2$. Using equation (3.12) we calculate:

$$WA_1(2) = \sum_{j=1}^{3} u_{j1}(x_k(c_{jk} - d_{jk}) + (d_{jk}^2 - c_{jk}^2)) + \sum_{j=1}^{2} w_j(a_{j1} - 2)$$

$$= 15\ [2(2 - 6) + (6^2 - 2^2)/2]$$
$$+ 21\ [2(2 - 7) + (7^2 - 2^2)/2]$$
$$+ 6\ [2(2 - 4) + (4^2 - 2^2)/2]$$
$$+ 45\ (6 - 2) + 6(7 - 2)$$
$$= 604.5.$$

Using Table 3.4 we calculate:

$$WA_1'(2) = \sum_{j=1}^{3} u_{j1}(c_{j1} - d_{j1}) + \sum_{j=1}^{2} (-w_j)$$

$$= 15(2 - 6) + 21(2 - 7) + 6(2 - 4) + (-45) + (-6)$$
$$= -228.$$

Graphs of $WA_1(x_1)$ and $WA_2(x_2)$ appear in Figures 3.5 and 3.6.

The figures (if accurate enough) show that $x_1^* = 4.83$ and $x_2^* = 6$. These coordinates can be obtained as the locations of median weights. Consider

Table 3.5 Points, Areas, and Weights.

j	u_j	c_{j1}	d_{j1}	u_{j1}	c_{j2}	d_{j2}	u_{j2}
1	5	2	6	15	1	4	20
2	7	2	7	21	7	10	35
3	2	2	4	6	4	7	4

j	w_j	a_{j1}	a_{j2}
1	45	6	6
2	6	7	4

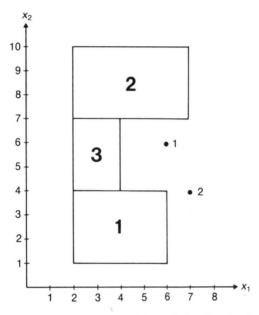

Figure 3.4   Three Area Destinations and Two Point Destinations.

the x_1-axis first. Figure 3.7 shows the areas and weights "dropped" on the x_1-axis. The rectangles can be thought of as being made of a material that has unit weight per unit volume; the thickness of each is then u_j.

Table 3.6   Calculation of $WA_1(x_1)$ and Its Derivative $WA_1'(x_1)$.

x_1	$WA_1(x_1)$	$WA_1'(x_1)$
2	604.5	−228
4	316.5	− 60
6	340.5	174
7	535.5	228

Table 3.7   Calculation of $WA_2(x_2)$ and Its Derivative $WA_2'(x_2)$.

x_2	$WA_2(x_2)$	$WA_2'(x_2)$
1	1174.5	−228
4	670.5	− 96
6	494.5	10
7	508.5	18
10	877.5	228

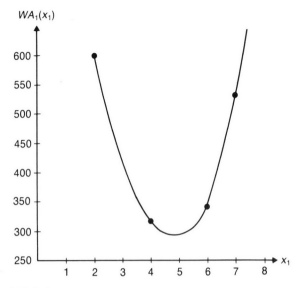

Figure 3.5 $WA_1(x_1)$.

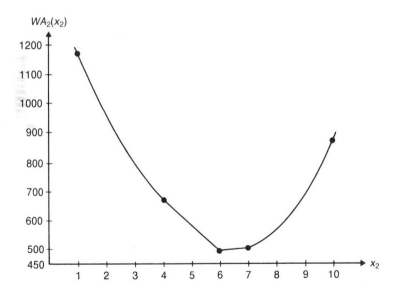

Figure 3.6 $WA_2(x_2)$.

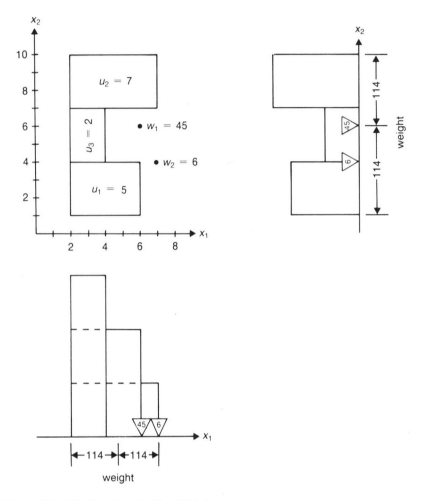

Figure 3.7   Finding the Median Weight.

We must find a point on the x_1-axis such that the weights are equal on either side. The total weight of points and areas is calculated as follows.

Area 1: $(d_{11} - c_{11})(d_{12} - c_{12})u_1 = (4)(3)(5) = 60$
Area 2: $(d_{21} - c_{21})(d_{22} - c_{22})u_2 = (5)(3)(7) = 105$
Area 3: $(d_{31} - c_{31})(d_{32} - c_{32})u_3 = (2)(3)(2) = 12$
Point 1: $w_1 = 45$
Point 2: $w_2 = \underline{6}$
Total weight   228

We have found that the point of median weight has a total weight of

$228/2 = 114$ to either side. We now do a bit of trial and error. The total weight in [2,4] is $(2)(3)(5) + (2)(3)(7) + (2)(3)(2) = 84$, whereas the weight in [2,6) is $84 + (2)(3)(5) + (2)(3)(7) = 156$. The point of median weight therefore falls in [4,6). Solving the equation

$$84 + (x_1^* - 4)(3)(5 + 7) = 114$$

produces $x_1^* = 4.8\overline{3}$. The reader will find that a similar procedure yields $x_2^* = 6$.

3.3 THE LOCATION OF A LINEAR FACILITY

In some applications, it may make sense to describe the new facility location by a line, rather than a point. In the design of some transportation networks, access roads or throughways may be treated as linear facilities that connect populations or industrial installations to a major transportation system. For example, MacKinnon and Barber (1972) presented the problem of designing a transportation network consisting of trunk lines (represented by line segments) and feeder routes (represented by least-distance line segments from the demand points to the lines). The cost of transportation along the trunk lines was assumed to be negligible compared with the transportation costs on the feeder routes. Another example would be a conveyor line that serves a plant floor by transporting materials produced at several different points.

Suppose there are n existing facilities each with an associated (positive) weight. The problem is to locate a line $x_2 = A^* + S^* x_1$, such that the sum of weighted perpendicular distances to the line (the total cost of the

Figure 3.8 Perpendicular Distances.

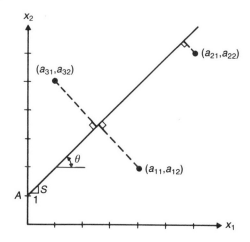

system) is minimized. Figure 3.8 illustrates a line $x_2 = A + Sx_1$ and the resulting perpendicular distances from three points.

The perpendicular distance from a point (a_{j1}, a_{j2}) to the line can be shown (see Exercise 3.10) to be:

$$\frac{|A - (a_{j2} - Sa_{j1})|}{(S^2 + 1)^{1/2}}, \tag{3.13}$$

which implies the location problem:

$$\underset{A,S}{\text{minimize}} \; P(A,S) = \sum_{j=1}^{n} \frac{w_j |A - (a_{j2} - SA_{j1})|}{(S^2 + 1)^{1/2}}. \tag{3.14}$$

Unfortunately, $P(A,S)$ is not convex and is, as we shall see, multimodal as a rule. However, given any S, the problem reduces to locating a point A on a line. We can see this by comparing equation (3.14) to problem (2.12) for any fixed S. We can therefore easily find $P^*(S)$ where:

$$P^*(S) = \underset{A}{\text{min}} \; P(A,S). \tag{3.15}$$

Minimizing $P^*(S)$ is more difficult because $P^*(S)$ is multimodal in S, the derivatives are discontinuous, and the range in S to be searched is awkward (S approaches ∞ as the line becomes vertical). As a result, we will reformulate the problem using not S but θ, the angle of the line with the

Figure 3.9 Rotation of Axes.

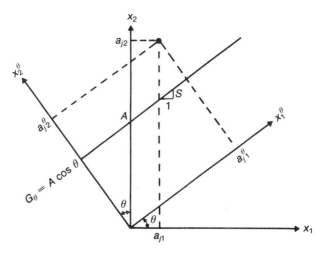

x_1-axis (see Figure 3.9). We will also find it expedient to rotate the co-ordinate axes by θ degrees to produce x_1^θ and x_2^θ. The new coordinates of point a_j are therefore:

$$(a_{j1}^\theta, a_{j2}^\theta) = (a_{j1}\cos\theta + a_{j2}\sin\theta, -a_{j1}\sin\theta + a_{j2}\cos\theta). \quad (3.16)$$

Figure 3.9 shows that the line $x_2 = A + Sx_1$ becomes $x_2^\theta = A\cos\theta = G_\theta$ after rotation.

The problem of minimizing the sum of weighted perpendiculars to the line now becomes:

$$\underset{G_\theta}{\text{minimize}} = P_\theta(G_\theta) = \sum_{j=1}^{n} w_j|G_\theta - a_{j2}^\theta|. \quad (3.17)$$

We must investigate θ in the range $[0,180°)$. Fortunately, only a finite set of values of θ in the range will be candidates. We will show how to identify these candidates by eliminating portions of the range from consideration. After a somewhat lengthy development the reader's patience will be re-warded by two examples intended to clarify matters.

Problem (3.17) is easily solved using methods developed in Section 2.2. Recall that a value of G_θ is optimal if it is a median weight point. That is, if we place the weight w_j on some line marked off with their locations, a_{j2}^θ, then G_θ^* is a median weight location. For example, if $a_{12}^\theta = 3$, $a_{22}^\theta = 1$, $a_{32}^\theta = 2$, and $w_1 = w_2 = w_3 = 2$, then the point of median weight is at a_{32}^θ and $G_\theta^* = 2$. However, if $w_1 = 1$, $w_2 = 2$, and $w_3 = 1$, then any point between a_{22}^θ and a_{32}^θ inclusive is a median weight loca-tion.

The essential idea in what follows is that a_{j2}^θ or $[a_{i2}^\theta, a_{j2}^\theta]$ may still define the median even if θ changes. The median changes from index j or from the pair of index values (i,j) only if the order of the a_{k2}^θ's, $k = 1,...,n$ changes sufficiently to upset the "balance" of weights. As θ changes, so do the values of a_{k2}^θ's. However, it should be evident that it is often possible to rotate the line through some angle $\Delta\theta$ without changing the value j or (i,j) at which G^θ is equal to a_{j2}^θ or $[a_{i2}^\theta, a_{j2}^\theta]$. Figure 3.10 illustrates this.

A line drawn through point a_1 with either angle θ_1 or θ_2 in Figure 3.10 minimizes the sum of weighted perpendiculars; in either case a_1 is the location of the median weight. However, it can also be verified that a line through a_1 is optimal for any angle in the range $[\theta_1,\theta_2]$. Note that at $\theta = \theta_1$ a line through a_2 is optimal, and that for $\theta = \theta_2$ a line through a_3 is optimal. We will now show that any line with an angle in the open interval (θ_1,θ_2) cannot be optimal with respect to θ. In other words, the best θ in the closed interval $[\theta_1,\theta_2]$ must occur at an endpoint.

Let $\phi_i = (\theta_1^i,\theta_2^i)$ be an open interval of angles for which $G_\theta^* = a_{i2}^\theta$ and

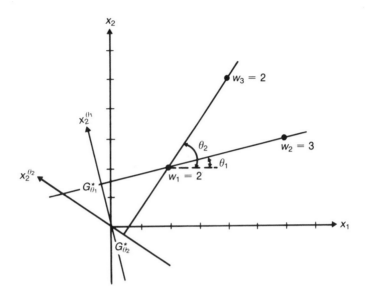

Figure 3.10   Range of θ for a_{11}^{θ} Optimal.

hence for which the line goes through a_i. Then in ϕ_i, the line goes through another point a_k only if $a_i = a_k$.

Property 3.6   [θ *cannot be optimal in* ϕ_i].

PROOF: Let:

$$L(\phi_i) = \{j \,|\, a_{j2}^{\theta} < a_{i2}^{\theta},\ \theta \epsilon \phi_i\} \tag{3.18a}$$

$$U(\phi_i) = \{j \,|\, a_{j2}^{\theta} > a_{i2}^{\theta},\ \theta \epsilon \phi_i\}. \tag{3.18b}$$

The sets $L(\phi_i)$ and $U(\phi_i)$ merely identify those points that are "below" and "above" G_{θ}^{*} in the range ϕ_i.

Using equation (3.16) we can restate equation (3.18) in a more operational form. For $j \epsilon L(\phi_i)$ we have:

$$-a_{i1} \sin\theta + a_{i2} \cos\theta > -a_{j1} \sin\theta + a_{j2} \cos\theta$$

and

$$(a_{i2} - a_{j2}) \cos\theta > (a_{i1} - a_{j1}) \sin\theta.$$

Performing similar calculations for $j \epsilon U(\phi_i)$, we find that for $j \epsilon L(\phi_i)$:

$$(a_{i2} - a_{j2}) \cos\theta > (a_{i1} - a_{j1}) \sin\theta, \tag{3.19a}$$

and for $j \epsilon U(\phi_i)$:

$$(a_{j2} - a_{i2}) \cos\theta > (a_{j1} - a_{i1}) \sin\theta. \tag{3.19b}$$

Conditions (3.19) can easily be used to find the endpoints of ϕ_i. This will be illustrated in Example 3.3. We now show that the optimum angle θ cannot occur in ϕ_i. For $\theta \epsilon \phi_i$:

$$P_\theta(G_\theta) = \sum_{j=1}^{n} w_j |a_{i2}^\theta - a_{j2}^\theta|$$

$$= \sum_{j \epsilon L(\phi_i)} w_j((a_{i2} - a_{j2}) \cos \theta - (a_{i1} - a_{j1}) \sin \theta)$$

$$+ \sum_{j \epsilon U(\phi_i)} w_j((a_{j2} - a_{i2}) \cos \theta - (a_{j1} - a_{i1}) \sin \theta)$$

$$= \cos \theta \left(\sum_{j \epsilon L(\phi_i)} w_j(a_{i2} - a_{j2}) + \sum_{i \epsilon U(\phi_i)} w_j(a_{j2} - a_{i2}) \right)$$

$$- \sin \theta \left(\sum_{j \epsilon L(\phi_i)} w_j(a_{i1} - a_{j1}) + \sum_{j \epsilon U(\phi_i)} w_j(a_{j1} - a_{i1}) \right).$$

It can easily be verified that:

$$\frac{\partial^2}{\partial \theta^2} P_\theta(G_\theta) = -P_\theta(G_\theta),$$

which is always negative. This means that $P_\theta(G_\theta)$ is concave in ϕ_i and that the minimum must occur at the endpoints of ϕ_i.

This leaves the possibility that G_θ^* is not a point but a range. Figure 3.11 illustrates such a case. It can be verified that $G_\theta^* = [a_{12}^\theta, a_{32}^\theta]$ for $\theta \epsilon [\theta_1, \theta_2]$. In general, let $\phi_i = (\theta_1^i, \theta_2^i)$ be an open interval of angles for which $G_\theta^* = [a_{i2}^\theta, a_{q2}^\theta]$, where $a_{i2}^\theta \leqslant a_{q2}^\theta$. Note that the angles θ_1^i and θ_2^i, where the line would pass through "new" points, are again not included in ϕ_1. Let:

$$L'(\phi_i) = \{j | a_{j2}^\theta < a_{i2}^\theta, \ \theta \epsilon \phi_i\} \tag{3.20a}$$

and

$$U'(\phi_i) = \{j | a_{j2}^\theta > a_{q2}^\theta, \ \theta \epsilon \phi_i\}. \tag{3.20b}$$

Using conditions (3.19) we can now identify the conditions that define ϕ_1.

For $j \epsilon L'(\phi_1)$: $(a_{i2} - a_{j2}) \cos \theta > (a_{i1} - a_{j1}) \sin \theta$. $\tag{3.21a}$

For $j \epsilon U'(\phi_1)$: $(a_{j2} - a_{q2}) \cos \theta > (a_{j1} - a_{q1}) \sin \theta$. $\tag{3.21b}$

But $a_{q2}^\theta \geqslant a_{i2}^\theta$.

Therefore, $(a_{q2} - a_{i2}) \cos \theta > (a_{q1} - a_{i1}) \sin \theta$. $\tag{3.21c}$

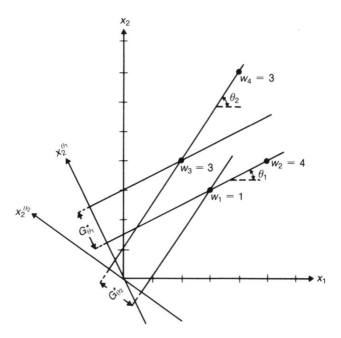

Figure 3.11 $G_\theta^* = [a_{12}^0, a_{32}^0]$.

Exercise 3.11 asks the reader to show that the optimum angle can also not occur in ϕ_1 for the case where G_θ^* is a range.

Finding θ^*, the best angle, can therefore be accomplished by systematically eliminating intervals ϕ_i from $[0°, 180°)$ and evaluating the cost function at the endpoints of these intervals. As can be verified by checking Figure 3.9, the slope and intercept of the best line are:

$$A^* = G_{\theta^*}^*/\cos \theta^* \tag{3.22a}$$

$$S^* = \tan \theta^*. \tag{3.22b}$$

Example 3.3 illustrates the notation and equations. Example 3.4 illustrates a graphical, nearly "equationless" version of the method that is simple to apply for small problems.

Example 3.3 Table 3.8 gives the coordinates and weights of three demand points.

We can start our search at $0°$. Table 3.9 reproduces Table 3.8, but with the points ordered by the magnitudes of a_{j2}^0 so that we can more easily find G_0^*. It is evident that the median weight is at a_{12}^0 and hence $G_0^* = 5$. We find that $L(\phi_1) = \{2\}$ and $U(\phi_1) = \{3\}$, and using conditions (3.19) we draw the following conclusions.

Table 3.8 Parameters for Example 3.3.

j	w_j	a_{j1}	a_{j2}
1	3	1	5
2	1	4	2
3	2	6	6

Table 3.9 Ordering of a_{j2}^θ at $\theta = 0°$.

j	w_j	a_{j1}	a_{j2}	a_{j2}
2	1	4	2	2
1	3	1	5	5
3	2	6	6	6

For $j \epsilon L(\phi_1)$: $(a_{12}^\theta - a_{22}^\theta) \cos \theta > (a_{11}^\theta - a_{21}^\theta) \sin \theta$

or $(5-2) \cos \theta > (1-4) \sin \theta$

or $\quad -\cos \theta < \sin \theta$,

which is true for θ in $(-45,135)$.

For $j \epsilon U(\phi_1)$: $(a_{32}^\theta - a_{12}^\theta) \cos \theta > (a_{31} - a_{11}) \sin \theta$

or $(6-5) \cos \theta > (6-1) \sin \theta$

$0.2 \cos \theta < \sin \theta$,

which is true for θ in $(-168.6901,11.3099)$.

This can be verified by setting:

$$Z = 0.2 \cos \theta - \sin \theta$$

$$= \cos \theta(0.2 - \tan \theta).$$

Z is positive for $\cos \theta > 0$ and $0.2 > \tan \theta$ or for $\cos \theta < 0$ and $\tan \theta < 0.2$. It follows that $\phi_1 = (-45,11.3099)$.

To eliminate the next interval, we consider in Table 3.10 the new ordering of a_{j2}^θ that begins at $11.3099°$. Conditions (3.21) now define ϕ_3. Hence, $L'(\phi_3) = \{2\}$ and $(6-2) \cos \theta > (6-4) \sin \theta$, which gives $2 \cos \theta > \sin \theta$. This inequality is true for $\theta \epsilon [-116.565,63.435]$. Note that $U'(\phi_3)$ is an empty set.

Since $q = 1$ and $i = 3$ in ϕ, $a_{q2}^\theta > a_{i2}^\theta$ and $(5-6) \cos \theta > (1-6) \sin \theta$.

Table 3.10 Ordering at $\theta = 11.31°$.

j	w_j	a_{j1}	a_{j2}	$a_{j2}^{11.31}$
2	1	4	2	1.1767
3	2	6	6	4.7068
1	3	1	5	4.7068

Table 3.11 Ordering at $\theta = 63.435°$.

j	w_j	a_{j1}	a_{j2}	$a_{j2}^{63.435}$
3	2	6	6	-2.6833
2	1	4	2	-2.6833
1	3	1	5	1.34174

Table 3.12 Comparison of Costs.

θ	G_θ^*	$P_\theta(G_\theta^*)$
11.3009	4.7068	3.5301
63.435	$[-2.6833, 1.34164]$	12.0748
135.0	-4.2426	8.4852

Therefore, $0.2 \cos\theta > \sin\theta$, which is true for $\theta\epsilon[11.3099, 191.3099]$. We now have $\phi_3 = (11.3099, 63.435)$. The a_{j2}^θ are reordered for the next interval in Table 3.11.

Again, conditions (3.21) apply: $(2-6)\cos\theta > (4-6)\sin\theta$ or $2\cos\theta < \sin\theta$, which is true for $\theta\epsilon[63.435, 243.43]$. Also, $(5-2)\cos\theta > (1-4)\sin\theta$ or $-\cos\theta < \sin\theta$, which is true for $(-45°, 135°)$. Hence, $\phi_2 = (63.435, 135)$.

Because a new line with $\theta = 135°$ is the same as one with $\theta = -45°$, we have exhausted 180°. We now need only evaluate the cost $P_\theta(G_\theta)$ at the endpoints of ϕ_1, ϕ_2, and ϕ_3 to find the best line. This is done in Table 3.12.

Using equation (3.22) gives $A^* = 4.7068/\cos 11.3099° = 4.8$, $S^* = \tan 11.3099° = 2$. The cost function $P_\theta(G_\theta^*)$ is plotted in Figure 3.12. We observe that cost is rather sensitive to changes in angle in the vicinity of the optimum. The concavity of the function in each region ϕ_i is also apparent.

Simplifications

Two simplifications suggest themselves. First, note that the optimum line *must* cut through *at least two* points. This suggests a simple search approach. We can simply calculate the intercepts A and slopes S of the $n(n-1)/2$ lines cutting all pairs of points and use $P(A,S)$ in problem (3.14) to choose the least-cost line. Second, the algorithm can be viewed as rotating the line and using pivot point after pivot point such that the line continues to be median. This can readily be done graphically for small problems. Both procedures are illustrated in the following example.

Example 3.4 Table 3.13 gives the coordinates and weights of four points.
There are six possible lines through two points at a time. The indices of the pairs of points are (1,2), (1,3), (1,4), (2,3), (2,4), and (3,4). Table

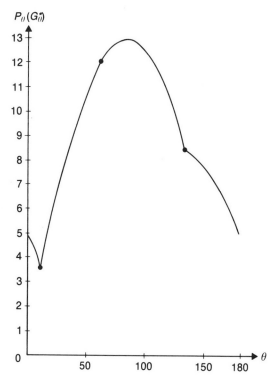

Figure 3.12 Plot of $P_\theta(G_\theta^*)$.

3.14 gives the intercepts, slopes, and costs of these lines. The line through points a_1 and a_2 is optimal.

Figure 3.13 illustrates the rotation procedure. If we begin with a horizontal line, it must go through point 1 in order to divide the weights in two. However, this line intersects only one point and cannot be optimal. We therefore rotate this line counterclockwise with point 1 as a pivot until we obtain line #1 in Figure 3.13. In order for the line to remain median, point 3 becomes the pivot until line #2 is produced. Then point 4 becomes the pivot until line #3 is produced. Point 1 then becomes a pivot to create line #4. It then remains a pivot until the line is again horizontal. Only four lines need now be evaluated. The lines through

Table 3.13 Parameters for Example 3.4.

j	w_j	a_{j1}	a_{j2}
1	2	1	5
2	1	4	4
3	1	6	6
4	1	3	4

Table 3.14 Evaluation of Candidate Lines.

Pair	A	S	$P(A,S)$
(1,2)	16/3	−1/3	2.846
(1,3)	24/5	1/5	2.942
(1,4)	11/2	−1/2	3.578
(2,3)	0	1	6.364
(2,4)	4	0	4.000
(3,4)	2	2/3	4.438

pairs (2,4) and (2,3) are eliminated. In larger examples, of course, the savings in computational time is much larger.

3.4 SINGLE-FACILITY DYNAMIC LOCATION

Let us assume that a facility is expected to serve over r periods of time. The facility may be relocated repeatedly during that time. To simplify matters, let us stipulate that this facility may be moved only at the beginning of each period. The reasons for relocating the facility may lie in changing costs of transportation, changing demands from the existing facilities, or even changes in the numbers and locations of the existing facilities themselves. It is obvious that if no costs were associated with moving the facility, we could relocate it optimally at the beginning of each period provided we knew the weights and locations of the existing

Figure 3.13 Candidate Lines.

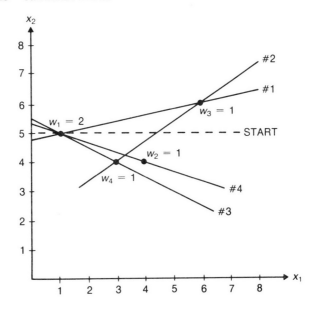

facilities for that period. The inclusion of relocation costs, however, may make relocation inadvisable in some periods. Again for simplicity, we assume that relocation costs are not affected by the distance that the facility must be moved through space, but are incurred only by the act of relocation.

The first question that arises is this: How do we balance present and future costs? One approach could be not even to try. We could compare the costs of the present location with the cost of the optimal location for the forthcoming period. If the difference is greater than the cost of re-location, then we would move the facility. This myopic approach has its faults. For example, relocation costs may be very low now but may be predicted to be very high several periods hence. It may be wise to move the facility now even though the move is not strictly justified in the immediately following period.

What is needed is some way of balancing present costs against future costs. First, however, we must know future costs. It is assumed in dynamic location that future costs and the future locations of demand points can be predicted. Of course, in practice, such predictions may have a measure of uncertainty attached to them. For the present we will assume "perfect" predictions for the sake of simplicity. If future costs are known, we can take their present values and thus treat present and future costs on a comparable basis.

As a first step toward formulation, let us recall the "nondynamic" single-facility location problem of Chapter 2 as expressed in problem (2.1). We will henceforth call this problem the *static* problem. Problem (2.1) (renumbered for convenience) is:

$$\text{minimize } W(X) = \sum_{j=1}^{n} w_j \ell_p(X, a_j). \tag{3.23}$$

We now wish to find not a single location for the facility, but a location for each of r periods. The notation of problem (3.23) must be modified to accommodate the dynamic problem. Let the weight w_{jk} be the present value of the cost per unit distance between the new facility and existing facility j in period k. The present value of a cost C that is k periods in the future is $C/(1+r_d)^k$. We will neglect the contentious practical issue of how to determine the discount rate r_d; much has been written about that elsewhere. Let the present value of the cost of relocating the facility in period k be c_k. The object, then, is to find a series of locations $X_k = (x_{1k}, x_{2k})$, $k = 1, ..., r$ that minimize the present value of the location-re-location *plan*. The dynamic location problem to be considered is:

$$\text{minimize } \sum_{k=1}^{r} \sum_{j=1}^{n} w_{jk} \ell_p(X_k, a_j) + \sum_{k=2}^{r} c_k z_k \tag{3.24}$$

$\quad\quad X, Z$

where:

$$z_k = \begin{cases} 1 \text{ if } X_k \neq X_{k-1} \text{ is allowed,} \\ 0 \text{ otherwise.} \end{cases}$$

The z's serve as indicator variables that tell us whether the facility is "permitted to move" from where it was the previous period. If it is so permitted, a relocation cost is incurred whether a move takes place or not. However, if $X_k = X_{k-1}$, then $z_k = 1$ cannot be optimal. This interpretation will be used shortly.

In the problem statement (3.24), the locations of the existing facilities do not have period subscripts, and it appears (as n has no subscript) that we are assuming that the number of existing facilities does not change over time. This is not necessarily so. We can assume the creation and deletion of existing facilities over time simply by changing w_{jk} from zero to some positive value, or from some positive value to zero. The difficulty is that n must equal the total number of the sites that will ever be used. We only do this to simplify notation. The problem could have posed with n_k and a_{jk}'s and the optimization methods to be discussed would be basically unchanged.

When $p = 1$ distances are rectangular and problem (3.24) can be expressed as a zero-one linear integer programming problem. This formulation is explored in Exercise 3.13. The method discussed here is more generally applicable and can be used with ℓ_p distances. Consider the vector $Z = (z_2, ..., z_r)$. Any particular vector is a plan for relocation. For example, (1,0,0,1) tells us that we can move the facility at the beginning of period 2 to a new location where it must stay for two periods (we pass up two chances for relocation). We can relocate again at the beginning of period 5. *Given* any such vector, problem (3.24) can be solved by the methods of Chapter 2 because $\sum_{k=2}^{r} c_k z_k$ is constant and does not enter into the optimization. The example vector causes $X_2 = X_3 = X_4$, which reduces problem (3.24) to a problem in the variables X_1, X_2, and X_5, which in turn can be solved as three *separate* static problems. It is evident that if we find the costs for all possible vectors Z and pick the best one, we will have found the optimal location-relocation plan.

Example 3.5 Table 3.15 gives the locations of three existing facilities and the predicted weights for three periods.

The relocation costs c_2 and c_3 at the beginning of the second and third periods are 2 and 10, respectively. For ease of computation assume that distances are rectangular ($p = 1$). If there were no relocation costs, we could use the weight w_{j1} to find the best location in period 1, the weights w_{j2} to find the best location in period 2, and the weights w_{j3} to find the

Table 3.15 Three Period Locations and Weights.

j	a_{j1}	a_{j2}	w_{j1}	w_{j2}	w_{j3}
1	1	2	2	1	5
2	3	3	2	2	2
3	4	5	1	4	4

best location in period 3. We can use the median weight method in Chapter 2 to find the best locations; these locations and the resulting transportation costs are given in Table 3.16.

Let us now consider a myopic location scheme. At the end of period 1 the facility is located at (3,3). If we leave it at (3,3), we can calculate the transportation cost during period 2 to be 15 (the reader should check this). If we move it to (4,5) the cost drops to 12. Because the cost of relocating at the beginning of period 2 is 2, the decisionmaker who does not look ahead to period 3 would relocate the facility to (4,5). Leaving the facility at (4,5) for the third period would mean a transportation cost of 36 (again, the reader should check this). The savings for moving back to (3,3), ie, $36 - 27 = 9$, is not as big as the cost of relocation (10), and therefore our myopic decisionmaker would leave the facility at (4,5). In terms of the relocation vector Z, the scheme was (1,0). The total cost was: $9 + 12 + 36 + 2 = 59$.

Of course, there are other schemes available, namely (1,1), (0,1), and (0,0). For example, let us calculate the best locations and cost for $Z = (0,1)$. Because the facility must stay put for the first two periods, we can combine the weights for the three existing facilities and get 3, 4, and 5, respectively. Using conditions (2.16) with these combined weights we find that the best location for the first two periods is (3,3), giving a transportation cost of 24. Although Z specifies a move in the third period, the "move" is to (3,3) because this remains the best location. The move cost must still be charged, and so the total cost for the scheme is $24 + 27 + 10 = 61$. The cost of all possible schemes is given in Table 3.17.

The above example has illustrated that we can solve problem (3.24) by evaluating all possible change plans and within each solving a set of static problems. Unfortunately, as the planning horizon increases, the number of change plans to be evaluated, 2^{r-1}, expands greatly. Exercise 3.14 asks the reader to show that the number of static problems that

Table 3.16 Best Static Locations and Costs.

Period (k)	x_{1k}^*	x_{2k}^*	Cost
1	3	3	9
2	4	5	12
3	3	3	27

Table 3.17 Total Costs for Z.

Z	Optimal Transportation Cost	Moving Cost	Total Cost
(1,1)	48	12	60
(1,0)	57	2	59
(0,1)	51	10	61
(0,0)	51	0	51

would have to be solved is $2^{r-1}((r-1)/2+1)$. For example, if $r = 10$, this number is 2816.

Fortunately, the amount of work involved can be greatly reduced by a simple branch-and-bound approach. The key is the following observation: Once a move is specified by the Z vector, subsequent optimal locations are not dependent on the preceding location "history." This leads to the conclusion that many of the static problems solved in the total enumeration of the Z vector are identical. The scheme to be explained avoids this duplication.

Let Z_k be that part of the Z vector pertaining to periods k through r. For example, if $Z = (0,1,1,0,1)$, $Z_4 = (1,0,1)$ and indicates that there is a move in the fourth period, none in the fifth, and a move again in the sixth. Let $C(Z_k)$ be the optimal cost connected with vector Z_k. This cost includes the lowest transportation costs possible in periods k through r inclusive given change plan Z_k, and includes the appropriate relocation costs. We begin our search for the best plan with period k. This search is illustrated in Figure 3.14. Inside each circle is a number; 1 indicates a relocation, 0 indicates that no relocation was made.

Costs where Z_k begins with 0, ie, $C(0,1,0)$ or $C(0,0)$, cannot be evaluated because the location of the facility at the beginning of period k is not known. Let us ignore this difficulty for the moment. Consider the costs $C(1,0)$ and $C(1,1)$ in Figure 3.14. Suppose $C(1,1) > C(1,0)$. We can then remove the branch below $C(1,1)$ from further consideration; in other words, we know that any plan that calls for a relocation in the $r-1^{st}$ period must require no change in the rth period in order to be optimal. We generalize this procedure as follows: At each period k, we cancel all branches where the cost $C(Z_k)$ is higher than the lowest.

Fortunately, we can do even more pruning. Let Z_k^0 be any vector that starts with zero and Z_k^1 be a vector identical except that it starts with one. For example, if $Z_k^0 = (0,1,1,0,1)$ then $Z_k^1 = (1,1,1,0,1)$. First we justify the following inequality:

$$C(Z_k^0) \geqslant C(Z_k^1) - c_k . \tag{3.25}$$

On the right-hand side, the kth period move cost is subtracted from the optimal cost of the scheme that allows a move in that period. This *net*

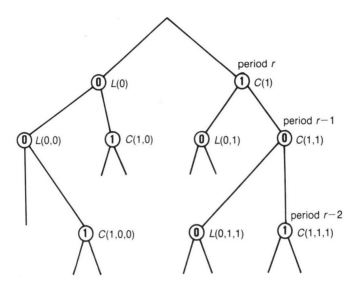

Figure 3.14   Decision Tree for Relocation.

amount cannot be larger than the optimal cost of the scheme that *doesn't* allow a move in the kth period. Now define:

$$L(Z_k^0) = C(Z_k^1) - c_k . \qquad (3.26)$$

The cost $L(Z_k^0)$ is the lower bound on what the cost of a branch (from period $k+1$ on) can be. If it is higher than some cost $C(Z_k)$, it follows that this branch also can be dropped. With some luck, and if we are not fussy about keeping ties, it is often possible to prune rather substantially the tree in Figure 3.14.

Example 3.6   The data in Example 3.5 were used to illustrate our "tree-pruning" method; Figure 3.15 gives the details. Note that the branches bearing the costs $L(0,1)$ and $C(1,1)$ were eliminated because they could not possibly be superior to the branch labeled $C(1,0)$. The final result is that $Z = (1,0)$ is the best location-relocation plan—the same solution that was found by complete enumeration of Z's in Example 3.5. The computation savings are not apparent in this small example, but would be in a larger one.

The basic concept of dynamic location was illustrated here with simple cost assumptions and with a simple single-facility location problem. Naturally, this concept can be extended to more complex problems.

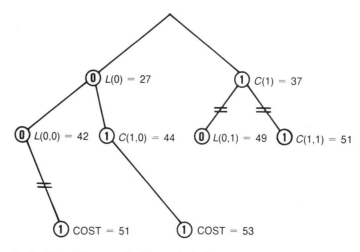

Figure 3.15 Tree Diagram for Example 3.6.

3.5 PROBABILISTIC DESTINATION LOCATIONS

So far we have assumed that both the locations of existing facilities and all costs in the system were known exactly. In practice, we seldom encounter this ideal. In this section we allow "knowledge" about the exact location of an existing facility to take the form of a probability distribution. In other words, though we may not know where the demand will be located, by using an appropriate distribution we are able to calculate the probability that it will occur in any given area of the plane. An example of such a situation arises when there is a large population of potential demand points and it is unknown which particular ones will become "active."

Let us consider a single-facility problem with rectangular distances. As usual, rectangular distances (versus ℓ_p distances) allow for considerable simplification in the problem. Let each of the n existing facilities (demand points) have random coordinates (Y_{j1}, Y_{j2}), as specified by a bivariate normal probability density $f(y_{j1}, y_{j2})$. We are required to find a facility location (x_1^*, x_2^*) that minimizes the expected sum of weighted rectangular distances in the system. Each distance is weighted by the known cost w_j. The total expected cost in the system is then:

$$EW(X) = \underset{Y}{E} \left(\sum_{i=1}^{n} w_j \ell_1(X, Y_j) \right) \qquad (3.27)$$

where:

$$Y_j = (Y_{j1}, Y_{j2})$$

$$Y = (Y_{j1}, Y_{j2}, ..., Y_{n1}, Y_{n2}).$$

It follows that:

$$EW(X) = \sum_{j=1}^{n} w_j \underset{Y_j}{E} \, (\ell_1(X, Y_j)),$$

$$= \sum_{j=1}^{n} w_j \underset{Y_j}{E} \, |x_1 - Y_{j1}| + \sum_{j=1}^{n} w_j \underset{Y_j}{E} \, |x_2 - Y_{j2}|,$$

$$= \sum_{j=1}^{n} w_j \underset{Y_{j1}}{E} \, |x_1 - Y_{j1}| + \sum_{j=1}^{n} w_j \underset{Y_{j2}}{E} \, |x_2 - Y_{j2}|,$$

$$= EW_1(x_1) + EW_2(x_2), \tag{3.28}$$

which means:

$$\min_{X} EW(X) = \min_{x_1} EW_1(x_1) + \min_{x_2} EW_2(x_2).$$

This makes it possible to concentrate on minimizing $EW_1(x_1)$, because the minimization of $EW_2(x_2)$ is analogous. From equation (3.28) we can write:

$$EW_1(x_1) = \sum_{j=1}^{n} w_j \int_{-\infty}^{\infty} |x_1 - y_{j1}| \, f(y_{j1}) dy_{j1}, \tag{3.29}$$

where $f(y_{j1})$ is the marginal (normal) distribution of Y_{j1}. Let Y_{j1} have mean μ_{j1} and standard deviation σ_{j1}. Then:

$$f(y_{j1}) = (\sqrt{2\pi} \, \sigma_{j1})^{-1} \exp(-((y_{j1} - \mu_{j1})^2/2)). \tag{3.30}$$

Note that the analysis is unaffected by whether or not Y_{j1} and Y_{j2} are correlated!

Fortunately, $EW_1(x_1)$ has a unimodal shape. As is shown in the Appendix, mathematical note 3.4, the derivative is:

$$EW_1'(x_1) = \sum_{j=1}^{n} w_j(1 - 2P_r(z \geqslant (x_1 - \mu_{j1})/\sigma_{j1})), \tag{3.31}$$

where z is the standardized normal variate and P_r denotes probability. As $EW_1'(x_1)$ is easily evaluated with the aid of cumulative normal tables, we may use a method such as interval bisection to find x_1^*.

Example 3.7 Table 3.18 gives the data for an example of three probabilistic destination locations.

Suppose the locations of the three points are deterministic at the means of their marginal distributions; that is, suppose that we were trying to

Table 3.18 Parameters for the Marginal Distributions of Three Points.

j	w_j	μ_{j1}	σ_{j1}	μ_{j2}	σ_{j2}
1	1	3	1	20	1
2	4	10	3	25	6
3	2	15	4	10	2

find the location of a facility among existing facilities located at (3,20), (10,25), and (15,10). Using the median weight method of Chapter 2, we find that $(x_1^*, x_2^*) = (10,25)$. This solution minimizes $EW(X)$ under the assumption that all standard deviations σ_{j1}, σ_{j2} are zero. We shall see that the solution is different when they are not all equal to zero.

As an illustration, let us find $EW_1'(3)$. By equation (3.31) and cumulative standardized normal probability tables:

$$EW_1'(3) = 1(1 - 2P_r(z \geqslant (3-3)/1)) + 4(1 - 2P_r(z \geqslant (3-10)/3))$$

$$+ 2(1 - 2P_r(z \geqslant (3-15)/4))$$

$$= -5.9947.$$

Table 3.19 shows the steps in the method of interval bisection as applied to finding the minimum of $EW(x_1)$. The interval [3,15] is a logical starting point. After three steps the derivative can be successively used to bisect the interval within which x_1^* must lie, because $EW_1(x_1)$ is unimodal. At $x_1^* = 10.602$, the expected cost $EW_1(x_1)$ is 27.2524. A similar computation shows that x_2^* is 20.632, and the cost $EW_2(20.632)$ is 46.2159. In sum-

Table 3.19 Steps in Interval Bisection.

x_1	$EW_1'(x_1)$
3	−5.99477
15	4.90467
9	−2.1174
12	2.06679
10.5	−0.145819
11.25	0.966502
10.875	0.40155
10.6875	0.124198
10.5937	−0.0119195
10.6406	0.0558858
10.6172	0.0219169
10.6055	0.00498343
10.5996	−0.00347376
10.6025	0.000754356
10.6011	−0.00135994
10.6018	−0.000303268
10.6022	0.000223637

mary, the facility location that gives the lowest expected cost $EW(X)$ is (10.602,20.632).

EXERCISES

3.1 Justify the following properties of problem (3.1).

    a. A point is a minimizer for $\sum_{j=1}^{n} w_j A(X,a_j)$ if, and only if, its antipode is a maximizer.

    b. A point and its antipode with equal weights can be added to the problem without a change in the optimal location of the facility.

    c. A point with weight w_j can be replaced by its antipode with weight $-w_j$ without changing the optimal location of the facility.

    d. Every problem can be transformed to an equivalent one that has only positive weights.

3.2 a. Write a computer program to perform the Weiszfeld procedure on the sphere. It should include a preliminary check of Property 3.4 for each point.

    b. Use an atlas to find the coordinates of 10 cities on the globe: two in North America, two in Europe, two in the Middle East, and four in Asia. Weight the cities by their approximate population size. Apply the program developed in Exercise 3.2a. Discuss your confidence in having found the optimum solution.

3.3 a. Find the optimum solution to problem (3.1) if the distance function $d(X,a_j) = \pi \sin^2 (A(X,a_j)/2)$ is used.

    b. When might $d(X,a_j)$ be used?

3.4 Derive equations (3.6) from equations (3.4). (Warning: This requires a bit of trigonometry.)

3.5 Drezner and Wesolowsky (1978a) Show that Property 3.3 is "tight" in the sense that an example with two or more local minima can be constructed if the radius is $\pi/4 + \epsilon$, where $\epsilon > 0$.

3.6 Show that $T_{jk}(x_k)$ in equation (3.10) is strictly convex.

3.7 Show that problem (3.8) can be solved for (x_1^*, x_2^*) by finding the location of the medians of weights on the respective axes. (Hint: Define a value x_k'' and divide the sums in problem (3.8) into three parts: areas and points to the left of x_k'', areas and points to the right of x_k'', and points coinciding with x_k''. Equate $dWA_k(x_k)/dx_k$ to zero and consider the implications.)

3.8 A post office box must be optimally located among three "area" destinations and four point destinations. Problem parameters are given in Table 3E.1.

Table 3E.1   Problem Parameters for Exercise 3.8.

j	c_{j1}	d_{j1}	c_{j2}	d_{j2}	u_j
1	2	3	8	9	3
2	2	4	4	8	3
3	4	6	4	6	3

j	w_j	a_{j1}	a_{j2}
1	5	2	3
2	8	4	3
3	2	3	5
4	17	5	7

a. Display the area and point destinations graphically.
b. Find the optimum location for the post office box.

3.9 Find an expression for $T_j(x_1, x_2)$ in equation (3.7) when straight-line distances are used. Perform any integration; then express $WA(X)$ in problem (3.8) for straight-line distances. Suggest a solution method.

3.10 Show that the shortest (or perpendicular) distance from a point (a_{j1}, a_{j2}) to the line $x_2 = A + Sx_1$ is:

$$\frac{|A - (a_{j2} - Sa_{j1})|}{(S^2 + 1)^{1/2}}.$$

3.11 Show that the optimum angle for a line that minimizes the sum of weighted perpendiculars cannot occur in a range ϕ_i, where ϕ_i is specified preceding Property 3.6.

3.12 Table 3E.2 gives the data for locating a linear facility.
a. Plot the seven points and their weights on a diagram.
b. By inspection, find the 12 lines whose slopes represent the only angles that can be optimal.
c. Use the results of Exercise 3.12b and $P(A, S)$ in problem (3.14) to evaluate the 12 candidate lines. Choose the best one.

Table 3E.2   Seven Points and Their Weights.

j	a_{j1}	a_{j2}	w_j
1	2	2	2
2	3	5	1
3	6	1	2
4	7	5	1
5	7	7	2
6	9	3	2
7	9	8	4

3.13 For the case $p = 1$, express problem (3.24) in the text as a zero-one linear programming problem. (Hint: A reading of the first part of Section 4.1 will help here.)

3.14 Show that if all possible change plans were to be evaluated in single-facility dynamic location, $2^{r-1}((r-1)/2+1)$ static problems would have to be solved.

3.15 Repeat Example 3.5 for straight-line distances.

3.16 Tables 3E.3 and 3E.4 give the data for a six-period dynamic facility location problem. Distances are rectangular. Find the optimal location plan by using the branch-and-bound method of Section 3.4. It is not necessary to find all tied solutions.

3.17 Assume that each demand point can occur within a rectangular area (this shape is chosen to make analysis easier) and that the probability density of occurrence anywhere within that area is the same (uniform). Note that overlapping rectangles of various sizes can be used to represent complex spatial configurations of probability.

Table 3E.3 Location of Destinations by Period.

Period k	Destination Number j	a_{j1k}	a_{j2k}
1	1	1	1
	2	4	2
	3	6	6
2	1	1	1
	2	4	2
	3	6	6
3	1	1	1
	2	4	2
	3	6	6
	4	6	7
4	1	1	1
	2	4	2
	3	6	6
	4	6	7
5	1	1	1
	2	4	2
	3	6	6
	4	6	7
	5	5	8
6	1	1	1
	2	4	2
	3	6	6
	4	6	7
	5	5	8

Table 3E.4 Weights by Period.

Period j	w_{jk}				
	1	2	3	4	5
1	3	1	1		
2	2	1	1		
3	2	1	1	2	
4	1	1	1	2	
5	1	1	1	1	1
6	1	1	1	1	1

Consider a rectangle bounded by the corners (c_{j1},c_{j2}), (d_{j1},c_{j2}), (d_{j1},d_{j2}), and (c_{j1},d_{j2}), with $d_{j1} > c_{j1}$ and $d_{j2} > c_{j2}$. Show that:

$$EW_1(x_1) = -\sum_{j=1}^{n} w_j R_j (I_j(x_1 - c_{j1})^2 + (x_1 - d_{j1})^2)/2(d_{j1} - c_{j1})$$

where: $R_j = 1$ when $c_{j1} \leqslant x_1 < d_{j1}$,

$\qquad = -1$ otherwise;

$\quad I_j = 1$ when $c_{j1} \leqslant x_1 < d_{j1}$,

$\qquad = -1$ otherwise,

and that:

$$EW_1'(x_1) = -\sum_{j=1}^{n} w_j R_j (x_1 - d_{j1} + I_j(x_1 - c_{j1}))/(d_{j1} - c_{j1}),$$

and that $EW_1(x_1)$ is convex, where E denotes expected value.

3.18 Derive a formula for finding a minimizer x_1^* for $EW_1(x_1)$ in Exercise 3.17, given that the values of the indicators I and R at the optimum are known.

3.19 Derive an efficient search procedure for solving the problem in Exercise 3.17. Apply this method to the problem defined by the data in Table 3E.5.

3.20 Discuss the relationship between the problem of minimizing $EW_1(x_1)$ in Exercise 3.17 and the problem in Section 3.2.

3.21 Show that equation (3.31) implies that x_1^* is, in a sense, the location of the median weight. (Hint: Be careful in defining "weight.")

3.22 Solve the problem of Example 3.7 by the median weight method.

3.23 The mean of a uniform probability distribution with range $[a,b]$ is $(b + a)/2$, and the standard deviation is $(b - a)/\sqrt{12}$. Solve the example in Table 3.18 assuming uniform distributions with the same means and standard deviations as the normal distributions.

Table 3E.5 Data for Exercise 3.19.

j	w_j	c_{j1}	d_{j1}	c_{j2}	d_{j2}
1	1	$-\ 7.12$	17.12	5.12	12.31
2	2	-17.71	37.71	3.15	14.51
3	1	-16.18	46.18	$-\ 5.12$	15.12
4	3	$-\ 1.18$	61.18	-12.12	42.12
5	1	19.22	60.78	5.12	12.12

REFERENCE NOTES

SECTION 3.1 This section is based primarily on the paper by Drezner and Wesolowsky (1978). This problem was previously investigated by, among others, Litwhiler (1977), and Katz and Cooper (1980); also, see Litwhiler and Aly (1979). For a summary of the literature on spherical surface location problems, see Wesolowsky (1982).

SECTION 3.2 The material presented here originally appeared in Wesolowsky and Love (1971a). The somewhat more complex problem created when straight-line distances are used was discussed by Love (1972), and Drezner and Wesolowsky (1980b).

SECTION 3.3 The discussion here is from Wesolowsky (1974). Related analysis was carried out by Morris and Norback (1980). There is evidence of increasing interest in the location literature in incorporating expressways and corridors into models.

The topic of orthogonal curve fitting has a long and interesting history. Early references include Adcock (1878), Kermack and Haldane (1950), and Pearson (1901). However, these works referred to the problem of fitting using the sum of *squared* perpendicular distances.

SECTION 3.4 This introduction to the topic follows Wesolowsky (1973). Further work includes Wesolowsky and Truscott (1975), Roodman and Schwarz (1977), Erlenkotter (1981), and Van Roy and Erlenkotter (1982).

SECTION 3.5 The corresponding problem with straight-line distances was introduced by Katz and Cooper (1974, 1976). The rectangular distance case was discussed by Wesolowsky (1977).

SECTION 3.6 For an extension of the problem to ℓ_p distances, see Drezner and Wesolowsky (1981).

APPENDIX—CHAPTER 3

Mathematical Notes

3.1 *Prove* Property 3.1

   $A(X,a_j)$ is convex on a spherical disk with radius $\pi/2$ centered on point j.

PROOF: To prove convexity for a continuous function such as $A(X,a_j)$, it is enough to prove [see equation (3.3)] that

$$f(V^{.5}) \leqslant .5f(Y) + .5f(Z).$$

We can choose the upper hemisphere for our disk of radius $\pi/2$ without loss of generality.

Choose any two points with coordinates $Y = (y_1,y_2)$ and $Z = (z_1,z_2)$ on the sphere provided that $y_1,z_1 \geqslant 0$. Let $p = (\pi/2,0)$ be the north pole. Then:

$$A(Y,p) = \pi/2 - y_1$$

$$A(Z,p) = \pi/2 - z_1$$

$$A(V^{.5},p) = \pi/2 - V_1^{.5}.$$

By the median formula [Donnay (1945), p. 59] $\sin V_1^5 = \sin ((y_1 + z_1)/2) \cos ((y_1 - z_1)/2) \cos (A(Y,Z)/2)$. Using equation (3.2) to evaluate $A(Y,Z)$, we can obtain:

$$\sin V_1^5 = \frac{\sin ((y_1 + z_1)/2}{(1 - t)^{1/2}},$$

where t is given by:

$$1 - \sin^2((y_2 - z_2)/2) \cos y_1 \cos z_1/\cos^2((y_1 - z_1)/2).$$

As $t \leqslant 1$, and $V_1^5 \leqslant \pi/2$,

$$V_1^5 \geqslant (y_1 + z_1)/2.$$

Therefore:

$$\pi/2 - V_1^5 \leqslant (\pi/2 - y_1 + \pi/2 - z_1)/2$$

and $A(V_1^5,p) \leqslant (A(Y,p) + A(Z,p))/2$,

which means $A(X,p)$ is a convex function north of the equator, and Property 3.1 follows immediately.

3.2 *Prove* Property 3.2
A local minimizer of a convex function $f(X)$ on a convex subset D of a sphere is also a global minimizer.

PROOF: Suppose that Y and Z are global and local minimizers on D, respectively. Because D is convex, the arc connecting Y and Z is included in D. Let V^λ be defined as in equation (3.3). Now:

$$f(V^\lambda) \leqslant \lambda f(Y) + (1 - \lambda) f(Z),$$

and if $f(Y) < f(Z)$, then $f(V^\lambda) < f(Z)$ for λ as small as desired. This contradicts the assumption that Z is a local minimizer. Thus Z cannot be a local minimizer without being a global minimizer.

3.3 *Prove* Property 3.4

$W(X)$ has a local minimum at a_r if, and only if, $CF_r \leqslant w_r$.

PROOF: It can be shown that for movement from point a_r:

$$dW(X) = w_r[(dx_1)^2 + \cos^2 a_{r1}(dx_2)^2]^{1/2}$$
$$-dx_1 \sum_{j \neq r} w_j(-\sin a_{r1} \cos a_{j1} \cos (a_{r2} - a_{j2})$$
$$+ \cos a_{r1} \sin a_{j1})/\sin A(a_r, a_j)$$
$$-dx_2 \sum_{j \neq r} w_j(\cos a_{r1} \cos a_{j1} \sin (a_{j2} - a_{r2})/\sin A(a_r, a_j).$$

For a local minimum, $dW(X) > 0$, and, hence, we must show

$$w_r((dx_1)^2 + \cos^2 a_{r1}(dx_2)^2)^{1/2} - F_{r1}dx_1 - F_{r2} \cos a_{r1}dx_1 > 0.$$

Letting $L = dx_2 \cos a_{r1}/dx_1$, we have:

$$|dx_1|w_r(1 + L^2)^{1/2} > dx_1(F_{r1} + LF_{r2}), \text{ and so:}$$
$$w_r > dx_1(F_{r1} + LF_{r2})(1 + L^2)^{-1/2}/|dx_1|.$$

Note that $dx_1/|dx_1|$ is ± 1. It can be shown that:

$$-(F_{r1}^2 + F_{r2}^2)^{1/2} \leqslant (F_{r1} + LF_{r2})/(1 + L^2)^{1/2}$$
$$\leqslant (F_{r1}^2 + F_{r2}^2)^{1/2}$$

and hence, the condition:

$$w_r \geqslant (F_{r1}^2 + F_{r2}^2)^{1/2}$$

is necessary and sufficient for $dW(X) > 0$ for every L.

3.4 *Derive* $EW_1'(x_1)$ in equation (3.31)

From equations (3.29) and (3.30), $EW_1(x_1) = \sum_{j=1}^{n} w_j \text{ INT}_j$, where:

$$\text{INT}_j = \int_{-\infty}^{\infty} |x_1 - y_{j1}|(\sqrt{2\pi} \sigma_j)^{-1} \exp (-((y_{j1} - \mu_{j1})/\sigma_{j\ell})^2/2)dy_{j1}.$$

We break up INT_j into two integrals:

$$\text{INT}_j = \int_{-\infty}^{x_1} (x_1 - y_{j1})(\sqrt{2\pi}\ \sigma_j)^{-1} \exp\left(-((y_{j1} - \mu_{j1})/\sigma_{j1})^2/2\right)dy_{j1}$$

$$+ \int_{x_1}^{\infty} (y_{j1} - x_1)(\sqrt{2\pi}\ \sigma_j)^{-1} \exp\left(-((y_{j1} - \mu_{j1})/\sigma_{j1})^2/2\right)dy_{j1}.$$

Differentiating with respect to x_1:

$$\frac{d\text{INT}_j}{dx_1} = \int_{-\infty}^{x_1} (\sqrt{2\pi}\ \sigma_j)^{-1} \exp\left(-((y_{j1} - \mu_{j1})/\sigma_{j1})^2/2\right)dy_{j1}$$

$$- \int_{x_1}^{\infty} (\sqrt{2\pi}\ \sigma_j)^{-1} \exp\left(-((y_{j1} - \mu_{j1})/\sigma_{j1})^2/2\right)dy_{j1}$$

$$= 1 - 2\int_{x_1}^{\infty} (\sqrt{2\pi}\ \sigma_j)^{-1} \exp\left(-((y_{j1} - \mu_{j1})/\sigma_{j1})^2/2\right)dy_{j1}$$

$$= 1 - 2\,P_r(z \geqslant (x_1 - \mu_{j1})/\sigma_{j1})$$

and hence,

$$EW_1'(x_1) = \sum_{j=1}^{n} w_j(1 - 2\,P_r(z \geqslant (x_1 - \mu_{j1})/\sigma_{j1})).$$

Chapter 4

Multi-Facility Location

It often occurs that more than one new facility must be located. If no pair of new facilities interact (have inter-facility flow), we can treat the location of each new facility as a separate problem and apply the techniques of Chapter 2. Otherwise, the new facility locations are interdependent and must be optimized simultaneously. The resultant problem is termed a multi-facility location problem. We will continue to assume that the cost per unit flow between any pair of facilities is proportional to the distance between them. In general form, the multi-facility problem is:

$$\underset{X}{\text{minimize }} WM(X) = \sum_{i=1}^{m} \sum_{j=1}^{n} w_{1ij} \ell_p(X_i, a_j) + \sum_{i=1}^{m-1} \sum_{r=i+1}^{m} w_{2ir} \ell_p(X_i, X_r), \quad (4.1)$$

where

m is the number of new facilities to be located,

n is the number of existing facilities,

w_{1ij} converts distance between new facility i and existing facility j into cost and $w_{1ij} \geqslant 0$,

w_{2ir} converts distance between new facility i and new facility r into cost and $w_{2ir} \geqslant 0$,

$X = (X_1,...,X_m)$ is the vector of new facility locations,

$X_i = (x_{i1}, x_{i2})$ is the location of new facility i,

$a_j = (a_{j1}, a_{j2})$ is the location of existing facility j,

$\ell_p(X_i, a_j)$ is the distance between new facility i and existing facility j, and

$\ell_p(X_i, X_r)$ is the distance between new facility i and new facility r.

The condition on the sum describing the cost of distances between pairs of the new facilities indicates that each distance is to be considered only once. If $m = 1$, the problem reverts in form to problem (2.1), the single-facility problem.

Example 4.1   To motivate the multi-facility model, we describe an actual application reported by Love and Yerex (1976). The Coastal Construction Company* is to introduce a new product, transmission poles for electrical utilities, and the location of two new production facilities is to be determined. Figure 4.1 shows a section of the yard area and the three relevant existing facilities. The concrete batching plant supplies the premixed concrete used in pole construction. The steel manufacturing area supplies the steel hardware used in pole production, about half of which is embedded in the concrete and forms part of the finished pole. All completed

Figure 4.1   Layout of Existing Facilities.
(Reprinted by permission, "Application of a Facilities Location Model in the Prestressed Concrete Industry," Love and Yerex, *Interfaces,* Vol. 6, No. 4, August 1976. Copyright 1976, The Institute of Management Sciences, 290 Westminster Street, Providence, RI 02903.)

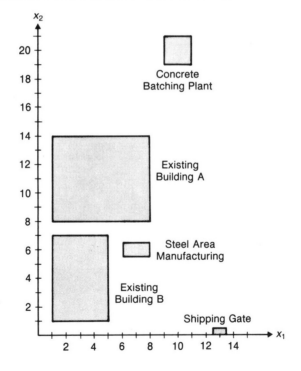

*This is a fictitious name.

production moves through the shipping gate, where it is checked and weighed before leaving the yard.

The two new facilities are a concrete casting area, where the poles are cast, and an assembly and storage area, where the remainder of the steel hardware is added. To develop numerical data, a sales estimate of 40 poles per day is used as a production norm. These 40 poles require approximately 10 cubic yards of concrete and 8400 pounds of manufactured steel. The required handling equipment is as follows:

Concrete (3 cubic-yard buckets)—flatbed trucks

Steel (in drums)—front-end loader

Poles—lift crane and flatbed trailer

A field accountant supplied historical costs for each piece of handling equipment based on studies of existing operations. The following cost-distance values were then computed:

Table 4.1 Cost Estimates for the Coastal Construction Problem.

Item	Cost per 100 feet	Trips required per 40 poles
Concrete delivery	$0.20	4
Steel delivery	0.08	10
Crane	0.40	10
Flatbed trailer	0.20	2

Based on these estimates, the following daily costs in dollars per 100 feet between all pairs of facilities were computed:

		Existing Facilities			New Facilities	
		1	2	3	1	2
New	1	0.80	0.80	0	0	4.00
facilities	2	0.80	0.80	0.40	0	0

Forbidden regions for location are shaded in Figure 4.1; the coordinates are in units of 100 feet. Locations are denoted as follows: concrete casting area, $X_1 = (x_{11}, x_{12})$; assembly and storage area, $X_2 = (x_{21}, x_{22})$; concrete batching plant, $a_1 = (10, 20)$; steel manufacturing area, $a_2 = (7, 6)$; and shipping gate, $a_3 = (13, 0)$. Temporarily ignoring the effect of the forbidden regions, the location problem is to determine the values of X_1 and X_2 that minimize:

$$WM(X) = 0.80 \; \ell_p(X_1, a_1) + 0.80 \; \ell_p(X_1, a_2) + 0.80 \; \ell_p(X_2, a_2)$$

$$+ 0.40 \; \ell_p(X_2, a_3) + 4.0 \; \ell_p(X_1, X_2)$$

Methods for solving problem (4.1) are generalized from those for solving problem (2.1). We will first discuss the rectangular distance case, of which the Coastal Construction Company problem is an example.

4.1 THE RECTANGULAR DISTANCE MODEL

For rectangular distances, $WM(X)$ in problem (4.1) becomes:

$$WM(X) = \sum_{i=1}^{m} \sum_{j=1}^{n} w_{1ij}(|x_{i1} - a_{j1}| + |x_{i2} - a_{j2}|)$$

$$+ \sum_{i=1}^{m-1} \sum_{r=i+1}^{m} w_{2ir}(|x_{i1} - x_{r1}| + |x_{i2} - x_{r2}|). \qquad (4.2)$$

As in the case of the single-facility problem, $WM(X)$ is separable (into two functions). In particular:

$$WM(X) = WM_1(x_{11}, \ldots, x_{m1}) + WM_2(x_{12}, \ldots, x_{m2})$$

where:

$$WM_k(x_{1k}, \ldots, x_{mk}) = \sum_{i=1}^{m} \sum_{j=1}^{n} w_{1ij}|x_{ik} - a_{jk}|$$

$$+ \sum_{i=1}^{m-1} \sum_{r=i+1}^{m} w_{2ir}|x_{ik} - x_{rk}|. \qquad (4.3)$$

The minimization of $WM(X)$ can therefore be accomplished in two separate steps: minimizing WM_1 with respect to $x_{11}, \ldots, x_{m1}$, and minimizing WM_2 with respect to $x_{12}, \ldots, x_{m2}$. We already know that the terms $w_{1ij}|x_{ik} - a_{jk}|$ are convex, and the convexity of the terms $w_{2ir}|x_{ik} - x_{rk}|$ is the subject of Exercise 4.1. Because the sum of convex functions is convex, WM_k is a convex function, as is WM itself.

A Linear Programming Approach

We will now show how to minimize WM_k by transforming the problem to linear form and using linear programming. To develop an appropriate formulation, new variables representing absolute deviations are first introduced. These deviational variables are intended to behave in the following way:

$$d^+_{ijk} = |x_{ik} - a_{jk}| \text{ if } x_{ik} \geqslant a_{jk} \text{ and is 0 otherwise;}$$

$$d^-_{ijk} = |x_{ik} - a_{jk}| \text{ if } x_{ik} \leqslant a_{jk} \text{ and is 0 otherwise.}$$

Similarly:

$$e^+_{irk} = |x_{ik} - x_{rk}| \text{ if } x_{ik} \geqslant x_{rk} \text{ and is 0 otherwise;}$$

$$e^-_{irk} = |x_{ik} - x_{rk}| \text{ if } x_{ik} \leqslant x_{rk} \text{ and is 0 otherwise.}$$

The function WM_k given by equation (4.3) can now be linearized as:

$$\sum_{i=1}^{m} \sum_{j=1}^{n} w_{1ij}(d^+_{ijk} + d^-_{ijk}) + \sum_{i=1}^{m-1} \sum_{r=i+1}^{m} w_{2ir}(e^+_{irk} + e^-_{irk}). \qquad (4.4)$$

However, we must ensure that the new variables behave as intended. This is accomplished by appending constraints to equation (4.4) to obtain the following linear programming problem for dimension k:

$$\text{minimize } Z_k = \sum_{i=1}^{m} \sum_{j=1}^{n} w_{1ij}(d^+_{ijk} + d^-_{ijk}) + \sum_{i=1}^{m-1} \sum_{r=i+1}^{m} w_{2ir}(e^+_{irk} + e^-_{irk})$$

subject to:

$$(4.5)$$

$$x_{ik} - d^+_{ijk} + d^-_{ijk} = a_{jk} \text{ for } i=1,...,m \text{ and } j=1,...,n,$$

$$x_{ik} - x_{rk} - e^+_{irk} + e^-_{irk} = 0 \text{ for } i=1,...,m-1; r=i+1,...,m,$$

and all $x_{ik}, d^+_{ijk}, d^-_{ijk}, e^+_{irk}, e^-_{irk} \geqslant 0$.

The formulation includes non-negativity constraints on the x_{ik}'s. This is innocuous if the origin of the coordinate system is chosen so that all of the existing facility locations fall in the first quadrant.

Now we claim that d^+_{ijk} and d^-_{ijk} cannot both be positive in an *optimal* solution. For example, let us say $d^+_{ijk} = 3$ and $d^-_{ijk} = 1$ in a given feasible solution. The relevant constraint specifies that $x_{ik} + 3 - 1 = a_{jk}$, and the associated cost $w_{1ij}(3+1)$ is registered in the objective function. However, this solution can be improved upon by setting $d^+_{ijk} = 2$ and $d^-_{ijk} = 0$ because the associated cost then drops to $w_{1ij}(2+0)$ while the difference of 2 between x_{ik} and a_{jk} is preserved. In this way it can be shown that from each pair of d^+_{ijk} and d^-_{ijk} variables, at least one variable must be zero in an optimal solution. (This assumes $w_{1ij} > 0$. However, if $w_{1ij} = 0$, the pair of variables is extraneous and is to be omitted from the formulation—together with the associated constraint.) Similar reflection will show that e^+_{irk} and e^-_{irk} cannot both be positive in an optimal solution. This implies the deviational variables behave as intended.

Assuming rectangular travel distances, we can solve the Coastal Construction Company location problem by solving the following pair of linear programming problems:

minimize $Z_1 = 0.80(d_{111}^+ + d_{111}^-)$

$\quad + 0.80(d_{121}^+ + d_{121}^-) +$

$0.80(d_{221}^+ + d_{221}^-) + 0.40(d_{231}^+ + d_{231}^-)$

$\quad + 4.00(e_{121}^+ + e_{121}^-)$

subject to:

$$x_{11} - d_{111}^+ + d_{111}^- = 10$$
$$x_{11} - d_{121}^+ + d_{121}^- = 7$$
$$x_{11} - d_{131}^+ + d_{131}^- = 13$$
$$x_{21} - d_{211}^+ + d_{211}^- = 10$$
$$x_{21} - d_{221}^+ + d_{221}^- = 7$$
$$x_{21} - d_{231}^+ + d_{231}^- = 13$$
$$x_{11} - x_{21} - e_{121}^+ + e_{121}^- = 0$$

minimize $Z_2 = 0.80(d_{112}^+ + d_{112}^-)$

$\quad + 0.80(d_{122}^+ + d_{122}^-) +$

$0.80(d_{222}^+ + d_{222}^-) + 0.40(d_{232}^+ + d_{232}^-)$

$\quad + 4.00(e_{122}^+ + e_{122}^-)$

subject to:

$$x_{12} - d_{112}^+ + d_{112}^- = 20$$
$$x_{12} - d_{122}^+ + d_{122}^- = 6$$
$$x_{12} - d_{132}^+ + d_{132}^- = 0$$
$$x_{22} - d_{212}^+ + d_{212}^- = 20$$
$$x_{22} - d_{222}^+ + d_{222}^- = 6$$
$$x_{22} - d_{232}^+ + d_{232}^- = 0$$
$$x_{12} - x_{22} - e_{122}^+ + e_{122}^- = 0$$

and all variables are non-negative.

The d_{ijk} variables may be interpreted intuitively in a given application. The first subscript refers to the new facility number and the second refers to the existing facility number. The third subscript indicates whether d_{ijk} corresponds to distance along the horizontal ($k = 1$ problem) or the vertical ($k = 2$ problem) direction in Figure 4.1. At optimality, $d_{111}^+ + d_{111}^-$ measures the horizontal distance between existing facility 1 (concrete batching plant) and new facility 1 (concrete casting area). If the location of the casting facility is to the left of the concrete batching plant, d_{111}^+ is zero and d_{111}^- measures the horizontal distance between these facilities. Otherwise, d_{111}^- is zero and d_{111}^+ measures this horizontal distance. In the same way, $d_{112}^+ + d_{112}^-$ measures the vertical distance between the concrete batching plant and the concrete casting area; d_{112}^- measures the distance when the casting area is below the batching plant, whereas d_{112}^+ measures this distance when the casting area is above the batching plant. Each new-to-existing facility pair has associated with it four of the d_{ijk} variables; two for the horizontal problem and two for the vertical problem. Similarly, the sum $e_{121}^+ + e_{121}^-$ measures the horizontal distance between the two new facilities, whereas $e_{122}^+ + e_{122}^-$ measures the vertical distance.

The optimal solutions to the linear programs for the Coastal Construction Company application are $x^*_{11} = x^*_{21} = 7$ and $x^*_{12} = x^*_{22} = 6$, respectively, with a total daily cost of $Z_1^* + Z_2^* = \$18.40$. This indicates that the two new facilities are to be located together *adjacent* to the (forbidden) steel manufacturing area for maximum materials handling cost savings. This solution was implemented by the company.

Management did not recognize the existence of a location problem in this form. The location study had not been specifically requested, but was suggested by a production analyst who was enrolled in a facilities location course! It is not possible to state with certainty the exact savings that were achieved by using the model, as management had not reached an earlier decision regarding the location of the new facilities. However, one possible set of sites that had been considered located the concrete casting area at location (10,18) and the assembly and storage area at location (13,10), with an associated daily cost of $69.60.

But what if the 40-poles-per-day sales forecast is not accurate? Conveniently, the optimal locations of the new facilities would not be different with a different sales volume, because all material flows between facilities are proportional to the flow of finished poles from the yard. For example, with a sales volume of 80 poles per day, all coefficients in the objective functions of the linear programs would be doubled. Because the constraints remain unchanged, the same facility placements would be optimal.

The linear programming approach allows for linear constraints on the locations of the new facilities. Had it been desirable to locate the concrete casting area below $x_2 = 6$ and to the right of $x_1 = 10$, the constraints $x_{11} \geq 10$ and $x_{12} \leq 6$ could have been added to the respective formulations. Several computer runs testing out various combinations of constraints may be necessary before the best locations are found when forbidden regions are present. If a constraint involves x_{i1} together with x_{i2}, such as $x_{11} + x_{12} \geq 10$, the linear programming problems cannot be solved separately. A combined formulation is then required.

Traveling Along Edges

We now describe an approach to minimizing WM_k that is computationally more efficient, but which (unless specially adapted) precludes constraints on the locations of the new facilities. The basic idea is this: The convex surface $WM_k(x_{11},...,x_{k1})$ is made up of plane segments. In two variables the three-dimensional surface may be visualized as the bottom of a diamond—sometimes of unorthodox cut (see Figure 4.2). We may imagine "travel" to a lowest level (minimum) along the edges. Because of convexity we are guaranteed that as long as we keep traveling downward, we will eventually reach the minimum. Fortunately, "edge travel" is straightforward and, in fact, is based on techniques developed in Section 2.2. The preceding, admittedly vague, description is illustrated with an example.

Example 4.2 In the following problem, two new facilities are to be located among four existing facilities. Table 4.2 gives the existing facility locations (a_{j1},a_{j2}); the new-to-existing facility weights, w_{1ij}; and the new-to-new facility weight, w_{212}. We will concentrate on minimizing $WM_1(x_{11},x_{21})$. According to equation (4.3), we can write:

$$WM_1(x_{11},x_{21}) = 1|x_{11} - 3| + 2|x_{11} - 2| + 0|x_{11} - 1| + 1|x_{11} - 5|$$
$$+ 0|x_{21} - 3| + 1|x_{21} - 2| + 3|x_{21} - 1| + 2|x_{21} - 5|$$
$$+ 2|x_{11} - x_{21}|.$$

We know that $WM_1(x_{11},x_{21})$ describes a surface in three dimensions. We make the following important observation: In a region of the $x_{11}x_{21}$ plane, the surface WM_1 itself is a plane—as long as none of the terms inside the absolute value brackets changes sign in that region. This is because within a given region absolute value brackets can be replaced unambiguously by parentheses to yield a *linear* function. Changes of sign can occur only across the lines: $x_{11} = 3$, $x_{11} = 2$, $x_{11} = 5$, $x_{21} = 2$, $x_{21} = 1$, $x_{21} = 5$, and $x_{11} = x_{21}$. These lines must therefore define edges of the surface WM_1. The surface WM_1 and its edges projected on the $x_{11}x_{21}$ plane are shown in Figure 4.2.

To illustrate the technique of edge travel, we need a starting point. A point at the intersection of at least two of the edge-defining lines will suffice. Let us arbitrarily choose the point (5,5) that is at the intersection of three of the lines and let us attempt downward travel along the edge defined by $x_{21} = 5$. In other words, we set $x_{21} = 5$ and minimize WM_1 with respect to x_{11}. Then:

$$WM_1(x_{11},5) = 1|x_{11} - 3| + 2|x_{11} - 2| + 1|x_{11} - 5|$$
$$+ 2|x_{11} - 5| + 15.$$

The constant 15 can be ignored in the optimization. When we apply the median weight approach of Example 2.5 in Section 2.2, we find that the best x_{11} is the range [3,5]. Setting $x_{11} = 5$, we minimize WM_1 with respect to x_{21}, where:

$$WM_1(5,x_{21}) = 1|x_{21} - 2| + 3|x_{21} - 1| + 2|x_{21} - 5|$$
$$+ 2|5 - x_{21}| + \text{a constant.}$$

Table 4.2 Problem Parameters for Example 4.2.

j	1	2	3	4
a_{j1}	3	2	1	5
a_{j2}	1	2	4	7
w_{11j}	1	2	0	1
w_{12j}	0	1	3	2
$w_{212} = 2$				

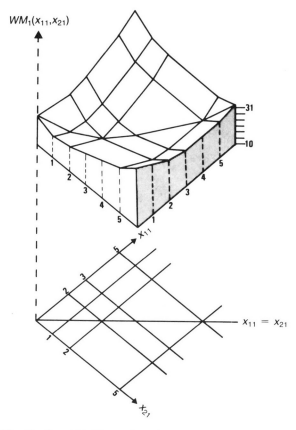

Figure 4.2 The Surface $WM_1(x_{11},x_{21})$ and the Projections of the Edges on the $x_{11}x_{21}$ Plane.

The best x_{21} is the range [2,5]. If we did not know better, we might conclude that the point (5,5) minimizes WM_1. However, let us investigate the edge $x_{11} = x_{21}$ that goes through the point (5,5). We have:

$$WM_1(x_{11},x_{11}) = 1|x_{11} - 3| + 2|x_{11} - 2| + 1|x_{11} - 5|$$
$$+ 1|x_{11} - 2| + 3|x_{11} - 1| + 2|x_{11} - 5|.$$

The minimum along this edge occurs at $x_{11} = x_{21} = 2$. We then find that $x_{11} = 2$ minimizes $WM_1(x_{11},2)$, and $x_{21} = 2$ minimizes $WM_1(2,x_{21})$; thus the procedure terminates at this point with $WM_1(2,2) = 13$.

There are, of course, alternative "rules of the road" that we could have followed. However, as long as we move downward and investigate *all* the edges going *through* a point before declaring it the optimum, we cannot go wrong. For three or more facilities, the surface WM_k is a bit more difficult to visualize. However, the edges are easy enough to determine. These (their projections) are:

$$x_{ik} = a_{jk} \text{ for } i=1,...,m; \ j=1,...,n, \text{ and}$$

$$x_{ik} = x_{rk} \text{ for } 1 \leqslant r < i \leqslant m.$$

The following algorithm, essentially a modified edge descent procedure, formalizes a strategy for exploiting this convex edge structure inherent in WM_k. The algorithm is applied once for each dimension ($k = 1,2$) of the location problem. It achieves edge descent by optimizing the locations of all single new facilities, all clusters and all subsets of all clusters of new facilities.

Juel-Love Algorithm

Step 0 Find an initial solution. (The initial solution may be found by solving m single-facility problems and ignoring the weights between pairs of new facilities).

Step 1 Improve the current solution by optimizing the location of single new facilities one at a time, until no further improvements are possible.

Step 2 Improve the current solution by optimizing the location of sets of coinciding new facilities, one set at a time, until no further improvements are possible.

Step 3 Check all subsets of each set of coinciding new facilities. If moving some subset improves the current solution, optimize the location of that subset and return to Step 1.

The algorithm continues cycling through steps 1 to 3. It terminates when a full cycle has been completed and no improvements have been made.

4.2 THE ℓ_p DISTANCE MODEL

The general case of WM in problem (4.1) lacks the structure for linearization when $1 < p < \infty$, and so we must rely on nonlinear optimization methods. However, some useful structure remains.

Property 4.1 [*Convexity of the ℓ_p distance function*]. *The function $\ell(X_i,X_r)$ is convex.*

A proof is given in the Appendix, mathematical note 4.1. As $WM(X)$ is a sum of weighted convex functions where the weights are all non-negative, $WM(X)$ is convex. However, for $m > 1$, the derivatives of $WM(X)$ may be undefined anywhere on the two-dimensional plane. This is in contrast to the single-facility ℓ_p distances problem, where the derivatives are discontinuous only at the existing facility locations a_j. This derivative discontinuity arises because two or more of the new facilities may occupy the *same* location *anywhere*.

Property 4.2 [*Discontinuities in the derivatives of the ℓ_p distance function*]. *The derivatives of $\ell_p(X_i, X_r)$ and, hence, $WM(X)$ may be undefined anywhere on the two-dimensional plane.*

A proof is given in the Appendix, mathematical note 4.2. To eliminate the problem of discontinuities in the derivatives, we will generalize problem (2.19) and approximate $WM(X)$ by:

$$WMH(X) = \sum_{i=1}^{m} \sum_{j=1}^{n} w_{1ij}[((x_{i1}-a_{j1})^2+\epsilon)^{p/2}+((x_{i2}-a_{j2})^2+\epsilon)^{p/2}]^{1/p}$$

$$+ \sum_{i=1}^{m-1} \sum_{r=i+1}^{m} w_{2ir}[((x_{i1}-x_{r1})^2+\epsilon)^{p/2}+((x_{i2}-x_{r2})^2+\epsilon)^{p/2}]^{1/p},$$

where $\epsilon > 0$.

All orders of derivatives of WMH are continuous everywhere. $WMH(X)$ is a strictly convex function when each new facility is chained to at least one existing facility.

Chained Facilities

New facilities i and r are said to have an exchange if $w_{2ir} > 0$ or $w_{2ri} > 0$. New facility i is said to be *chained* to existing facility j if there exists a sequence of distinct new facilities $i, i_1,...,i_q$ such that there is an exchange between i and i_1, and i_1 and $i_2,...,i_q$, and $w_{1i_q j} > 0$. We will not consider problem (4.1) to be well stated unless each new facility is chained to at least one existing facility.

Property 4.3 [*Maximum difference between $WMH(X)$ and $WM(X)$*].

$$\max_{X} \{WMH(X) - WM(X)\} \leqslant \Delta_M(\epsilon) = 2^{1/p}\epsilon^{1/2}(\sum_{i=1}^{m} \sum_{j=1}^{n} w_{1ij}$$

$$+ \sum_{i=1}^{m-1} \sum_{r=i+1}^{m} w_{2ir})$$

The proof follows analogously the proof of Property 2.8. By taking $\partial WMH(X)/\partial x_{rk}$, equating to zero, and "isolating" x_{rk} on the left-hand side, the Weiszfeld procedure given by equation (2.6) generalizes to the multi-facility case as:

$$x_{rk}^{(\ell+1)} = \frac{SX_{rk}^{(\ell)} + SA_{rk}^{(\ell)}}{S_{1rk}^{(\ell)} + S_{2rk}^{(\ell)}} \quad \text{for } r=1,2,...,m; \text{ and } k=1,2, \qquad (4.6)$$

where:

$$SX_{rk}^{(\ell)} = \sum_{i=1}^{m} \frac{w_{2ri}x_{ik}^{(\ell)}}{\{[(x_{r1}^{(\ell)} - x_{i1}^{(\ell)})^2 + \epsilon]^{p/2} + [(x_{r2}^{(\ell)} - x_{i2}^{(\ell)})^2 + \epsilon]^{p/2}\}^{(p-1)/p}[(x_{rk}^{(\ell)} - x_{ik}^{(\ell)})^2 + \epsilon]^{(2-p)/2}},$$

$$SA_{rk}^{(\ell)} = \sum_{j=1}^{n} \frac{w_{1rj}a_{jk}}{\{[(x_{r1}^{(\ell)} - a_{j1})^2 + \epsilon]^{p/2} + [(x_{r2}^{(\ell)} - a_{j2})^2 + \epsilon]^{p/2}\}^{(p-1)/p}[(x_{rk}^{(\ell)} - a_{jk})^2 + \epsilon]^{(2-p)/2}},$$

$$S_{1rk}^{(\ell)} = \sum_{j=1}^{n} \frac{w_{1rj}}{\{[(x_{r1}^{(\ell)} - a_{j1})^2 + \epsilon]^{p/2} + [(x_{r2}^{(\ell)} - a_{j2})^2 + \epsilon]^{p/2}\}^{(p-1)/p}[(x_{rk}^{(\ell)} - a_{jk})^2 + \epsilon]^{(2-p)/2}},$$

$$S_{2rk}^{(\ell)} = \sum_{i=1}^{m} \frac{w_{2ri}}{\{[(x_{r1}^{(\ell)} - x_{i1}^{(\ell)})^2 + \epsilon]^{p/2} + [(x_{r2}^{(\ell)} - x_{i2})^2 + \epsilon]^{p/2}\}^{(p-1)/p}[(x_{rk}^{(\ell)} - x_{ik}^{(\ell)})^2 + \epsilon]^{(2-p)/2}}.$$

It is important to note that w_{2ri} must be evaluated as w_{2ir} whenever $r > i$. The sequence is relatively simple to program, relatively efficient, and requires very little computer memory space.

A stopping criterion for procedure (4.6) must consider the suboptimality of the current iterate $X^{(\ell)}$ with respect to minimizing WMH, as well as the error of approximating WM by WMH. The following property defines such a criterion. Let X^* and X^{**} minimize WM and WMH, respectively. Let

$$\bar{\Omega} = \{X = (X_1, X_2,...,X_m) \mid X_i \in \Omega, i=1,...,m\},$$

where Ω is the convex hull of the existing facility locations, and let

$$\sigma_M(X^{(\ell)}) = \max_{X \in \bar{\Omega}} \{\ell_2(X^{(\ell)}, X)\}.$$

Analogous arguments to those preceding Property 2.4 and succeeding Property 2.8 can be used to justify:

Property 4.4 [*Lower bounds on WMH(X**) and WM(X*)*].

$$WMH(X^{**}) \geqslant LBMH^{(t)} = WMH(X^{(t)}) - \|\nabla WMH(X^{(t)})\|\sigma_M(X^{(t)}), \text{ and}$$

$$WM(X^*) \geqslant LBM^{(t)} = LBMH^{(t)} - \Delta_M(\epsilon).$$

Example 4.3 Tables 4.3 through 4.6 give the parameters and numerical results for a problem with $m = 3$, $n = 5$, $p = 1.8$, and $\epsilon = 0.001$.

For problems in which one or more of the new facilities are constrained to lie in some subset of the plane (or three-dimensional space if the problem is three-dimensional in nature), it is usually necessary to employ a nonlinear programming algorithm. In this case, it is advisable to replace $WM(X)$ by $WMH(X)$ in order to ensure convergence of most nonlinear programming algorithms.

Table 4.3 Existing Facility Locations.

j	1	2	3	4	5
a_j	(2,3)	(4,2)	(5,4)	(3,5)	(6,7)

Table 4.4 New-to-Existing Facility Weights w_{1ij}.

			j		
i	1	2	3	4	5
1	1	1	10	1	6
2	4	1	1	1	1
3	1	1	1	1	1

Table 4.5 New-to-New Facility Weights w_{2ir}.

		r	
i	1	2	3
1	—	1	1
2	—	—	1

Table 4.6 Computation Results for Example 4.3.

Iteration Number ℓ	$(x_{11}^{(\ell)}, x_{12}^{(\ell)})$	$(x_{21}^{(\ell)}, x_{22}^{(\ell)})$	$(x_{31}^{(\ell)}, x_{32}^{(\ell)})$	$WMH(X^{(\ell)})$	Magnitude of $\nabla WMH(X^{(\ell)})$	$LBMH^{(\ell)}$	$[WMH(X^{(\ell)}) - LBMH^{(\ell)}]/LBMH^{(\ell)}$
0	(0.0000,0.0000)	(0.0000,0.0000)	(0.0000,0.0000)	210.7866	21.8458	0.000	—
1	(0.0030,0.0132)	(0.0023,0.0102)	(0.0183,0.0445)	210.1930	22.3861	0.000	—
2	(0.0347,0.1906)	(0.1544,0.4791)	(0.3065,0.8064)	201.2360	23.2518	0.000	—
3	(1.8084,3.2586)	(1.3233,2.5660)	(2.6273,3.2464)	108.6370	20.3162	0.000	—
4	(3.3494,3.9221)	(2.4800,3.2035)	(2.7707,3.4146)	75.0533	12.4520	0.000	—
5	(4.3133,4.1231)	(2.5473,3.2736)	(2.9978,3.5704)	63.7436	9.6475	0.000	46.6367
6	(4.8041,4.0844)	(2.6383,3.3290)	(3.1973,3.6766)	59.0732	7.8966	1.240	4.5216
7	(4.9541,4.0412)	(2.7380,3.3770)	(3.4117,3.7518)	57.6079	6.6123	10.433	2.5725
8	(4.9882,4.0187)	(2.8389,3.4184)	(3.5803,3.8012)	57.1308	5.8829	15.989	2.1037
9	(4.9961,4.0084)	(2.9326,3.4546)	(3.7054,3.8326)	56.9143	5.6086	18.337	1.8762
10	(4.9985,4.0037)	(3.0129,3.4852)	(3.7963,3.8528)	56.7980	5.4583	19.748	1.5759
11	(4.9993,4.0017)	(3.0732,3.5088)	(3.8623,3.8664)	56.7365	5.1638	22.026	0.9834
12	(4.9997,4.0008)	(3.1259,3.5435)	(3.9101,3.8756)	56.7001	4.2147	28.587	0.3769
13	(4.9998,4.0004)	(3.1694,3.5435)	(3.9447,3.8819)	56.6787	2.3391	41.165	0.1033
14	(4.9999,4.0002)	(3.2050,3.5560)	(3.9696,3.8664)	56.6661	0.8027	51.359	0.0311
15	(4.9999,4.0002)	(3.2338,3.5661)	(3.9873,3.8895)	56.6585	0.2584	54.947	0.0179
16	(4.9999,4.0002)	(3.2570,3.5743)	(3.9994,3.8916)	56.6540	0.1499	55.658	0.0135
17	(4.9999,4.0002)	(3.2757,3.5808)	(4.0063,3.8930)	56.6514	0.1141	55.892	0.0108
18	(4.9999,4.0002)	(3.2906,3.5862)	(4.0117,3.8938)	56.6497	0.0905	56.046	0.0086
19	(4.9999,4.0002)	(3.3026,3.5905)	(4.0157,3.8944)	56.6486	0.0723	56.164	0.0087
20	(4.9999,4.0002)	(3.3122,3.5939)	(4.0186,3.8948)	56.6479	0.0073	56.161	0.0057
21	(4.9999,4.0002)	(3.3199,3.5967)	(4.0208,3.8951)	56.6475	0.0470	56.328	0.0055
22	(4.9999,4.0002)	(3.3261,3.5989)	(4.0224,3.8954)	56.6472	0.0456	56.337	0.0037
23	(4.9999,4.0002)	(3.3309,3.6007)	(4.0236,3.8955)	56.6471	0.0305	56.436	0.0032
24	(4.9999,4.0002)	(3.3349,3.6021)	(4.0244,3.8957)	56.6469	0.0258	56.466	0.0026
25	(4.9999,4.0002)	(3.3381,3.6032)	(4.0251,3.8957)	56.6469	0.0207	56.499	0.0015
30	(4.9999,4.0002)	(3.3467,3.6063)	(4.0265,3.8959)	56.6468	0.0108	56.563	0.0012
35	(4.9999,4.0002)	(3.3495,3.6074)	(4.0269,3.8959)	56.6468	0.0092	56.574	0.0012
40	(4.9999,4.0002)	(3.3505,3.6077)	(4.0270,3.8959)	56.6467	0.0090	56.575	0.0012

EXERCISES

4.1 Show that $w_{2ir}|x_{ik} - x_{rk}|$ is a convex function of x_{ik} and x_{rk}, where w_{2ir} is a positive constant.

4.2 Using the observation that $|x - a| = \max\{(x - a),(a - x)\}$, find a linear programming formulation for the minimization of $WM_k(x_{1k},...,x_{mk})$ that is different from that of problem (4.5) in the text. (Hint: Consider the construction: minimize d, subject to $d \geqslant x - a$ and $d \geqslant a - x$.)

4.3 Verify that if all weights are positive (all variables are present), the number of variables in problem (4.5) in the text is $m^2 + 2mn$ and the number of constraints is $mn + (m^2 - m)/2$. (Recall that k is fixed.)

4.4 Find the dual of problem (4.5) in the text. Show that the majority of the constraints in the dual are of the bounded-variable type, ie, variables are bounded from below and above by constants. (Bounded-variable constraints are handled implicitly and thus quite efficiently by some linear programming computer codes.)

4.5 Consider the data given in Table 4.2.
 a. Use linear programming to minimize $WM_2(x_{12},x_{22})$.
 b. Use either the edge descent method or the Juel-Love algorithm to minimize $WM_2(x_{12},x_{22})$.

Figure 4E.1 Locations of Existing Machines.

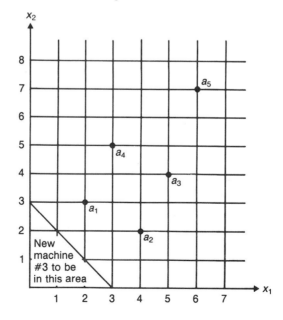

Table 4E.1   Weights for the Three-Machine Location Problem.

	w_{1ij}					w_{2ir}		
	j					r		
i	1	2	3	4	5	1	2	3
1	1	1	2	1	4	–	1	1
2	4	1	1	1	1	–	–	1
3	1	1	1	1	1	–	–	–

4.6 Three new machines are to be optimally located among five existing ones. Figure 4E.1 gives the relative positions of the existing machines and of the constraint on the position of new machine #3. Table 4E.1 gives the relevant weights. Assume rectangular distances.

   a. Use linear programming to find optimal locations for the three new machines.

   b. Use the iterative scheme given by procedure (4.6) to locate the three new machines (*ignoring* the constraint on the location of new machine #3).

   c. Suppose the only restriction on the placement of new machine #3 is that it *not* be located inside the rectangle whose corners are at the points $(1,1)$, $(1,8)$, $(7,8)$, and $(7,1)$. Describe a method for solving this problem.

   d. Assume that there is no constraint on the location of new machine #3 and that the new machine interaction weights are: $w_{212} = 8$, $w_{223} = 10$, $w_{213} = 7$. Find the optimum coordinates x^*_{11}, x^*_{21} and x^*_{31} using either the edge descent method or the Juel-Love algorithm.

REFERENCE NOTES

SECTION 4.1 An early treatment of the Euclidean distance multi-facility problem was given by Miehle (1958) who rediscovered the Weiszfeld iterative procedure. Francis (1964) introduced the rectangular distance version of the multi-facility problem. Werson, Quon, and Charnes (1962) and Wesolowsky and Love (1971b) applied the linear programming approach for absolute value minimization to the rectangular distance facility location context. Cabot, Francis, and Stary (1970) developed a network flow algorithm for the dual problem. Discussion of the edge descent method is from Wesolowsky (1970). The method is related to one due to Pritsker and Ghare (1970), subsequently studied by Rao (1973); the difference lies in the fact that edge descent optimizes along an edge instead of taking the next lowest grid point. The Juel-Love algorithm is further detailed in Juel and Love (1976).

SECTION 4.2 The chaining assumption for well-structured problems follows Francis and Cabot (1972). Using a differentiable hyperboloid approximation procedure (HAP), Eyster, White, and Wierwille (1973) extended the Weiszfeld iterative procedure to multi-facility problems with rectangular and Euclidean distances. Modifications to accelerate HAP were suggested by Ostresh (1977) and Charalambous (1985). The ℓ_p distance extension was given by Morris and Verdini

(1979); Morris (1981) discussed convergence. Nonlinear programming approaches were taken in Love (1967a,1969), where constraints were prominent and the concept of a differentiable approximation method was introduced; in Wesolowsky and Love (1972), wherein a different approximating function was used; and in Love and Morris (1975b). The use of a stopping criterion involving a lower bound was described by Love and Yeong (1981); a generalized bound for the multi-facility ℓ_p distance case was given by Love and Dowling (1986). Calamai and Conn (1987) presented a second-order algorithm that does not modify the objective function to remove discontinuities in the derivatives.

APPENDIX—CHAPTER 4

Mathematical Notes

4.1 *Prove* Property 4.1

The function $\ell_p(X_i, X_r)$ is convex, where X_i and X_r are two variable points.

PROOF: Let $(x_{i1}, x_{r1}, x_{i2}, x_{r2}) = (y_1, y_2, y_3, y_4) \equiv Y$, then $\ell_p(X_i, X_r) = f(Y) = (|y_1 - y_2|^p + |y_3 - y_4|^p)^{1/p}$.
We have

$$f(\lambda Y' + (1-\lambda)Y'') = [|(\lambda y_1' + (1-\lambda)y_1'') -$$

$$(\lambda y_2' + (1-\lambda)y_2'')|^p + |(\lambda y_3' + (1-\lambda)y_3'') -$$

$$(\lambda y_4' + (1-\lambda)y_4'')|^p]^{1/p} \leq [|\lambda(y_1' - y_2')|^p +$$

$$|\lambda(y_3' - y_4')|^p]^{1/p} + [|(1-\lambda)(y_1'' - y_2'')|^p +$$

$$|(1-\lambda)(y_3'' - y_4'')|^p]^{1/p} \qquad \text{(Minkowski inequality)}$$

$$= \lambda f(Y') + (1-\lambda)f(Y''), \text{ since } 0 \leq \lambda \leq 1,$$

which completes the proof.

4.2 *Prove* Property 4.2

The derivatives of $\ell_p(X_i, X_r)$ may be undefined anywhere on the two-dimensional plane.

PROOF: Following note 4.1, let $\ell_p(X_i, X_r)$ be given by:

$$f(Y) = [|y_1 - y_2|^p + |y_3 - y_4|^p]^{1/p}.$$

A direction in R^4 is determined by the vector $\mu = (\mu_1, \mu_2, \mu_3, \mu_4)$, where $\|\mu\| = 1$. The first directional derivative at point Y is given by $D_\mu f(Y)$. The first derivatives of $f(Y)$ do not exist at any point in the set $Z =$

$\{Y \epsilon R^4 | y_1 = y_2, y_3 = y_4\}$. If $D_\mu f(Y)$ existed for $Y \epsilon Z$, it would be given by:

$$D_\mu f(Y) = \lim_{\lambda \to 0} \frac{f(Y + \lambda\mu) - f(Y)}{\lambda}$$

$$= \lim_{\lambda \to 0} \frac{|\lambda|[|\mu_1 - \mu_2|^p + |\mu_3 - \mu_4|^p]^{1/p}}{\lambda}, \text{ since } Y \epsilon Z$$

$$= \begin{cases} [|\mu_1 - \mu_2|^p + |\mu_3 - \mu_4|^p]^{1/p}, & \lambda > 0, \\ - [|\mu_1 - \mu_2|^p + |\mu_3 - \mu_4|^p]^{1/p}, & \lambda < 0, \end{cases}$$

and so the limit does not exist. Since the points X_i and X_r are taken anywhere on the two-dimensional plane, the derivatives of $\ell_p(X_i, X_r)$ are undefined anywhere on the two-dimensional plane where new facilities i and r coincide.

Chapter 5

Duality

This chapter is concerned with the development of dual mathematical programs for the single- and multi-facility location models of Chapters 2 and 4.* As opposed to the case of linear programming, dual programs for general nonlinear programming models as developed by Wolfe (1961) and described by Balinski and Baumol (1968) include primal variables. The dual problems described here are formulated entirely from the data of the primal location problem, and they are "pure" in the sense that they contain only dual variables (the models of Chapters 2 and 4 will henceforth be referred to as primal). The solution of the primal problem is a by-product of having solved the dual, and vice versa. Dual variables will be shown to have physical interpretations as direction vectors that point to optimal facility locations in the primal problem.

5.1 THE SINGLE-FACILITY EUCLIDEAN DUAL

The primal problem we will consider first is:

$$\text{minimize } W(X) = \sum_{j=1}^{n} w_j[(x_1-a_{j1})^2 + (x_2-a_{j2})^2]^{1/2}. \quad (5.1)$$

We will use a strictly convex approximating function to eliminate the problem of discontinuities of the derivatives of $W(X)$. The dual of the approximating problem will then be formulated and the dual of problem (5.1) is then developed as a limiting case. The smooth approximation to problem (5.1) employed here is given by:

---

*This chapter assumes the reader has a background in nonlinear programming.

$$\text{minimize } Wh(X) = \sum_{j=1}^{n} w_j[(x_1-a_{j1})^2+(x_2-a_{j2})^2 + \epsilon^2]^{1/2}, \quad (5.2)$$

which is slightly different from that used in problem (2.19).

There are several ways to develop a dual problem. We will use an approach based on the observation that:

$$w_j[(x_1-a_{j1})^2 + (x_2-a_{j2})^2+\epsilon^2]^{1/2}$$
$$= \max_{[u_j^2+v_j^2+z_j^2]^{1/2}=w_j} [(x_1-a_{j1})u_j+(x_2+a_{j2})v_j-\epsilon z_j]. \quad (5.3)$$

To see how this equality follows, recall that the inner product of two vectors equals the product of their lengths times the cosine of the angle between them. In terms of the vectors $(x_1 - a_{j1}, x_2 - a_{j2}, -\epsilon)$ and (u_j, v_j, z_j) this means:

$$[(x_1-a_{j1})u_j + (x_2-a_{j2})v_j-\epsilon z_j]$$
$$= [(x_1-a_{j1})^2 + (x_2-a_{j2})^2 + \epsilon^2]^{1/2}[u_j^2+v_j^2+z_j^2]^{1/2} \cos\theta$$

where θ is the angle between the vectors. Hence the optimization on the right-hand side of equation (5.3) can be posed as:

$$\max_{[u_j^2+v_j^2+z_j^2]^{1/2}=w_j} [(x_1-a_{j1})^2 + (x_2-a_{j2})^2 + \epsilon^2]^{1/2}w_j \cos\theta,$$

for which the maximum is attained when $\cos\theta = 1$. This establishes equation (5.3) and shows that the angle between the two vectors is to be $0°$; the vector (u_j, v_j, z_j) is a positive multiple of $(x_1 - a_{j1}, x_2 - a_{j2}, - \epsilon)$. The multiple is seen to be $w_j/[(x_1-a_{j1})^2 + (x_2-a_{j2})^2 + \epsilon^2]^{1/2}$. In particular, the values of u_j, v_j, and z_j that enable equation (5.3) to hold are given by:

$$u_j = \frac{w_j(x_1 - a_{j1})}{[(x_1 - a_{j1})^2 + (x_2 - a_{j2})^2 + \epsilon^2]^{1/2}},$$

$$v_j = \frac{w_j(x_2 - a_{j2})}{[(x_1 - a_{j1})^2 + (x_2 - a_{j2})^2 + \epsilon^2]^{1/2}},$$

$$z_j = \frac{- w_j\epsilon}{[(x_1 - a_{j1})^2 + (x_2 - a_{j2})^2 + \epsilon^2]^{1/2}}. \quad (5.4)$$

The transformation defined by equation (5.3) has been termed quasi-linearization. We have chosen the quasilinearization approach since it allows a relatively self-contained development of the dual problem. Since the primal problem is a minimization problem we expect that the dual will be a maximization problem.

Let $U = (U_1, U_2, ..., U_n)$, where $U_j = (u_j, v_j)$, and let $Z = (z_1, z_2, ..., z_n)$. From equation (5.3) we have:

$$\text{minimize } Wh(X) = \min_X \max_{U,Z} \sum_{j=1}^{n} [(x_1 - a_{j1})u_j + (x_2 - a_{j2})v_j - \epsilon z_j]$$

$$= \min_X \max_{U,Z} [x_1 \sum_{j=1}^{n} u_j + x_2 \sum_{j=1}^{n} v_j$$

$$- (\sum_{j=1}^{n} a_{j1} u_j + a_{j2} v_j + \epsilon z_j)],$$

subject to $\hspace{6cm}$ (5.5)

$$(u_j^2 + v_j^2 + z_j^2)^{1/2} = w_j, \, j = 1, ..., n.$$

From equations (5.4) we can write the necessary and sufficient conditions for minimizers of $Wh(X)$ as:

$$\frac{\partial Wh(X)}{\partial x_1} = \sum_{j=1}^{n} u_j = 0, \text{ and} \hspace{2cm} (5.6)$$

$$\frac{\partial Wh(X)}{\partial x_2} = \sum_{j=1}^{n} v_j = 0. \hspace{2cm} (5.7)$$

Using conditions (5.6) and (5.7) to optimize X out of problem (5.5), and letting Dh denote the hyperbolic dual objective function, we obtain:

$$\text{minimize } Wh(X) = \max_{U,Z} Dh(U,Z)$$

$$= - \sum_{j=1}^{n} (a_{j1} u_j + a_{j2} v_j + \epsilon z_j)$$

subject to $\hspace{6cm}$ (5.8)

$$\sum_{j=1}^{n} u_j = 0,$$

$$\sum_{j=1}^{n} v_j = 0,$$

$$(u_j^2 + v_j^2 + z_j^2)^{1/2} = w_j, \, j = 1, ..., n,$$

which is the dual of the approximating problem (5.2). Because $Wh(X)$ is uniformly convergent [Love and Morris (1975b)] to $W(X)$ as $\epsilon \to 0$, the dual of problem (5.1) is the limit of problem (5.8) as $\epsilon \to 0$. Since $|z_j| \leq w_j$ by the nonlinear equality constraints, the limiting dual problem (with objective function denoted by D) is:

$$\max_{U,Z} D(U) = -\sum_{j=1}^{n} (a_{j1}u_j + a_{j2}v_j)$$

subject to   (5.9)

$$\sum_{j=1}^{n} u_j = 0,$$

$$\sum_{j=1}^{n} v_j = 0,$$

$$(u_j^2 + v_j^2 + z_j^2)^{1/2} = w_j, \ j = 1,...,n.$$

Upon omitting the z_j variables, we arrive at a standard form of the dual problem given by:

$$\max_{U} D(U) = -\sum_{j=1}^{n} (a_{j1}u_j + a_{j2}v_j)$$

subject to   (5.10)

$$\sum_{j=1}^{n} u_j = 0,$$

$$\sum_{j=1}^{n} v_j = 0,$$

$$(u_j^2 + v_j^2)^{1/2} \leq w_j, \ j = 1,...,n.$$

It is proved in the Appendix, mathematical note 5.2, that if $X^* \neq a_j$, then $(u_j^{*2} + v_j^{*2})^{1/2} = w_j$; whereas if $(u_j^{*2} + v_j^{*2})^{1/2} < w_j$ then $X^* = a_j$ where * denotes optimality. If $X^* = a_j$, then $(u_j^* + v_j^*)^{1/2} \leq w_j$.

The dual form (5.10) is "pure" in the sense that no primal variables are present. As min $W(X)$ has been transformed into max $D(U)$ over
     X U
feasible U, a feasible solution to the dual provides a lower bound for $W(X^*)$. The inequality constraints in problem (5.10) can be equivalently posed as $u_j^2 + v_j^2 \leq w_j^2$ to produce a differentiable problem. The dual problem can then be solved for a global optimum using a standard non-linear programming algorithm. The optimal solution to the primal problem can be calculated from an optimal solution to the dual problem utilizing a physical interpretation of the dual variables that will be discussed. Or X^* may be obtained directly as the vector of Lagrange multipliers for the two equality constraints of problem (5.10).

Let $\bar{0}$ denote the null vector. Then, writing $\|U\| = (u_j^2 + v_j^2)^{1/2}$, and letting $a_j U_j$ denote the scalar product $a_{j1} u_j + a_{j2} v_j$, the dual may be written conveniently in vector notation as:

$$\max_{U} D(U) = - \sum_{j=1}^{n} a_j U_j$$

subject to   (5.11)

$$\sum_{j=1}^{n} U_j = \bar{0}$$

$$\|U_j\| \leqslant w_j, \, j = 1,...,n.$$

Property 5.1 [*Solving the primal problem*]. *The optimal Lagrange multipliers for the equality constraints of problem (5.11) solve the primal problem (5.1).*

A proof is given in the Appendix, mathematical note 5.2. There it is shown (see equation 5A.1) that for $j = 1,...,n$, $X^* = a_j + k_j U^*_j$ where $k_j \geqslant 0$. We conclude that each line through an a_j with *direction* U^*_j goes through X^*. This provides a simple approach to finding X^*, having solved problem (5.11). If all $\|U^*_j\| = w_j$, then four equations in four unknowns can be solved for X^* using any two of the a_j. Otherwise, if some $\|U^*_r\| < w_r$, we have the immediate result that $X^* = a_r$. From the same proof we have that the optimal Lagrange multiplier for the jth inequality in problem (5.11) is given by:

$$\pi^*_j = \frac{\|X^* - a_j\|}{2w_j} = k_j/2.$$

Example 5.1 The data of Example 2.2 are used to illustrate the dual structure. The associated dual problem is:

$$\max_{U} D(U) = - (u_1 + v_1 + u_2 + 4v_2 + 2u_3 + 2v_3 + 4u_4 + 5v_5)$$

subject to

$$u_1 + u_2 + u_3 + u_4 = 0$$

$$v_1 + v_2 + v_3 + v_4 = 0$$

$$u_1^2 + v_1^2 \leqslant 1$$

$$u_2^2 + v_2^2 \leqslant 4$$

$$u_3^2 + v_3^2 \leqslant 4$$

$$u_4^2 + v_4^2 \leqslant 16.$$

A nonlinear programming algorithm produced the following:

$$u_1^* = 0.4880, \ u_2^* = 1.9871, \ u_3^* = 0.6043, \ u_4^* = -3.0794,$$

$$v_1^* = 0.8728, \ v_2^* = -0.2265, \ v_3^* = 1.9065, \ v_4^* = -2.529.$$

The optimal multipliers corresponding to the six constraints are:

$$x_1^* = 2.5769, \ x_2^* = 3.8203, \ \pi_1^* = 1.6156,$$

$$\pi_2^* = 0.3968, \ \pi_3^* = 0.4774, \ \pi_4^* = 0.2311.$$

Using existing facilities 1 and 2, the following vector equations can be written:

$$(1,1) + k_1(0.4880, 0.8728) = (x_1^*, x_2^*)$$

$$(1,4) + k_2(1.9871, -0.2265) = (x_1^*, x_2^*).$$

Solving these equations gives $x_1^* = 2.57686$, $x_2^* = 3.82026$, $k_1 = 3.23128$, and $k_2 = 0.793551$. Figure 5.1 illustrates the physical interpretation of U_1^* and U_2^* as direction vectors.

Example 5.2 The effect on an optimal dual solution of the case $\|U_r^*\| < w_r$ can be shown by using the data from Example 2.2 with the exception that $w_4 = 4.9$. From Table 2.2 $CR_4 = 4.754 < w_4 = 4.9$. This indicates that $X^* = a_4 = (4,5)$. The nonlinear programming algorithm produced the dual solution:

$$u_1^* = 0.5999, \ u_2^* = 1.8967, \ u_3^* = 1.1149, \ u_4^* = -3.6115$$

$$v_1^* = 0.8000, \ v_2^* = 0.6343, \ v_3^* = 1.6604, \ v_4^* = -3.0948,$$

Figure 5.1 Interpreting the U_j as Direction Vectors.

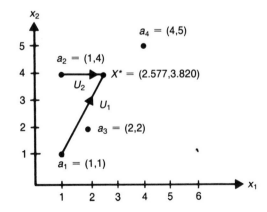

and the optimal multipliers:

$$x_1^* = 4.0000, \; x_2^* = 5.0000, \; \pi_1^* = 2.5000,$$

$$\pi_2^* = 0.7906, \; \pi_3^* = 0.9014, \; \pi_4^* = 0.0000.$$

We observe that $\|U_4^*\| = 4.7561 < 4.9 = w_4$.

5.2 THE DUAL FORM WITH LINEAR CONSTRAINTS

When linear constraints augment problem (5.2), we have:

$$\text{minimize } Wh(X) = \sum_{j=1}^{n} w_j[(x_1 - a_{j1})^2 + (x_2 - x_{j2})^2 + \epsilon^2]^{1/2}$$

$$\text{subject to } \quad GX \geq b, \tag{5.12}$$

where G is a $t \times 2$ matrix of real numbers whose i^{th} row is (g_{i1}, g_{i2}) and b is a $t \times 1$ vector whose i^{th} element is a real number b_i. Let the ith linear constraint be given by $g_i(X) = g_{i1}x_2 + g_{i2}x_2 \geq b_i$. For example, the constraint might be $4x_1 + 3x_2 \geq 12$. This restricts the facility location to a specific half-plane. Imposition of t linear constraints restricts the location to the intersection of t half-planes and models a particular feasible region for the facility. Since location studies frequently involve some form of restrictions, linear constraints can be quite useful.

We subtract the surplus variables s_i^2 to convert the constraints to equalities, ie,

$$g_i(X) - s_i^2 - b_i = 0, \; i = 1, \dots, t.$$

Using the Lagrangian function, problem (5.12) can be solved as:

$$\max_{\lambda \geq \bar{0}} \min_{X} Lh(X, \lambda) = Wh(X) + \sum_{i=1}^{t} \lambda_i[g_i(X) - s_i^2 b_i]$$

where $\lambda = (\lambda_1, \lambda_2, \dots, \lambda_t)$. From problem (5.5) this can be written:

$$\max_{\lambda \geq \bar{0}} \min_{X} \max_{U,Z} \{x_1 \sum_{j=1}^{n} u_j + x_2 \sum_{j=1}^{n} v_j - \sum_{j=1}^{n} (a_{j1}u_j + a_{j2}v_j + \epsilon z_j)$$

$$+ \sum_{i=1}^{t} \lambda_i[g_i(X) - s_i^2 - b_i]\}$$

$$\text{subject to } (u_j^2 + v_j^2 + z_j^2)^{1/2} = w_j, \; j = 1, \dots, n.$$

Setting $\partial Lh(X,\lambda)/\partial x_k = \partial Lh(X,\lambda)/\partial s_i = \partial Lh(X,\lambda)/\partial \lambda_i = 0$ yields the extremal conditions:

$$\sum_{j=1}^{n} u_j + \sum_{i=1}^{t} \lambda_i g_{i1} = 0$$

$$\sum_{j=1}^{n} v_j + \sum_{i=1}^{t} \lambda_i g_{i2} = 0$$

$$s_i \lambda_i = 0, \; i = 1,...,t,$$

$$g_i(X) - s_i^2 - b_i = 0, \; i = 1,...,t. \tag{5.14}$$

The extremal conditions (5.14) imply:

$$x_1 \sum_{j=1}^{n} u_j + x_2 \sum_{j=1}^{n} v_j = -x_1 \sum_{i=1}^{t} \lambda_i g_{i1} - x_2 \sum_{i=1}^{t} \lambda_i g_{i2}$$

$$= - \sum_{i=1}^{t} \lambda_i g_i(X) = - \sum_{i=1}^{t} \lambda_i(s_i^2 + b_i) = - \sum_{i=1}^{t} \lambda_i b_i. \tag{5.15}$$

Applying conditions (5.14) and (5.15) to problem (5.13) we have the limiting case of the dual to problem (5.12) as $\epsilon \rightarrow 0$ given by:

$$\max_{U,\lambda} D(U,\lambda) = b\lambda - \sum_{j=1}^{n} a_j U_j$$

subject to $\tag{5.16}$

$$\lambda G + \sum_{j=1}^{n} U_j = \bar{0},$$

$$\|U_j\| \leqslant w_j, \; j = 1,...,n,$$

$$\lambda \geqslant \bar{0}.$$

5.3 THE MULTI-FACILITY EUCLIDEAN DUAL

The approximation in problem (5.2) extended to the multi-facility Euclidean primal problem is:

$$WMh(X) = \sum_{i=1}^{m} \sum_{j=1}^{n} w_{1ij} \|X_i - a_j\|_\epsilon + \sum_{i=1}^{m-1} \sum_{r=i+1}^{m} w_{2ir} \|x_i - x_r\|_\epsilon \tag{5.17}$$

where:

$$\|X_i - a_j\|_\epsilon = [(x_{i1} - a_{j1})^2 + (x_{i2} - a_{j2})^2 + \epsilon^2]^{1/2}, \text{ and}$$

$$\|X_i - X_r\|_\epsilon = [(x_{i1} - x_{r1})^2 + (x_{i2} - x_{r2})^2 + \epsilon^2]^{1/2}, \; \epsilon > 0.$$

We use the triple-bar notation to indicate that this is not a distance function (since $\|X_i - X\|_\epsilon \neq 0$). Defining $U_{1ij} = (u_{1ij}, v_{1ij})$ and $U_{2ir} = (u_{2ir}, v_{2ir})$, and following equation (5.3), the quasilinearization of terms of WMh is given by:

$$w_{1ij}\|X_1 - a_j\|_\epsilon = \max_{U_{1ij}, z_{1ij}} \ [(X_i - a_j)U_{1ij} - \epsilon z_{1ij}]$$

$$\text{subject to } [\|U_{1ij}\|^2 + z_{1ij}^2]^{1/2} = w_{1ij}. \tag{5.18}$$

The equality holds for:

$$u_{1ij} = \frac{w_{1ij}(x_{i1} - a_{j1})}{\|X_i - a_j\|_\epsilon}, \ v_{1ij} = \frac{w_{1ij}(x_{i2} - a_{j2})}{\|X_i - a_j\|_\epsilon},$$

$$z_{1ij} = \frac{-w_{1ij}\epsilon}{\|X_i - a_j\|_\epsilon}. \tag{5.19}$$

Similarly:

$$w_{2ir}\|X_i - X_r\|_\epsilon = \max_{U_{2ir}, z_{2ir}} \ [(X_i - X_r)U_{2ir} - \epsilon z_{2ir}]$$

$$\text{subject to } [\|U_{2ir}\|^2 + z_{2ir}^2]^{1/2} = w_{2ir}. \tag{5.20}$$

In this case the equality holds for:

$$u_{2ir} = \frac{w_{2ir}(X_{i1} - x_{r1})}{\|X_i - X_r\|_\epsilon}, \ v_{2rr} = \frac{w_{2ir}(x_{i2} - x_{r2})}{\|X_i - X_r\|_\epsilon},$$

$$z_{2ir} = \frac{-w_{2ir}\epsilon}{\|X_i - X_r\|_\epsilon}. \tag{5.21}$$

Problem (5.17) can now be stated as:

$$\min_X WMh(X) = \min_X \max_{U,Z} \sum_{i=1}^m \sum_{j=1}^n [(X_i - a_j)U_{1ij} - \epsilon z_{1ij}]$$

$$+ \sum_{i=1}^{m-1} \sum_{r=i+1}^m [(X_i - X_r)U_{2ir} - \epsilon z_{2ir}]$$

$$= \min_X \max_{U,Z} \ [\sum_{i=1}^m X_i(\sum_{j=1}^n U_{1ij} - \sum_{r=1}^{i-1} U_{2ri} + \sum_{r=i+1}^m U_{2ir})$$

$$- \sum_{i=1}^m \sum_{j=1}^n (a_j U_{1ij} + \epsilon z_{1ij}) - \sum_{i=1}^{m-1} \sum_{r=i+1}^m \epsilon z_{2ir}]$$

subject to (5.22)

$$[\|U_{1ij}\|^2 + z_{1ij}^2]^{1/2} = w_{1ij}, \ i = 1,...,m; \ j = 1,...,n,$$

$$[\|U_{2ir}\|^2 + z_{2ir}^2]^{1/2} = w_{2ir}, \ i = 1,...,m-1; \ r = i+1,...,m.$$

From equations (5.19) and (5.21) we can write the necessary and sufficient conditions for minimizers of $WMh(X)$ as:

$$\frac{\partial WMh(X)}{\partial X_i} = -\sum_{r=1}^{i-1} U_{2ri} + \sum_{r=i+1}^{m} U_{2ir} + \sum_{j=1}^{n} U_{1ij} = \bar{0}, \; i = 1,...,m. \quad (5.23)$$

Using conditions (5.23) in problem (5.22), we arrive at:

$$\min_{X} WMh(X) = \max_{U,Z} DMh(U,Z) = -\sum_{i=1}^{m} \sum_{j=1}^{n} (a_j U_{1ij} + \epsilon z_{1ij})$$

$$-\sum_{i=1}^{m-1} \sum_{r=i+1}^{m} \epsilon z_{2ir} \quad (5.24)$$

subject to

$$-\sum_{r=1}^{i-1} U_{2ri} + \sum_{r=i+1}^{m} U_{2ir} + \sum_{j=1}^{n} U_{1ij} = \bar{0}, \; i = 1,...,m,$$

$$[\|U_{1ij}\|^2 + z_{1ij}^2]^{1/2} = w_{1ij}, \; i = 1,...,m; \; j = 1,...,n,$$

$$[\|U_{2ir}\|^2 + z_{2ir}^2]^{1/2} = w_{2ir}, \; i = 1,...,m-1; \; r = i+1,...,m.$$

Now $|z_{1ij}| \leq w_{1ij}$ and $|z_{2ir}| \leq w_{2ir}$, so the limit of problem (5.24) as $\epsilon \to 0$ (and Z is omitted thereafter) is:

$$\max_{U} DM(U) = -\sum_{i=1}^{m} \sum_{j=1}^{n} a_j U_{1ij}$$

subject to $\qquad\qquad\qquad\qquad\qquad\qquad\qquad\qquad\quad (5.25)$

$$-\sum_{r=1}^{i-1} U_{2ri} + \sum_{r=i+1}^{m} U_{2ir} + \sum_{j=1}^{n} U_{1ij} = \bar{0}, \; i = 1,...,m,$$

$$\|U_{1ij}\| \leq w_{1ij}, \; i = 1,...,m; \; j = 1,...,n,$$

$$\|U_{2ir}\| \leq w_{2ir}, \; i = 1,...,m-1; \; r = i+1,...,m.$$

The corresponding dual form when linear constraints are present in the primal problem is a special case of the dual model derived in the following section.

5.4 THE MULTI-FACILITY ℓ_p DUAL

From problem (4.1), the multi-facility ℓ_p distance primal problem is:

$$\text{minimize } WM(X) = \sum_{i=1}^{m} \sum_{j=1}^{n} w_{1ij}[|x_{i1} - a_{j1}|^p + |x_{i2} - a_{j2}|^p]^{1/p} \quad (5.26)$$

$$+ \sum_{i=1}^{m-1} \sum_{r=i+1}^{m} w_{2ir}[|x_{i1} - x_{r1}|^p + |x_{i2} - x_{r2}|^p]^{1/p}.$$

The methods used to derive the Euclidean dual in the preceding sections are now applied to the ℓ_p problem for $p > 1$. (When $p = 1$, problem (5.26) can be posed as the linear programming problem (4.5), for which duality results are well known.) Let $Y = (y_1, y_2)$. Here we use the notation $\|Y\|_p$ to denote $[|y_1|^p + |y_2|^p]^{1/p}$. In this notation $\ell_p(X_i, X_r)$ becomes $\|X_i - X_r\|_p$. The approximation in equation (5.17) extended to ℓ_p distances is:

$$WMh(X) = \sum_{i=1}^{m} \sum_{j=1}^{n} w_{1ij}\|X_i - a_j\|_{\epsilon,p} + \sum_{i=1}^{m-1} \sum_{r=i+1}^{m} w_{2ir}\|X_i - X_r\|_{\epsilon,p}$$

(5.27)

where:

$$\|X_i - a_j\|_{\epsilon,p} = [|x_{i1} - a_{j1}|^p + |x_{i2} - a_{j2}|^p + \epsilon^p]^{1/p}, \text{ and}$$

$$\|X_i - X_r\|_{\epsilon,p} = [|x_{i1} - x_{r1}|^p + |x_{i2} - x_{r2}|^p + \epsilon^p]^{1/p}, \epsilon > 0.$$

Let $q = p/(p - 1)$. Then using the construction in the Appendix, mathematical note 5.1, quasilinearization of terms of WMh_p is given by:

$$w_{2ir}\|X_i - X_r\|_{\epsilon,p} = \max_{U_{2ir}, z_{2ir}} [(X_i - X_r)U_{2ir} - \epsilon z_{2ir}]$$

$$\text{subject to } [(\|U_{2ir}\|_q)^q + |z_{2ir}|^q]^{1/q} = w_{2ir}. \tag{5.28}$$

The values of U_{2ir} and z_{2ir} that make the equality hold in this case are given by:

$$U_{2ir} = w_{2ir}[\text{sign}(x_{i1} - x_{r1})(|x_{i1} - x_{r1}|/\|X_i - X_r\|_{\epsilon,p})^{p-1},$$

$$\text{sign}(x_{i2} - x_{r2})(|x_{i2} - x_{r2}|/\|X_i - X_r\|_{\epsilon,p})^{p-1}] \tag{5.29a}$$

and $z_{2ir} = - w_{2ir}\epsilon^{p-1}/(\|X_i - X_r\|_{\epsilon,p})^{p-1}.$ (5.29b)

Similarly:

$$w_{1ij}\|X_i - a_j\|_{\epsilon,p} = \max_{U_{1ij}, z_{1ij}} [(X_i - a_j)U_{1ij} - \epsilon z_{1ij}]$$

$$\text{subject to } [(\|U_{1ij}\|_q)^q + |z_{1ij}|^q]^{1/q} = w_{1ij},$$

with values for U_{1ij} and z_{1ij} given by the analog of equations (5.29).

Carrying through the same development as that from problem (5.22) to problem (5.24), we have:

$$\min_{X} WMh(X) = \max_{U,Z} DMh(U,Z)$$

$$= \max - \sum_{i=1}^{m} \sum_{j=1}^{n} (a_j U_{1ij} + \epsilon z_{1ij}) - \sum_{i=1}^{m-1} \sum_{r=i+1}^{m} \epsilon z_{2ir}$$

subject to   (5.30)

$$-\sum_{r=1}^{i-1} U_{2ri} + \sum_{r=i+1}^{m} U_{2ir} + \sum_{j=1}^{n} U_{1ij} = \bar{0}, \; i = 1,...,m,$$

$$[(\|U_{1ij}\|_q)^q + |z_{1ij}|^q]^{1/q} = w_{1ij}, \; i = 1,...,m; \; j = 1,...,n,$$

$$[(\|U_{2ir}\|_q)^q + |z_{2ir}|^q]^{1/q} = w_{2ir}, \; i = 1,...,m-1; \; r = i+1,...,m.$$

Because the primal approximating objective $WMh(X)$ in equation (5.27) is uniformly convergent to $WM(X)$ in problem (5.26) as $\epsilon \to 0$, we seek the dual problem in the limiting case as $\epsilon \to 0$. Since $|z_{1ij}| \leqslant w_{1ij}$ and $|z_{2ir}| \leqslant w_{2ir}$, the limiting form of problem (5.30) as $\epsilon \to 0$ (and Z is omitted thereafter) is:

$$\max_{U} DM(U) = -\sum_{i=1}^{m}\sum_{j=1}^{n} a_j U_{1ij}$$

subject to   (5.31)

$$-\sum_{r=1}^{i-1} U_{2ri} + \sum_{r=i+1}^{m} U_{2ir} + \sum_{j=1}^{n} U_{1ij} = \bar{0}, \; i = 1,...,m,$$

$$\|U_{1ij}\|_q \leqslant w_{1ij}, \; i = 1,...,m; \; j = 1,...,n,$$

$$\|U_{2ir}\|_q \leqslant w_{2ir}, \; i = 1,...,m-1; \; r = i+1,...,m.$$

The multi-facility ℓ_p dual problem ($p > 1$) can be solved using a standard nonlinear programming algorithm upon raising both sides of the inequality constraints to the power q to produce a differentiable problem. The m optimal facility locations will be the m optimal Lagrange multiplier vectors corresponding to the equality constraints.

When linear constraints $GX \geqslant b$ augment the primal problem (5.26), an analysis entirely analogous to that of Section 5.2 can be used to derive the augmented multi-facility ℓ_p dual form. Let G be a $t \times 2m$ matrix and let $\lambda = (\lambda_i,...,\lambda_t)$ be the vector of associated Lagrange multipliers. Let the ith constraint be given by $g_i(X) = g_{i1}x_{11} + g_{i2}x_{12} + g_{i3}x_{21} + ... + g_{i,2m}x_{m2} \geqslant b_i$. The constrained primal problem can be solved as:

$$\max_{\lambda \geqslant \bar{0}} \min_{X} LMh(X,\lambda) = WMh(X) + \sum_{i=1}^{t} \lambda_i[g_i(X) - s_i^2 - b_i]. \quad (5.32)$$

Let the jth column of G be given by $G_j, j = 1,2,...,2m$. Applying conditions analogous to equations (5.14) and (5.15) to the analog of problem (5.13) and letting $\epsilon \rightarrow 0$, we arrive at the following limiting case of the dual of problem (5.26) in the presence of linear constraints:

$$\max_{U,\lambda} DM(U,\lambda) = \lambda b - \sum_{i=1}^{m} \sum_{j=1}^{n} a_j U_{1ij}$$

subject to   (5.33)

$$\lambda(G_{2i-1}, G_{2i}) - \sum_{r=1}^{i-1} U_{2ri} + \sum_{r=i+1}^{m} U_{2ir} + \sum_{j=1}^{n} U_{1ij} = \bar{0}, \; i = 1,\ldots,m,$$

$$\|U_{1ij}\|_q \leq w_{1ij}, \; i = 1,\ldots,m; \; j = 1,\ldots,n,$$

$$\|U_{2ir}\|_q \leq w_{2ir}, \; i = 1,\ldots,m-1; \; r = i+1,\ldots,m,$$

$$\lambda \geq \bar{0}$$

5.5 SOLUTION METHODS FOR THE DUAL FORM

The multi-facility ℓ_p primal problem (with or without linear constraints) can be solved by solving the dual problem using a standard nonlinear programming algorithm. (For $p = 1$ both the primal and dual problems can be posed as linear programming problems, following the discussion in Section 4.1.) However, computational experience seems to indicate that using nonlinear programming algorithms, and one of the differentiable approximating objective functions, the primal problem may be solved faster than the dual. Yet the dual problem has a much simpler functional form in the objective function and constraints (after raising each nonlinear constraint to the qth power). The ease of setting up the dual problem for solution by a nonlinear programming algorithm may outweigh any extra computing time.

Decomposition procedures have also been developed to solve the dual problem. They require special computer programs to be written and are computationally efficient only when large numbers of constraints are present in the primal problem. Sources for the methods are given in Reference Note 5.3.

EXERCISES

5.1 Kuhn (1967,1976) Consider problem (5.1) with $n = 3$ and $w_1 = w_2 = w_3 = 1$. Figure 5E.1 depicts the geometry of the situation described by Mr. Tho. Moss in Section 1.3. The locations a_1, a_2, and a_3 are the locations of the three trees mentioned there. Equilateral triangles have been constructed on the sides of the triangle $\Delta a_1 a_2 a_3$. The point X^* is the Toricelli point described in

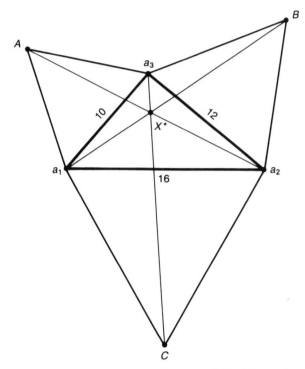

Figure 5E.1   Geometrical Arrangement for Primal-Dual Example.

Section 1.3. The line segments $\overline{a_2A}$, $\overline{a_1B}$, and $\overline{a_3C}$ correspond to so-called Simpson lines that intersect at X^*.

a. Using the observation of Rochat, Vecten, Fanguier, and Pilatte in Section 1.3, graph the equilateral triangle requested by Mr. Moss (the "Moss triangle").

b. By direct measurement verify that the altitude of the Moss triangle equals the sum of the lengths of the segments $\overline{a_1X^*}$, $\overline{a_2X^*}$, and $\overline{a_3X^*}$.

c. Let the locations of the three trees be given by $a_1 = (0,0)$, $a_2 = (16,0)$, and $a_3 = (6.6250,7.4906)$. Then $X^* = (6.8149,4.5425)$ and $W(X^*) = 2.1391$. Solve the associated dual problem (5.10) using a nonlinear programming algorithm and perform an analysis similar to that carried out in Example 5.1. Comment on the relationship between the direction vectors U_1^*, U_2^*, and U_3^* and the Simpson lines.

5.2 a. Perform the analysis to arrive at problem (5.31) starting with problem (5.27).

b. Show how to incorporate linear constraints into the development of Exercise 5.2a to arrive at problem (5.33).

5.3 Francis and Cabot (1972)

a. Consider problem (5.25). Show that $\|U_{2ir}\| < w_{2ir}$ implies $X_i^* = X_r^*$, whereas $X_i^* \neq X_r^*$ implies $\|U_{2ir}\| = w_{2ir}$. (Hint: Consider the analysis demonstrated in the Appendix, mathematical note 5.2.)

b. Generalize the "line through each a_j..." statement after Property 5.1 to the case of new facility locations X_i^* and X_r^* in problem (5.25). Justify the result.

5.4 Use a nonlinear programming algorithm to solve the constrained multi-facility location problem posed in Exercise 4.6, assuming Euclidean distances. Do this by solving a dual problem.

5.5 Verify that the quasilinearization implemented in equations (5.28) and (5.29) satisfies the requirements of mathematical note 5.1 in the Appendix.

REFERENCE NOTES

SECTION 5.1 An historical perspective on the dual problem is contained in Kuhn (1976). Using quasilinearization, Bellman (1965) implicitly gave a form to the single-facility Euclidean dual that is close to that of problem (5.10); however, the nonlinear constraints were written as equalities. This occurred because Bellman assumed away the discontinuities in the derivatives of the primal. The first formally published development of the single-facility Euclidean dual was given by Kuhn (1967). There Witzgall and Rockafellar are mentioned as having independently discovered the same dual [see Witzgall (1964)]. For general background on duality, the reader is referred to Geoffrion (1971) who provided an applications-oriented synthesis of duality in nonlinear programming.

SECTION 5.2 Francis and Cabot (1972) obtained and interpreted the multi-facility Euclidean dual, and a method for treating linear constraints was discussed.

SECTION 5.3 Love (1974) developed the constrained multi-facility ℓ_p dual using quasilinearization. Juel and Love (1981a) formulated the linearly constrained dual with generalized distance norms using conjugate function theory as exposited by Witzgall (1964). A decomposition method tailored to solving the constrained Euclidean dual problem was described in Love and Kraemer (1973), and subsequently extended to ℓ_p distance problems by Love (1974). Another version of the decomposition method was given by Planchart and Hurter (1975) for mixed Euclidean and rectangular distances.

APPENDIX—CHAPTER 5

Mathematical Notes

5.1 [Quasilinearization]. Let $\alpha = (\alpha_1, \alpha_2, ..., \alpha_K)$ and $\beta = (\beta_1, \beta_2, ..., \beta_K)$ be vectors whose components are real numbers. Denote the scalar product $\sum_{k=1}^{K} \alpha_k \beta_k$ by $\alpha\beta$ and denote $[\sum_{k=1}^{K} |\alpha_k|^p]^{1/p}$ by $\|\alpha\|_p$. Let $p > 1$ and $1/p + 1/q = 1$. Then $w\|\alpha\|_p = \max_{\|\beta\|_q = w} \alpha\beta$.

PROOF: [Beckenbach and Bellman (1965)]. Hölder's inequality can be stated: $\sum_{k=1}^{K} |\alpha_k \beta_k| \leqslant \|\alpha\|_p \|\beta\|_q$. Equality holds if and only if $|\beta_k|^q = c|\alpha_k|^p$, $k = 1,...,K$, where c is a non-negative scalar. Thus, if β_k has the same sign as α_k, $k = 1,...,K$ and $\|\beta\|_q = w$ (through a suitable choice of c) we have $\alpha\beta = \sum_{k=1}^{K} |\alpha_k \beta_k| = \|\alpha\|_p w$, as required.

In equation (5.3), where $p = 2$ and $K = 3$ we have $\alpha_1 = (x_1 - a_{j1})$, $\alpha_2 = (x_2 - a_{j2})$ and $\alpha_3 = \epsilon$, whereas $\beta_1 = u_j$, $\beta_2 = v_j$ and $\beta_3 = -z_j$. A geometrical perspective is gained by noting $\alpha\beta = \|\alpha\|_2 \|\beta\|_2 \cos\theta$, where θ is the angle between α and β (representable as directed line segments in three-dimensional space). We have

$$\max_{\|\beta\|_2 = w_j} \alpha\beta = \max_{\|\beta\|_2 = w_j} \|\alpha\|_2 \|\beta\|_2 \cos\theta.$$

The maximum is attained $\theta = 0°$, which means $\beta = c\alpha$ for $c \geqslant 0$. ($c > 0$ unless $w_j = 0$, an uninteresting case.) From equation (5.4) it is seen that $c = w_j / \|\alpha\|_2$. The case $\|\alpha\|_2 = 0$ is avoided because α_3 is always positive.

5.2 *Prove* Property 5.1

The optimal Lagrange multipliers for the equality constraints of problem (5.11) solve the primal problem (5.1).

PROOF: For the dual form given by problem (5.11), let the vector of multipliers for the two equality constraints be $X = (x_1, x_2)$. To attain differentiability, let the inequality constraints be written $U_j^2 \leqslant w_j^2$, where $U_j^2 = \|U_j\|^2$. Let the vector of associated multipliers be $\pi = (\pi_1, \pi_2,...,\pi_n)$. The Lagrangian function to be used is:

$$L(U,X,\pi) = -\sum_{j=1}^{n} U_j a_j + X \sum_{j=1}^{n} U_j + \sum_{j=1}^{n} \pi_j(w_j^2 - U_j^2).$$

Applying the Karush-Kuhn-Tucker necessary conditions for problem (5.10) and setting $\partial L / \partial U_j = \bar{0}$ gives:

$$- a_j + X - 2\pi_j U_j = \bar{0} \text{ for } j = 1,...,n, \qquad (5A.1)$$

and setting $\partial L / \partial X = \bar{0}$ gives:

$$\sum_{j=1}^{n} U_j = \bar{0}. \qquad (5A.2)$$

As $\partial L / \partial \pi_j \geqslant 0$, $\pi_j \geqslant 0$, and $\pi_j(\partial L / \partial \pi_j) = 0$, it follows that:

$$w_j^2 - U_j^2 \geqslant 0, \text{ and } \pi_j(w_j^2 - U_j^2) = 0. \qquad (5A.3)$$

These conditions are also sufficient for problem (5.10). There are two cases to consider.

Case 1

All $\pi_j^* > 0$. Then from condition (5A.3), $\|U_j^*\| = w_j$ for all j; and from equation (5A.1), $\pi_j^* = \|X - a_j\|/2w_j$. Upon substituting π_j^* into (5A.1) we have $U_j^* = w_j(X^* - a_j)/\|X^* - a_j\|$. Substituting the U_j^* into equation (5A.2), yields the necessary and sufficient conditions for optimality in problem (5.1) when $X^* \neq a_j$, for all $j = 1,...,n$ [see equation (2.3)].

Case 2

Some $\pi_r^* = 0$. From equation (5A.1), $X^* = a_r$, and because no existing facilities coincide, $\pi_j > 0$ for $j \neq r$. From condition (5A.3), $\|U_r^*\| \leq w_r$, and $\|U_j^*\| = w_j$ for $j \neq r$. The three conditions are satisfied with:

$$\pi_j^* = \frac{\|X^* - a_j\|}{2w_j}, \quad U_j^* = \frac{w_j(a_r - a_j)}{\|X^* - a_j\|} \text{ for } j \neq r, \text{ and } U_r^* = \sum_{\substack{j=1 \\ \neq r}}^{n} U_j^*.$$

If $\|U_r^*\| < w_r$, this is equivalent to condition (2.4) holding with strict inequality.

Chapter 6

Site Generation Under the Minimax Criterion

In previous chapters the adopted criterion for optimal locations has been the minimization of a sum of distances multiplied by non-negative weights such as:

$$WM(X) = \sum_{i=1}^{m} \sum_{j=1}^{n} w_{1ij}\ell_p(X_1, a_j) + \sum_{i=1}^{m-1} \sum_{r=i+1}^{m} w_{2ir}\ell_p(X_i, X_r).$$

But a minimizer for $WM(X)$ is also a minimizer for $WM(X)/C$ where $C > 0$. Let

$$C = \sum_{i=1}^{m} \sum_{j=1}^{n} w_{1ij} + \sum_{i=1}^{m-1} \sum_{r=i+1}^{m} w_{2ir}.$$

Then it becomes clear that minimizing $WM(X)$ is equivalent to minimizing the (weighted) average distance. This *efficiency* criterion is not appropriate if system performance is directly related to extreme distances. Consider the radio reception problem described by Brady and Rosenthal (1980).

Suppose a set of radio transmitters are located at points $a_1,...,a_n$ and are broadcasting mutually incoherent signals with intensities $I_1,...,I_n$. The problem is to choose the size and the site of a receiver with two considerations entering into the decision: first, the receiver should be as small (i.e., insensitive) as possible yet able to monitor every signal; second, the receiver's location X must not fall within a previously specified (and arbitrarily configured) forbidden zone. ... The rationale for the second consideration is obvious; the reasons for the first are cost, speed of construction, and possibly, vulnerability. By the inverse-square law, a signal's intensity diminishes with the square of Euclidean distance as it leaves its source. Thus the

113

problem to be solved, ie, of maximizing the signal strength of the weakest signal to be received at X, may be formulated as . . .

$$\text{maximize } \min\{I_j/[\ell_2(X,a_j)]^2, j = 1,...,n\}$$
$$X \epsilon F$$

where F is the feasible region. This *maximin* problem is equivalent to the minimization over $X \epsilon F$ of:

$$M(X) = \max\{w_j\ell_2(X,a_j), j = 1,...,n\}, \tag{6.1}$$

with (positive) weights given by $w_j = 1/\sqrt{I_j}$. This, in turn, is an example of a *minimax* criterion applied to a location problem.

Let $C_j(x_0) = \{X \mid w_j\ell_2(X,a_j) \le x_0\}$, and let $C(x_0)$ denote the intersection of all the circular sets $C_j(x_0), j = 1,...,n$. Then $x_0^* = M(X^*)$ is the smallest value of x_0 such that the intersection of $C(x_0)$ and F is not empty. These concepts have direct graphic expressions.

Example 6.1   Let there be five radio transmitters located at (3,2), (6,2), (4,4), (8,1), and (5,7) with intensities 1, 1/4, 1/4, 1, and 1, respectively. The weights w_j are therefore 1, 2, 2, 1, and 1, respectively. Figure 6.1

Figure 6.1   Graphic Analysis of Example 6.1.

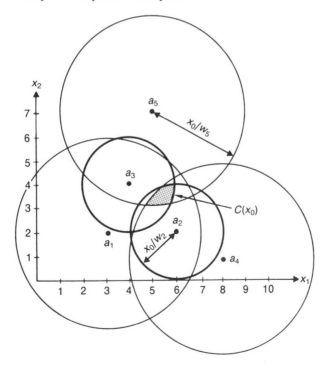

illustrates construction of the intersection set $C(x_0)$ for $x_0 = 4$. The circular region $C_2(x_0)$, for example, is the "listening area" enclosed by the circle centered at a_2 with radius x_0/w_2. A receiver located therein with sensitivity x_0 can monitor the signal sent by the transmitter at location a_2. Then $C(x_0)$ represents the region within which to place the receiver to monitor the signals of all n transmitters. The feasible region here is the entire plane (no forbidden zones). As x_0 is reduced to 3.474, $X^* = (5.689, 3.595)$ emerges as the single member of $C(x_0)$, and therefore is the optimal location of the receiver. If F implied location along a road or outside a body of water, the analysis would include a graphic display of F in order to consider the intersection of $C(x_0)$ and F.

The minimax criterion might be adopted when the facilities to be located provide goods or services under conditions of urgency, or when system response depends on the "weakest locational link." Examples of applications include locating industrial services (rapid delivery, troubleshooting); locating public facilities (fire alarm boxes, ambulance bases); or designing detection or signaling systems (radar systems, early warning sirens).

There are two important observations that can be made upon careful consideration of Figure 6.1. First, there will exist a subset of two or three existing points a_j such that $C(x_0^*)$ is the intersection of the circular regions for these points. In the example, transmitters at a_3, a_4, and a_5 determine X^*. If w_4 were changed to $\frac{1}{2}$, then a_2 and a_5 would determine $X^* = (5.664, 3.666)$. The second observation is that the minimax criterion is a "grease-the-squeaky-wheel" criterion, because only the extreme existing facility locations determine X^*. No account is taken of the average distances. Whether this sensitivity to outliers is problematic must be determined within the context of the application. Minimax formulations imply "equity" considerations since the poorest service is made to be as good as possible.

Further lessons can be gained from graphic analysis. Suppose a helicopter ambulance base is to be located and the population to be served is spread over a convex polygon (H) with a finite number (n) of corner points. (Convert any nonconvex polygon to a convex polygon by joining the vertices.) Figure 6.2, which is based on a similar figure in Nair and Chandrasekaran (1971), illustrates that a minimax location will be at the center of the smallest circle that encloses H. The circle in Figure 6.2(b) is not a minimum covering circle and so X is not the minimax location. Figure 6.2(a) illustrates that a minimum covering circle will pass through at least two corner points. Only corner points will determine the extreme distances to the facility. Thus, letting the a_j's correspond to the corner points and the w_j's $= 1$, the helicopter base location problem may be solved by minimizing $M(X)$ in equation (6.1).

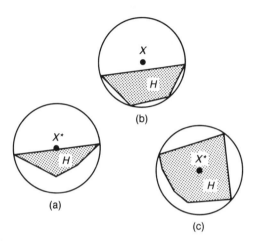

Figure 6.2   Covering Points and Covering Circles.

A formal definition of the (unconstrained) ℓ_p distance multi-facility problem is to find X^* that minimizes $MM(X)$, given by:

$$MM(X) = \max \{w_{1ij}\ell_p(X_i,a_j),\ i = 1,...,m,\ j = 1,...,n;$$

$$w_{2ir}\ell_p(X_i,X_r),\ i = 1,...,m-1;\ r = i+1,...,m\} \quad (6.2)$$

where $X = (X_1,...,X_m)$, $X_i = (x_{i1},x_{i2})$, and the weights are non-negative. We shall assume that each new facility is *chained* (Section 4.2) to at least one existing facility. The single-facility case is given by omitting the elements $w_{2ir}\ell_p(X_i,X_r)$ from the set that determines $MM(X)$. Otherwise these terms reflect interaction between the new facilities themselves.

It is appropriate to consider whether $MM(X)$ indeed takes on a minimum value. Because $w_{1ij}\ell_p(X_i,a_j)$ and $w_{2ir}\ell_p(X_i,X_r)$ are continuous functions, $MM(X)$ is continuous. For any X', say, with an X_i outside the smallest rectangle enclosing all existing facility locations a_j, there is an X'' with all X_i inside the rectangle such that $MM(X'') \leqslant MM(X')$. The *existence* of a minimizer X^*, say, for $MM(X)$ is thus guaranteed by the extreme value theorem.

A mathematical programming formulation that facilitates subsequent discussion of solution procedures and derives from the intuition gained from Figure 6.1 is:

$$\text{minimize } x_0$$
$$x_0,X$$

$$\text{subject to} \qquad\qquad\qquad\qquad\qquad\qquad\qquad (6.3a)$$

$$x_0 \geqslant w_{1ij}\ell_p(X_i,a_j),\ i = 1,...,m;\ j = 1,...,n$$

$$x_0 \geqslant w_{2ir}\ell_p(X_i,X_r),\ i = 1,...,m-1;\ r = i+1,...,m.$$

During the course of minimization the value of x_0 will be reduced. The effect is to reduce the largest of the weighted distances. When x_0 is minimized, the binding constraints correspond to the weighted distances that are equal to the minimax weighted distance.

Let $z_0 = x_0^p$, then formulation (6.3a) can be put into a computationally convenient form. Upon raising both sides of the constraints to the power p, we obtain:

minimize z_0
z_0, X

subject to   (6.3b)

$$z_0 \geqslant w_{1ij}^p[|x_{i1} - a_{j1}|^p + |x_{i2} - a_{j2}|^p], \; i = 1,...,m; \; j = 1,...,n$$

$$z_0 \geqslant w_{2ir}^p[|x_{i1} - x_{r1}|^p + |x_{i2} - x_{r2}|^p], \; i = 1,...,m-1; \; r = i+1,...,m.$$

As well as avoiding p^{th} root operations, formulation (6.3b) is differentiable for $p > 1$, ie, the constraint functions are now differentiable everywhere. Discussion of the $p = 1$ case is deferred to Section 6.2.

As noted, the minimax criterion is insensitive to the magnitude of weighted distances that are *less* than $MM(X^*)$. Remedies include mandatory closeness constraints such as $\ell_p(X_i, a_j) \leqslant b$, feasibility constraints such as $g_1 x_{i1} + g_2 x_{i2} \leqslant b$, or the embedding of formulation (6.3) in a multi-objective framework. The first two remedies are considered after the ensuing discussions of solution approaches for Euclidean and rectangular distance problems.

6.1 EUCLIDEAN DISTANCES

Unweighted Single-Facility Problems

A convenient quadratic program is an immediate consequence of formulation (6.3b) for the unweighted (all $w_j = 1$) single-facility Euclidean distance problem. Using the substitution $x_3 = z_0 - (x_1^2 + x_2^2)$ reduces formulation (6.3b) to the following:

minimize $x_1^2 + x_2^2 + x_3$
x_1, x_2, x_3

subject to   (6.4)

$$2x_1 a_{j1} + 2x_2 a_{j2} + x_3 \geqslant a_{j1}^2 + a_{j2}^2, \; j = 1,...,n.$$

This formulation gains access to finite quadratic programming algorithms.

Graphic methods also have natural appeal here. These are motivated by the following property from Nair and Chandrasekaran (1971), which was observed in Figure 6.2.

Property 6.1 [*Minimum covering circles and corner points*]. *The minimum covering circle of a convex polygon will pass through two or more of its corner points, and all such corner points cannot be on less than half the perimeter of the circle.*

An example of the use of these observations is contained in the following algorithm. When reduced to algebraic terms and implemented on a computer, the algorithm is very efficient.

Elzinga-Hearn Algorithm

Step 1   Plot the existing facility locations as points on a graph. Construct the convex hull H of the points. Choose the two corner points of H that are farthest apart. Construct the minimum covering circle for the two points. If this is also a minimum covering circle for H, terminate. Otherwise, choose a (likely) corner point outside the circle, and proceed to Step 2.

Step 2   If the three points define a right triangle or an obtuse triangle, exclude the point at the angle greater than or equal to 90°, and return to Step 1 with the remaining two corner points. Otherwise, proceed to Step 3.

Step 3   Construct the minimum covering circle for the three defining points. If this is also a minimum covering circle for H, terminate. Otherwise, choose a (likely) corner point outside, call it D, and label as A a point from among the three defining points that is farthest from D. Extend the diameter of the current circle through point A to divide the plane into two half-planes. Label as B the defining point in the same half-plane with D, and label the remaining point as C. Return to Step 2 with points A, C, and D.

If in Step 2 the three points are on a straight line, consider this a degenerate triangle with a 180° angle at the intermediate point. To construct a circle through the three points in Step 3, construct perpendicular bisectors of any two sides of the (acute) triangle; the intersection of the two bisectors is the center of the circle. Convergence of the algorithm derives from the increasing radii of the circles created and the finite number of possible two-point and three-point circles. The user's visual inspection of the problem (using interactive computer graphics) will produce "likely" candidates in Steps 2 and 3.

Weighted Single-Facility Problems—Interactive Computer Graphics

The strategy of the Elzinga-Hearn algorithm can be extended to weighted problems. However, we will describe an approach that represents a distinct departure from the mathematical programming orientation of most techniques in this text. Here we require a person at a computer graphics terminal to test visually for intersection of circular regions. This idea is attractive because human pattern recognition can be used to detect whether $C(x_0)$, for a given x_0, intersects with a feasible region F of irregular (perhaps nonconvex) shape possibly dictated by the inclusion of forbidden regions (also of irregular shape).

Let $\tilde{x}_0$ denote the *constrained* minimum value of $M(X)$ in equation (6.1), for which X is constrained to be in F. Then observe that $C(x_0)$ and F do not intersect if $x_0 < \tilde{x}_0$ whereas there is an intersection if $x_0 \geqslant \tilde{x}_0$. This dichotomy enables the following iterative bisection search for $\tilde{x}_0$.

Brady-Rosenthal Interactive Graphics Minimax Algorithm

Step 0 Choose $\epsilon > 0$, and set $LB = 0$, $UB = M$ where M is a finite number sure to exceed $\tilde{x}_0$.

Step 1 Set $x_0 = (UB+LB)/2$. If $UB-LB < \epsilon$, terminate; $\tilde{x}_0 \simeq x_0$.

Step 2 Otherwise, display F and $C_j(x_0)$, $j = 1,...,n$, graphically. The user observes whether or not $C(x_0)$ intersects F. If so, set $UB = x_0$; otherwise set $LB = x_0$. Return to Step 1.

It is envisioned that the algorithm would be implemented in two phases using color graphics. The circular sets $C_j(x_0)$ might be shaded blue, whereas the background might be white. Once easily discernible, the set $C(x_0)$ might be red. In the first phase the user would apply the approach to find the *unconstrained* minimum x_0^*, say, where F is temporarily the entire plane. The second phase would begin with $UB = M$ and $LB = x_0^*$ and require the user only to determine if $C(x_0)$ and (the original) F intersect. The region F might conveniently be drawn by the user with a light pen.

The more complicated first phase might necessitate a verification procedure in Step 2 to avoid human error. If the user indicates $C(x_0) = \phi$, the user would be required to identify j_1, and j_2 such that $C_{j_1}(x_0)$ and $C_{j_2}(x_0)$ do not intersect. If $C(x_0) \neq \phi$ is indicated, a light pen would be used to indicate a point in $C(x_0)$. Alternatively, a mathematical algorithm, such as that described in the next section, could be used in the first phase to find x_0^* without human intervention. This avoids a possibly difficult recognition task in the first phase.

Addenda

Suppose an ambulance base is to be located. If a trip is made from a base located at X to the jth response zone, centered at a_j, a trip must then be made to the hospital nearest to a_j. Let g_j measure the expected trip time from a_j to the hospital and let w_j convert distance into expected minutes of travel time to the jth zone. Then equation (6.1) would be amended to:

$$M(X) = \max\{w_j \ell_2(X, a_j) + g_j, j = 1,...,n\}. \tag{6.1'}$$

The interactive graphics algorithm can be used upon defining the circular regions as:

$$C_j(x_0) = \{X \mid \ell_2(X, a_j) \leqslant e_j(x_0)\},$$

where

$$e_j(x_0) = \max[0, (x_0 - g_j)/w_j].$$

Multi-Facility Problems

We now describe a convenient iterative approach which complements the Weiszfeld method for minimum sum location problems. The approach produces successively improved approximations to a solution to the Karush-Kuhn-Tucker conditions that are sufficient for this problem. These conditions are stated in Property 6.2. (When derivatives are taken, it will be important to recall the convention that whenever $i > r$, w_{2ir} is evaluated as w_{2ri}.)

Property 6.2 [*Necessary and sufficient conditions for optimality using Euclidean distances*]. *The Karush-Kuhn-Tucker necessary (and sufficient) conditions for* (z_0^*, X^*) *to solve problem (6.3b) with* $p = 2$ *are given by the constraints of problem (6.3b) together with:*

$$\sum_{j=1}^{n} v_{ij}^* w_{1ij}^2 (x_{ik}^* - a_{jk}) + \sum_{\substack{r=1 \\ \neq i}}^{m} u_{ir}^* w_{2ir}^2 (x_{ik}^* - x_{rk}^*) = 0 \tag{6.5}$$

$$i = 1,...,m; \ k = 1,2$$

$$\sum_{i=1}^{m} \sum_{j=1}^{n} v_{ij}^* + \sum_{i=1}^{m-1} \sum_{r=i+1}^{m} u_{ir}^* = 1 \tag{6.6}$$

$$v_{ij}^*(z_0^* - w_{1ij}^2[\ell_2(X_i^*, a_j)]^2) = 0 \quad i = 1,...,m; \ j = 1,...,n \tag{6.7}$$

$$u_{ir}^*(z_0^* - w_{2ir}^2[\ell_2(X_i^*, X_r^*)]^2) = 0 \quad i = 1,...,m-1; \ r = i+1,...,m \tag{6.8}$$

and all $v_{ij}^* \geqslant 0$, $u_{ir}^* \geqslant 0$. $\tag{6.9}$

The v_{ij}^* and u_{ir}^* are the Lagrange multipliers (dual variables). Before describing the algorithm, we define a particular minimum sum problem.

For *given* values of v_{ij} and u_{ir} (indicated by overbars), we will need to:

$$\text{minimize } W(X;\bar{u},\bar{v}) = \sum_{i=1}^{m} \sum_{j=1}^{n} \bar{w}_{1ij}[(x_{i1} - a_{j1})^2 + (x_{i2} - a_{j2})^2]$$

$$+ \sum_{i=1}^{m-1} \sum_{r=i+1}^{m} \bar{w}_{2ir}[(x_{i1} - x_{r1})^2 + (x_{i2} - x_{r2})^2], \qquad (6.10)$$

where $\bar{w}_{1ij} = \bar{v}_{ij}w_{1ij}^2$, $\bar{w}_{2ir} = \bar{u}_{ir}w_{2ir}^2$. Problem (6.10) is a squared-Euclidean distance problem that has an analytical solution. This is discussed in the Appendix, mathematical note 6.1.

Property 6.3 [*Lagrange multipliers and primal variables*]. *If* $\bar{v} = v^*$ *and* $\bar{u} = u^*$, *then* X^* [*which solves problem (6.3b) with* $p = 2$] *is a global minimizer of* $W(X,u^*,v^*)$.

PROOF: $W(X;\bar{u},\bar{v})$ is a convex differentiable function of X. Hence, setting partial derivatives to zero and solving the system of linear equations will produce a global minimizer of W, ie, solving:

$$\frac{\partial W}{\partial x_{ik}} = \sum_{j=1}^{n} v_{ij}^* w_{1ij}^2 (x_{ik} - a_{jk}) + \sum_{\substack{r=1 \\ \neq i}}^{m} u_{ir}^* w_{2ir}^2 (x_{ik} - x_{rk}) = 0$$

$$i = 1,...,m; \; k = 1,2 \qquad (6.10')$$

will produce a global minimizer for W. But these equations are the same as those in expression (6.5), which X^* must satisfy; this means X^* minimizes $W(X;u^*,v^*)$, as claimed.

If u^* and v^* were known in advance, we could solve the problem analytically by solving problem (6.10). This leads to an iterative procedure for estimating u^* and v^*. Let $X^{(t)}$ be a minimizer of $W(X;u^{(t)}, v^{(t)})$, where $u^{(t)}$ and $v^{(t)}$ are the tth estimates of u^* and v^*. Define:

$$v_{ij}^{(t+1)} = v_{ij}^{(t)} w_{1ij} \ell_2(X_i^{(t)}, a_j)/s \text{ and} \qquad (6.11)$$

$$u_{ir}^{(t+1)} = u_{ir}^{(t)} w_{2ir} \ell_2(X_i^{(t)}, X_r^{(t)})/s, \qquad (6.12)$$

where:

$$s = \sum_{i=1}^{m} \sum_{j=1}^{n} v_{ij}^{(t)} w_{1ij} \ell_2(X_i^{(t)}, a_j) + \sum_{i=1}^{m-1} \sum_{r=i+1}^{m} u_{ir}^{(t)} w_{2ir} \ell_2(X_i^{(t)}, X_r^{(t)}).$$

By construction, $v_{ij}^{(t+1)} \geqslant 0$, $u_{ir}^{(t+1)} \geqslant 0$ and

$$\sum_{i=1}^{m} \sum_{j=1}^{n} v_{ij}^{(t+1)} + \sum_{i=1}^{m-1} \sum_{r=i+1}^{m} u_{ir}^{(t+1)} = 1. \qquad (6.13)$$

Because $X^{(t)}$ minimizes W, the partial derivatives of $W(X;u^{(t)}, v^{(t)})$ must be zero at $X^{(t)}$. Using equations (6.11) and (6.12) to eliminate $v_{ij}^{(t)}$ and $u_{ir}^{(t)}$, we obtain:

$$\sum_{i=1}^{m}\sum_{j=1}^{n} v_{ij}^{(t+1)} \frac{w_{1ij}^2}{w_{1ij}\ell_2(X_i^{(t)},a_j)}(x_{ik}^{(t)} - a_{jk})$$

$$+ \sum_{\substack{r=1 \\ \neq i}}^{m} u_{ir}^{(t+1)} \frac{w_{2ir}^2}{w_{2ir}\ell_2(X_i^{(t)},X_r^{(t)})}(x_{ik}^{(t)} - x_{rk}^{(t)}) = 0 \qquad (6.14)$$

for $i = 1,...,m$; $k = 1,2$.

Now suppose $v_{ij}^{(t+1)} = v_{ij}^*$ and $u_{ir}^{(t+1)} = u_{ir}^*$. Then by the complementary slackness conditions (6.7) and (6.8)

$$x_0^* = w_{1ij}\ell_2(X_i^*,a_j) = w_{2ir}\ell_2(X_i^*,X_r^*) \text{ for } v_{ij}^* \neq 0, u_{ir}^* \neq 0.$$

Hence the denominators in equation (6.14) could be replaced by 1 in this case. [Terms in equation (6.14) for which the denominator is zero are to be omitted because the associated terms in problem (6.3b) do not define z_0^*.] Considering conditions (6.9) and comparing equations (6.13) and (6.14), with denominators replaced by 1, to equations (6.6) and (6.5) suggests $u^{(t+1)}$ and $v^{(t+1)}$ are approximations to u^* and v^*. The following algorithm is based on this observation.

Lawson-Charalambous Algorithm

Step 0 Set all $v_{ij}^{(0)}$ and $u_{ir}^{(0)} = 1$; set $t = 1$ and choose $\epsilon > 0$.

Step 1 Find a minimizer $X^{(t)}$ for $W(X;u^{(t)},v^{(t)})$. Then set $v^{(t+1)}$ and $u^{(t+1)}$ according to equations (6.11) and (6.12).

Step 2 Calculate $\bar{x}_0 = MM(X^{(t)})$ according to equation (6.2) with $p = 2$ and set

$$\underline{x}_0 = \sum_{i=1}^{m}\sum_{j=1}^{n} v_{ij}^{(t+1)}w_{1ij}\ell_2(X_i^{(t)},a_j)$$

$$+ \sum_{i=1}^{m-1}\sum_{r=i+1}^{m} u_{ir}^{(t+1)}w_{2ir}\ell_2(X_i^{(t)},X_r^{(t)}).$$

If $(\bar{x}_0 - \underline{x}_0)/\underline{x}_0 < \epsilon$, stop. Otherwise, set $t = t+1$ and return to Step 1.

The lower bound on $MM(X^*)$ in Step 2 is justified in the Appendix, mathematical note 6.1. Use of the algorithm will be illustrated by two examples. Let us return to Example 6.1 wherein $M(X)$ of equation (6.1)

Table 6.1 Results for Example 6.1.

Iterations	1	2	10	20	50	78
$\bar{x}_0$	3.9101	3.8167	3.5153	3.5132	3.4869	3.4771
$\underline{x}_0$	3.2076	3.2884	3.4420	3.4549	3.4705	3.4738

$v^{(78)} = (0.00005, 0.00287, 0.14351, 0.51925, 0.33433)$
$X^{(78)} = (5.6916, 3.5987)$
$M(X^{(78)}) = \bar{x}_0 = 3.4771$ is within 0.1% of $M(X^*)$

is to be minimized. In this single-facility case (see Exercise 1.2), the squared-Euclidean problem (6.10) is solved by setting:

$$x_k = \sum_{j=1}^{n} \bar{w}_{11j} \, a_{jk} / \sum_{j=1}^{n} \bar{w}_{11j}, \quad k = 1,2.$$

Progress of the algorithm is traced in Table 6.1 where $\epsilon = 10^{-3}$.

Although 78 iterations were required, the computational time was minimal. This was expected because the computational work per iteration is minimal. Only v_3, v_4, and v_5 appear to be nonzero. From equation (6.7) we conclude $\ell_2(X^*,a_3) = \ell_2(X^*,a_4) = \ell_2(X^*,a_5) = x_0^*$ and the minimum covering circle for a_3, a_4, and a_5 is the minimum covering circle for all the points. To verify this and to obtain a more precise answer, the algorithm could be continued from the 78th iteration *excluding* points a_1 and a_2. This would further reduce the computational burden per iteration. That the right points were excluded could be verified upon termination of this second phase.

The Elzinga-Hearn algorithm extended to weighted problems has been shown to be more efficient than the present algorithm for single-facility problems, but hasn't been extended to multi-facility problems. This, plus the simplicity of the present algorithm, accounts for its elaboration here; see Reference Notes for competing algorithms.

Example 6.2 Returning to the context of Example 6.1, suppose there are now eight transmitters. Receiver 1 is to monitor the signals of transmitters 1, 2, 3, and 4, whereas receiver 2 is to monitor the remaining signals. Furthermore, receiver 2 also serves as a transmitter of data to receiver 1 with intensity indicated by $w_{212} = 1/\sqrt{I_{212}} = 1.5$. Other transmitter intensities are indicated by:

$$W_1 = (w_{1ij}) = \begin{bmatrix} 3 & 3 & 3 & 3 & 0 & 0 & 0 & 0 \\ 0 & 0 & 0 & 0 & 3 & 3 & 3 & 3 \end{bmatrix}.$$

Transmitter locations are $a_1 = (4,5)$, $a_2 = (2,2)$, $a_3 = (3,3)$, $a_4 = (5,1)$, $a_5 = (7,6)$, $a_6 = (8,4)$, $a_7 = (9,3)$, and $a_8 = (9,6)$. Table 6.2 summarizes results obtained with $\epsilon = 10^{-4}$.

Table 6.2 Results for Example 6.2.

Iterations	1	2	10	20	50	118
$\bar{x}_0$	6.8718	6.5369	6.4389	6.4373	6.4178	6.4107
$\underline{x}_0$	5.6938	5.9450	6.2562	6.3259	6.3910	6.4101

$v_{11} = 0.412507$, $v_{12} = 0.210835$, $v_{13} = 0.0$, $v_{14} = 0.375364$,
$v_{25} = v_{26} = 0.0$, $v_{27} = 0.000158$, $v_{28} = 0.000367$,
$u_{12} = 0.000769$,
$w_{11j}\ell_2(X_1,a_j) = (6.410706, 6.409900, 2.892103, 6.410720)$,
           where $j = 1,2,3,4$,
$w_{12j}\ell_2(X_2,a_j) = (4.901313, 1.835351, 6.059212, 6.059135)$,
           where $j = 5,6,7,8$,
$w_{212}\ell_2(X_1,X_2) = 6.059177$
$X_1 = (3.954334, 2.863586)$ and $X_2 = (7.647476, 4.500006)$.

Only v_{11}, v_{12}, and v_{14} appear to be nonzero. Figure 6.3 confirms this. The location for receiver 1 is uniquely determined, while receiver 2 can be located anywhere in the shaded area labeled $C^2(x_0^*)$. Indeed, with computer graphics capability such a figure could be part of the output of the computer package that implements the algorithm.

Define indicators of inactive constraints in problem (6.3a) in the following way. Let:

$$I_v^{(t)} = \{(i,j) \mid w_{1ij}\ell_2(X_i^{(t)},a_j) < (1-\epsilon_1)\,\underline{x}_0\ ,v_{ij}^{(t)} < \epsilon_1\},$$

and

$$I_u^{(t)} = \{(i,r) \mid w_{2ir}\ell_2(X_i^{(t)},X_r^{(t)}) < (1-\epsilon_1)\,\underline{x}_0\ ,u_{ir}^{(t)} < \epsilon_1\},$$

Figure 6.3 Graphic Solution of Example 6.2.

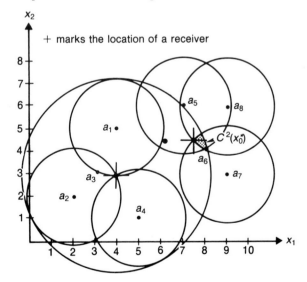

where, for example, $\epsilon_1 = 0.01$. As $X^{(t)}$ approaches X^* elements of I_u and I_v will indicate which of the constraints $x_0^* \geqslant w_{1ij}\ell_2(X_i^*,a_j)$ and $x_0^* \geqslant w_{2ir}\ell_2(X_i^*,X_r^*)$ are inactive. A second phase of the algorithm is to exclude terms involving elements in I_u and I_v and continue iterations after having terminated on the basis of ϵ in the first phase. The algorithm tends to distinguish the sets I_u and I_v rather quickly. Early exclusion of the indicated terms accelerates the algorithm and enhances numerical stability.

Lawson (1965) observed that the algorithm can fail if at some iteration it occurs that a multiplier u_{ir} or v_{ij} becomes zero for some critical term in equation (6.7) or (6.8); ie, if the associated weighted distance term was omitted from the problem, the value of x_0^* would be reduced. In practice, this is a very unlikely prospect. That results are valid can be checked at termination by verifying that terms with u_{ir} or $v_{ij} = 0$ have weighted distances not exceeding x_0^*. The algorithm cannot fail in the single-facility case (unless all a_j are identical). The inactivity of the omitted constraints can be verified using the second-phase solution.

But what of the indeterminacy of X_2^* in Example 6.2? We know X_2^* is any point in the set $C^2(x_0^*)$, say, that is the intersection of the sets:

$C_j^2(x_0^*)$, $j = 5,6,7,8,9$, where:

$C_j^2(x_0^*) = \{X_2 \mid w_{12j}\ell_2(X_2,a_j) \leqslant^* x_0\}$ $j = 5,6,7,8$ and

$C_9^2(x_0^*) = \{X_2 \mid w_{212}\ell_2(X_1^*,X_2) \leqslant x_0^*\}$.

Because location is to be guided by the minimax criterion, it would seem appropriate to choose X_2^* to minimize:

$$M(X_2) = \max \{w_{12j}\ell_2(X_2,a_j), j = 5,\ldots,8; w_{212}\ell_2(X_1^*,X_2)\}.$$

This is a single-facility problem that could be solved by the algorithm. However, it is intriguing that X_2^* as reported above minimizes $M(X_2)$. This is because X_1^* is unique, and as iterations proceed, $X_1^{(t)}$ approaches X_1^* and begins to act like an existing facility location with respect to X_2. To see the result of this, consider v_{27}, v_{28}, and u_{12} from Table 6.2. When these weights are normalized (to sum to one), we obtain 0.122, 0.284, and 0.594, respectively. These are the weights (to three decimal digits) found using the algorithm to minimize $M(X_2)$. The minimal value of $M(X_2)$ was 6.059621, which agrees with the information in Table 6.2.

6.2 RECTANGULAR DISTANCES

Suppose that in Example 6.1 the existing facilities locations represent response neighborhoods and the facility to be located is an ambulance base. The weights might represent probabilities of demand for service (upon division by their sum). If the locational setting is an urban area, rectangular distances may adequately approximate actual travel distances. In this case the x_0–distance sets become:

$$C_j(x_0) = \{X = (x_1, x_2) \mid w_j[|x_1 - a_{j1}| + |x_2 - a_{j2}|] \leq x_0\}.$$

Figure 6.4 illustrates the intersection set $C(x_0)$ for $x_0 = 5$. It is unlikely that $C(x_0^*)$ will contain only a single point because the sides of the $C_j(x_0)$ sets are parallel. This means problem (6.3) will typically have multiple optima when distances are rectangular, even in the single-facility case.

The interactive graphics method of the previous section is directly applicable here, with diamond-shaped $C_j(x_0)$ sets replacing the circular shapes. However, the Lawson-Charalambous algorithm is replaced by a linear programming approach when distances are rectangular.

A Linear Programming Representation

The following property enables a linear programming formulation.

Figure 6.4   Graphic Analysis with Rectangular Distances.

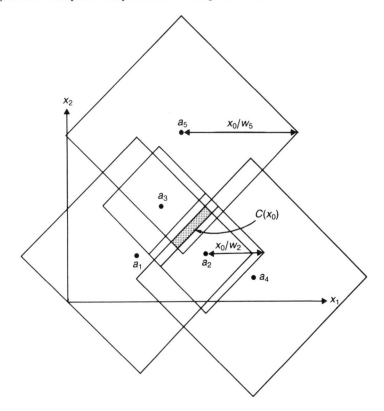

Property 6.4 [*Transformation of absolute value constraints*]. *The inequality:*

$$x_0 \geq w_{1ij} \left[|x_{i1} - a_{j1}| + |x_{i2} - a_{j2}| \right] \qquad (6.15)$$

is equivalent to the following quadruple of inequalities:

$$x_0 \geq w_{1ij} \left[\;\;(x_{i1} - a_{j1}) + (x_{i2} - a_{j2}) \right]$$
$$x_0 \geq w_{1ij} \left[-(x_{i1} - a_{j1}) + (x_{i2} - a_{j2}) \right]$$
$$x_0 \geq w_{1ij} \left[\;\;(x_{i1} - a_{j1}) - (x_{i2} - a_{j2}) \right]$$
$$x_0 \geq w_{1ij} \left[-(x_{i1} - a_{j1}) - (x_{j2} - a_{j2}) \right]. \qquad (6.16)$$

The equivalence follows because at least one constraint in inequalities (6.16) is equivalent to that in inequality (6.15), and the greatest lower bound on x_0 in inequalities (6.16) must equal the lower bound on x_0 in inequality (6.15). (The d-dimensional extension of inequality (6.15) can be replaced by an analogous set of 2^d inequalities.) Problem (6.3), for location in the plane using rectangular distances, can now be written as the following linear program:

minimize x_0
x_0, X

subject to $\qquad\qquad\qquad\qquad\qquad\qquad\qquad\qquad\qquad$ (6.17)

$$x_{i1} + x_{i2} + x_0/w_{1ij} \geq \;\;\;a_{j1} + a_{j2}$$
$$-\,x_{i1} + x_{i2} + x_0/w_{1ij} \geq -a_{j1} + a_{j2}$$
$$x_{i1} - x_{i2} + x_0/w_{1ij} \geq \;\;\;a_{j1} - a_{j2}$$
$$-\,x_{i1} - x_{i2} + x_0/w_{1ij} \geq -a_{j1} - a_{j2}$$
$$i = 1,...,m; \; j = 1,...,n$$
$$x_{i1} - x_{r1} + x_{i2} - x_{r2} + x_0/w_{2ir} \geq 0$$
$$-x_{i1} + x_{r1} + x_{i2} - x_{r2} + x_0/w_{2ir} \geq 0$$
$$x_{i1} - x_{r1} - x_{i2} + x_{r2} + x_0/w_{2ir} \geq 0$$
$$-x_{i1} + x_{r1} - x_{i2} + x_{r2} + x_0/w_{2ir} \geq 0$$
$$i = 1,...,m-1; \; r = i+1,...,m.$$

Constraints corresponding to zero weights are to be omitted; variables are unrestricted in sign. Problem (6.17) has $4mn + 2(m^2 - m)$ constraints and $2m + 1$ variables when all weights are positive. If all a_{j1}, $a_{j2} \geqslant 0$, then all x_{i1}^*, x_{i2}^* will be non-negative and problem (6.17) could be augmented with non-negativity conditions. x_0^* is a weighted distance and therefore must be non-negative. (An alternative approach decomposes the original problem into two relatively small independent linear programs; this is the subject of Exercise 6.5.)

Unweighted Single-Facility Problems

The single-facility problem can be solved in closed form when all weights are equal. In this case the second set of constraints is absent and the problem reduces to:

$$\text{minimize } x_0$$
$$x_0, x_1, x_2$$

subject to   (6.18)

$$x_1 + x_2 + x_0 \geqslant \max_j (\ a_{j1} + a_{j2}) = m_1$$

$$- x_1 + x_2 + x_0 \geqslant \max_j (-a_{j1} + a_{j2}) = m_2$$

$$x_1 - x_2 + x_0 \geqslant \max_j (\ a_{j1} - a_{j2}) = m_3$$

$$- x_1 - x_2 + x_0 \geqslant \max_j (-a_{j1} - a_{j2}) = m_4.$$

There are four constraints, regardless of the number of existing facilities. Adding the first and fourth constraints gives $x_0 \geqslant (m_1 + m_4)/2$, and adding the second and third constraints gives $x_0 \geqslant (m_2 + m_3)/2$. If $m_5 = \max \{(m_1 + m_4), (m_2 + m_3)\}$, then $m_5/2$ is a lower bound on x_0^*. By direct substitution we find that this lower bound is attained for (x_1, x_2) $= \frac{1}{2}(m_3 - m_4, -m_3 - m_4 + m_5)$ or $\frac{1}{2}(m_1 - m_2, m_1 + m_2 - m_5)$, and each of these two-tuples represents an optimal location for the new facility. As convex combinations (non-negative weighted averages) of optimal solutions to linear programming problems are also optimal solutions, all points on the line segment between the two optimal locations are also optimal.

Example 6.3 A hub facility for a rapid delivery service in a city is to be located in relation to five distribution sectors (idealized as points). Their locations are as given in Example 6.1; but all $w_j = 1$. We find m_1

$= 12$, $m_2 = 2$, $m_3 = 7$, $m_4 = -5$ and $m_5 = $ max $\{12-5, 2+7\} = 9$. Then, $x_0^* = 4.5$ and:

$$X^* \epsilon \{\lambda(6.0, 3.5) + (1-\lambda)(5.0, 2.5); 0 \leqslant \lambda \leqslant 1\}$$

represents the line segment of optimal locations. This segment is depicted in Figure 6.5.

The Dual Problem

Because the computational effort in solving a linear programming problem depends primarily on the number of constraints, it is expedient to solve the dual of problem (6.17), given by:

$$\begin{array}{c} \text{maximize} \\ u,v \end{array} \sum_{i=1}^{m} \sum_{j=1}^{n} (a_{j1} + a_{j2})v_{ij1} + (-a_{j1} + a_{j2})v_{ij2}$$

$$+ (a_{j1} - a_{j2})v_{ij3} + (-a_{j1} - a_{j2})v_{ij4}$$

Figure 6.5 Graphic Solution of Hub Facility Problem.

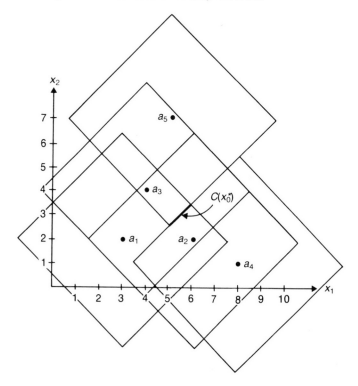

subject to   (6.19)

$$\sum_{j=1}^{n} (v_{ij1} - v_{ij2} + v_{ij3} - v_{ij4}) + \sum_{r=1}^{i-1} (-u_{ri1} + u_{ri2} - u_{ri3} + u_{ri4})$$

$$+ \sum_{r=i+1}^{m} (u_{ir1} - u_{ir2} + u_{ir3} - u_{ir4}) = 0 \qquad i = 1,...,m$$

$$\sum_{j=1}^{n} (v_{ij1} + v_{ij2} - v_{ij3} - v_{ij4}) + \sum_{r=1}^{i-1} (-u_{ri1} - u_{ri2} + u_{ri3} + u_{ri4})$$

$$+ \sum_{r=i+1}^{m} (u_{ir1} + u_{ir2} - u_{ir3} - u_{ir4}) = 0 \qquad i = 1,...,m$$

$$\sum_{i=1}^{m} \sum_{j=1}^{n} (v_{ij1} + v_{ij2} + v_{ij3} + v_{ij4})/w_{1ij}$$

$$+ \sum_{i=1}^{m-1} \sum_{r=i+1}^{m} (u_{ir1} + u_{ir2} + u_{ir3} + u_{ir4})/w_{2ir} = 1,$$

where all variables are non-negative.

Sums have no terms whenever the initial subscript value is greater than the terminal subscript value. Problem (6.19) has only $2m+1$ constraints, regardless of the number of existing facilities. The variable v_{ijs} corresponds to the rectangular distance between existing facility j and new facility i. The value of the subscript s, $s = 1,2,3,4$, refers to that primal constraint of the first four forms in problem (6.17) to which the dual variable is related. In similar fashion u_{irs} corresponds to the distance between new facilities i and r. The pair (x_{i1}^*, x_{i2}^*) is the pair of dual variables associated with the ith and $m+i^{th}$ constraints, respectively, when problem (6.19) is solved.

From the theory of linear programming, the following complementary slackness conditions must hold at optimality:

$$v_{ijs}^*[\pm x_{i1}^* \pm x_{i2}^* + x_0^*/w_{1ij} - (\pm a_{j1} \pm a_{j2})] = 0$$

$$i = 1,...,m, j = 1,...,n, s = 1,...,4,$$

and

$$u_{irs}^*[\pm x_{i1}^* \mp x_{r1}^* \pm x_{i2}^* \mp x_{r2}^* + x_0^*/w_{2ir}] = 0$$

$$i = 1,...,m-1; r = i+1,...,m; s = 1,...,4.$$

The signs in the brackets are to be in accordance with the signs in the sth form of the associated constraint in problem (6.17). As in Example

6.2, these conditions can be used to indicate the full set of optimal locations, analogous to the situation depicted in Figure 6.3.

6.3 ADDENDA TO MINIMAX LOCATION

Upper bound constraints, such as:

$$\ell_p(X_i,a_j) \leqslant \alpha_{ij} \text{ and/or } \ell_p(X_i,X_r) \leqslant \beta_{ir}$$

may be included in problem (6.3) to avoid unacceptable placement. When included in problem (6.17) where $p = 1$, these constraints become:

$$\left.\begin{aligned} x_{i1}+x_{i2} &\leqslant \alpha_{ij}+a_{j1}+a_{j2} \\ -x_{i1}+x_{i2} &\leqslant \alpha_{ij}-a_{j1}+a_{j2} \\ x_{i1}-x_{i2} &\leqslant \alpha_{ij}+a_{j1}-a_{j2} \\ -x_{i1}-x_{i2} &\leqslant \alpha_{ij}-a_{j1}-a_{j2} \end{aligned}\right\} \text{ and/or } \left\{\begin{aligned} x_{i1}-x_{r1}+x_{i2}-x_{r2} &\leqslant \beta_{ir} \\ -x_{i1}+x_{r1}+x_{i2}-x_{r2} &\leqslant \beta_{ir} \\ x_{i1}-x_{r1}-x_{i2}+x_{r2} &\leqslant \beta_{ir} \\ -x_i+x_{r1}-x_{i2}+x_{r2} &\leqslant \beta_{ir}. \end{aligned}\right.$$

The need for such constraints may naturally arise in a service-oriented application.

Linear constraints can also be included to limit feasible locations of the new facilities. For example, if the constraints $-x_{31} - x_{32} \geqslant -40$, $x_{31} \geqslant 10$, and $x_{32} \geqslant 10$, were appended to problem (6.17), the third new facility location would be constrained to be within or on the boundaries of the triangle with vertices (30,10), (10,30), and (10,10). If new facility i is to be located along a linear corridor, an equality constraint will serve the purpose. A constraint of the form $x_{i2} - ax_{i1} = b$ is imposed. It is a straightforward matter to alter the form of problem (6.19) when linear constraints and/or interfacility distance constraints are included in problem (6.17). The effect on computational efficiency is minimal because to add constraints to problem (6.17) is to add variables to problem (6.19).

Contours

The mathematically "optimal" solution to a location problem frequently represents a point of departure, a reference point against which to measure the goodness of alternative solutions. Decision problems are typically multi-objective in nature. Location under the minimax criterion satisfies but a single objective. Construction of contour lines (points with equal objective value) provides a convenient visual means of comparing satisfaction of other locational goals against the suboptimality induced by deviations from a minimax location. For example, the set of points on the boundary of the shaded region in Figure 6.1 constitutes the contour for $M(X) = 4$. There, Euclidean distances define $M(X)$.

Consider the single-facility rectangular distance criterion function given by $M(X) = \max \{w_j(|x_1 - a_{j1}| + |x_2 - a_{j2}|), j = 1,...,n\}$. Contours of $M(X)$ are defined by the set:

$$S(x_0) = \{X = (x_1,x_2) \mid M(X) = x_0\}.$$

Let:

$$s_1(x_0) = \min \{(x_0/w_j) + a_{j1} + a_{j2}, j = 1,...,n\},$$

$$s_2(x_0) = \max \{(-x_0/w_j) + a_{j1} + a_{j2}, j = 1,...,n\},$$

$$s_3(x_0) = \min \{(x_0/w_j) - a_{j1} + a_{j2}, j = 1,...,n\}, \text{ and}$$

$$s_4(x_0) = \max \{(-x_0/w_j) - a_{j1} + a_{j2}, j = 1,...,n\}.$$

Then the set $S(x_0)$ is comprised of the sides of a (possibly degenerate) rectangle with corners at $\frac{1}{2}(s_1(x_0) - s_3(x_0), s_1(x_0) + s_3(x_0))$, $\frac{1}{2}(s_1(x_0) - s_4(x_0), s_1(x_0) + s_4(x_0))$, $\frac{1}{2}(s_2(x_0) - s_4(x_0), s_2(x_0) + s_4(x_0))$, and $\frac{1}{2}(s_2(x_0) - s_3(x_0), s_2(x_0) + s_3(x_0))$.

In Example 6.3, the contour for $x_0 = 4.5$ should correspond to the degenerate rectangle given by the line segment between $(6.0,3.5)$ and $(5.0,2.5)$. Indeed, we find that $s_1(4.5) = 9.5$, $s_2(4.5) = 7.5$, $s_3(4.5) = -2.5$, and $s_4(4.5) = -2.5$, which means the corners of the rectangle are at $(6.0,3.5)$, $(6.0,3.5)$, $(5.0,2.5)$, and $(5.0,2.5)$, respectively.

A Convex Programming Approach

Let us return to formulation (6.3b). The functions in the brackets are convex, as they are compositions of increasing convex functions of convex functions, ie, $[\ell_p(X_i,a_j)]^p$ and $[\ell_p(X_i,X_r)]^p$, respectively. As mentioned, these composite functions are everywhere differentiable for $p > 1$. Together with the linear objective function this formulation represents a differentiable convex programming problem. These facts guarantee that standard convex programming algorithms will converge to an optimum solution.

Limitations on interfacility distances can be included as:

$$\alpha_{ij}^p - [|x_{1i} - a_{1j}|^p + |x_{2i} - a_{2j}|^p] \geq 0 \text{ and/or}$$

$$\beta_{ir}^p - [|x_{1i} - x_{1r}|^p + |x_{2i} - x_{2r}|^p] \geq 0,$$

where α_{ij} and β_{ir} are the bounds on the respective ℓ_p distances. The addends introduced in equation (6.1') are easily accommodated within this convex programming approach. With the increasing availability of convenient computer codes for nonlinear programming for use even on personal computers, this general approach to ℓ_p distance problems will likely gain practical appeal.

Maximin Location

Let $f(X) = \min\{w_j \ell_2(X, a_j), j = 1,...,n\}$. Then, f measures the least Euclidean distance from the new facility to an existing facility. An example of location under the *maximin* criterion is:

$$\text{maximize } f(X), \qquad (6.20)$$
$$X \epsilon F$$

where $F \{X | \ell_2(X, a_j) \leqslant \alpha_j, j = 1,...,n\}$. The constraints that make up F impose mandatory closeness requirements. We note that some of the existing facility locations may be dummy points to produce a desired geometrical shape for F. This model might be appropriate when locating an "obnoxious" facility.

$$\text{Let } \bar{C}(x_0) = \{X = (x_1, x_2) \mid f(X) \geqslant x_0\}.$$

Then $\bar{C}(x_0)$ can be realized graphically by constructing a circle with radius x_0/w_j about each existing facility, and then considering the region that is outside all these circles simultaneously.

Example 6.4 To illustrate, consider Table 6.3, which gives data from Drezner and Wesolowsky (1980c) for three existing facilities. Figure 6.6 shows the intersection of $\bar{C}(x_0)$ and F for $x_0 = 3$ as the two darkly shaded areas. The solid circle about each existing facility represents the associated mandatory closeness constraint; the lightly shaded region is F. The dotted circles have radius $x_0/w_j = 3/w_j$. As x_0 is increased, the two darkly shaded areas will shrink until $X^* = (-0.94425, 0.66550)$ emerges as the only point in the intersection of $\bar{C}(x_0)$ and F.

Let $f(X^*) = f^*$ denote the optimal value in problem (6.20). Then the following property is self-evident.

Property 6.5 [*Relating f^* to x_0*]. *If for a given value of x_0, $\bar{C}(x_0)$ and F do not intersect, then $f^* < x_0$; otherwise, $f^* \geqslant x_0$.*

This suggests an interactive graphics bisection search procedure to solve problem (6.20). Color graphics capability would enhance the appeal of this approach.

Table 6.3 Locations, Weights, and Maximum Distances.

Existing Facility	a_j	w_j	α_j
1	(0,0)	3	4.5
2	(3,0)	1	4.0
3	(0,4)	1	4.0

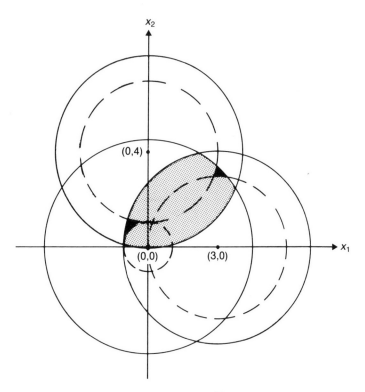

Figure 6.6 Illustration of the Intersection of $\bar{C}(3)$ and F.
(Figure from "A Maximin Location Problem with Maximum Distance Constraints" by Z. Drezner and G. Wesolowsky, *AIIE Transactions*, vol. 12, no. 3. Copyright Institute of Industrial Engineers, 25 Technology Park/Atlanta, Norcross, GA 30092.)

Drezner-Wesolowsky Algorithm

Step 0 Choose $\epsilon > 0$, establish $LB = f_{min}$ and $UB = f_{max}$ and determine if problem (6.20) is feasible (see below). Display the sets $C_j(\alpha_j)$ = $\{X \mid \ell_2(X,a_j) \leq \alpha_j\}$, $j = 1,...,n$ graphically and determine their intersection, which is F.

Step 1 Set $x_0 = (UB+LB)/2$. If $UB-LB < \epsilon$, terminate.

Step 2 Otherwise, display the sets $C_j(x_0) = \{X \mid \ell_2(X,a_j) \leq x_0/w_j\}$, $j = 1,...,n$ graphically and determine $\bar{C}(x_0)$ as the area outside the union of these sets. The user observes whether or not $\bar{C}(x_0)$ and F intersect. If not, set $UB = x_0$; otherwise, set $LB = x_0$. Return to Step 1.

Some detail is needed to implement Step 0. To find a point in the feasible region F, consider solving the *minimax* problem of minimizing $M(X)$ given by equation (6.1) where $w_j = 1/\alpha_j$. We could use the Lawson-

Charalambous algorithm for this. Let X^M solve this problem. If, $M(X^M)$ $\leqslant 1$, then $\ell_2(X^M, a_j) \leqslant \alpha_j$, for all $j = 1,...,n$ and so $X^M \epsilon F$. Otherwise, problem (6.20) is infeasible, and the α_j bounds must be reconsidered. We have found an unexpected use of the minimax model!

Suppose $M(X^M) \leqslant 1$. Then we can use $LB = f_{min} = f(X^M)$ in Step 0 of the algorithm. To value f_{max}, we compute:

$$f_{max} = \min\{w_i(\alpha_j + \ell_2(a_i, a_j)), \ i \neq j = 1,...,n\}.$$

To justify the calculation of f_{max}, consider the requirement that for feasibility each pair of sets $C_i(\alpha_i)$ and $C_j(\alpha_j)$ must have a nonempty intersection. The farthest point from a_i that is within $C_j(\alpha_j)$ can be no further away than $\ell_2(a_i, a_j) + \alpha_j$, or the intersection wouldn't be possible.

Hence, the computer provides f_{min} and f_{max}. The human user provides recognition skills in Step 2. With the benefit of human pattern recognition, F could actually be of general shape—not restricted to the intersection of circles. A verification step could be added to the algorithm to assure "infallibility," much like that discussed for the interactive graphics minimax algorithm.

EXERCISES

6.1 Use rectangular distances and solve the problem given in Example 6.1 as a linear programming problem using formulation (6.17).

6.2 Show the calculations to verify that $\bar{x}_0 = 3.9101$ and $\underline{x}_0 = 3.2076$ after one iteration of the Lawson-Charalambous algorithm applied to Example 6.1, as reported in Table 6.1.

6.3 a. Use rectangular distances and solve Example 6.2 using formulation (6.17).
  b. Repeat Exercise 6.3a using formulation (6.19) instead of formulation (6.17).
  c. Provide a graphic exposition as was done in Figure 6.3.

6.4 Prove that $h(x) = w|x - a|^p$ is everywhere differentiable for $p > 1$, where $w > 0$ and a are given constants.

6.5 Dearing and Francis (1974) The transformation $T(x_1, x_2) = (x_1 + x_2, -x_1 + x_2) = (x_1', x_2')$, say, both rotates the coordinate axes counterclockwise through a 45° angle and expands the axes.
  a. Show that $|x_1 - a_1| + |x_2 - a_2| = \max(|x_1' - a_1'|, |x_2' - a_2'|)$. You will have shown that $\ell_1(X, a) = \ell_\infty(X', a')$ where X and a are points in the plane, and X' and a' are the images of those points under T, respectively. (Figure 10.1 motivates this idea.)
  b. Exercise 6.5a enables the following formulation of the constrained multifacility rectangular distance problem with addends:

minimize z_0

subject to

$$z_0 \geq w_{1ij} \max(|x'_{i1} - a'_{j1}|, |x'_{i2} - a'_{j2}|) + g_i$$

$$i = 1,...,m; \ j = 1,...,n$$

$$z_0 \geq w_{2ir} \max(|x'_{i1} - x'_{r1}|, |x'_{i2} - x'_{r2}|)$$

$$i = 1,...,m-1; \ r = i+1,...,m$$

$$\max(|x'_{i1} - a'_{j1}|, |x'_{i2} - a'_{j2}|) \leq \alpha_{ij}$$

$$i = 1,...,m; \ j = 1,...,n$$

$$\max(|x'_{i1} - x'_{r1}|, |x'_{i2} - x'_{r2}|) \leq \beta_{ir}$$

$$i = 1,...,m-1; \ r = i+1,...,m.$$

Show how this problem can be solved by solving two independent linear programming problems, one in the variables z_1, x'_{i1}, x'_{r1}, and the other in the variables z_2, x'_{i2}, x'_{r2}.

c. Use rectangular distances and solve Example 6.1 using the approach in Exercise 6.5b.

d. Use rectangular distances and solve Example 6.2 using the approach in Exercise 6.5b.

6.6 Chatelon, Hearn, and Lowe (1978) Two ships are to be stationed in the Caribbean sea "and must be ready to intervene, in case of trouble at any one of nine given cities of the Caribbean Islands." Need for assistance occurs with estimated probabilities that are the weights (scaled). The Euclidean distance between the two ships is to have weight 1, reflecting the need for the two ships to communicate.

Parameters for the problem are given in Table 6E.1. The p-value for the ℓ_p distance between ship i and city j is denoted p_{ij}. The differing p-values

Table 6E.1 Caribbean Islands Problem.

			Ship 1		Ship 2	
j	Cities	a_j	w_{11j}	p_{1j}	w_{12j}	p_{2j}
1	Colon (Panama Canal)	(11.4,11.6)	2.0	2.0	1.0	2.0
2	Caracas-LaGuaira (Venezuela)	(35.3,13.5)	1.0	2.0	2.0	2.0
3	Havana (Cuba)	(8.8,37.2)	1.5	1.1	1.0	1.4
4	Guantanamo (Cuba)	(20.9,30.6)	1.5	1.5	1.0	1.9
5	Port-au-Prince (Haiti)	(25.5,28.0)	1.5	1.4	1.5	1.2
6	Santo Domingo (Dom. Rep.)	(29.7,27.7)	1.0	2.0	1.5	2.0
7	San Juan (Puerto Rico)	(36.2,27.8)	0.5	1.8	1.0	1.7
8	Fort-de-France (Martinique)	(45.5,21.3)	0.5	2.0	0.5	2.0
9	Montego Bay (Jamaica)	(15.8,28.2)	0.5	1.1	0.5	1.8

Source: Chatelon, Hearn and Lowe, 1978, *Mathematical Programming,* Amsterdam, North Holland.

represent *anticipated* indirect paths that must be taken by the ships to avoid
land masses.

6.6 a. Use a nonlinear programming software package and the convex programming approach based on problem (6.3b) in the text to locate the
two ships under the minimax criterion. Verify that $x_0^* = 26.0836$, with
$X_1^* = (13.817,24.358)$ and $X_2^* = (25.818,22.454)$.

b. Obtain the optimal values of the dual variables for this problem and give
their interpretation here.

6.7 a. Write a computer program to implement the Lawson-Charalambous algorithm for single-facility problems. Use the algorithm to locate ship 1
in Table 6E.1, letting all $p_{1j} = 2$ and ignoring the distance to ship 2.
Verify that $x_0^* = (15.19,21.77)$.

b. Let $a_1 = (0,1)$, $a_2 = (1,0)$, $a_3 = (0,-1)$, and $a_4 = (a_{41},0)$. Use the algorithm
to solve the single-facility problem with all $w_j = 1$, $\epsilon = 10^{-4}$, and $a_{41} = -1.0$, -0.99, and -0.9999, successively. Comment on the results.

6.8 a. Retracing the developmental steps, attempt to generalize the single-facility Lawson-Charalambous algorithm to three-dimensional problems.
Describe a practical application.

b. Retracing the developmental steps, attempt to generalize the single-facility Lawson-Charalambous algorithm to accommodate addends.

c. Attempt to generalize the single-facility Lawson-Charalambous algorithm
to the case of ℓ_p distances.

6.9 a. Verify that the lower bound on x_0 in problem (6.18) is attained for (x_1,x_2)
$= \frac{1}{2}(m_3 - m_4, -m_3 - m_4 + m_5)$. Show that this is a feasible solution.

b. State the dual of problem (6.18). Then consider all possible basic feasible
solutions for the dual and show that an optimal basic solution has value
$m_5/2$. Derive an optimal primal solution from an optimal dual solution.

6.10 Using the data from Example 6.3, graph the contours $S(4)$, $S(6)$, and $S(8)$,
as defined in Section 6.3. Give a practical example of the use of such contours.

6.11 Francis and White (1974)   Write the constraints of problem (6.17) in the
text for the single-facility case, as:

$$x_1 + x_2 \geqslant -x_0/w_j + a_{j1} + a_{j2}$$

$$-x_1 + x_2 \geqslant -x_0/w_j - a_{j1} + a_{j2}$$

$$-x_1 + x_2 \leqslant x_0/w_j - a_{j1} + a_{j2}$$

$$x_1 + x_2 \leqslant x_0/w_j + a_{j1} + a_{j2}$$

$$j = 1,...,n,$$

or $$x_1 + x_2 \geqslant s_2(x_0)$$

$$-x_1 + x_2 \geqslant s_4(x_0)$$

$$-x_1 + x_2 \leqslant s_3(x_0)$$

$$x_1 + x_2 \leqslant s_1(x_0),$$

where the s notation is from the discussion of contours in Section 6.3. Consider the rectangle defined by these constraints.

a. Show that the corners of the rectangle are as given in the text.

b. Show that in the case of addends [see equation (6.1′)] the expressions for $s_r(x_0)$, $r = 1,2,3,4$, are as before, except that x_0 is replaced by (x_0-g_j).

6.12 a. Solve Example 6.3 using Euclidean distances and the Elzinga-Hearn graphic algorithm.

   b. Sketch two contours for the problem.

   c. Solve Example 6.3 using Euclidean distances and formulation (6.4) with the constraint $x_1 + x_2 \leqslant 5$.

   d. Attempt to generalize formulation (6.4) to accommodate a fixed addition g_j to each Euclidean distance.

   e. Attempt to generalize formulation (6.4) to three-dimensional problems.

   f. Attempt to generalize formulation (6.4) to weighted problems.

   g. Attempt to generalize formulation (6.4) to unweighted multi-facility problems.

6.13 The *one-dimensional*, single-facility case of problem (6.19) is given by the linear programming problem:

$$\text{maximize } \sum_{j=1}^{n} a_j(v_{j1} - v_{j2})$$

subject to   (6E.1)

$$\sum_{j=1}^{n} v_{j1} - v_{j2} = 0$$

$$\sum_{j=1}^{n} (v_{j1} + v_{j2})/w_j = 1$$

$$v_{j1},v_{j2} \geqslant 0 \qquad j = 1,...,n.$$

a. Show that problem (6E.1) reduces to finding $\max\{w_q w_r |a_q - a_r|/(w_q+w_r)$, $q \neq r = 1,...,n\}$, where a_j is the coordinate of existing facility j on the line. (Hint: As there are only two constraints, there will be two basic variables in an optimal basic feasible solution.)

b. Using primal-dual complementary slackness conditions, show that this means $X^* = (a_{q*}w_{q*} + a_{r*}w_{r*})/(w_{q*} + w_{r*})$, where * indicates optimality.

6.14 Kolen (1986)   Consider the minimization of:

$$M(X) = \max\{w_j(|x_1 - a_{j1}| + |x_2 - a_{j2}|) + g_j, j = 1,...,n\}. \qquad (6E.2)$$

From Exercise 6.5 we know that minimizing $M(X)$ given by equation (6E.2) is equivalent to:

   minimize z_0

   subject to

   $$z_0 \geqslant w_j(\max\{|x_1' - a_{j1}'|, |x_2' - a_{j2}'|\}) + g_j \qquad j = 1,...,n.$$

a. Show that this means we can minimize $M(X)$ given by equation (6E.2) by solving two ($k = 1,2$) independent, *one-dimensional* problems of the form:

$$\text{minimize } z_k$$

$$\text{subject to} \qquad\qquad\qquad\qquad\qquad\qquad (6E.3)$$

$$x'_k + z_k/w_j \geqslant \quad a'_{jk} + g_j/w_j$$

$$-x'_k + z_k/w_j \geqslant -a'_{jk} + g_j/w_j$$

$$j = 1,...,n.$$

b. Using insight from Exercise 6.13, show that problem (6E.3) can be written as:

$$z_k^* = \max \{w_q w_r(|a'_q - a'_r| + g_q/w_q + g_r/w_r)/(w_q + w_r), q \neq r = 1,...,n\}.$$

6.15 Suppose Example 6.3 represents an ambulance base location problem and the existing facilities are centers of response neighborhoods. Use the result developed in Exercise 6.14 (or a straightforward linear programming approach) to locate the base. Assume that multiplying 0.95 times ℓ_1 distances closely approximates actual travel distances. Also assume that all medical service is performed at a hospital located at (5,2.5).

6.16 Späth (1978)
a. Develop the three-dimensional analog of formulation (6.18).
b. Consider six existing facilities with locations given by (0,0,0), (0,0,1), (2,1,3), (4,0,0), (0,2,0), and (3,2,0). Then verify that the optimal solution sets for the problems with the first 3, 4, 5, and then all 6 of the points are given by:

$$n = 3 \quad 0 \leqslant x_1^* \leqslant 2, 0 \leqslant x_2^* \leqslant 1, 0 \leqslant 2(x_1^* + x_2^*) \leqslant 5,$$

$$x_1^* + x_2^* + x_3^* = 3, x_0^* = 3$$

$$n = 4 \quad x_1^* = 2, x_2^* = 1 - x_3^*, 1 \leqslant 2x_3^* \leqslant 2, x_0^* = 3$$

$$\begin{array}{l} n = 5 \\ n = 6 \end{array} \quad (x_1^*, x_2^*, x_3^*) = \tfrac{1}{4}(7,3,1), x_0^* = 13/4.$$

c. Describe a practical application for this problem.

6.17 Consider Example 6.4.
a. Illustrate the intersection of the sets $\bar{C}(4)$ and F using the shading conventions adopted in Figure 6.6.
b. Compute f_{min} and f_{max}.
c. Perform one iteration of the associated interactive graphics algorithm.
d. Verify (graphically) that $X^* = (-0.94425, 0.66550)$.

REFERENCE NOTES

SECTION 6.1 The quadratic programming formulation is from Nair and Chandrasekaran (1971), as is the previous discussion centered on Figure 6.2. A dual quadratic program was given in Elzinga and Hearn (1972a). The Elzinga-Hearn algorithm for unweighted problems was introduced in Elzinga and Hearn (1972b). Hearn and Vijay (1982) provided a computational study and classification scheme for algorithms that solve the Euclidean single-facility problem. They extended the Elzinga-Hearn algorithm to weighted problems, and their computational study, which includes starting-point generators, shows this to be the most efficient among the competitors considered.

The interactive computer graphics approach is from Brady and Rosenthal (1980) and Brady, Rosenthal and Young (1983). Lawson (1965) gave an algorithm that successively approximates the dual variables for the unweighted single-facility Euclidean problem, in the applications context of "multiple airborne target tracking with a ground-based radar." The discussion here and in the Appendix follows that of Charalambous (1981), who provided a generalization to weighted, multi-facility Euclidean problems. Convergence and the generalization to ℓ_p distances were discussed in Morris (1982).

SECTION 6.2 Francis (1967) provided early results for rectangular distances. The closed-form result for problem (6.18) is from Francis (1972) and Elzinga and Hearn (1972b). Wesolowsky (1972) provided an early linear programming formulation, and Elzinga and Hearn (1973) and Morris (1973) studied the linear programming approach further. Dearing and Francis (1974) offered a network flow approach.

SECTION 6.3 Convex programming approaches were suggested in Love, Wesolowsky, and Kraemer (1973) and Chatelon, Hearn, and Lowe (1978). Drezner and Wesolowsky (1978b) developed a numerical analytic approach. The discussion of the maximin problem is from Drezner and Wesolowsky (1980c) who described implementation of the algorithm in algebraic terms.

APPENDIX–CHAPTER 6

Mathematical Notes

6.1 *Solving* problem (6.10)

When $m > 1$, the analytical solution of problem (6.10) can be conveniently stated in matrix form. Setting

$$\frac{\partial W}{\partial x_{ik}} = 2\sum_{j=1}^{n} \bar{w}_{1ij}(x_{ik} - a_{jk}) + 2\sum_{\substack{r=1 \\ \neq i}}^{m} \bar{w}_{2ir}(x_{ik} - x_{rk})$$

$$k = 1,2; \ i = 1,...,m,$$

to zero and rearranging produces the system of equations:

$$x_{ik}\left(\sum_{j=1}^{n} \bar{w}_{1ij} + \sum_{\substack{r=1 \\ \neq i}}^{m} \bar{w}_{2ir}\right) - \sum_{\substack{r=1 \\ \neq i}}^{m} \bar{w}_{2ir}x_{rk} = \sum_{j=1}^{n} \bar{w}_{1ij}a_{jk}$$

$$k = 1,2; \ i = 1,...,m.$$

Now, define $m \times 1$ column vectors $\bar{x}_k$ and $\bar{a}_k$ as

$$\bar{x}_k = \begin{bmatrix} \bar{x}_{1k} \\ \bar{x}_{2k} \\ \cdot \\ \cdot \\ \cdot \\ \bar{x}_{mk} \end{bmatrix} \qquad \bar{a}_k = \begin{bmatrix} \sum_{j=1}^{n} \bar{w}_{11j} a_{jk} \\ \sum_{j=1}^{n} \bar{w}_{12j} a_{jk} \\ \cdot \\ \cdot \\ \cdot \\ \sum_{j=1}^{n} \bar{w}_{1mj} a_{jk} \end{bmatrix}.$$

Let $\beta_i = \sum_{j=1}^{n} \bar{w}_{1ij} + \sum_{\substack{r=1 \\ \neq i}}^{m} \bar{w}_{2ir}$ and then define the $m \times m$ matrix A given by:

$$A = \begin{bmatrix} \beta_1 & -\bar{w}_{212} & \cdots & -\bar{w}_{21m} \\ -\bar{w}_{212} & \beta_2 & \cdots & -\bar{w}_{22m} \\ \cdot & \cdot & & \cdot \\ \cdot & \cdot & & \cdot \\ \cdot & \cdot & & \cdot \\ -\bar{w}_{21m} & -\bar{w}_{22m} & & \beta_m \end{bmatrix}.$$

Then the system of equations can be expressed as:

$$A\bar{x}_k = \bar{a}_k, \ k = 1,2. \tag{6A.1}$$

If $\beta_i = 0$, then the ith row of A, the ith column of A, and the ith element of both $\bar{a}_1$ and $\bar{a}_2$ are all equal to zero and should be *removed* before solving for $\bar{x}_1$ and $\bar{x}_2$. The location of the ith facility is not unique in this case. The matrix A is positive semidefinite and symmetric.

6.2 *Prove* $\underline{x}_0 \leq x_0^*$ in Step 2 of the Lawson-Charalambous algorithm

PROOF: We have $x_0^* = \min_X MM(X) =$

$$\min_X (\sum_{i=1}^{m} \sum_{j=1}^{n} v_{ij}^{(t+1)} MM(X) + \sum_{i=1}^{m-1} \sum_{r=i+1}^{m} u_{ir}^{(t+1)} MM(X))$$

[as $v^{(t+1)}$ and $u^{(t+1)}$ satisfy equation (6.13)]

$$\geq \min_{X}(\sum_{i=1}^{m} \sum_{j=1}^{n} v_{ij}^{(t+1)} \, w_{1ij}\ell_2(X_i,a_j)$$

$$+ \sum_{i=1}^{m-1} \sum_{r=i+1}^{n} u_{ir}^{(t+1)} \, w_{2ir}\ell_2(X_i,X_r))$$

[from the definition of $MM(X)$]

$$= \sum_{i=1}^{m} \sum_{j=1}^{n} v_{ij}^{(t+1)} \, w_{1ij}\ell_2(X_i^{(t)},a_j)$$

$$+ \sum_{i=1}^{m-1} \sum_{r=i+1}^{m} u_{ir}^{(t+1)} \, w_{2ir}\ell_2(X_i^{(t)},X_r^{(t)})$$

[from equation (6.14) which indicates $X^{(t)}$ is a minimizer]

$$= \underline{x}_0.$$

Chapter 7

Site-Generating Location-Allocation Models

Heretofore we have been concerned with location models where the flows between the new facilities and the existing facilities are given. However, in situations where there is more than one new facility to be located, determining the flows is often part of the problem. Figure 7.1 shows 19 demand locations over a geographical area. Each of these locations has a requirement, which is the associated decimal number. The numbers could be tonnage to be shipped, sales dollars, or simply units demanded. It is only important that all numbers be in a common unit and that it is possible to calculate shipping cost per unit requirement per unit distance. Figure 7.2 shows one possible solution to the problem of locating three distribution centers. The indicated allocations are arbitrary, but the locations of the centers (marked by crosses) minimize the sums of weighted distances with respect to the allocations. When the distances are rectangular and in kilometers, and the requirements are in tons, the total weighted-distance cost for this solution is 17,389 ton-kilometers. Figure 7.3 shows the optimal solution, which has a cost of 15,203 ton-kilometers.

The number of new facilities may also be part of the problem. The cost of adding a new facility must then be balanced against the transportation cost saved by utilizing that new facility. In this chapter, we develop techniques for addressing this general problem.

We first consider the location-allocation problem when the number of new facilities is *known*. The structure of this problem may be characterized by a set of existing facility locations a_j and their known requirements, $w_j > 0, j = 1,...,n$. The problem is to determine the optimal location for each of the m new facilities and the optimal allocation of existing facility requirements to the new facilities so that all requirements are satisfied.

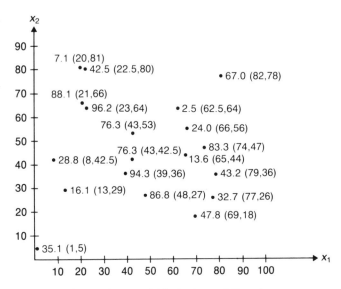

Figure 7.1 Demand Locations and Their Annual Requirements.

Let the amount supplied by the ith new facility to the jth existing facility be given by w_{ij}. Then, to minimize total weighted (ℓ_p) distances:

$$\text{minimize } L(X,W) = \sum_{i=1}^{m} \sum_{j=1}^{n} w_{ij}\ell_p(X_i,a_j)$$
$$X,W$$

subject to   (7.1)

$$\sum_{i=1}^{m} w_{ij} = w_j, \, j = 1,...,n,$$

$$w_{ij} \geqslant 0, \, i = 1,...,m; \, j = 1,...,n,$$

where $X = (X_1,...,X_m)$, $W = (w_{11},w_{12},...,w_{1n},w_{21},...,w_{mn})$.

Problem (7.1) has a nonlinear objective function that is neither concave nor convex, and generally contains many *local* minimizers. This means standard nonlinear programming algorithms may fail to produce a global minimizer.

We call this model the location-allocation problem. However, we do not mean to imply that all actual location-allocation problems can be adequately represented by problem (7.1). Among the prominent factors that may impair the use of the model are the following: The requirements w_j may depend on the new facility locations. Transportation costs may not be adequately expressed as weights times distances. The total cost may involve other significant components besides transportation costs.

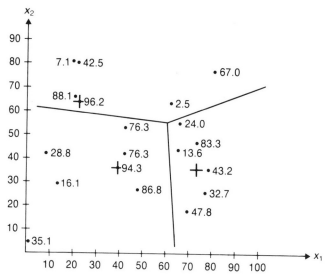

Figure 7.2 Possible Location and Allocation for Three Distribution Centers.

There may be flows between the new facilities. Finally, it may be more appropriate to maximize profit.

We emphasize that this is a site-generating model. It is intended to give a rough cut at an optimal distribution design, perhaps for input to

Figure 7.3 Optimal Location and Allocation for Three Distribution Centers.

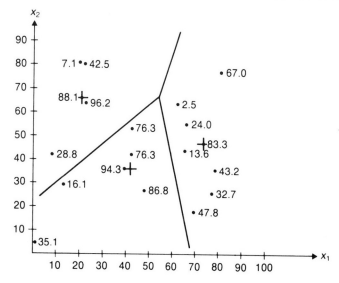

the more detailed models of the following chapter. Yet there are applications for which formulation (7.1) is quite appropriate (see the Blue Water Farms problem, Exercise 7.4). As observed by Ostresh (1975), "Applications of the analysis of continuous space problems (site-generating models here) include the locating of helicopter serviced emergency medical units, in which travel time is essentially proportional to distance; and the whole realm of long range facilities location planning, in which today's costs and times are probably a less reliable estimate of future costs than measures derived from distances."

7.1 ONE-DIMENSIONAL LOCATION-ALLOCATION BY DYNAMIC PROGRAMMING

Suppose all existing facilities are situated on one route, or equivalently on a straight line given by the x-axis. This means $\ell_p(X_i, a_j) = |X_i - a_j|$ because X_i and a_j are now one-tuples and $[|x - a|^p]^{1/p} = |x - a|$. One type of application is the placement of supply, storage, or processing facilities along transportation or flow arteries. An example of the location of sewage treatment plants along a river basin is given by Converse (1972). To illustrate the difficult nature of problem (7.1), even in this one-dimensional context, consider the following example where two new facilities are to be located with respect to five existing facilities. The requirements w_j and locations a_j are given as:

$$w_1 = 2, \; w_2 = 2, \; w_3 = 2, \; w_4 = 2, \; w_5 = 1,$$

$$a_1 = 1, \; a_2 = 2, \; a_3 = 3, \; a_4 = 6, \; a_5 = 15.$$

An early heuristic solution approach used was to alternate between locating the new facilities and allocating the existing facilities to their nearest new facility until neither the locations nor the allocations changed. Suppose this procedure led to:

$$X_1 = 2, \; w_{11} = w_1 = 2, \; w_{12} = w_2 = 2, \; w_{13} = w_3 = 2, \; w_{14} = w_{15} = 0,$$

$$X_2 = 6, \; w_{21} = w_{22} = w_{23} = 0, \; w_{24} = w_4 = 2, \; w_{25} = w_5 = 1,$$

with $L(X, W) = 13$. Since the values of X_1 and X_2 are optimal given the values of the w_{ij}, and the values of the w_{ij} are optimal given the values of the X_i, the procedure terminates. The following solution is optimal, however:

$$X_1^* \epsilon [2,3], \; w_{11}^* = w_1 = 2, \; w_{12}^* = w_2 = 2, \; w_{13}^* = w_3 = 2, \; w_{14}^* = w_4 = 2, \; w_{15}^* = 0,$$

$$X_2^* = 15, \; w_{21}^* = w_{22}^* = w_{23}^* = w_{24}^* = 0, \; w_{25}^* = w_5 = 1,$$

with $L(X^*, W^*) = 12$.

A dynamic programming approach can be used to produce optimal solutions to the one-dimensional case of problem (7.1). For notational convenience, let the existing facilities be numbered so that $a_j < a_{j+1}$, $j = 1,...,n-1$. As there are no capacity constraints, each existing facility is optimally allocated to the nearest new facility (ties broken arbitrarily). This observation together with the numbering convention used for the existing facilities leads to a *fundamental insight*: Existing facilities will be optimally allocated to new facilities in sequence. For example, if existing facilities 1 and 4 are optimally allocated to a given new facility, so also will existing facilities 2 and 3. Let the *stages* of the dynamic programming formulation be the number of new facilities yet to be located. The stage number is given by i, $i = 1,...,m$. The *state* is measured by s, the index of the lowest numbered unallocated existing facility. Then $m-i+1 \leq s \leq n-i+1$ if $i < m$, and $s = 1$ if $i = m$. Let $A_i(s)$ be the set of all possibly optimal subsets of allocations of existing facilities to the ith new facility, given s. Each such subset is represented by an index t_i, $s \leq t_i \leq n-i+1$ if $i \neq 1$ and $t_i = n$ otherwise. Let $W^*(s,t_i)$ denote the minimum weighted-distance cost of the ith new facility optimally located with respect to allocated existing facilities s, $s+1,...,t_i$. Let $X_i^*(s,t_i)$ be an optimal location that produces $W^*(s,t_i)$. This means $X_i^*(s,t_i)$ is a minimizer for:

$$W(X_i;s,t_i) = \sum_{j=s}^{t_i} w_j|X_i - a_j|.$$

Efficient techniques have been discussed (in Section 2.2) for finding $X_i^*(s,t_i)$.

The recursive dynamic programming relationship is:

$$f_i^*(s) = \min_{t_i \in A_i(s)} \{f_i(s,t_i)\}, \tag{7.2}$$

where $f_i(s,t_i) = W^*(s,t_i) + f_{i-1}^*(t_i+1)$. Stated in words, $f_i^*(s)$ is the minimum weighted-distance cost of allocating existing facilities s, $s+1,...,n$, to i new facilities. The approach is probably best "explained" by an example.

Example 7.1 The location and requirements of seven demand points are given in Table 7.1. Three distribution centers are to be located. Com-

Table 7.1 Data for Example 7.1.

j	1	2	3	4	5	6	7
a_j	1	2	3	5	7	8	10
w_j	2	1	2.5	1.5	2.5	4	3

putations for the three dynamic programming stages are shown in Tables 7.2, 7.3, and 7.4 where t_i^* denotes the minimizer in equation (7.2).

We find $f_3^*(1) = 10.5$, with $t_3^* = 4$, $t_2^* = 6$, and $t_1^* = 7$. In the notation of problem (7.1), this means:

$$X_3^* = X_3^*(1,4), w_{31}^* = w_1 = 2, w_{32}^* = w_2 = 1, w_{33}^* = w_3 = 2.5, w_{34}^* = w_4 = 1.5,$$

$$X_2^* = X_2^*(5,6), w_{25}^* = w_5 = 2.5, w_{26}^* = w_6 = 4,$$

$$X_1^* = X_1^*(7,7), w_{17}^* = w_7 = 3,$$

and all other w_{ij}^*'s equal zero.

We have implemented the algorithm on a computer. For simplicity the value of $X_i^*(s,t_i)$ was determined by evaluating $W(X_i;s,t_i)$ at successive a_j's for $j = s, s+1,...,t_i$ until a minimizer is found using conditions (2.15). The shapes of sample computing time functions are shown in Figures 7.4 and 7.5.

The shapes are not unexpected. The number of minimizations of $W(X_i;s,t_i)$ at each stage is of order $n-m$ and the number of stages is m. The average computation time to do one minimization will be of order $n-m$ because t_i ranges from s to $n-i+1$, and s ranges from $m-i+1$ to $n-i+1$. Total computation time then should be of order $m(n-m)^2$. With

Table 7.2 $i = 1, t_1^* = t_1 = 7$.

s	$f_1(s,7)$	$f_1^*(s)$	$X_1^*(s,7)$
7	0	0	10
6	6	6	8
5	8.5	8.5	8
4	13	13	8
3	25.5	25.5	8

Table 7.3 $i = 2$.

s/t_2	$f_2(s,t_2)$					$f_2^*(s)$	t_2^*	$X_2^*(s,t_2^*)$
	2	3	4	5	6			
6					0	0	6	8
5				6	2.5	2.5	6	8
4			8.5	9	7	7	6	[7,8]
3		13	11.5	16	17	11.5	4	3
2	25.5	14	12.5	19	22	12.5	4	3

Table 7.4 $i = 3$.

s/t_3	$f_3(s,t_3)$					$f_3^*(s)$	t_3^*	$X_3^*(s,t_3^*)$
	1	2	3	4	5			
1	12.5	12.5	11.5	10.5	18	10.5	4	3

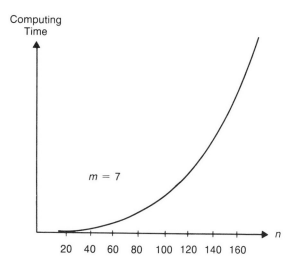

Figure 7.4 Computing Time in Relation to n for $m = 7$.

n fixed and m variable, the maximum of $m(n-m)^2$ occurs at $m = n/3$. Figure 7.5 shows that this a good prediction for $n = 100$.

Unfortunately, the dynamic programming approach doesn't generalize to two-dimensional problems. This is because the fundamental insight is no longer valid. (There are some exceptions—see Exercise 7.2.)

Determining the Number of New Facilities

When each new facility has the same constant operating cost per unit time, problem (7.1) can be extended to determine the optimal number of new facilities, as well as the optimal locations and allocations. For a warehouse location problem the fixed operating cost might correspond to the monthly fixed rental charges. The optimal weighted-distance cost is computed for increasing numbers of new facilities and added to the total fixed operating cost. Performing this analysis for Example 7.1 gives weighted-distance costs of: 43, 16.5, 10.5, 6.5, 3.5, 1.0, and 0.0, respectively, for $m = 1,2,....,7$. Augmenting these costs with an operating cost of 10 per unit time for each new facility gives the results depicted in Figure 7.6. The weighted-distance cost is strictly decreasing in m, whereas the operating cost increases linearly. It is best to use $m^* = 2$ distribution centers with an optimal total cost of $16.5+2(10) = 36.5$.

Notice that the total cost for the best configuration of $m = 3$ distribution centers is 40.5 which is about 11% higher than the least cost for an optimal number of centers. This is not an unusual finding in distribution studies. The total cost curve for an optimally configured distri-

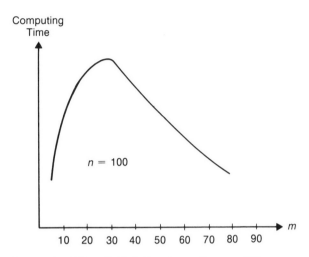

Figure 7.5   Computing Time in Relation to m for $n = 100$.

bution system with $m \neq m^*$ distribution centers is relatively flat in the neighborhood of m^*.

7.2 SOLVING THE TWO-FACILITY EUCLIDEAN DISTANCE PROBLEM

Suppose that two distribution centers are to be located in relation to the demand points depicted in Figure 7.1, and that Euclidean distances are used in problem (7.1). Imagine a line drawn between the points labeled with weights 2.5 and 86.8. Call these points A and B, respectively. The line defines two possible allocations of the 19 demand points. One allocation includes demand point A with the group of points to one side of the line and includes demand point B with the group of points to the other side of the line. The second allocation reverses the group associations of demand points A and B. Another conceptualization is to think of the line as being rotated slightly, first clockwise and then counterclockwise about an axis on the segment between points A and B. In this way the two different partitions of the 19 demand points are graphically apparent. This is a useful construction because it is readily proven that there is an optimal partitioning of the demand points such that the two groupings of the points are strictly separated by some straight line.

More formally, let J be the index set $\{1,2,...,n\}$; let (J_1,J_2) be a partition of the set J, ie, J_1 and J_2 are mutually exclusive and collectively exhaustive with respect to J. Then the two-facility location-allocation problem with Euclidean distances has an optimal partition (J_1^*,J_2^*) such that locations of existing facilities with indices in J_1^* are strictly separated by some straight line from the locations of those with indices in J_2^*. There are

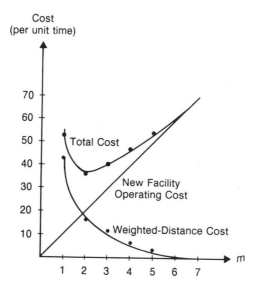

Figure 7.6   Cost Versus the Number of New Facilities.

$n(n-1)/2$ pairs of existing facility locations. Each pair determines a line, which in turn determines a pair of partitions. Hence we need only consider $n(n-1)$ partitions if no three existing facility locations lie on the same line, and fewer otherwise. The maximum number $n(n-1)$ of these candidate partitions is much smaller than the total number $2^{n-1}-1$ of partitions of J that would have to be examined using an exhaustive enumeration approach.

Perhaps the case of three collinear existing facility locations needs amplification. Suppose the line through the demand points labeled with weights 24.0 and 67.0 in Figure 7.1 also passes through the point labeled with weight 86.8, that we have called B. Call these additional points C and D, respectively. This single line corresponds to the three point pairs BC, BD, and CD. Potentially there are two partitions to be considered for each point pair. However, we see that only four partitions need actually be considered in this collinear case. These are the two partitions for which points B and C are in one grouping while point D is in the other grouping, and the two partitions for which points C and D are in one grouping while point B is in the other grouping. By the strictly separating line property of an optimal partition, points B and D cannot be in one grouping while the point C (between B and D on the same line) is in the other grouping.

There are several ways to implement these ideas to create an algorithm. In the discussion to follow we will not distinguish between a subset I of the index set J and the corresponding subset $\{a_j | j \epsilon I\}$ of the existing facility locations. Consider an optimal partition (J_1^*, J_2^*) and an associated strictly separating line. Move the line parallel to itself toward the grouping of points in J_1^* until it first passes through one or more points in J_1^* (J_1^* cannot be empty in an optimal partition). This means there exists a line passing through a point of J_1^* such that all points on the line or to one side belong to J_1^*, while the points on the other side of the line belong to J_2^*. Summing up, we need only consider those partitions (J_1, J_2) as candidates for optimality for which J_1 and J_2 are separated by a line passing through some existing facility location in J_1, termed the "pivot." If for each such partition we solve the corresponding pair of single-facility *location* problems defined by J_1 and J_2, and the least pair-wise sum of minimized single-facility objective values is chosen, then the two-facility location-allocation problem with Euclidean distances will have been solved. The following is a method for determining candidate partitions.

Drezner Algorithm

For each $j = 1, 2, ..., n$, let a_j be the pivot point. Then for each $r \neq j$, calculate the angle, say θ_r, that the ray originating at the pivot a_j and passing through a_r makes with the positive x_1-axis. Sort these $n-1$ angles in nondecreasing order. Then, for a given angle θ, let $J_1(\theta)$ include a_j together with existing facility locations a_r such that $\theta \leq \theta_r \leq \theta + \pi$, and let $J_2(\theta) = J - J_1(\theta)$. To obtain the candidate partitions with a_j as the pivot, begin with $\theta = 0°$ and generate $(J_1(0°), J_2(0°))$. Then choose the least angle θ from among $\theta_1, \theta_2, ..., \theta_{j-1}, \theta_{j+1}, ..., \theta_n$ for which $J_1(\theta)$ is different from $J_1(0°)$. In general, suppose $\hat{\theta}$ has just been considered. Calculate $\alpha = \min\{\theta_r | \theta_r > \hat{\theta}\}$ and $\beta = \min\{\theta_r | \theta_r > \hat{\theta} + \pi\}$. Then $\tilde{\theta} = \min\{\alpha, \beta - \pi\}$ is the next angle θ after $\hat{\theta}$ for which $J_1(\theta)$ is different from $J_1(\hat{\theta})$. Increase θ from $\hat{\theta}$ to $\tilde{\theta}$ and continue until $\tilde{\theta} \geq \pi$.

A logical question is whether or not an analog of the strictly separating line property for the two-facility problem exists for the three-facility problem with Euclidean distances. Viewing Figure 7.3 we see that a three-way partition of a set of points is based on a configuration of three rays emanating from a single point. That point may or may not be inside the convex hull of the existing facility locations. The way to an efficient algorithm that checks all three-way partitions using this observation is not yet clear.

7.3 SOLVING RECTANGULAR DISTANCE PROBLEMS AS m-MEDIAN PROBLEMS

In this section we single out the case of problem (7.1) with $p = 1$. The two-dimensional rectangular distance location-allocation problem contains structure inherited from the location problem that can be exploited.

Furthermore, optimal allocations are often close to the optimal allocations for the ℓ_p distance problem.

As we are not considering capacity restrictions in problem (7.1), the requirement w_j of each existing facility will be optimally allocated entirely to the closest new facility. Hence, before the location-allocation problem is solved, every existing facility is potentially in the allocation set of every new facility. This means that the set of candidate points for optimal location of each new facility is the same as that for a single new facility serving all n of the existing facilities. From Property 2.5 we observe that at least one optimal location for the single-facility rectangular distance *location* problem is included in the set I, say, consisting of *intersection points* of lines drawn vertically and horizontally through the existing facility locations. Call this the *inclusion property*. As set I satisfies the inclusion property, I must include a set of optimal locations for the *location-allocation* problem when distances are rectangular.

We now show how to construct a subset I_R, say, of set I that also satisfies the inclusion property. Figure 7.7 shows six existing facility locations and their associated convex hull. The intersection points marked by a circle together with the existing facility locations make up the set I_R. These are points in set I that are also in the so-called rectangular hull of the existing facility locations. Let the rectangular hull be denoted by H_R, and as in the previous section, let $J = \{1,...,n\}$ be the index set for the existing facilities. Then H_R is defined as the set of points $X = (x_1,x_2)$ that satisfy the following four conditions simultaneously:

$$x_1 \leqslant a_{j1} \text{ and } x_2 \geqslant a_{j2} \text{ for some } j\epsilon J,$$

$$x_1 \geqslant a_{j1} \text{ and } x_2 \leqslant a_{j2} \text{ for some } j\epsilon J,$$

$$x_1 \leqslant a_{j1} \text{ and } x_2 \leqslant a_{j2} \text{ for some } j\epsilon J, \qquad (7.3)$$

$$x_1 \geqslant a_{j1} \text{ and } x_2 \geqslant a_{j2} \text{ for some } j\epsilon J.$$

Figure 7.7 Intersection Points for Six Existing Facilities.

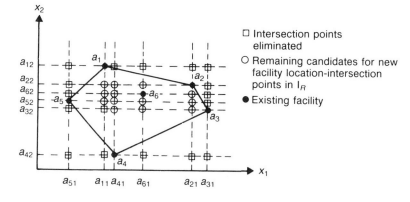

These four inequalities specify that for each point X in H_R: at least one existing facility lies no farther west and no farther north than X; at least one lies no farther east and no farther south than X; at least one lies no farther west and no farther south than X; and at least one lies no farther east and no farther north than X, respectively. This implies a geometrical interpretation of the rectangular hull. H_R is the set of points that cannot be reached by translation of any quadrant of the coordinate system without including one of the existing facility locations as an interior point of the quadrant. In Figure 7.8 the shaded region (including its boundary) plus all the outlying existing facility points together with their connecting lines to the shaded region constitute H_R. From Figure 7.7 we observe that the intersection point (a_{11}, a_{32}) marked by a square is in the convex hull, but is not in the rectangular hull H_R, and is therefore not in I_R. The following property establishes the significance of H_R.

Property 7.1 [*Inclusion property of the rectangular hull*]. *An optimal solution to the single-facility rectangular distance location problem given by problem (2.10) is included in H_R.*

The proof is given in the Appendix, mathematical note 7.1. As a simple example of the inclusion property of H_R consider the case: $n = 2$, $w_1 = w_2 = 1$, $a_1 = (2,0)$, and $a_2 = (0,1)$. Then $I = \{(0,0), a_1, a_2, (2,1)\}$ and $H_R = \{a_1, a_2\} = I_R$, as I_R is the intersection of H_R and I. Points in the entire rectangle with corners at a_1 and a_2 are optimal for problem (2.10). We see that unless the optimal location is unique, H_R doesn't necessarily include the entire set of the optimal locations. Typically, four distinct existing facilities are needed to satisfy the four pairs of inequalities in conditions (7.3). An exception occurs when $X = a_r$, in which case a_r alone suffices. This shows that the existing facility locations are always in H_R and, hence, in I_R.

Figure 7.8   Rectangular Hull H_R.

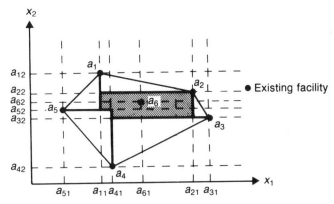

The set I_R may be determined from the intersection set I using conditions (7.3). For reference we state this central result as a property. Define the index sets $G_k = \{j\epsilon J | x_k \leq a_{jk}\}$ and $L_k = \{j\epsilon J | x_k \geq a_{jk}\}$ for $k = 1,2$.

Property 7.2 [*Determining the set I_R*]. *The point $X = (x_1,x_2)\epsilon I$ satisfies conditions (7.3) and is hence a member of I_R, if, and only if, no pair of sets, G_1, L_2 or L_1, G_2 or G_1, G_2 or L_1, L_2 is disjoint.*

For example, the intersection point $X = (a_{11},a_{32})$ in Figure 7.7 defines the sets $L_1 = \{5,1\}$, $L_2 = \{3,4\}$, $G_1 = \{1,4,6,2,3\}$ and $G_2 = \{3,5,6,2,1\}$. Because the pair of sets L_1, L_2 is disjoint, the fourth pair of inequalities in conditions (7.3) is violated, and we conclude $X \notin I_R$.

Transformation to an *m*-Median Problem

Suppose we wish to solve problem (7.1) with $p = 1$. We have established that an optimal set of locations for the new facilities will be contained in I_R. Let the points in I_R be denoted by P_k, $k = 1,...,K$, and let:

$c_{kj} = w_j\ell_1(P_k,a_j)$, which is the weighted-distance cost of allocating the entire requirement w_j of existing facility j to a new facility at location P_k,

$y_{kj} = $ proportion of requirement w_j of existing facility j allocated to a new facility at location P_k,

$z_k = 1$ if P_k is chosen as a location for a new facility; or 0 otherwise.

Then an optimal solution can be found by solving:

$$\text{minimize} \sum_{k=1}^{K} \sum_{j=1}^{n} c_{kj}y_{kj}$$
$$y,z$$

subject to   (7.4)

$$\sum_{k=1}^{K} y_{kj} = 1 \qquad \text{for all } j$$

$$z_k - y_{kj} \geq 0 \qquad \text{for all } k,j$$

$$\sum_{k=1}^{K} z_k = m$$

$$z_k = 0 \text{ or } 1, \; y_{kj} \geq 0 \qquad \text{for all } k,j.$$

The first set of constraints ensures that the requirement of each existing facility is fully allocated. The second set ensures that there is no allocation to location P_k unless a new facility is located there. The final constraint requires that exactly m new facilities are to be located. Problem (7.4) is a mixed-integer linear programming problem that has been termed the m-median problem. Special purpose solution methods are discussed in the following chapter. We note that compared to solving the resulting m-median problem, the computing time required to generate I_r is negligible.

More on Hulls

There is a hull related to H_R that must contain the *entire* set of optimal solutions to problem (2.10). We will denote this hull by E_R. For the example given after the statement of Property 7.1 where $n = 2$, $a_1 = (2,0)$, and $a_2 = (0,1)$, the elements of E_R are the points in the rectangle with corners at a_1 and a_2. If $w_1 = w_2 = 1$, this is indeed the entire set of optimal solutions. The following property indicates when a point cannot solve (the d-dimensional case of) problem (2.10), and is therefore *not* in E_R.

Property 7.3 [*Exclusion property for E_R*]. *If for $X = (x_1,x_2,...,x_d)$ any two sets, say A and B, chosen from among the 2d sets L_k and G_k, $k = 1,2,...,d$ are disjoint, and if A and B are* not *collectively exhaustive with respect to J, then $X \notin E_R$ and X cannot be optimal in the d-dimensional case of problem (2.10).*

Property 7.3 implies that H_R is a subset of E_R. Reconsidering the intersection point $X = (a_{11},a_{32})$ in Figure 7.7 the only disjoint pair of sets is L_1 and L_2. As the union of L_1 and L_2 is $\{1,3,4,5\} \neq J$, we find that X is neither in H_R nor in E_R. The following example illustrates the use of Property 7.3 to analyze a three-dimensional problem.

Example 7.2 There are four offices in a two-story building, with coordinates as given in Table 7.5. A copying machine is to be located to minimize the sum of weights times distances to the existing offices.

The intersection set I (which must contain an optimal location) contains eight points, of which four are existing office locations. The remaining four points are analyzed in Table 7.6, using Property 7.3. As a

Table 7.5   Present Office Locations and Weights.

j	w_j	a_j
1	2	(0,0,0)
2	2	(0,1,1)
3	2	(1,1,0)
4	1	(1,1,1)

Table 7.6 Using Property 7.3.

x_1	G_1, L_1	x_2	G_2, L_2	x_3	G_3, L_3	Comment
0	{1,2,3,4} {1,2}	0	{1,2,3,4} {1}	1	{2,4} {1,2,3,4}	eliminated: $L_2 \cap G_3 = \phi$, and $L_2 \cup G_3 \neq J$.
0	{1,2,3,4} {1,2}	1	{2,3,4} {1,2,3,4}	0	{1,2,3,4} {1,3}	not eliminated
1	{3,4} {1,2,3,4}	0	{1,2,3,4} {1}	0	{1,2,3,4} {1,3}	eliminated: $G_1 \cap L_2 = \phi$, and $G_1 \cup L_2 \neq J$.
1	{3,4} {1,2,3,4}	0	{1,2,3,4} {1}	1	{2,4} {1,2,3,4}	eliminated: $L_2 \cap G_3 = \phi$, and $L_2 \cup G_3 \neq J$.

result, we conclude that the set $\{a_1, a_2, a_3, a_4, (0,1,0)\}$ must contain an optimal location.

The total cost values $W(X) = \sum_{j=1}^{3} w_j \ell_1(X, a_j)$ for each $X \epsilon I$ are shown in Table 7.7. The optimal location of the copy machine is $X^* = (0,1,0)$. We note that X^* is *outside* the convex hull of existing office locations.

Table 7.7 Values of $W(X)$ for Each $X \epsilon I$.

X	$W(X)$	X	$W(X)$
(0,0,0)	11	(1,0,0)	12
(0,0,1)	12	(1,0,1)	13
(0,1,0)	8	(1,1,0)	9
(0,1,1)	9	(1,1,1)	10

For two-dimensional location problems of the form (2.17) such that the new facilities are chained and $1 < p < \infty$, the smallest set that must contain the entire set of optimal solutions is the convex hull of the existing facility locations. Because the convex hull contains an infinite number of points, the transformation of the associated location-allocation problem to the m-median formulation [where K in problem (7.4) must be finite] is no longer possible. Even if $p = 1$ but K is a large number, the m-median approach becomes impractical. The need for heuristic solution procedures becomes apparent.

7.4 LOCATION-ALLOCATION HEURISTICS

In this section we present heuristics for solving relatively large instances of problem (7.1). We first formulate the problem as a concave minimization problem with linear constraints (concave minimization problems are nonlinear programming problems whose objective is to minimize a concave objective function). A heuristic strategy is then developed based on this structure.

Structural Properties

When W in problem (7.1) is temporarily held *fixed* (such that each $w_{ij} \geq 0$), the problem reduces to a pure location problem. Then from problem (5.31) (with all $w_{2ir} = 0$), letting $U_{1ij} \equiv U_{ij}$, the dual location problem with $p > 1$ can be written as:

$$\max_{U} DM(U) = -\sum_{i=1}^{m} \sum_{j=1}^{n} a_j U_{ij}$$

subject to   (7.5)

$$\sum_{j=1}^{n} U_{ij} = \bar{0}, \qquad i = 1,...,m,$$

$$\|U_{ij}\|_q \leq w_{ij}, \qquad i = 1,...,m; j = 1,...,n,$$

where $q = p/(p-1)$ and $\bar{0}$ denotes a vector of zeros. From Chapter 4 we know that when $p = 1$, we can write the pure location problem as a linear programming problem. Hence, for $p = 1$, the dual location problem also can be written as a linear programming problem. Problem (7.5) is a nonlinear programming problem.

Consider the *perturbation function* $v(W)$ which is defined as the optimal value of problem (7.5) for a given $W \geq \bar{0}$. When $p = 1$, $v(W)$ is the optimal value of the associated linear programming dual problem. We invoke the following result for $v(W)$.

Property 7.4 [*Concavity of the perturbation function*]. $v(W)$ is a concave function on the set of W's such that $W \geq \bar{0}$.

A proof found in Geoffrion (1971) shows that $-v(W)$ is convex and hence that $v(W)$ is concave. Using Property 7.4, we may state problem (7.1) as the following concave minimization problem:

$$\min_{W} v(W)$$

subject to   (7.6)

$$\sum_{i=1}^{m} w_{ij} = w_j, \quad j = 1,...,n,$$

$$w_{ij} \geq 0, \quad i = 1,...,m; j = 1,...,n.$$

Heuristics

Although algorithms for concave minimization problems are available, large instances of problem (7.6) are yet beyond their computational reach. One property of problem (7.1) that follows from the concavity of $v(W)$ is that the optimal solution must lie at an extreme point of the feasible region in (7.6). A logical computational strategy, therefore, is to search along such extreme points. [We should emphasize here that an objective function value in problem (7.6) is realized only when, given the current w_{ij} values, the locations for all new facilities are optimal.] An algorithm that proceeds from one extreme point (basic solution) to an adjacent extreme point (one basic variable changed) is not guaranteed to reach optimality for concave minimization problems in general, however. The H1, H2, and H3 heuristics given below are of this type. A more elaborate heuristic is to change two basic variables at a time in order to "step over" adjacent extreme points, in addition to investigating adjacent extreme points. The H4 and H5 heuristics are of this type.

The H4 and H5 procedures are analogous in linear programming to testing all possible *pairs* of nonbasic variables for entry into the basis at each step of the simplex method, in addition to testing all single nonbasic variables for entry to the basis. For linear programming problems, the examination of pairs of nonbasic variables for entry into the basis is not necessary, as a single variable entry method (the simplex method) converges to optimality. However, because problem (7.1) typically has many local minima, testing pairs of variables for possible entry into the basis at each iteration enables the algorithm to step over a local optimum, thus increasing the chances of reaching a global optimum.

Because problem (7.6) contains n linear equality constraints, there will be n basic variables in a basic solution. Furthermore, each constraint must include one basic variable. Since basic feasible solutions correspond to extreme points of the feasible region, each extreme point corresponds to allocating each of the n existing facilities to a single new facility. Consideration of a pair of variables for entry into the basis corresponds to changing the allocations of two existing facilities.

All of the tested heuristics start with a trial solution to problem (7.1). Then the solution is perturbed by changing the allocations systematically, each time determining the associated optimal locations. Five procedures with varying degrees of perturbation are investigated. Each of the methods starts with an arbitrary allocation. Each method stops when the perturbations do not produce any further improvement. The following describes the perturbations employed for each heuristic.

H1: For each new facility i_1, $i_1 = 1,2,...,m$, the new facility i_2 closest to i_1 is found. Among the existing facilities allocated to i_2, the one closest to i_1 is tentatively reallocated to i_1. Once an improvement is found, the perturbation scheme is restarted.

H2: For each new facility i, each existing facility is tentatively reallocated to i (if not already allocated to i). Once an improvement is found, the perturbation scheme is restarted.

H3: This heuristic is identical to H2 except that all tentative reallocations are checked in order to adopt the best one before the perturbation scheme is restarted.

H4 and H5: These heuristics are similar to H2 and H3, respectively, except that reallocations here additionally involve two existing facilities. In H5 all possible pairs as well as all possible single existing facilities are tried at each iteration.

Specifically, the procedure for H5 is as follows:

Procedure for H5

Step 0   Initialize "least cost achieved thus far" to a large number.

Step 1   Set $i = 0$.

Step 2   Set $i = i+1$. If $i > m$, go to Step 9. Otherwise set $j_1 = 0$ and go to Step 3.

Step 3   Set $j_1 = j_1 + 1$. If $j_1 > n$, go to Step 2. Otherwise, set $j_2 = j_1$ and go to Step 4.

Step 4   Set $j_2 = j_2 + 1$. If $j_2 > n$, go to Step 3.

Step 5   If existing facilities j_1 and j_2 are both allocated to new facility i, go to Step 4.

Step 6   Allocate existing facilities j_1 and j_2 to new facility i. (Note that either of the existing facilities j_1 or j_2 may already be allocated to new facility i. In this case, a single existing facility is being reallocated.)

Step 7   Check to see if any new facility has no existing facilities allocated to it. If so, reverse Step 6 and go to Step 4.

Step 8   Optimally locate all m new facilities and compute the total cost. If this cost is less than the least cost achieved thus far, record this new cost, the corresponding allocations of existing facilities, and the locations of new facilities. Go to Step 4.

Step 9   Check if i has been completely indexed from 0 to m once without recording an improved solution. If not, go to Step 1. Otherwise, the best solution recorded to date in Step 8 is reported, and the procedure terminates.

The procedure for H4 is identical to H5 with the exception that as soon as a pair change produces a reduction in total cost, that pair change is adopted and the perturbation procedure is restarted at Step 1. Heuristics H2 and H3 are less likely to produce optimal solutions, but require less computation time than H4 and H5.

To test the five heuristics, data sets (a_j's and w_j's) for 28 problems with rectangular distances were generated randomly. Optimal solutions were found by determining I_R and solving the m-median formulation (7.4). Table 7.8 shows the percentage by which the cost of the solution found exceeds the optimal cost (0% means less than 0.5%). A dash (–) indicates that an optimal solution was found. Optimal solutions were found in all cases by H4 and H5. Computation times were minimal.

A second set of 74 randomly generated rectangular distance test problems ranging in size from $m = 2$, $n = 11$ to $m = 3$, $n = 16$ were optimally solved using the m-median approach and then resolved by H5. Again, optimal solutions were produced in all cases. Further testing indicated that problems with $m = 2$, $n = 100$ and $m = 5$, $n = 60$ can be "solved"

Table 7.8 Sample Results for the Heuristics.

m	n	H1	H2	H3	H4	H5
2	12	–	–	–	–	–
2	13	2%	–	–	–	–
2	14	–	–	–	–	–
2	15	2%	1%	1%	–	–
2	16	0%	–	–	–	–
2	17	10%	3%	3%	–	–
2	18	2%	–	–	–	–
2	19	–	–	–	–	–
2	20	–	–	–	–	–
2	25	–	–	–	–	–
2	30	–	–	–	–	–
2	35	–	–	–	–	–
3	12	4%	–	–	–	–
3	13	–	–	–	–	–
3	14	–	–	–	–	–
3	15	0%	–	–	–	–
3	16	–	–	–	–	–
3	17	–	–	–	–	–
3	18	–	–	–	–	–
3	19	5%	5%	5%	–	–
3	20	–	28%	–	–	–
4	12	–	–	–	–	–
5	12	30%	–	–	–	–
6	12	0%	0%	–	–	–
7	12	190%	–	–	–	–
8	12	–	–	–	–	–
9	12	180%	–	–	–	–
10	12	190%	–	–	–	–

by H5 in a few minutes of computer CPU time. It is not known for these larger problems whether all the solutions produced were optimal.

Rectangular distances were used for testing, although any ℓ_p distance would have been suitable. Rectangular distances were chosen because large numbers of location problems must be solved during the computations, and rectangular problems can be solved rapidly and exactly. It is difficult to compare computing times between solving location problems with, say $p = 1$ and $1 < p \leq 2$. This is because it is possible to compute exact solutions rapidly by simple arithmetic in the former case, but only approximations to the solution by relatively slow convergent algorithms are possible in the latter case.

7.5 LOCATION-ALLOCATION WITH CONTINUOUS EXISTING FACILITIES

When there are a great many existing facilities, it is convenient to return to the notion of area destinations introduced in Section 3.2, and to develop a so-called auxiliary model. Geoffrion (1976c) lists the intended benefits of an auxiliary model as:

1. Reduce the level of detail and complexity of the location-allocation model until it can be solved by "back-of-the-envelope" calculations.
2. Educate intuition concerning the behavior of the optimal solution of a full model, including sensitivities of the solution as certain parameters are changed systematically.
3. Develop insights to be tested using a full model.
4. Use the insights that are confirmed as a conceptual framework for understanding the numerical results generated by a full model.

Consider a consumer products manufacturer with a single plant and a range of products to be considered as a single product group. Goods are distributed nationally through full-line distribution centers (DCs). The model is constructed from the following assumptions (cwt denotes gross shipping hundred-weight):

(A1) Demand is uniformly distributed in an area A with a constant density of ρ (cwt/square kilometer).

(A2) All DCs are identical and arbitrarily relocatable.

(A3) The supply cost for each DC is s (dollars/cwt) regardless of its location.

(A4) The fixed cost of each DC is f (dollars).

(A5) The variable throughput cost of each DC is v(dollars/cwt).

(A6) The outbound freight rate for each DC is t(dollars/cwt-kilometer).

(A7) There are no throughput limits for the DCs.

(A8) Distances are adequately estimated as inflated Euclidean distances.

The model is given by:

$$\text{minimize } TC(m) = \rho A(v + s) + fm + T(m), \qquad (7.7)$$

where $T(m)$ is the (weighted-distance) transportation cost for m optimally located DCs. Initially, suppose each market area is circular and the respective DC is located at the center of the circle. The optimum size A^* of the area for a given DC is determined by the radius, r, of the circle. The assumptions adopted imply that each market area will be A^*.

We will use polar coordinates to compute $T(1)$. The demand density at any point (r',θ) is ρ. The quantity $\rho r'\,dr'\,d\theta$ costs $tr'(\rho r'\,dr'\,d\theta)$ to transport over a distance r'. Thus $T(1)$ can be calculated as:

$$T(1) = \int_0^{2\pi} \int_0^r \rho t(r')^2 \, dr'\,d\theta = \frac{2}{3}\,\pi\rho tr^3. \qquad (7.8)$$

The assumptions imply that $T(m)$ is $mT(1) = 2/3\,\pi m\rho tr^3$. If A is "divided" into m equal-sized nonoverlapping circles, the common radius will satisfy $A = m\pi r^2$, which means $r = (A/m\pi)^{1/2}$. We have:

$$TC(m) = \rho A(v + s) + fm + \frac{2}{3}\,\rho t(A^3/\pi m)^{1/2}$$

$$= \rho A(v + s) + fm + 0.37613\,\rho t\,A^{3/2}/m^{1/2}. \qquad (7.9)$$

Using standard calculus methods, we find:

$$m^* = (\rho t/f)^{2/3}\,A/3.047 \qquad (7.10)$$

and so each nonoverlapping market area should be:

$$A^* = 3.047\,(\rho t/f)^{-2/3}.$$

Of course, circles cannot divide A. The only identical market shapes that can divide the plane are the square, the equilateral triangle, and the regular hexagon. Of these, hexagons cover a given area with least transportation cost $T(m)$. However, using hexagonal market areas instead of circular areas, the change in m^* would be approximately $+0.2\%$; square areas would change m^* by approximately $+1.1\%$; and even equilateral triangular market areas would change m^* by about $+4.8\%$. This means the analytical solution for m^* based on circular market areas is quite robust with respect to the actual shapes of the market areas that will be used. The actual shapes can be tailored to the shape of the area A. Therefore, under the stated assumptions we have simultaneously answered these complex questions: How many DCs should there be? Where should they be? What service areas should there be to cover the total area A, which is essentially of unspecified shape?

As intended, sensitivity analysis is facilitated using the model. For instance, a 10% increase in ρ or t changes m^* by $+6.6\%$, as $(1.10)^{2/3} = 1.066$. Sensitivity predictions can be surprisingly accurate for small changes in ρ, t, and f when compared with results from a full model to be discussed in Section 8.3. Using $TC(m)$ in equation (7.9), a figure such as Figure 7.6 can easily be constructed from the data of the problem.

EXERCISES

7.1 A subway is planned through an urban area. There are to be three access stations to serve a section of the line that crosses under eight streets as follows:

Street No.	1	2	3	4	5	6	7	8
Distance	100	200	500	100	100	200	100	

The distances between consecutive streets (in meters) are shown. The estimated number of passengers arriving at each intersection per hour (during peak periods) is given by:

Street No.	1	2	3	4	5	6	7	8
No. of Passengers Arriving per Hour	350	200	500	600	150	400	250	450

Determine the three subway station locations that minimize total passenger travel on the upper street surface.

7.2 It is required to find the location of three distribution centers to serve six existing facilities in an urban area. Data are as follows (assume rectangular distances):

Existing Facility	1	2	3	4	5	6
Location	(2,1)	(4,3)	(6,2)	(7,5)	(9,7)	(11,6)
Requirement	2	3	1	4	2.5	7

a. Graphically display H_R and then find the set I_R using Property 7.2.
b. Using Property 7.3 determine which of the points in the set $I-I_R$ are not in E_R.
c. Solve the location-allocation problem using dynamic programming.

7.3 Demand zone locations with their monthly requirements are given as follows. Coordinates are in kilometers on a rectangular coordinate system.

Demand Zone	1	2	3	4	5	6
Location	(1,2)	(2,3)	(2,5)	(4,7)	(9,6)	(10,8)
Monthly Requirement (tons)	1	2	3	4	5	6

Two warehouses are to be located and allocated to minimize total ton-kilometer shipping costs. Assume as a starting point that demand zones 1 and 2 are served by one warehouse and that zones 3, 4, 5, and 6 are served by a second warehouse.

a. Try to improve this solution using heuristic H5. Assume rectangular distances.

b. Assume Euclidean distances. Find all the candidate partitions that are generated using the location of demand zone 3 as the pivot point in the Drezner algorithm.

7.4 Recently, Blue Water Farms, a hog and white bean farming operation in Huron County, Ontario, was faced with a severe water shortage. Extensive field draining in the area had lowered the water table and the existing shallow wells were not able to produce sufficient water to meet livestock, field, and multi-family needs. Figure 7E.1 shows the location of the seven main house-barn locations where water is consumed. The farm manager decided to drill at least one deep well to supply the needs of the complex. In this section of the county there is an unlimited water supply approxi-

Figure 7E.1 Blue Water Farms—Geographical Configuration.

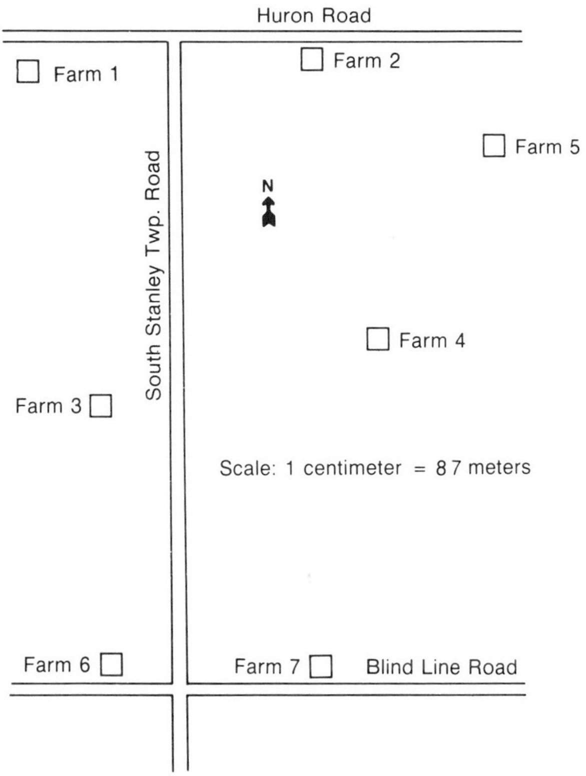

mately 75 meters below the ground surface. From discussions with a drilling contractor and an agricultural engineer, the following information was collected.

Approximate well cost (includes drilling, casing, pump, etc.) is $5200.00. The best way to distribute water from a well to another location is by polyvinyl chloride plastic piping buried 1.5 meters below ground level (to prevent winter freezing). A trench must be dug and the pipe laid and buried. Cost estimates were:

Trenching—$1.00/meter

Piping—polyvinyl chloride pipe (100 psi bursting strength) 1.25 inch, $2.29/meter; 1.5 inch, $3.00/meter; and 2 inch, $4.45/meter.

Because of differing requirements, the seven locations would require varying pipe sizes, as shown in Table 7E.1. Any line length greater than 760 meters would result in an excessive pressure drop with these pipe sizes and required flows. The trenches can follow straight-line paths from the new wells to the user locations.

How many wells should be drilled and where should they be located? What is the optimal cost?

7.5 Suppose that market areas are hexagonal as shown in Figure 7E.2. The quantity $\rho r' dr' d\theta$ costs $tr'(\rho r' dr' d\theta)$ to transport over the distance r'. Thus, the hexagonal analog of equation (7.8) is:

$$T(1) = 12 \int_0^{\pi/6} \int_0^r t\rho(r')^2 dr' d\theta.$$

Observe that $r = b/\cos\theta$ and that $c = 2b/\sqrt{3}$. Find a formula for m^* when market areas are taken to be hexagonal. Verify that the change in m^* from that in equation (7.10) is approximately $+0.2\%$.

7.6 Find m^* for square market areas, then for equilateral triangular areas. Verify that the percentage changes in m^* from that in equation (7.10) are approximately $+1.1\%$ and $+4.8\%$, respectively.

7.7 Explain why parameters s and v in problem (7.7) have no bearing on m^* or on the optimal service area shape. What shapes would you expect to

Table 7E.1   Pipe Requirements for Blue Water Farms.

Farm	Pipe Size Required (Inches)
1	1.5
2	2.0
3	1.5
4	1.25
5	1.5
6	2.0
7	1.5

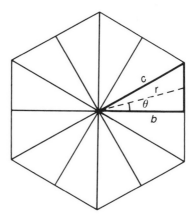

Figure 7E.2 Hexagonal Market Area.

evolve for market areas for the distribution centers of a consumer products manufacturer? Why? What are the major pitfalls of the model? How should the model be used?

7.8 It will be difficult to find precise values for the parameters in equation (7.10). Suppose A, ρ, and f have been measured accurately, but t has not. Let t_a be the actual value of the outbound freight rate and t be the estimated value. Let the *optimal* number of DCs using t_a be m_a and the *estimated* number using t be m^*. Determine an equation relating $TC(m^*)/TC(m_a)$ to t/t_a. Explain the usefulness of such an equation. Is it worse to overestimate or underestimate t_a? Determine an equation relating m^*/m_a to t/t_a.

7.9 Leamer (1968) Suppose demand density is not uniform over the total area A as is assumed in problem (7.7), but A is divided into n circular market areas $A_j, j = 1,...,n$, each with uniform demand density ρ_j. If market area j has m_j DCs, then transportation cost in that area is:

$$T_j(m_j) = 0.37613 \; \rho_j t \; A_j^{3/2}/m_j^{1/2}.$$

Use the Lagrange-multiplier technique to minimize $T(m) = \sum_{j}^{n} T_j(m_j)$ subject to $\sum_{j}^{n} m_j = m$. Interpret the result.

7.10* The township of Rio Rancho has hitherto not had its own emergency facilities. It has secured funds to erect two emergency facilities next year,

*This problem was used in the 1986 Mathematical Competition in Modeling administered by the Consortium for Mathematics and Its Applications (COMAP). It is included here with the permission of COMAP and the author, J. C. McGrew, Department of Geography & Regional Planning, Salisbury State College, Maryland.

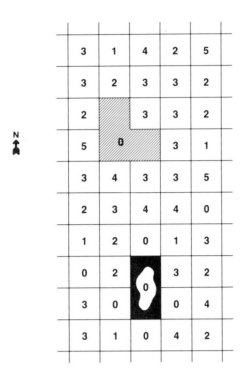

Figure 7E.3   Township of Rio Rancho—Geographical Configuration of Demand.

each of which will combine ambulance, fire, and police services. Figure 7E.3 indicates the demand, or number of emergencies per square block for the past year. The "L" region in the north is an obstacle, while the rectangle in the south is a park with a shallow pond. It takes an emergency vehicle an average of 15 seconds to go one block in the N-S direction and 20 seconds in the E-W direction. Your task is to locate the two facilities so as to minimize the total response time.

a. Assume that the demand is concentrated at the center of the block and that the facilities will be located on corners.

b. Assume that the demand is uniformly distributed on the streets bordering each block and that the facilities may be located anywhere on the streets.

Suggested Outline for Solution Report

1. A clarification or restatement of the problem, as appropriate.
2. A clear exposition of all assumptions and hypotheses.
3. An analysis of the problem justifying or motivating the modeling approach to be used.

4. The design of the model.
5. A discussion of how the model can be tested.
6. A discussion of the strengths and weaknesses of the model, including error analysis and such things as stability (eg, conditioning, sensitivity).
7. A one-page summary of results attached to the front.

REFERENCE NOTES

SECTION 7.1 This section is based on Love (1976).

SECTION 7.2 Ostresh (1973, 1975) used the strictly separating line property to suggest an algorithm based on choosing pairs of existing facility locations through which to pass a line, which is then rotated slightly. The implementation presented here is from Drezner (1984) who also considered the analogous problem under the minimax criterion. O'Kelly (1986) discussed an application to locating interacting hub facilities.

SECTION 7.3 Construction of the set I_R and the associated m-median approach are from Love and Morris (1975a). The definition of the rectangular hull and the proof of Property 7.1 are from Juel (1975). The set E_R was discussed by Juel and Love (1983b). Wendell, Hurter, and Lowe (1977), Chalmet, Francis, and Kolen (1981), and Thisse, Ward, and Wendell (1984) discussed a related set of "efficient points." A point X^* solves problem (2.10) for some choice of the positive weights w_j if and only if X^* is an efficient point.

Wendell and Hurter (1973) proved that an optimal location exists in the convex hull for two-dimensional single-facility location problems for any norm. Their conjecture that this result would extend to the multi-facility problem (4.1) was proved by Hansen, Perreur, and Thisse (1980). Juel and Love (1983b) showed that if the new facilities are chained and $1 < p < \infty$, all optimal solutions for problem (4.1) must be in the convex hull.

SECTION 7.4 The development here is from Love and Juel (1982). A survey of global concave minimization techniques is contained in Pardalos and Rosen (1986). Cooper (1963, 1964, 1972) did foundation work on formulating location-allocation models and solving them using heuristic procedures. Gelders, Pintelon, and Van Wassenhove (1987) discussed an application to a large Belgian brewery.

Techniques for exact solutions to problem (7.1) have been suggested by Kuenne and Soland (1972) for $p = 2$ and by Sherali and Shetty (1977) and Marucheck and Aly (1981) for $p = 1$. Chen and Handler (1987) considered the minimax problem.

SECTION 7.5 This section is based on Geoffrion (1976c), who used the model here to discuss the insight value of an auxiliary model. The work of Bos (1965) and Leamer (1968) supported the model development.

APPENDIX–CHAPTER 7

Mathematical Notes

7.1 *Prove* Property 7.1
The rectangular hull H_R includes an optimal solution to problem
(2.10).

PROOF: We will use the index set notation of Property 7.2. Let $\bar{G}_k$
and $\bar{L}_k$ be the complements of the index sets G_k and L_k with respect
to J; and for any index set A, let

$$S(A) = \sum_{j \in A} w_j.$$

Initially, suppose problem (2.10) has a *unique* optimal solution
(x_1^*, x_2^*). Then the necessary and sufficient conditions (2.15) for a given
point (x_1, x_2) to solve problem (2.10) become:

$$S(\bar{G}_k) < S(G_k) \text{ and } S(L_k) > S(\bar{L}_k) \text{ for } k = 1, 2.$$

Now to show $(x_1^*, x_2^*) \in H_R$, we must show that each of the pairs of
sets in Property 7.2 have an element in common. On the contrary,
suppose one of the pairs, say A and B, is disjoint. Then $\bar{A}$ contains
B, and $\bar{B}$ contains A, and we have

$$S(B) \leqslant S(\bar{A}) \text{ and } S(A) \leqslant S(\bar{B}).$$

We also have the optimality conditions:

$$S(\bar{A}) < S(A) \text{ and } S(\bar{B}) < S(B).$$

Combining we get

$$S(A) \leqslant S(\bar{B}) < S(B) \leqslant S(\bar{A}) < S(A),$$

which is a contradiction. Thus each of the pairs of sets in Property
7.2 must have an element in common. By conditions (7.3), this means
$(x_1^*, x_2^*) \in H_R$.
If the optimal solution to problem (2.10) is not unique, then the
optimality conditions (2.15) can be stated:

$$S(\bar{G}_k) \leqslant S(G_k) \text{ and } S(L_k) \geqslant S(\bar{L}_k) \text{ for } k = 1, 2.$$

We see that the contradiction above breaks down only if both subproblems have multiple optima, and A and B are complements. This

means that any location in a rectangle is optimal, and A and B consist of indices for existing facilities NW and SE (or NE and SW) to this rectangle. Thus two opposite corners of the rectangle belong to H_R.

Chapter 8

Site-Selecting Location-Allocation Models

Models of previous chapters are termed site-generating models, or "continuous" location models, because location takes place in a continuous space. The facility locations generated would indicate plausible "neighborhoods" within which to implement solutions, qualified by practical realities. Models in this chapter assume the decision-maker can specify a *list* of plausible sites for facility location. The list may be constructed from solutions of site-generating models and supplemented by sites that are appealing from a multi-objective perspective. For warehouse location, the list might include gateway cities relative to important demand points, and cities where the company or its competitors presently have facilities.

Models of this chapter will treat location of facilities and allocation of demand points simultaneously (existing facilities are demand points in this chapter). Typical questions addressed include: How many facilities should there be? Where should they be located? What size should each facility be? Which facility should serve which demand points? We begin with a model to minimize the number of facilities required to satisfy service level constraints.

8.1 SET-COVERING MODELS FOR SITE SELECTION

Horses pulling a fire wagon, it was once decided, can run no farther than ten city blocks. For that reason, fire stations in many American cities were located 20 blocks apart.

Today Wichita, Kansas, is saving nearly $3 million in construction and operating costs. . . . The city had planned to construct five new stations during the 1970's. But, after a computer analysis, the Fire Department decided to relocate two stations, construct only two new stations and transfer three existing companies to them.*

Example 8.1 Plane and Hendrick (1977) performed such an analysis in Denver. We will explain their approach using a hypothetical example similar to theirs. There are four possible fire station sites in a city and five response neighborhoods that require coverage by a pumper company. We will need a relation between expected fire engine travel time, $T(d)$, and travel distance, d, to determine if coverage is adequate. In an empirical study, Kolesar, Walker, and Hausner (1975) validated the model $T(d) = 2(d/a)^{1/2}$ if $d \leqslant 2d_c$ and $T(d) = v_c/a + d/v_c$ if $d > 2d_c$. The parameter a can be interpreted as acceleration, v_c is cruising velocity, and d_c is distance required to achieve cruising velocity. Considerations of time of day and regional traffic conditions (within a city) appeared to create only minor differences in average response velocities.

Table 8.1 shows the maximum allowable response time (T_ℓ) for each response neighborhood (RN_ℓ) and the expected fire engine travel times. The objective is to locate a minimum number of fire stations while satisfying response time requirements. The problem can be cast in the form of a zero-one linear programming problem given by:

$$\text{minimize } q = z_1 + z_2 + z_3 + z_4$$

subject to

$$0z_1 + 1z_2 + 1z_3 + 0z_4 \geqslant 1$$
$$1z_1 + 0z_2 + 0z_3 + 1z_4 \geqslant 1$$
$$0z_1 + 0z_2 + 0z_3 + 1z_4 \geqslant 1$$
$$1z_1 + 1z_2 + 1z_3 + 1z_4 \geqslant 1$$
$$0z_1 + 0z_2 + 1z_3 + 1z_4 \geqslant 1$$
$$z_1, z_2, z_3, z_4 = 0 \text{ or } 1.$$

This is an example of an unweighted set-covering problem (SC), with general form given by:

$$\text{minimize } q = \sum_k z_k \tag{8.1}$$

subject to

$$\sum_k a_{k\ell}z_k \geqslant 1 \qquad \text{for all } \ell \tag{8.2}$$

$$z_k = 0 \text{ or } 1 \qquad \text{for all } k. \tag{8.3}$$

*Advertisement for IBM in *mba*, Vol. 12, No. 5, May 1978

Table 8.1 Hypothetical Response Time Data.

Response Neighborhood	Maximum Response Time Requirements for First-Due Pumper (seconds)	Expected Response Time (seconds) from Fire Station Candidate Sites			
		1	2	3	4
1	120	145	115	95	150
2	90	70	180	110	85
3	90	110	130	190	90
4	180	155	160	95	105
5	150	180	160	140	120

In a related application, Kolesar and Walker (1974) let demand points correspond to response neighborhoods presently uncovered because their fire companies are in service. Site k corresponds to the kth empty fire station. The problem is to minimize the number of empty fire stations to be filled by relocating available fire companies so that all response neighborhoods are covered. In this context $a_{k\ell} = 1$ if filling the kth empty fire station covers RN_ℓ and $a_{k\ell} = 0$ otherwise.

In another instance, site k is a potential ambulance station. Let $t_{k\ell}$ be the travel time between site k and RN_ℓ, and let t_ℓ be the travel time from RN_ℓ to the nearest hospital. If the maximum permissible round-trip time is T_ℓ for an ambulance serving RN_ℓ from the nearest station, then $a_{k\ell} = 1$ if $t_{k\ell} + t_\ell \leq T_\ell$, and $a_{k\ell} = 0$ otherwise.

Still another instance arises indirectly. Walker (1974) described a model for use by the New York City Fire Department to add a fleet of tower ladders to its ladder companies. The Rand Institute of New York City was asked to suggest which of 138 existing conventional aerial ladder locations should be replaced by tower ladders. The fire department's goal was to deploy as many tower ladders as possible while maintaining at least one conventional ladder (which is preferred in certain situations) as one of the two closest ladders to every alarm box in the city. For each alarm box, the two closest ladder houses are called a response pair. If there are K ladder houses that can accept a tower ladder and L alarm boxes, the implied optimization is:

$$\text{maximize } Q = \sum_k y_k$$
$$y$$

subject to

$$\sum_k a_{k\ell} y_k \leq 1 \qquad \text{for all } \ell$$

$$y_k = 0 \text{ or } 1 \qquad \text{for all } k.$$

Here $y_k = 1$ if a tower ladder should be located in house k and 0 otherwise, and $a_{k\ell} = 1$ if house k is one of the *two* ladder houses in response pair ℓ and 0 otherwise. Now set $y_k = 1 - z_k$ and observe that $\sum_k a_{k\ell}(1-z_k)$ $\leqslant 1$ can be written as $2 - \sum_k a_{k\ell}z_k \leqslant 1$. The problem can now be put into the form of problem (SC), where $z_k = 0$ if ladder house k *should* receive a tower ladder, and $z_k = 1$ otherwise.

Although many solution procedures have been proposed for problem (SC) we will discuss three that are particularly expedient.

Solution Procedures

(a) *Reduction Rules.*

The following rules are often effective in reducing problem (SC).

> R1. Redundant demand points may be ignored. If for some demand point ℓ there exists another demand point r such that $a_{k\ell} \geqslant a_{kr}$ for all k (the ℓth demand point is covered whenever the rth demand point is covered), the constraint for demand point ℓ may be eliminated.
>
> (For example, using R1 and letting $r = 3$, the constraints for demand points 2, 4, and 5 may be eliminated in Example 8.1.)

> R2. Redundant sites may be deleted. If for some site k there exists another site r such that $a_{r\ell} \geqslant a_{k\ell}$ for all ℓ (all demand points covered by site k are also covered by site r), the variable z_k may be eliminated.
>
> (Using R2, the variables z_1 and z_2 may be eliminated in Example 8.1.)

> R3. Essential sites may be chosen immediately. If for some demand point ℓ, $a_{r\ell} = 1$ whereas $a_{k\ell} = 0$ for $k \neq r$ (site r is the only satisfactory service point for demand point ℓ), z_r may be set equal to 1. Further, demand point ℓ and all other demand points j such that a_{rj} have thereby been covered and their associated constraints may be eliminated.
>
> (In Example 8.1 variable z_4 may be set equal to 1; the second, third, fourth, and fifth constraints may be eliminated using R3.)

Large problems may be reduced considerably (and often solved when the $a_{k\ell}$'s are based on real data) by successive application of R1 through R3. When reductions do not produce an optimal solution, the reduced problem may be solved using the following procedure.

(b) *Cutting Plane Procedure.*

Define the linear programming relaxation of problem (SC) as:

$$\text{minimize } \{q = \sum_k z_k \mid \sum_k a_{k\ell}z_k \geq 1, \text{ for all } \ell$$

$$\text{and } z_k \geq 0, \text{ for all } k\}.$$

(8.4)

Step 1 Append the cutting plane constraint:

$$\sum_k z_k \geq LB$$

(8.5)

to the constraints of problem (8.4) with $LB = 1$. (LB is a lower bound on the optimal value of problem (SC).) Solve the resulting linear programming problem. Let q_{LP} denote the optimal objective value. If the optimal solution is integer, stop. Otherwise, if q_{LP} is an integer, set $LB = q_{LP}$ and go to Step 3. If q_{LP} is not an integer, set LB to $[q_{LP}] + 1$, where $[q_{LP}]$ denotes the greatest integer in q_{LP}, and proceed to Step 2.

Step 2 Solve the resulting linear programming problem. If this solution is integer, stop. Otherwise, proceed to Step 3.

Step 3 Use a branch-and-bound analysis to determine whether an integer solution exists with value LB. If not, set $LB = LB + 1$ and return to Step 2.

Typically, problem (SC) is solved on the first pass through Step 2. If, however, as in the dynamic relocation of fire companies, problem (SC) is large and must be solved *quickly*, a heuristic procedure may be necessary. The following procedure is efficient and has proved effective.

(c) *Kolesar-Walker Heuristic.*

Step 0 Set $h = 1$ and $UB = +\infty$.

Step 1 Choose site k (set $z_k = 1$) such that site k covers ($a_{k\ell} = 1$) the hth largest number of demand points.

Step 2 Assuming site k has been chosen, eliminate all demand points ℓ for which $a_{k\ell} = 1$. If any demand points remain, set $z_k = 1$, which covers the greatest number (break ties arbitrarily) of remaining demand points, and repeat Step 2. Otherwise, go to Step 3.

Step 3 Let q equal the number of sites chosen. If $q < UB$, store the solution and set $UB = q$. If $h = H$, terminate; otherwise, set $h = h + 1$ and return to Step 1.

The value of H is arbitrary. Computational experience using H equal to about one-third of the number of candidate sites indicates optimal solutions are produced with high frequency; otherwise, near optimal solutions are generated.

Perils and Perspectives

At this point it is appropriate to warn of the perils of integer programming. Integer programming problems are often very hard to solve exactly. Hence, there is often a need for good heuristics to "solve" location models of realistic dimension posed as integer programs.

An opposing caveat must be registered, however. Using a heuristic cannot ensure that the solution generated is optimal. Efforts at sensitivity analysis and comparative analysis are therefore confounded. Typically individual computer runs of a model are designed to gain insights based on different scenarios. Consider the view expressed by Geoffrion (1976b):

> Not only does an optimizing capability enhance the value of most individual runs [for validation and gaining insights], but it also provides the opportunity to make valid *comparisons* between results of different runs. This is an extremely important consideration because the conclusions reached by a planning project typically rely far more heavily on comparisons between computer runs than on runs considered individually. With [heuristic programs] . . . one never knows whether different results are due to different inputs or to the vagaries of the computer program.

Solving problem (SC) to develop configurations of emergency service units represents only a first approximation in many applications. The model focuses on intradistrict responses and ignores design issues relating to interdistrict response. The model also lacks service capacity considerations and fails to incorporate the probabilistic nature of the service system. See Walker, Chaiken, and Ignall (1980) and Larson and Odoni (1981) for models addressing these issues.

Set-Covering Addenda

(a) *Set-Covering Under the Minimax Criterion.*

Let m be the optimal value of problem (SC). Frequently there are *several* feasible solutions that use only m facilities. Some of these "optimal" configurations may appear very unattractive to a decisionmaker. Secondary criteria must guide selection from among the alternate optima. The following formulation chooses m sites for facilities to minimize the *maximum* time (or distance) for all the demand points to their nearest located facility. Let I_m denote a set of m indices of chosen sites. The maximum response time is:

$$T(I_m) = \max_\ell\{\min_{k\in I_m}\{t_{k\ell}\}\}.$$

Let $I = \{1,2,...,K\}$. The problem is to:

$$\text{minimize } T(I_m) \text{ such that } I_m \text{ is a subset of } I. \tag{8.6}$$

Problem (8.6) is sometimes referred to as the m-center problem. To retain the requirement from problem (SC) that response neighborhood ℓ is assigned to at least one located facility within the threshold time (distance) T_ℓ, set $t_{k\ell} = M$, an arbitrarily large number for all k and ℓ such that $t_{k\ell} > T_\ell$. This implicitly enforces the constraints $\min_{k\in I_m}\{t_{k\ell}\} \leq T_\ell$, for all ℓ. An optimal solution to problem (8.6) is denoted by $\hat{I}_m$. The following algorithm determines $\hat{I}_m$.

Minieka's Algorithm

Step 0   Choose an initial I_m from I. (Perhaps start with an optimal solution to problem (SC) that located m facilities.)

Step 1   Calculate $T(I_m)$ and define $a_{k\ell} = 1$ if $t_{k\ell} < T(I_m)$, and $a_{k\ell} = 0$ otherwise. Then solve problem (SC) with *these* definitions. Let q^* denote the optimal objective value obtained.

Step 2   If $q^* > m$, or if problem (SC) is infeasible, terminate with $\hat{I}_m = I_m$. Otherwise, an improved solution is at hand. Update I_m as the set of indices k, such that $z_k^* = 1$ in the solution of problem (SC). If $q^* < m$, then a judiciously chosen set of $m - q^*$ additional indices may be used to complete the update. Return to Step 1.

The rationale for Step 1 is that if $q^* \leq m$, then the new set I_m yields a reduced value of $T(I_m)$, over the previous set. To see this, consider a typical constraint of problem (SC). Because $\sum_k a_{k\ell}z_k^* \geq 1$ is satisfied, some $z_k^* = 1$ for which $a_{k\ell} = 1$. This means the response time to demand point ℓ from chosen site k is less than the previous maximum response time. Because all such constraints must be satisfied, *all* demand points are closer to their nearest facility than the previous maximum response time. The number of zero values for the $a_{k\ell}$'s increases by at least one at each iteration. This guarantees finite convergence of the algorithm.

The following example illustrates the construction of a trade-off curve of m versus $T(\hat{I}_m)$ to show service coverage versus the number of facilities required.

Example 8.2   Figure 8.1 and Table 8.2 are from Scott (1971). The demand points, indicated as nodes on the graph, are candidate sites for

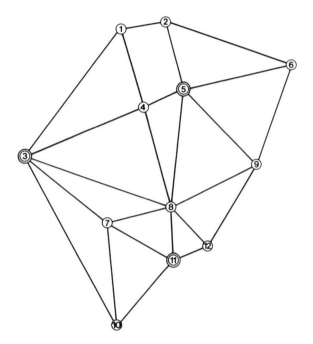

Figure 8.1 Geographical Configuration of Demand Points.
(Source: Scott, 1971, *Combinatorial Programming, Spatial Analysis and Planning,* Methuen, London.)

locating ($m = 3$) ambulance bases. No $t_{k\ell} \leq T_{\ell}$ constraints are used. An arbitrary initial choice, $I_3 = \{3,5,11\}$ with $T(I_3) = 43$, is indicated in the figure. Proceeding to Step 1 in the algorithm, the $a_{k\ell}$'s produced are

Table 8.2 Symmetric Shortest Distance Matrix (in kilometers).

						To						
	1	2	3	4	5	6	7	8	9	10	11	12
From												
1	0	17	57	29	43	66	91	67	81	116	86	87
2		0	74	42	26	49	92	68	64	117	87	88
3			0	46	62	102	38	56	91	69	66	76
4				0	16	56	62	38	54	87	57	58
5					0	40	66	42	38	91	61	62
6						0	97	73	38	116	86	72
7							0	24	59	37	28	42
8								0	35	49	19	20
9									0	78	48	34
10										0	30	44
11											0	14
12												0

Table 8.3 Constraint Coefficients $a_{k\ell}$ for Example 8.1.

k	\multicolumn{12}{c}{ℓ}

k	1	2	3	4	5	6	7	8	9	10	11	12
1	1	1	0	1	0	0	0	0	0	0	0	0
2	1	1	0	1	1	0	0	0	0	0	0	0
3	0	0	1	0	0	0	1	0	0	0	0	0
4	1	1	0	1	1	0	0	1	0	0	0	0
5	0	1	0	1	1	1	0	1	1	0	0	0
6	0	0	0	0	1	1	0	0	1	0	0	0
7	0	0	1	0	0	0	1	1	0	1	1	1
8	0	0	0	1	1	0	1	1	1	0	1	1
9	0	0	0	0	1	1	0	1	1	0	0	1
10	0	0	0	0	0	0	1	0	0	1	1	0
11	0	0	0	0	0	0	1	1	0	1	1	1
12	0	0	0	0	0	0	1	1	1	0	1	1

as given in Table 8.3. A zero-one linear programming algorithm found $q^* = 3$. Several alternate optima were reported. Of these, $z^* = (1,0,0,0,0,1,0,1,0,0,0)$ gave the least maximum response distance. At Step 2 then, I_3 is updated to $\{1,7,9\}$, for which $T(I_3) = 38$. Returning to Step 1, we find $q^* = 5$. The algorithm then terminates with an improvement of 5 over the initial I_3. A partially complete trade-off curve of maximum distance T versus m is given in Figure 8.2. Determining $\hat{I}_3 = \{1,7,9\}$ with $T(\hat{I}_3) = 38$, $\hat{I}_2 = \{5,7\}$, with $T(\hat{I}_2) = 43$, and $\hat{I}_1 = \{8\}$ with $T(\hat{I}) = 73$ provides the left endpoints of the steps in the graph. Evidently optimal solutions to problem (SC) defined by $38 \leqslant T_\ell < 43$, for all ℓ, require three facilities. The set $\hat{I}_3$ is a minimax choice from among those optimal solutions.

Figure 8.2 Example of a Trade-off Curve of Maximum Distance (T) Versus Number of Facilities (m) to Be Located.

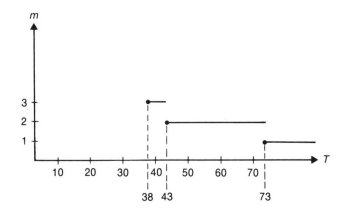

(b) *Maximal Covering with Mandatory Closeness Constraints.*

The minimax approach to choosing from alternate optima for problem (SC) ignores the *average* closeness of response neighborhoods to their nearest service center. The following approach seeks locations for m facilities to maximize coverage (population covered) within a desired time (distance) T. Let $T_\ell \geqslant T(\hat{I}_m)$ be a *required* upper bound on the response time (or distance) to RN_ℓ from the nearest service center location. Let w_ℓ be the population at (or weight for) RN_ℓ. Then solve the following problem:

$$\text{minimize} \sum_\ell w_\ell x_\ell \qquad (8.7)$$
$$\underset{x,z}{}$$

subject to

$$\sum_{k \in K1_\ell} z_k \geqslant 1 \qquad \text{for all } \ell \qquad (8.8)$$

$$\sum_k z_k = m \qquad (8.9)$$

$$\sum_{k \in K2_\ell} z_k + x_\ell \geqslant 1 \qquad \text{for all } \ell \qquad (8.10)$$

$$z_k, x_\ell = 0 \text{ or } 1 \qquad \text{for all } k, \ell, \qquad (8.11)$$

where:

$$z_k = \begin{cases} 1, \text{ if a facility is to be located at site } k \\ 0, \text{ otherwise} \end{cases}$$

$$x_\ell = \begin{cases} 1, \text{ if demand point } \ell \text{ is } not \text{ assigned to a facility, within } T \\ 0, \text{ otherwise} \end{cases}$$

$$K1_\ell = \{k \mid t_{k\ell} \leqslant T_\ell\} \text{ and } K2_\ell = \{k \mid t_{k\ell} \leqslant T\}.$$

The objective is to minimize the population *not* covered within T and, hence, to maximize the population *covered* within T. Constraints of type (8.10) force $x_\ell = 1$ if no facility is located within T of demand point ℓ. If any $z_k = 1$ for $k \in K1_\ell$, then due to the sense of the optimization, x_ℓ will be zero in the optimal solution. Constraint (8.9) restricts the number of service facilities to m, whereas constraints (8.8) enforce the mandatory closeness requirements. Limited computational experience indicates that solving the linear programming relaxation frequently produces integer solutions as required.

Example 8.3   Church and ReVelle (1974) provide the following example. Suppose there are 55 response neighborhoods for ambulance service and *all* must be covered within 15 minutes. Thus, all $T_\ell = 15$. Figure 8.3(a) indicates an optimal solution to problem (SC); $m = 5$ ambulance bases are needed. Solid-line partitions denote 15-minute coverage. Suppose a choice among alternate optima to problem (SC) is to be made on the

Population inside 10 201
Population outside 10 but inside 15 ... 439
Population outside 15 0

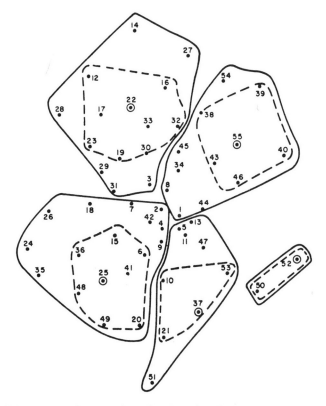

Figure 8.3(a)   A Location Set-Covering Solution for $T = 15$.
(Source: Church and ReVelle, 1974, in *Papers of the Regional Science Association* 32:101–118.)

basis of best coverage within $T = 10$ minutes. Dashed-line partitions indicate 10-minute coverage. Figure 8.3(b) shows an optimal solution to problem (8.7)-(8.11) using all $T_\ell = 15$, $T = 10$, and $m = 5$. The rectangular insert tallies the (improved) 10-minute coverage. Finally, Figure 8.3(c) shows an optimal solution ignoring the mandatory closeness constraints (8.8). The rectangular insert indicates a great improvement in 10-minute coverage. This benefit must be balanced against the cost of some of the population now lying outside 15-minute coverage.

(c) *The Weighted Set-Covering Problem.*

Fire station location analysis may include the goal of choosing from among the multiple optima for problem (SC) that alternative which utilizes the

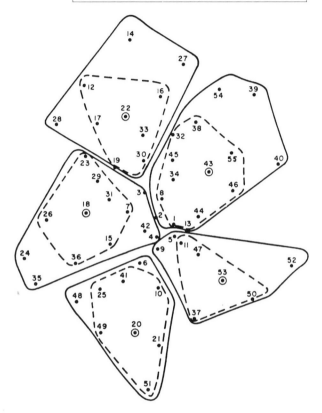

```
Population inside 10 . . . . . . . . . . . . . . .354
Population outside 10 but inside 15 . . .286
Population outside 15 . . . . . . . . . . . . . .  0
```

Figure 8.3(b)   An Optimal Solution to the Maximal Covering Location Problem with Mandatory Closeness Constraints.
(Source: Church and ReVelle, 1974, in *Papers of the Regional Science Association* 32:101–118.)

maximum number of existing fire stations. This avoids capital expenditures where possible and avoids the political "cost" of moving a fire station. A two-pass approach would be to first find the minimum number of fire stations necessary to satisfy the response time constraints. Then, holding this number constant, maximize the number of existing stations in the solution. Exercise 8.3a asks the reader to justify that the following hierarchical objective function combined with the response time covering constraints (8.2) achieves the intent in one step. The hierarchical objective is:

$$\text{minimize} \sum_{k=1}^{p} z_k + \sum_{k=p+1}^{k} (1 + w)z_k \qquad (8.12)$$

```
Population inside 10 . . . . . . . . . . . . . . 609
Population outside 10 but inside 15 . . . 19
Population outside 15 . . . . . . . . . . . . 12
```

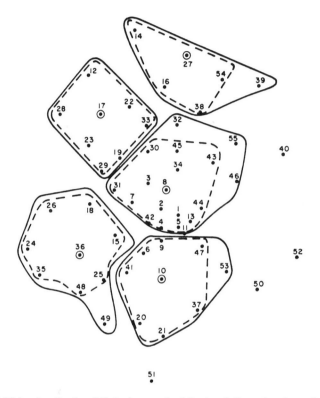

Figure 8.3(c)   An Optimal Solution to the Maximal Covering Location Problem Without Mandatory Closeness Constraints.
(Source: Church and ReVelle, 1974, in *Papers of the Regional Science Association* 32:101–118.)

where $0 < w < (1/L)$, L is the number of response neighborhoods, and the *existing* fire station locations are indexed from 1 to p.

This is an example of a *weighted* set-covering problem that replaces objective (8.1) with: minimize $\sum_k c_k z_k$, where $c_k > 0$. For problems beyond the computational reach of standard zero-one linear programming algorithms, specialized algorithms are necessary. Most integer programming texts contain a section on specialized approaches to solving set-covering problems.

8.2 SINGLE-STAGE, SINGLE-COMMODITY DISTRIBUTION SYSTEM DESIGN

Here we consider the design of a distribution system. Analysis begins with a single-stage distribution system for a single commodity (or standard product mix). The following notation is adopted:

D_ℓ = demand for the commodity in demand zone ℓ,

$t_{k\ell}$ = average unit cost of transporting the commodity from a facility at site k to demand zone ℓ,

v_k = average manufacturing and/or handling costs per unit of the commodity supplied from a facility at site k,

$y_{k\ell}$ = fraction of D_ℓ supplied from a facility at site k,

$c_{k\ell}$ = $(t_{k\ell} + v_k)D_\ell$,

f_k = non-negative fixed cost of operating and/or locating a facility at site k,

z_k = a zero-one variable equal to 1 if a facility is to be located at site k, and equal to 0 otherwise,

K = number of candidate sites for facility location,

L = number of demand zones.

The basic mixed-integer linear program is:

$$\text{minimize}_{y,z} \sum_k \sum_\ell c_{k\ell} y_{k\ell} + \sum_k f_k z_k \tag{8.13}$$

subject to

$$\sum_k y_{k\ell} = 1 \qquad \text{for all } \ell \tag{8.14}$$

$$z_k - y_{k\ell} \geq 0 \qquad \text{for all } k,\ell \tag{8.15}$$

$$\sum_k z_k \leq m \tag{8.16}$$

$$z_k, y_{k\ell} \geq 0 \qquad \text{for all } k,\ell \tag{8.17}$$

$$z_k = 0 \text{ or } 1 \qquad \text{for all } k. \tag{8.18}$$

Constraints (8.14) stipulate that each demand zone is to be totally supplied. Constraints (8.15) guarantee that no demand zone is to be supplied from a site not chosen for facility location. Constraint (8.16) states that no more than m facilities are to be located. The optimal number of facilities may be determined as an element of the solution by omitting constraint (8.16). As there are no capacity restrictions on the facilities, at optimality each demand zone will be supplied entirely from the most cost-effective located facility (ties can be broken arbitrarily). This may be fortuitous because many firms require single sourcing of customers to gain efficiencies and ensure good customer service.

Data Considerations

Individual demand points are often aggregated into demand zones in order to reduce L to a manageable number. The zones may be defined by postal zip codes and be represented by a key city with significant demand together with neighboring areas with relatively small associated demand. Using zip-coded zones facilitates linking customer demand records such as invoices with customer locations. However, more detailed demand data by geographical area are often required because billing address and delivery address frequently differ. This naturally leads to construction of an appropriate data base and anticipates development of a comprehensive distribution planning system as suggested by Geoffrion and Powers (1980).

This model does not require that transportation costs be proportional to distance, in contrast to the site-generating (continuous) models. As Geoffrion (1975) stated,

> One serious limitation of continuous location models is the impossibility of achieving a realistic cost structure for transportation flows. Consider, for instance, plant-to-warehouse flows. For any particular warehouse location one can look up the unit transportation rates by mode, weight, and product and combine these appropriately to achieve a suitable composite unit transportation cost. It is well known that such costs in many cases cannot be reliably predicted based on a knowledge of distance alone. Yet this is exactly what must be attempted in a continuous location model: all transportation costs must be expressed as explicit well-behaved functions of distance (no look-ups allowed).

In such cases continuous models might be used to generate sites based on approximate cost relationships. Site-selecting models can then be used to assist final locational decisions based on more accurate cost data (table look-ups allowed).

It is important to note that some source-destination combinations are not practicable in a given application. The associated assignment variables $y_{k\ell}$ can therefore be omitted from the model, together with the associated assignment constraints, $z_k - y_{k\ell} \geq 0$. This reduces data requirements *and* computational difficulty.

Most organizations have multiple products. When multiple products share manufacturing and distribution facilities, the single commodity treated here would be a "standard commodity bundle." This is a combination of the multiple products proportional to their respective demands. However, if the relative demands for the products differ significantly in different demand zones, or if some products are not supplied from some facilities, this approach breaks down. Treatment of the then necessary multi-commodity model is deferred until the succeeding section.

The model structure has been found useful in contexts other than distribution of a commodity. When $K = L$, and k and ℓ are the nodes of a graph, all $f_k = 0$ and equality is used in constraint (8.16), the problem becomes the so-called *m-median problem*. The m-median problem was encountered in Chapter 7 as problem (7.4). (Constraints such as $z_k \leq 1$ may need to be added when attempting to solve the m-median problem using its linear programming relaxation.)

Model Representation and Linear Programming Relaxation

A more compact problem formulation is possible. This is obtained by summing constraints (8.15) over ℓ to produce:

$$Lz_k - \sum_\ell y_{k\ell} \geq 0 \qquad \text{for all } k, \qquad (8.15a)$$

and substituting these for constraints (8.15). This reduces the number of constraints substantially. There is a pitfall here, however.

Let the linear programming relaxations (8.13) through (8.17) corresponding to using constraints (8.15) and (8.15a) be denoted as the "strong relaxation" (SR) and the "weak relaxation" (WR), respectively. Problem (SR) is a stronger relaxation than problem (WR), as every feasible solution to problem (SR) is also a feasible solution to problem (WR), but not conversely. Problem (SR) renders the original mixed-integer program and the linear programming relaxation more nearly the same. In fact, computational experience indicates that problem (SR) usually produces solutions that are integer in the z_k variables, as required by the omitted constraint (8.18). This is not true for problem (WR). In problem (SR), but not problem (WR), the z_k's corresponding to chosen sites will frequently have unit values, ie, the associated facility will supply some demand zones *entirely*, and, $z_k - y_{k\ell} \geq 0$ becomes $z_k - 1 \geq 0$ for those zones. The remaining z_k's will usually have zero value. If the solution to problem (SR) does not satisfy constraint (8.18), some form of branch-and-bound analysis would be required.

Example 8.4 Let Figure 8.1 represent a problem with 12 demand zones (population centers), which are the nodes of the graph. Let the demand zone locations be the only candidate sites for locating health outreach clinics. Let all $f_k = 0$ and define each $c_{k\ell}$ as the shortest travel distance (from Table 8.2) between nodes k and ℓ. Solving problem (SR) with constraint (8.16) written as an equality, and letting $m = 3$, produces the optimal integer solution indicated in Figure 8.1, with an objective value of 284 kilometers. The minimized average distance from a demand zone to the nearest clinic is therefore 23.67 kilometers. This m-median problem would likely be solved for different values of m to construct the trade-off curve for m versus minimized average travel distance.

The assignment constraints (8.15) expand rapidly in number as K and L increase. A computational expedient that saves required storage (and usually computational time) is to solve problem (SR) initially excluding constraints (8.15). Those assignment constraints violated by the solution are augmented to the problem and dual simplex iterations are performed to obtain the next solution. The process continues until no assignment constraints are violated.

Indeed, mechanics of the (revised) simplex method may be altered to represent constraints (8.15) implicitly when solving problem (SR). Striking computational efficiency is gained because $K \cdot L$ constraints may be represented implicitly. For example, problems with $K = L = 33$ require only $L + 1 = 34$ of 1123 constraints to be considered explicitly. The relatively minor computational burden of a great number of implicitly represented constraints (8.15) suggests that large-scale problems are within computational reach of the linear programming method.

We now turn to an in-depth discussion of a special purpose algorithm called DUALOC, which solves a classic location problem. We provide this detailed account because the algorithm has been found to be very efficient.

DUALOC

Problem (8.13)-(8.18), with the *omission* of constraint (8.16), is often referred to as the *simple plant location problem* (SPLP); "simple" implies the absence of plant capacity constraints. For ease of exposition we state problem (SPLP) here:

$$\underset{y,z}{\text{minimize}} \sum_k \sum_\ell c_{k\ell} + \sum f_k z_k \qquad (8.13)$$

subject to

$$\sum_k y_{k\ell} = 1 \qquad \text{for all } \ell \qquad (8.14)$$

$$z_k - y_{k\ell} \geqslant 0 \qquad \text{for all } k,\ell \qquad (8.15)$$

$$z_k, y_{k\ell} \geqslant 0 \qquad \text{for all } k,\ell \qquad (8.17)$$

$$z_k = 0 \text{ or } 1 \qquad \text{for all } k. \qquad (8.18)$$

DUALOC solves problem (SPLP). The efficiency of DUALOC derives from the high frequency of integer solutions derived from the linear programming relaxation (constraints (8.18) omitted) of problem (SPLP), denoted here by problem (SRS). However, the algorithm operates on the dual of problem (SRS) denoted problem (DSRS), given by:

$$\underset{v,w}{\text{maximize}} \sum_{\ell} v_{\ell}$$

subject to

$$\sum_{\ell} w_{k\ell} \leqslant f_k \qquad \text{for all } k$$

$$v_{\ell} - w_{k\ell} \leqslant c_{k\ell} \qquad \text{for all } k,\ell$$

$$w_{k\ell} \geqslant 0 \qquad \text{for all } k,\ell.$$

Let $v[\cdot]$ denote the optimal value of an optimization problem. Then evidently $v[\text{SPLP}] \geqslant v[\text{SRS}] = v[\text{DSRS}]$, where the equality holds by the strong duality property of linear programming. The idea, then, is to solve problem (DSRS) in order to have a lower bound on $v[\text{SPLP}]$.

A first attempt at solving problem (DSRS) is called dual ascent. Throughout the discussion, v_{ℓ} is to be evaluated as $\min_k\{c_{k\ell} + w_{k\ell}\}$. Let an assignment (k,ℓ) be called *admissible* if $v_{\ell} = c_{k\ell} + w_{k\ell}$. Dual ascent begins with all $w^0_{k\ell} = 0$ and attempts to increase the w's in order to increase the v's. (The superscript indicates the iteration number.) To illustrate the method, consider the following example employed in Erlenkotter (1978). Cost data are from Khumawala (1972).

Example 8.5a The M's represent large positive numbers and indicate prohibited assignments. Let the vector (f_k) of fixed costs be (100, 70, 60, 110, 80). Then $(v^0_{\ell}) = (\min_k\{c_{k\ell}\}) = (120, 150, 100, 150, 50, 120, 110, 120)$. The procedure cycles through the v_{ℓ}'s, attempting to increase each to the next higher value of $c_{k\ell}$. To maintain feasibility in problem (DSRS),

Table 8.4 Total Demand Cost $c_{k\ell}$ for an Instance of Problem (SPLP).

	ℓ							
k	1	2	3	4	5	6	7	8
1	120	180	100	M	60	M	180	M
2	210	M	150	240	55	210	110	165
3	180	190	110	195	50	M	M	195
4	210	190	150	180	65	120	160	120
5	170	150	110	150	70	195	200	M

$w_{k\ell}$'s corresponding to admissible assignments must be increased simultaneously. If the $\sum_\ell w_{k\ell} \leqslant f_k$ constraint blocks the increase of v_ℓ to the next highest $c_{k\ell}$, then v_ℓ is increased as much as the constraint allows.

To specify the procedure formally, reindex the $c_{k\ell}$ for each ℓ in nondecreasing order as c_ℓ^k, $k = 1,...,K$, and include a cost parameter $c_\ell^{K+1} = +\infty$. Let L^+ be the index set $\{1,2,...,L\}$. Then observe that for any feasible choice of v_ℓ we can set $w_{k\ell} = \max\{0, v_\ell - c_{k\ell}\}$. This allows the $w_{k\ell}$'s to remain implicit in the following procedure.

Dual Ascent Procedure

Step 1 Set $(v_\ell) = (c_\ell^1)$, $(s_k) = (f_k - \sum_\ell \max\{0, v_\ell - c_{k\ell}\})$, and $k(\ell) = 2$.

Step 2 Initialize $\ell = 1$ and $\delta = 0$.

Step 3 If $\ell \notin L^+$, go to Step 7.

Step 4 Set $\Delta_\ell = \min_k \{s_k | v_\ell - c_{k\ell} \geqslant 0\}$.

Step 5 If $\Delta_\ell > c_\ell^{k(\ell)} - v_\ell$, set $\Delta_\ell = c_\ell^{k(\ell)} - v_\ell$ and $\delta = 1$. Increment $k(\ell)$ by 1.

Step 6 Decrease s_k by Δ_ℓ for each k with $v_\ell - c_{k\ell} \geqslant 0$; then increase v_ℓ by Δ_ℓ.

Step 7 If $\ell \neq L^+$, increment ℓ by 1 and return to Step 3.

Step 8 If $\delta = 1$, return to Step 2; otherwise, terminate the procedure.

At the end of the first cycle we have $(v_\ell^1) = (170, 180, 110, 180, 55, 195, 160, 155)$. The slacks in the potentially blocking constraints are $(s_k^1) = (40, 20, 55, 0, 20)$. All v's have been increased to the next higher values of $c_{k\ell}$, respectively, except $v_8^1 = 155$, which is blocked by $s_4^1 = 0$.

After another cycle we have $(v_\ell^2) = (180, 190, 110, 180, 60, 195, 160, 155)$, whereas $(s_k^2) = (20, 15, 50, 0, 0)$. The only unblocked v_ℓ is v_5^2. We find $(v_\ell^3) = (180, 190, 110, 180, 65, 195, 160, 155)$, with $(s_k^3) = (15, 10, 45, 0, 0)$, and the dual ascent procedure terminates with $\sum_\ell v_\ell^3 = 1235$.

The question of whether v^3 is optimal in problem (DSRS) must now be investigated. To do this we derive a feasible (integer) solution to problem (SRS), and hence to problem (SPLP), and check optimality via linear programming optimality conditions. Let (v_ℓ^+) be the solution vector generated by the dual ascent procedure. Let

$$K^+ = \{k \mid \sum_\ell \max\{0, v_\ell^+ - c_{k\ell}\} = f_k\}$$

and let

$c_\ell^+ = c_{k^+(\ell),\ell} = \min_{k\epsilon K^+} c_{k\ell}$, for all ℓ. Then for all k and ℓ, let:

$$z_k^+ = \begin{cases} 1, & \text{for } k\epsilon K^+ \\ 0 & \text{otherwise,} \end{cases} \qquad y_{k\ell}^+ = \begin{cases} 1, & k\epsilon k^+(\ell) \\ 0 & \text{otherwise.} \end{cases}$$

Ties in the min operation defining c_ℓ^+ are broken arbitrarily. The solutions (z^+,y^+) and (v^+,w^+) are feasible for problem (SRS) and problem (DSRS), respectively. They are optimal for the respective problems if they satisfy the following primal-dual complementary slackness conditions of linear programming:

$$(c_{k\ell} + w_{k\ell} - v_\ell)\, y_{k\ell} = 0 \qquad \text{for all } k,\ell \qquad (8.19)$$

$$(f_k - \sum_\ell w_{k\ell})\, z_k = 0 \qquad \text{for all } k \qquad (8.20)$$

$$(z_k - y_{k\ell})\, w_{k\ell} = 0 \qquad \text{for all } k,\ell. \qquad (8.21)$$

Now $y_{k\ell}^+ = 1$ implies (k,ℓ) is an admissible assignment, ie, $(c_{k\ell} + w_{k\ell}^+ - v_\ell^+) = 0$. Also $z_k^+ = 1$ implies $k\epsilon K^+$, ie, $(f_k - \sum_\ell w_{k\ell}^+) = 0$. This means the first two conditions are automatically satisfied due to the methods used to determine (v^+,w^+) and (z^+,y^+). If the final condition is satisfied, then the integer solution (z^+,y^+) is not only optimal for problem (SRS), but also for problem (SPLP).

In the example at hand we find $K^+ = \{4,5\}$. The indicated solution to problem (SRS) is $z_4^+ = z_5^+ = 1$ and $y_{51}^+ = y_{52}^+ = y_{53}^+ = y_{54}^+ = y_{45}^+ = y_{46}^+ = y_{47}^+ = y_{48}^+ = 1$, with all other variables at zero level. The objective value of this solution is 1235. We indeed find that condition (8.21) is satisfied, and so we have found an optimal solution to problem (SRS) *and* to problem (SPLP).

A violation of condition (8.21) occurs if, say, for some $\ell = \ell'$, more than one $k\epsilon K^+$ has $w_{k\ell'}^+ > 0$, because exactly one $y_{k\ell'}^+$ is equal to one. In this case a so-called dual adjustment procedure is initiated to attempt to close the gap between the integer primal and the linear programming dual objective values by reducing these violations. Specifically, reducing $v_{\ell'}$ creates slack in at least two binding constraints $v_{\ell'}^+ - w_{k\ell'}^+ \leq c_{k\ell'}$ as all positive $w_{k\ell}^+$ appear in admissible assignments only.

Example 8.5b To elaborate, let $(f_k) = (200, 200, 200, 400, 300)$. The initial pass through dual ascent terminates with $(v_\ell^1) = (210, 190, 150, 240, 65, 285, 195, 195)$, $(s_k^1) = (30, 0, 70, 65, 0)$, and $\sum_\ell v_\ell^1 = 1530$. For $K^+ = \{2,5\}$ the primal objective value is 1605. However, $v_6^1 > c_{26} > c_{56}$, so the associated primal solution violates condition (8.21). An adjustment in the value of v_6^1 is required. This leads to the dual-adjustment procedure. We refer the interested reader to Erlenkotter (1978) for details of the remainder of DUALOC.

Generating Trade-off Curves

Optimal solutions are often desired for a range of the number of facilities located to examine the trade-off with cost. These solutions can be generated conveniently by obtaining optimal solutions to problem (SPLP) using DUALOC for various levels of a surcharge added uniformly to the fixed charges f_k. This approach may not generate solutions for all numbers of facilities, however. To see this let problem (SPLP;m) denote problem (8.13)-(8.18), with constraint (8.16) *included* in *equality* form.

Let s_m denote a surcharge constant that, when added to each f_k, causes problem (SPLP) (in which constraint (8.16) is *excluded*) to have an optimal solution with exactly m sites chosen for facility location. Then s_m must satisfy:

$$v[\text{SPLP};m] + ms_m \leq v[\text{SPLP};m+1] + (m+1)s_m$$

and:

$$v[\text{SPLP};m] + ms_m \leq v[\text{SPLP};m-1] + (m-1)s_m.$$

This means every surcharge constant s_m satisfying:

$$\underline{s}_m = v[\text{SPLP};m] - v[\text{SPLP};m+1] < s_m$$

$$< v[\text{SPLP};m-1] - v[\text{SPLP};m] = \bar{s}_m$$

will cause problem (SPLP) to have an optimal solution with exactly m facilities located. But it is possible that $\underline{s} > \bar{s}_m$, in which case no such s_m exists.

Cost Structures and Capacity Restrictions

The distribution model (8.13)-(8.18) enables piecewise-linear representations of facility cost curves. Three cases are considered.

Case 1

Figure 8.4 represents the case for which $c_{k\ell} = (t_{k\ell} + v_k)D_\ell$. The annual throughput of a facility at site k is $\sum_\ell y_{k\ell}D_\ell$, and the annual throughput cost is $v_k \sum_\ell D_\ell y_{k\ell} + f_k$.

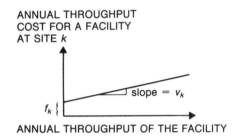

Figure 8.4 Linear Approximation of Facility Cost.

Case 2

The case in Figure 8.5 can be conveniently handled by associating z_k^1 and z_k^2, respectively, with the solid segments in Figure 8.5 representing two versions of a potential facility at site k. An automatic economic consequence is that the optimal solution will have at most one of z_k^1 or z_k^2 at unit value. The throughput cost will therefore be measured along the appropriate linear segment if a facility is located at the site.

Case 3

Case 3 emerges when capacity restrictions are included in the model. When total throughput at site k must be between an upper limit of $\bar{V}_k$ and a lower limit of $\underline{V}_k$ if a facility is located at the site, the model (omitting constraint 8.16) is generalized to:

$$\underset{y,z}{\text{minimize}} \sum_k \sum_\ell c_{k\ell} y_{k\ell} + \sum_\ell f_k z_k \qquad (8.22)$$

Figure 8.5 Piecewise-Linear Approximation of Facility Cost Under Economies-of-Scale.

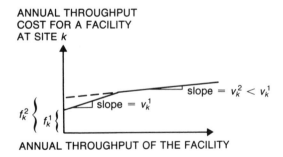

subject to

$$\sum_k y_{k\ell} = 1 \qquad \text{for all } \ell \qquad (8.23)$$

$$\underline{V}_k z_k \leqslant \sum_\ell D_\ell y_{k\ell} \leqslant \bar{V}_k z_k \qquad \text{for all } k \qquad (8.24)$$

$$0 \leqslant y_{k\ell} \leqslant 1 \qquad \text{for all } k,\ell \qquad (8.25)$$

$$z_k = 0 \text{ or } 1 \qquad \text{for all } k. \qquad (8.26)$$

Denote this capacitated plant location problem formulation as problem (CPLP). The lower bound on throughput can be used to preclude a facility at site k from operating below an acceptable level of activity. Bounds on facility size can also be used to restrict throughput to a range over which the cost structure is adequately modeled by a straight line, as in Figure 8.6. When f_k is used in this way, traditional accounting definitions of fixed cost no longer apply directly.

Using problem (CPLP), several alternative size ranges can be considered for a facility. For example, piecewise-linear representation of the cost function for small, medium, and large operational alternatives would require three pieces, each with an associated variable z_k and particularized f_k and v_k parameters. Size ranges would be controlled by the $\underline{V}_k$ and $\bar{V}_k$ bounds. If the entire range is characterized by economies-of-scale, at most one of the alternative versions of the facility would be chosen for operation at a given site. There may be diseconomies-of-scale, such as portrayed in Figure 8.6 for high throughput levels. Or there may be jump

Figure 8.6 Linear Approximation of the Classic S-Shaped Facility Cost Curve. (Reprinted by permission of Harvard Business Review. An exhibit from "Better distribution planning with computer models" by A.M. Geoffrion, (July–August 1976), p. 92 ©1976 by the President and Fellows of Harvard College; all rights reserved.)

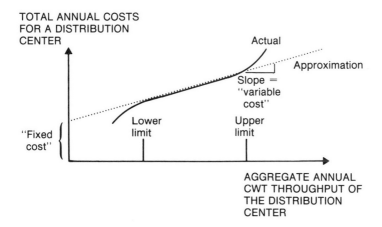

discontinuities corresponding to possible expansion projects at an existing facility ($z_k = 1$ is included in the model for the existing facility). Piece-wise-linear approximation of these cost structures requires additional constraints such as $z_1 + z_2 + \ldots + z_n \leq 1$ to ensure that, at most, one of the n versions of the facility could be chosen for use at a given site.

Another significant modeling issue is the extent to which demand points should be aggregated in defining the demand zones. The following section presents an a priori upper bound on the degree of suboptimality induced in problem (CPLP) by any given demand point aggregation.

Demand Point Aggregation Versus Suboptimality

Let L_1 be the index set of demand points to be aggregated. The aggregation will be assumed to be pro rata by demand, which means:

$$\text{for each } k, \text{ the } y_{k\ell}\text{'s must be the same for all } \ell \epsilon L_1. \qquad (8.27)$$

An implied qualification is that:

$$\text{for each } \ell \epsilon L_1, \text{ the same } k\ell \text{ links have been included} \qquad (8.28)$$
$$\text{in the model.}$$

The sought after benefit of condition (8.27) is that a number of variables and constraints are eliminated from the model. The model structure remains unchanged; however, there are $|L_1|$-1 fewer ℓ indices in the model, where $|L_1|$ denotes the number of elements of the set L_1. The reduced problem size is purchased at the price of model accuracy, ie, aggregation results in a possibly suboptimal solution in the full problem. The following property places an a priori bound on that price.

Property 8.1 [Customer aggregation error bound]. Let L_1 be any subset of demand point indices satisfying qualification (8.28). Then:

$$v[\text{CPLP}] \leq v[\text{CPLP}; (8.27)] \leq v[\text{CPLP}] + \epsilon_1 \qquad (8.29)$$

$$\text{where } \epsilon_1 \equiv \sum_{\ell \epsilon L_1} \max_k \left\{ \frac{D_\ell \sum_{\ell' \epsilon L_1} c_{k\ell'}}{\sum_{\ell' \epsilon L_1} D_{\ell'}} - c_{k\ell} \right\},$$

and $v[\text{CPLP}; (8.27)]$ denotes the optimal value of problem (CPLP) with condition (8.27) appended. Moreover, if $(\tilde{y}, \tilde{z})$ is feasible for problem (CPLP) augmented by condition (8.27) and is within ϵ of $v[\text{CPLP}; (8.27)]$, then $(\tilde{y}, \tilde{z})$ is feasible for problem (CPLP) and is within $\epsilon + \epsilon_1$ of $v[\text{CPLP}]$. That is, if $(\tilde{y}, \tilde{z})$ is ϵ-optimal for the aggregated problem, then $(\tilde{y}, \tilde{z})$ is $(\epsilon + \epsilon_1)$-optimal for the full problem.

The appeal of Property 8.1 is that ϵ_1 is calculated from problem data. Hence, no optimization problem need be solved. Potential reduction in model accuracy can therefore be determined a priori for any proposed customer aggregation defined by L_1.

Example 8.6   The error bound is useful even if no facility location decisions are to be made. Taking all $f_k = 0$ and all $\underline{V}_k = 0$, problem (CPLP) reduces to a classical transportation problem because all z_k's are defined equal to 1 (if a facility is operated at site k) or 0 (if no facility is operated at site k). We will use this simplified version of the problem for exposition. The company in question has facilities in Seattle (SEA), Los Angeles (LA), and Houston (HOU), with customers in Dallas (DAL), Chicago (CHI), Atlanta (ATL), Pittsburgh (PIT), New York (NY), and Boston (BOS). An aggregation of northeastern customers is proposed. Approximate transportation costs would have been determined from regression relationships of cost versus distance. Distance estimates may be obtained from empirical distance functions (see Chapter 10) knowing only the locational coordinates of the customers and the facilities. More accurate cost estimates would then be obtained when solving the smaller (aggregated) problem. Table 8.5 gives the *full* transportation problem data using the approximate transportation costs ($t_{k\ell}$'s) measured as dollars/cwt/1000 kilometers, where cwt is gross shipping hundredweight. Supplies and demands are in units of 1000 cwt. The optimal solution, indicated parenthetically, is to be ignored initially.

If all northeastern customers are to be aggregated, the aggregated problem becomes that portrayed in Table 8.6. The unit transportation costs to PIT/NY/BOS are weighted averages, weighted pro rata by demand, and $D_{\text{PIT/NY/BOS}} = D_{\text{PIT}} + D_{\text{NY}} + D_{\text{BOS}} = 35$ (units of 1000 cwt).

For example, $t_{\text{SEA,PIT/NY/BOS}} = (10/35)(2.465) + (15/35)(2.815) + (10/35)(2.976) = 2.761$ dollars/cwt. This method of aggregation honors the requirement of condition (8.27). As self-demonstrated in Exercise 8.13, the a priori error bound is $\epsilon_{\text{PIT/NY/BOS}} = \$500$. If this is too high relative

Table 8.5   Full Transportation Problem (Optimal Solution Indicated; Optimal Value = \$116,005).

	DAL	CHI	ATL	PIT	NY	BOS	Supplies
SEA	2.078	2.013	2.618	2.465	2.815	2.976	
		(10)				(5)	15
LA	1.387	2.054	2.182	2.426	2.786	2.960	
	(10)			(10)		(5)	25
HOU	0.243	1.067	0.789	1.313	1.608	1.804	
			(5)		(15)		20
Demands	10	10	5	10	15	10	

Table 8.6 First Proposed Aggregation (Optimal Solution Indicated; Optimal Value = $116,445).

	DAL	CHI	ATL	PIT/NY/BOS	Supplies
SEA	2.078	2.013	2.618	2.761	
		(10)		(5)	15
LA	1.387	2.054	2.182	2.733	
	(10)			(15)	25
HOU	0.243	1.067	0.789	1.580	
			(5)	(15)	20
Demands	10	10	5	35	

to the expected magnitude of total transportation costs, another aggregation must be sought. Table 8.7 characterizes an alternative.

Setting $L_I = \{NY, BOS\}$ and using $c_{k\ell} = t_{k\ell}D_\ell$,

$$\epsilon_{NY/BOS} = \max_{k=1,2,3} \left\{ \frac{D_{NY}(t_{k,NY}D_{NY} + t_{k,BOS}D_{BOS})}{D_{NY} + D_{BOS}} - t_{k,NY}D_{NY} \right\}$$

$$+ \max_{k=1,2,3} \left\{ \frac{D_{BOS}(t_{k,NY}D_{NY} + t_{k,BOS}D_{BOS})}{D_{NY} + D_{BOS}} - t_{k,BOS}D_{BOS} \right\}$$

$$= 15,000 \max\{(2.879 - 2.815), (2.856 - 2.786), (1.686 - 1.608)\}$$

$$+ 10,000 \max\{(2.879 - 2.976), (2.856 - 2.960), (1.686 - 1.804)\}$$

upon factoring D_{NY} and D_{BOS} out of the respective braces. Thus, $\epsilon_{NY/BOS}$ = 15,000(0.078) + 10,000(−0.097) = $200 for this aggregation. For the two proposed aggregations, Property 8.1 is exemplified by the following:

v[full problem] ≤ v[PIT/NY/BOS aggregation] ≤ v[full problem] + $\epsilon_{PIT/NY/BOS}$,

ie, 116,005 ≤ 116,445 ≤ 116,505, and

v[full problem] ≤ v[NY/BOS aggregation] ≤ v[full problem] + $\epsilon_{NY/BOS}$,

ie, 116,005 ≤ 116,170 ≤ 116,205.

Table 8.7 Second Proposed Aggregation (Optimal Solution Indicated; Optimal Value = $116,170).

	DAL	CHI	ATL	PIT	NY/BOS	Supplies
SEA	2.078	2.013	2.618	2.465	2.879	
		(10)			(5)	15
LA	1.387	2.054	2.182	2.426	2.856	
	(10)			(10)	(5)	25
HOU	0.243	1.067	0.789	1.313	1.686	
			(5)		(15)	20
Demands	10	10	5	10	25	

Owing to the nature of the pro rata demand aggregation scheme, an optimal solution of an aggregated model can be disaggregated into a feasible solution to the full problem with the *same cost* as the optimal value of the aggregated problem. In the second aggregation the SEA→NY/BOS flow of 5000 cwt has an associated cost of 5000(2.879) = 5000[(15/25)2.815 + (10/25)2.976]. This flow would be disaggregated into (15/25)5000 cwt to New York and (10/25)5000 cwt to Boston with the identical cost in the full problem. Similar results hold for disaggregating the remaining flows to NY/BOS. The value of the disaggregated solution is guaranteed to be within $200 of optimality. Indeed, the suboptimality is actually only $116,170 − $116,005 = $165.

Considering H sequential applications of Property 8.1 leads to its extension given below.

Property 8.2 [*Extended customer aggregation error bound*]. *Let $L_1, L_2, ..., L_H$, be disjoint subsets of demand point indices such that each subset L_h individually satisfies qualification (8.28). Then:*

if for $h = 1, ..., H$ and all k, the $y_{k\ell}$'s are identical

over all $\ell \epsilon L_h$, $\quad\quad\quad\quad\quad\quad\quad\quad\quad\quad\quad$ (8.30)

$$v[\text{CPLP}] \leqslant v[\text{CPLP}; (8.30)] \leqslant v[\text{CPLP}] + \sum_{h=1}^{H} \epsilon_h.$$

Modeling Philosophy

Solving the linear programming relaxation of problem (CPLP) augmented by the constraints $0 \leqslant z_k \leqslant 1$, for all k, will generally produce fractional values for the z_k variables if any throughput constraints are binding. The convenience of using linear programming directly as a solution approach is lost. However, Kuehn and Hamburger (1963) issued an early caveat: "Care must also be taken to avoid the chase for optimal solutions to simple problems and thereby miss the actual problem of business—the solution of large-scale problems containing many customers buying various mixes of a full product line, many potential warehouse sites, alternate warehouse types with different cost structures, several factories and, perhaps, a number of potential factory sites." The following section presents a computationally practicable approach for treating the complex problem described in the caveat.

8.3 TWO-STAGE, MULTI-COMMODITY DISTRIBUTION SYSTEM DESIGN

A large food products company is engaged in distribution planning [Geoffrion and Graves (1974)], and a computer-based model is adopted to plan the configuration and flow aspects of the distribution system design for the next five years. Hundreds of products must be aggregated into several product groups or "standard commodity bundles." Examples of groupings are bottled cooking oil, packaged shortenings, and catsup. These commodity bundles, hereafter called commodities, are produced at several existent plants with known production capacities (cwt/year). Not every plant can produce every group. There is a known demand for each of the commodities at each of several demand zones (customer aggregations). Commodities may be shipped through distribution centers (DCs). Each demand zone is to be assigned uniquely to a DC. This feature has accounting, marketing, and transportation advantages. There may be upper and lower bounds on the throughput of the DCs. There is a list of candidate sites for DCs developed from current locations, competitor DC locations, major demand centers, hub cities, or sites generated from continuous models. There is a fixed cost of establishing and operating a DC as well as a variable throughput cost. The transportation system is characterized by transportation costs that are linear in the amount shipped.

The primary design questions are: which DC sites to use, what throughput to plan for at each DC, what demand zones to assign to each DC, and what pattern of flows should there be for each commodity. The distribution system is to be designed to satisfy customer demand at minimum total cost while honoring plant capacity constraints, DC throughput bounds, and any additional constraints on the system configuration. The model presumes that all plants are previously established. However, the potential exists for including additional zero-one variables to select among alternative plant sites for some or all plants as well as among plant capacity expansion projects. The reader is encouraged to consider these possibilities as the narrative unfolds. The following symbols are used throughout this section:

i = index for commodities,

j = index for plants (or, more generally, procurement zones),

k = index for DC candidate sites,

ℓ = index for demand zones,

S_{ij} = supply (production capacity) of commodity i at plant j (cwt/year),

$D_{i\ell}$ = demand for commodity i in demand zone ℓ (cwt/year),

$\underline{V}_k, \bar{V}_k$ = minimum, maximum allowed total annual throughput for a DC at site k (cwt/year),

f_k = fixed cost of establishing a DC at site k (dollars/year),

v_k = average variable unit cost of throughput for a DC at site k (dollars/cwt),

$c_{ijk\ell}$ = average unit cost of producing and shipping commodity i from plant j through a DC at site k to demand zone ℓ (dollars/cwt),

$x_{ijk\ell}$ = amount of commodity i shipped from plant j through a DC at site k to demand zone ℓ (cwt),

$y_{k\ell}$ = a zero-one variable equal to 1 if a DC at site k serves demand zone ℓ and equal to 0 otherwise,

z_k = a zero-one variable equal to 1 if a DC is established at site k, and equal to 0 otherwise.

The distribution design model denoted problem (DD) is given by:

$$\text{minimize}_{x,y,z} \sum_i \sum_j \sum_k \sum_\ell c_{ijk\ell} x_{ijk\ell} + \sum_k \left(f_k z_k + v_k \sum_i \sum_\ell D_{i\ell} y_{k\ell} \right) \qquad (8.31)$$

subject to

$$\sum_k \sum_\ell x_{ijk\ell} \leq S_{ij} \qquad \text{for all } i,j \qquad (8.32)$$

$$\sum_j x_{ijk\ell} = D_{i\ell} y_{k\ell} \qquad \text{for all } i,k,\ell \qquad (8.33)$$

$$\sum_k y_{k\ell} = 1 \qquad \text{for all } \ell \qquad (8.34)$$

$$\underline{V}_k z_k \leq \sum_i \sum_\ell D_{i\ell} y_{k\ell} \leq \bar{V}_k z_k \qquad \text{for all } k \qquad (8.35)$$

linear configuration constraints on y's and/or z's   (8.36)

$$x_{ijk\ell} \geq 0, \ y_{k\ell}, z_k = 0 \text{ or } 1 \qquad \text{for all } i,j,k,\ell. \qquad (8.37)$$

Summations are understood to extend only over practicable combinations of indices, ie, certain ij links will be omitted if plant j doesn't produce commodity i and certain jk and $k\ell$ links will be clearly uneconomical. There may only be a small subset of potential DC sites for supplying any given demand zone. The omitted subscript combinations reduce the number of variables actually present in the model. The quadruple subscripting scheme used for the flow variables $x_{ijk\ell}$ preserves the identity of the origin of commodities. This permits imposition of restrictions on certain $jk\ell$ routes for perishable commodities by omitting the associated $x_{ijk\ell}$ variables. The quadruple subscripting scheme is also useful when a commodity price depends on the originating plant or when some transportation costs are determined on the basis of direct plant-to-customer shipments even though a stopover is made at the assigned DC, a "storage-in-transit" privilege. If certain demand zones are actually to be supplied directly from plants, a dummy DC site, say, k_o, can be included. The associated z_{k_o} and $y_{k_o\ell}$'s would be set to 1 and the $c_{ijk_o\ell}$'s would be specified appropriately.

The linear configuration constraints (8.36) can be used as a technical device to select among projects for expansion or contraction of capacity at existing DCs, or to ensure that, at most, one version of a DC will be opened at a given site. Discussions with management uncovered the need to include service level constraints such as $(\sum_k \sum_\ell t_{ik\ell} D_{i\ell} y_{k\ell}) / \sum_\ell D_{i\ell} \leqslant T_i$, where $t_{ik\ell}$ is the average time to deliver an order for commodity i to demand zone ℓ from a DC at site k, and T_i is an upper bound on average delivery time for commodity i. The latter concern can also be addressed by assigning $y_{k^+\ell}$ a comparatively large objective function coefficient whenever site k^+ is unacceptably distant from demand zone ℓ.

Data Considerations

The unit production cost (dollars/cwt) component of $c_{ijk\ell}$ measures the real cash flow change for changing the output rate of commodity i at plant j. The directly assignable portion of production cost can be derived from an existing standard cost accounting system. Actual, rather than standard, raw material costs should be used to measure the influence of regional raw material prices on location. The overhead portion requires estimation of variable components of indirect cost accounts (such as energy, indirect labor, management, maintenance, etc.) and the allocation of the variable component to the given commodity.

The distribution cost (dollars/cwt) component of $c_{ijk\ell}$ has two parts. For inbound $j \rightarrow k$ transportation links, the transportation rate may adequately be modeled as a weighted average reflecting the mix of modes and shipment sizes judged most likely to be used. (Pipeline inventory costs might be included.) For $k \rightarrow \ell$ links to large volume demand zones, unit transportation rates are developed by dividing estimated total annual freight cost by the volume that must flow on the link. This flow is known because $D_{i\ell}$ is known and demand zones must be supplied entirely from a single DC. If shipment is by truck delivering to small volume demand zones on a delivery tour, distribution cost for $k \rightarrow \ell$ links must be approximated. The following has been applied by Mairs, Wakefield, Johnson, and Spielberg (1978) to give quick and reasonably accurate estimates:

$$t_{ik\ell} = \frac{(\text{constant}) \times d_{k\ell} \times m_k \times o_{k\ell} \times r_{k\ell}}{s_k \times u_\ell \times p_i}, \text{ where}$$

$d_{k\ell}$ = travel distance from site k to demand zone ℓ,
m_k = freight cost per mile from site k,
s_k = factor for trailer size, depending on site k,
u_ℓ = factor for trailer utilization, depending on the destination,
p_i = density factor in cwt/cubic feet,
$o_{k\ell}$ = one-way trip factor—normally is 2 to reflect two-way trip; otherwise, less than 2 if the trip includes pickup of supplies from plant at an interchange point,
$r_{k\ell}$ = circuit cost factor, approximated by $2.38 - 0.18 \log_e(d_{k\ell})$, which reflects the fact that demand zone ℓ is supplied on delivery route.

The DC variable cost v_k (dollars/cwt) includes handling, inventory costs, and other variable operating expenses. The DC fixed cost f_k (dollars/year) captures amortized capital costs and fixed components of operating costs. However, as in Figure 8.6, f_k may function only to provide a straight-line approximation of DC throughput cost over a range of interest.

Solution by Benders Decomposition

The distribution design problem is a large-scale mixed-integer programming problem for this application. There are 17 product groups (commodities), 14 plants, 45 DC sites, and 121 demand zones. The solution approach to be presented decomposes the problem. The approach capitalizes on the property that when the zero-one variables y and z are held fixed at feasible values, the flow partition of the problem separates into independent classical transportation problems, one for each commodity. To see this, consider the flow partition of the problem that involves all the transportation variables and the temporarily held fixed y variables, say $y_{k\ell}^H$. The problem becomes:

$$\text{minimize } \sum_i \sum_j \sum_k \sum_\ell c_{ijk\ell} x_{ijk\ell}$$
$$x$$

subject to $\qquad\qquad\qquad\qquad\qquad\qquad\qquad$ (8.38)

$$\sum_k \sum_\ell x_{ijk\ell} \leqslant S_{ij} \qquad \text{for all } i,j$$

$$\sum_j x_{ijk\ell} = D_{i\ell} y_{k\ell}^H \qquad \text{for all } i,k,\ell$$

$$x_{ijk\ell} \geqslant 0 \qquad \text{for all } i,j,k,\ell.$$

Define $\bar{k}(\ell)$ as the k index value such that $y_{k\ell}^H = 1$ for a particular value of the ℓ index. In words, $\bar{k}(\ell)$ is the DC that serves demand zone ℓ. Since $\bar{k}(\ell)$ is unique by constraint (8.34), $x_{ijk\ell} = 0$ for all $ijk\ell$ with $k \neq \bar{k}(\ell)$. These facts provide the basis for stating the transportation problem for the ith commodity as:

$$\text{minimize } \sum_j \sum_\ell c_{ij\bar{k}(\ell)\ell} x_{ij\bar{k}(\ell)\ell}$$
$$x$$

subject to $\qquad\qquad\qquad\qquad\qquad\qquad\qquad$ (8.39)

$$\sum_\ell x_{ij\bar{k}(\ell)\ell} \leqslant S_{ij} \qquad \text{for all } j$$

$$\sum_j x_{ij\bar{k}(\ell)\ell} = D_{i\ell} \qquad \text{for all } \ell$$

$$x_{ij\bar{k}(\ell)\ell} \geqslant 0 \qquad \text{for all } j,\ell.$$

The Benders decomposition procedure (described in the Appendix, mathematical note 8.1) requires the solution of the dual of problem (8.38), which can be stated as:

$$\text{maximize} \sum_i \sum_j (-S_{ij})u_{ij} + \sum_i \sum_k \sum_\ell (-D_{i\ell}y^H_{k\ell})\pi_{ik\ell}$$
$$u,\pi$$

subject to   (8.40)

$$-u_{ij} - \pi_{ik\ell} \leq c_{ijk\ell} \qquad \text{for all } i,j,k,\ell$$

$$u_{ij} \geq 0 \qquad \text{for all } i,j$$

and $\pi_{ik\ell}$ is unrestricted in sign for all i, k, ℓ.

Because problem (8.38) is to be solved efficiently by solving an independent transportation problem (8.39) for each commodity, the optimal dual solution to problem (8.38) must be synthesized from the optimal solutions for problem (8.39), one for each commodity. Let μ_{ij} be the dual variables of problem (8.39) associated with the supply constraints. An optimal solution to problem (8.40) is:

$$u^*_{ij} = \mu^*_{ij} \tag{8.41a}$$

$$\pi^*_{ik\ell} = \max_j \{-u^*_{ij} - c_{ijk\ell}\} \text{ for all } i,k,\ell. \tag{8.41b}$$

Conditions (8.41a) and (8.41b) are derived in the Appendix, mathematical note 8.2. The necessary results are now in place for stating the solution procedure.

The Algorithm

Step 0 Select a suboptimality tolerance parameter $\epsilon \geq 0$. Initialize $UB = +\infty$, $LB = -\infty$, $H = 0$. If zero-one vectors y^1 and z^1 are available (as from a heuristic solution procedure) that satisfy constraints (8.34) through (8.36), go to Step 2. Otherwise, proceed to Step 1.

Step 1 Solve the Benders master problem, denoted problem (BDD^H), in the y and z variables given by:

$$\text{minimize } B$$
$$B,y,z \tag{8.42}$$
subject to constraints (8.34) through (8.36) and:

$$B \geq \sum_k (f_k z_k + v_k \sum_i \sum_\ell D_{i\ell}y_{k\ell}) - \sum_i \sum_k \sum_\ell (\pi_{ik\ell}D^h_{i\ell})y_{k\ell}$$

$$- \sum_i \sum_j u^h_{ij}S_{ij}, \quad h = 1,...,H \tag{8.43}$$

$$y_{k\ell}, z_k = 0 \text{ or } 1 \qquad \text{for all } k,\ell. \tag{8.44}$$

Denote an optimal solution by $(B^{H+1}, z^{H+1}, y^{H+1})$. Set $LB = B^{H+1}$; LB is a lower bound on the optimal value of the distribution design problem (DD), denoted by $v[DD]$. Terminate if $UB - LB \leq \epsilon$; the incumbent solution is an ϵ-optimal solution of problem (DD). Otherwise, proceed to Step 2.

Step 2 Solve the x-partition of problem (DD), given by problem (8.38), with $y = y^{H+1}$ by solving the independent classical transportation problems given by problem (8.39). Denote the optimal solution to problem (8.38) as x^{H+1} and the optimal value:

$$\sum_i (\sum_j \sum_\varrho c_{ij\overline{k}(\varrho)\varrho} x^{H+1}_{ij\overline{k}(\varrho)\varrho})$$

as $T(y^{H+1})$. Then following the properties discussed in the Appendix, mathematical note 8.1, an upper bound on $v[DD]$ is given by:

$$\sum_k (f_k z^{H+1}_k + v_k \sum_i \sum_\varrho D_{i\varrho} y^{H+1}_{k\varrho}) + T(y^{H+1}). \qquad (8.45)$$

If the value of expression (8.45) is less than the current upper bound UB, replace UB by the value of expression (8.45) and store $(y^{H+1}, z^{H+1}, x^{H+1})$ as the new incumbent solution. Terminate if $UB - LB \leq \epsilon$; the incumbent solution is an ϵ-optimal solution of problem (DD). Otherwise, go to Step 3.

Step 3 Determine an optimal dual solution to problem (8.38) with $y = y^{H+1}$ using equations (8.41). The necessary data for equations (8.41) are available from having solved problem (8.39) for each commodity in Step 2. Denote the dual solution by (u^{H+1}, π^{H+1}), set $H = H+1$, and return to Step 1.

Figure 8.7 is a schematic of the algorithm. The procedure sequentially identifies improved designs of the distribution system until it is determined that no significant cost improvement can be achieved. It is assumed that problem (8.38), and therefore problem (8.39), is feasible for every choice of $y^H_{k\varrho}$ satisfying constraint (8.34). This is ensured if $\sum_j S_{ij} \geq \sum_\varrho D_{i\varrho}$ for all i (if not, the design problem is infeasible) and if all possible jk links are in the model. (However, as discussed, impracticable combinations of indices should be dropped if possible.) These assumptions suffice to guarantee that problem (8.39) is feasible for each i and therefore has a finite minimum value for any zero-one y satisfying constraint (8.34). Convergence of the algorithm is guaranteed for any $\epsilon \geq 0$ because problem (DD) possesses a finite minimum

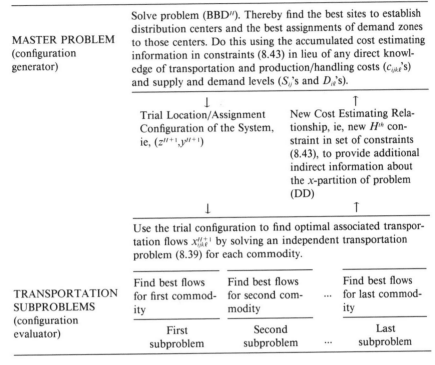

MASTER PROBLEM (configuration generator)	Solve problem (BBD^H). Thereby find the best sites to establish distribution centers and the best assignments of demand zones to those centers. Do this using the accumulated cost estimating information in constraints (8.43) in lieu of any direct knowledge of transportation and production/handling costs ($c_{ijk\ell}$'s) and supply and demand levels (S_{ij}'s and $D_{i\ell}$'s).

↓	↑
Trial Location/Assignment Configuration of the System, ie, (z^{H+1}, y^{H+1})	New Cost Estimating Relationship, ie, new H^{th} constraint in set of constraints (8.43), to provide additional indirect information about the x-partition of problem (DD)

↓	↑

Use the trial configuration to find optimal associated transportation flows $x_{ijk\ell}^{H+1}$ by solving an independent transportation problem (8.39) for each commodity.

TRANSPORTATION SUBPROBLEMS (configuration evaluator)	Find best flows for first commodity	Find best flows for second commodity	...	Find best flows for last commodity
	First subproblem	Second subproblem	...	Last subproblem

Figure 8.7   Schematic of the Decomposition Procedure.
(Adapted from: Geoffrion, Graves, and Lee, 1982, in *INFOR* 20:287–314.)

and the extreme point-generating problem (8.40) has a finite number of extreme points.

Insights from the information processing system delineated in Figure 8.7 suggest the following variant of the algorithm. When H is small in the master problem, problem (BDD^H), too little information is included by way of the transportation dual variables u_{ij}^h and $\pi_{ik\ell}^h$, $h = 1,...,H$, about transportation subproblems to justify optimizing the master problem. There are too few constraints in the master problem to expect that the optimal value will provide a sharp lower bound on the optimal value of the design problem. Thus the current master problem is solved only to the extent that a feasible solution is produced having a value less than $UB - \epsilon$. A lower bound LB is therefore no longer available, thus inactivating the termination criterion in Step 2. Termination in Step 1 occurs if problem (BDD^H) has no feasible solution with a value of B below $UB - \epsilon$. This scheme implies an adaptive increase in the optimization of the master problem. The minimal value of the solution to the master problem increases as H increases and the "threshold" $UB - \epsilon$ decreases with each new incumbent. The master problem in Step 1 becomes feasibility-seeking only, ie, a feasible solution is sought for:

$$UB - \epsilon > \sum_k (f_k z_k + v_k \sum_i \sum_\ell D_{i\ell} y_{k\ell}) - \sum_i \sum_k \sum_\ell (\pi^h_{ik\ell} D_{i\ell}) y_{k\ell}$$

$$- \sum_i \sum_j u^h_{ij} S_{ij} \qquad h = 1,...,H \qquad (8.46)$$

together with constraints (8.34) through (8.36), and (8.44).

Any convenient objective function in y and z could be augmented to these constraints to produce a feasible solution. A natural choice is to use the latest cost-estimating relationship, which is the Hth function on the right-hand side of constraint (8.46). This choice has proved computationally sound. The master problem, in Step 1, then becomes:

$$\underset{y,z}{\text{minimize}} \sum_k (f_k z_k + v_k \sum_i \sum_\ell D_{i\ell} y_{k\ell}) - \sum_i \sum_k \sum_\ell (\pi^H_{ik\ell} D_{i\ell}) y_{k\ell} - \sum_i \sum_j u^H_{ij} S_{ij}$$

subject to
$$(8.47)$$

constraints (8.34) through (8.36), (8.44), and (8.46).

Problem (8.47) is conveniently a pure zero-one integer programming problem. Problem (BDD^H) is a mixed-integer programming problem due to the inclusion of B. This adds to the advantage of using problem (8.47). To repeat, the minimize instruction in (8.47) is not to be taken seriously because it is only a feasible solution that is required.

Example 8.7 The structure of a two-stage distribution system is exemplified in Figure 8.8. We will associate the location of each distribution system entity with the coordinates of that entity in Figure 8.8. For example, distribution center site 2 is at (4,3). There are two commodities. To preserve the visual appeal of the figure, the average unit cost of producing and shipping commodity i from plant j through DC at site k to demand zone ℓ is arbitrarily defined as the rectangular distance involved for commodity 1, and that plus 2 for commodity 2. Values of the $c_{ijk\ell}$ are thus obtained. These and other problem parameters are given in Table 8.8.

Although this is a miniature distribution design problem, there are already 64 variables. There are 16 zero-one variables, 48 transportation variables, and 39 constraints. No constraints of type (8.36) are included.

Step 0   Set $UB = +\infty$, $LB = -\infty$, and $H = 0$. To force an *optimal* solution, set $\epsilon = 0$ for the example.

Step 1   As $H = 0$, solve:

$$\text{minimize} \sum_{k=1}^4 (f_k z_k + v_k \sum_{i=1}^2 \sum_{\ell=1}^3 D_{i\ell} y_{k\ell})$$

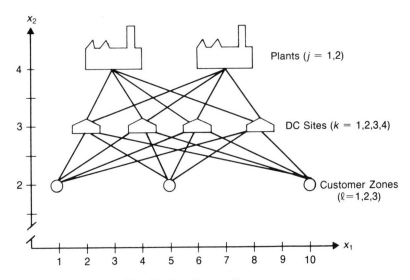

Figure 8.8 Two-Stage Distribution System Structure.

subject to constraints (8.34), (8.35), and (8.44), which is:

minimize $3000z_1 + \ldots + 3000z_4 + 175y_{11} + 350y_{21}$
$$+ \ldots + 150y_{32} + \ldots + 950y_{33} + 475y_{43}$$

subject to

$$y_{11} + y_{21} + y_{31} + y_{41} = 1$$
$$y_{12} + y_{22} + y_{32} + y_{42} = 1$$
$$y_{13} + y_{23} + y_{33} + y_{43} = 1$$
$$175y_{11} + 75y_{12} + 475y_{13} \leqslant 650z_1$$
$$175y_{21} + 75y_{22} + 475y_{23} \leqslant 650z_2$$
$$175y_{31} + 75y_{32} + 475y_{33} \leqslant 650z_3$$
$$175y_{41} + 75y_{42} + 475y_{43} \leqslant 650z_4$$
$$175y_{11} + 75y_{12} + 475y_{13} \geqslant 100z_1$$
$$175y_{21} + 75y_{22} + 475y_{23} \geqslant 100z_2$$
$$175y_{31} + 75y_{32} + 475y_{33} \geqslant 100z_3$$
$$175y_{41} + 75y_{42} + 475y_{43} \geqslant 100z_4$$

Table 8.8 Data for Example 8.5.

$$c_{ijk\ell}$$

$i = 1, j = 1$				$i = 1, j = 2$		
ℓ				ℓ		
k	1	2	3	k	1	2	3
1	4	6	11	1	8	10	15
2	6	4	9	2	8	6	11
3	10	6	9	3	8	4	7
4	16	12	9	4	12	8	5

$i = 2, j = 1$				$i = 2, j = 2$		
ℓ				ℓ		
k	1	2	3	k	1	2	3
1	6	8	13	1	10	12	17
2	8	6	11	2	10	8	13
3	12	8	11	3	10	6	9
4	18	14	11	4	14	10	7

DC Data

	1	2	3	4
			k	
$\underline{V}_k$	100	100	100	100
$\overline{V}_k$	650	650	650	650
f_k	3000	3000	3000	3000
v_k	1	2	2	1

	$D_{i\ell}$				S_{ij}		$y_{k\ell}$ coefficients in objective function (8.31)		
	ℓ				j		ℓ		
i	1	2	3	i	1	2	k	1	2	3
1	150	50	450	1	600	600	1	175	75	475
2	25	25	25	2	50	50	2	350	150	950
							3	350	150	950
							4	175	75	475

$$y_{11}, y_{21}, y_{31}, y_{41}, y_{12}, ..., y_{33}, y_{43}, z_1, z_2, z_3, z_4 = 0 \text{ or } 1.$$

The optimal solution (found using a zero-one integer programming computer code) is $y_{11} = y_{42} = y_{43} = z_1 = z_4 = 1$ and all other variables equal to zero. This is (y^1, z^1). The optimal objective value is 6725 and so $LB = 6725$, presently.

Step 2 We have $\bar{k}(1) = 1$, $\bar{k}(2) = 4$, and $\bar{k}(3) = 4$. The objective function coefficients for the transportation subproblems are given below.

$\dfrac{c_{1j\bar{k}(\ell)\ell}}{\ell}$				$\dfrac{c_{2j\bar{k}(\ell)\ell}}{\ell}$			
j	1	2	3	k	1	2	3
1	4	12	9	1	6	14	11
2	8	8	5	2	10	10	7

Each transportation subproblem involves 2 sources (plants) and 3 destinations (demand zones). The solutions are shown below. These represent x^1 and μ^1 with the understanding that all $x_{ijk\ell} = 0$ for $k \neq \bar{k}(\ell)$.

$\dfrac{x_{1j\bar{k}(\ell)\ell}}{\ell}$						$\dfrac{c_{2j\bar{k}(\ell)\ell}}{\ell}$				
j	1	2	3	S_{1j}	μ_{1j}	j	1	2	3	S_{2j}	μ_{2j}
1	150	0	0	600	0	1	25	0	0	50	0
2	0	50	450	600	0	2	0	25	25	50	0
$D_{1\ell}$	150	50	450			$D_{2\ell}$	25	25	25		
MINIMUM COST $= 3250$						MINIMUM COST $= 575$				

$T(y^1) = 3250 + 575 = 3825$, so $UB = 6725 + 3825 = 10550$, presently. Store (y^1, z^1, x^1) as the incumbent solution to the distribution design problem (DD). As $UB - LB = 10550 - 6725 = 3825 > \epsilon = 0$, proceed to Step 3.

Step 3 $u_{ij}^1 = \mu_{ij}^1 = 0$ (as found in Step 2) for all i, j
$\pi_{ik\ell}^1 = \max_j\{-0 - c_{ijk\ell}\} = \max\{-c_{i1k\ell}, -c_{i2k\ell}\}$, which gives the following:

$\dfrac{\pi_{1k\ell}^1}{\ell}$				$\dfrac{\pi_{2k\ell}^1}{\ell}$			
k	1	2	3	k	1	2	3
1	-4	-6	-11	1	-6	-8	-13
2	-6	-4	-9	2	-8	-6	-11
3	-8	-4	-7	3	-10	-6	-9
4	-12	-8	-5	4	-14	-10	-7

Set $H = 0 + 1 = 1$ and return to Step 1.

Step 1   For convenience, use problem (8.47) for the master problem in Step 1, and therefore we must solve:

$$\text{minimize } 3000z_1 + 3000z_2 + 3000z_3 + 3000z_4$$

$$+ \sum_{k=1}^{4} \sum_{\ell=1}^{3} [\sum_{i=1}^{2} (v_k D_{i\ell} - \pi_{ik\ell}^1 D_{i\ell})] y_{k\ell}$$

subject to

constraints (8.34), (8.35), (8.44), and

$$3000z_1 + 3000z_2 + 3000z_3 + 3000z_4$$

$$+ \sum_{k=1}^{4} [\sum_{\ell=1}^{3} \sum_{i=1}^{2} (v_k D_{i\ell} - \pi^1_{ik\ell} D_{i\ell})] y_{k\ell} - 0 < UB - \epsilon = 10550.$$

The coefficients for $y_{k\ell}$ in the objective function and in the $UB - \epsilon$ constraint are given in the following display.

	$\sum_{i=1}^{2} (v_k D_{i\ell} - \pi^1_{ik\ell} D_{i\ell}) = \sum_{i=1}^{2} v_k D_{i\ell} - \sum_{i=1}^{2} \pi^1_{ik\ell} D_{i\ell}$		
		ℓ	
k	1	2	3
1	$175-[-4(150)$ $-6(25)]=925$	$75-[-6(50)$ $-8(25)]=575$	$475-[-11(450)$ $-13(25)]=5750$
2	$350-[-6(150)$ $-8(25)]=1450$	$150-[-4(50)$ $-6(25)]=500$	$950-[-9(450)$ $-11(25)]=5275$
3	$350-[-8(150)$ $-10(25)]=1800$	$150-[-4(50)$ $-6(25)]=500$	$950-[-7(450)$ $-9(25)]=4325$
4	$175-[-12(150)$ $-14(25)]=2325$	$75-[-8(50)$ $-10(25)]=725$	$475-[-5(450)$ $-7(25)]=2900$

Though only a feasible solution is required, the problem was solved optimally to produce $z_1 = z_4 = y_{11} = y_{12} = y_{43} = 1$ and all other variables equal to zero. This represents (y^2, z^2). The optimal objective value is 10400. As $H = 1$, this is also the optimal value of B in Step 1. Hence we have a viable lower bound given by $LB = 10400$. Presently $UB - LB = 10550 - 10400 = 150 > \epsilon$, so we proceed to Step 2.

Step 2   Now $\bar{k}(1) = 1, \bar{k}(2) = 1, \bar{k}(3) = 4$. Objective function coefficients for the independent transportation problems are:

	$c_{1j\bar{k}(\ell)\ell}$					$c_{2j\bar{k}(\ell)\ell}$		
		ℓ					ℓ	
j	1	2	3		j	1	2	3
1	4	6	9		1	6	8	11
2	8	10	5		2	10	12	7

The respective solutions are:

$\dfrac{x_{1jk(\ell)\ell}}{\ell}$						$\dfrac{x_{2jk(\ell)\ell}}{\ell}$					
j	1	2	3	S_{1j}	μ_{1j}	j	1	2	3	S_{2j}	μ_{2j}
1	150	50	0	600	0	1	25	25	0	50	0
2	0	0	450	600	0	2	0	0	25	50	0

$D_{1\ell}$	150	50	450			$D_{2\ell}$	25	25	25
	MINIMUM COST = 3150						MINIMUM COST = 525		

$T(y^2) = 3150 + 525 = 3675$. Using expression (8.45), compute:

$$\sum_{k=1}^{4} (f_k z_k^2 + v_k \sum_{i=1}^{2} \sum_{\ell=1}^{3} D_{i\ell} y_{k\ell}^2) + T(y^2) = 3000z_1 + 3000z_4$$

$$+ \ 175y_{11} + 75y_{12} + 475y_{43} + 3675 = 10400 < UB = 10550,$$

so UB becomes 10400 and (y^2, z^2, x^2) becomes the new incumbent solution. This solution is optimal because $UB - LB = 0$. It calls for locating a DC at site 1 to serve demand zones 1 and 2, and locating a DC at site 4 to serve demand zone 3. The optimal transportation variables are given by:

$$x_{1111} = 150, \ x_{1212} = 50, \ x_{1243} = 450, \ x_{2111} = 25, \ x_{2243} = 25, \text{ and}$$
all others equal to zero.

Only two iterations were needed for convergence even though the sub-optimality bound ϵ was set to zero, requiring an exact optimal solution. (To gain a greater appreciation of this decomposition approach, the reader is invited to attempt solving the problem in its original form using any available mixed-integer programming computer code.) It must be emphasized that successful computer implementation of the algorithm is not straightforward. This would involve sophisticated computer science, and some cleverness.

8.4 DEMAND POINT AGGREGATION ISSUES REVISITED

The demand point aggregation error bound given by Property 8.2 for single-stage distribution models provides a convenient yet powerful basis for evaluating potential demand point aggregations in single-commodity distribution planning. The property extends to two-stage distribution system design for the case of a *single* commodity when single sourcing of customer is *not* required. The following model serves as a frame of reference:

$$\text{minimize} \sum_{j} \sum_{k} c_{jk} x_{jk} + \sum_{k} \sum_{\ell} a_{k\ell} y_{k\ell} + \sum_{k} f_k z_k \qquad (8.48)$$
$$x,y,z$$

subject to

$$\underline{S}_j \leqslant \sum_k x_{jk} \leqslant \bar{S}_j \qquad \text{for all } j \qquad (8.49)$$

$$\sum_j x_{jk} = \sum_\ell D_\ell y_{k\ell} \qquad \text{for all } k \qquad (8.50)$$

$$\sum_k y_{k\ell} = 1 \qquad \text{for all } \ell \qquad (8.51)$$

$$\underline{V}_k z_k \leqslant \sum_\ell D_\ell y_{k\ell} \leqslant \bar{V}_k z_k \qquad \text{for all } k \qquad (8.52)$$

$$x_{jk} \geqslant 0,\ 0 \leqslant y_{k\ell} \leqslant 1,\ z_k = 0 \text{ or } 1 \text{ for all } j,k,\ell. \qquad (8.53)$$

Slightly revised interpretations are used here:

x_{jk} = annual amount of flow from *procurement* zone j to a facility at site k,

$y_{k\ell}$ = fraction of demand D_ℓ satisfied by a facility at site k,

c_{jk} = average unit cost of procurement plus transportation from procurement zone j to site k,

$a_{k\ell}$ = annual variable costs incurred if demand point ℓ is served fully by a facility at site k; typically includes transportation plus facility-related costs.

All other notation has been used previously and is self-evident. The amount of flow from a facility at site k to demand point ℓ is exactly $D_\ell y_{k\ell}$. Therefore, the outbound transportation flow information resident in the ℓ subscript of $x_{jk\ell}$ is superfluous, given the y's, and has been dropped. Property 8.2 can now be restated for the present context.

Property 8.3 [*Customer aggregation error bound—two-stage distribution*]. *Let* $L_1,...,L_H$ *be disjoint subsets of demand point indices satisfying, for each h, the condition: for each* $\ell \epsilon L_h$*, the same* $k\ell$ *links exist. Then, if:*

for $h = 1,...,H$ and all k, the $y_{k\ell}$'s are identical over $\ell \epsilon L_h$,   (8.54)

$$v[\text{problem } (8.48)-(8.53)] \leqslant v[\text{problem } (8.48)-(8.54)]$$

$$\leqslant v[\text{problem } (8.48)-(8.53)] + \sum_{h=1}^{H} \epsilon_h,$$

where $\epsilon_h = \sum_{\ell \epsilon L_h} \max_k \left\{ \dfrac{D_\ell \sum_{\ell' \epsilon L_h} a_{k\ell'}}{\sum_{\ell' \epsilon L_h} D_{\ell'}} - a_{k\ell} \right\}$

An analogous aggregation property has not been developed for the multi-commodity single-sourcing distribution design problem (DD).

EXERCISES

8.1 Complete the trade-off curve started in Figure 8.2.

8.2 Kolesar and Walker (1974) Consider the dynamic fire company relocation problem described in Section 8.1. The output of the associated set-covering problem is a set of empty fire houses to be filled so that all RNs are covered with a minimum number of fire company relocations. A second-stage problem is to decide which available fire companies to relocate into the empty houses identified in the first stage. However, this two-stage strategy may yield suboptimal solutions because there may be multiple optima in the first-stage problem. All alternate optima for the first-stage problem must be considered in the second stage to guarantee an optimal relocation. The following problem considers both stages simultaneously:

$$\text{minimize} \sum_{i=1}^{N} \sum_{k=1}^{K} (c_{ik} + w)x_{ik},$$
$$x$$

subject to

$$\sum_{k=0}^{K} x_{ik} = 1 \qquad \text{for all } i$$

$$\sum_{i=1}^{N} \sum_{k=1}^{K} a_{k\ell}x_{ik} + \sum_{i=1}^{N} a_{i\ell}x_{i0} \geqslant 1 \qquad \text{for all } \ell$$

$$x_{ik} = 0 \text{ or } 1 \quad \text{for all } i \text{ and } k,$$

where $i = 1,...,N$ refers to available fire companies, $k = 1,...,K$ refers to empty houses, and $\ell = 1,...,L$ refers to RNs associated with both empty houses and houses occupied by available companies, $x_{i0} = 1$ indicates company i isn't relocated, c_{ik} is the "cost" in increased system response time for relocating company i into empty house k, and w is a large positive number.

a. Explain the model in detail.

b. Give another location application for this model and explain why the model applies.

c. Consider an alternative approach. Solve the first-stage problem to obtain q^*, say, the minimum number of companies that need to be relocated. Then solve the following problem:

$$\text{minimize max } \{c_{ik} \mid x_{ik} = 1\}$$
$$x$$

subject to

$$\sum_{i=1}^{N} \sum_{k=1}^{K} x_{ik} = q^*$$

together with the constraints above. Contrast this approach to relocation with the approach implied by the combined problem.

d. Describe how Minieka's algorithm might be adapted to solve the program in Exercise 8.2c.

8.3 a. Plane and Hendrick (1977)   Explain how the objective in problem (8.12) accomplishes the intended purpose.
   b. Daskin and Stern (1981) Emergency medical service (EMS) vehicle deployment might be guided by the following hierarchical set-covering model:

$$\text{minimize } w \sum_{k} z_k - \sum_{\ell} x_\ell$$
$$\underset{x,z}{}$$

subject to

$$\sum_{k} a_{k\ell} z_k - x_\ell \geqslant 1 \qquad \text{for all } \ell$$

$$z_k = 0 \text{ or } 1 \qquad \text{for all } k$$

$$x_\ell \geqslant 0 \text{ and integer} \qquad \text{for all } \ell,$$

where $a_{k\ell}$ is 1 if the expected response time of an EMS unit traveling from zone k to RN_ℓ is acceptable and is 0 otherwise; $x_\ell =$ number of additional EMS units capable of responding to RN_ℓ in an acceptable time; $z_k = 1$ if a unit is to be located in zone k and 0 otherwise; w is a positive weight.
   Explain how the model works and how to determine w; then solve the problem with $a_{k\ell}$ coefficients from Table 8.3 and $w = 13$.

8.4 Schilling, Elzinga, Cohon, Church and ReVelle (1979)   The problem is to locate engine (pumper) companies and truck (ladder) companies in a study of the Baltimore City Fire Protection System. A model considered is the following:

$$\underset{x,z^c,z^l}{\text{maximize }} \sum_{\ell} a_\ell x_\ell$$

subject to

$$\sum_{k \in K^c_\ell} z^c_k \geqslant x_\ell \qquad \text{for all } \ell$$

$$\sum_{k \in K^l_\ell} z^l_k \geqslant x_\ell \qquad \text{for all } \ell$$

$$\sum_{k} z^c_k = n^c$$

$$\sum_{k} z^l_k = n^l$$

$$z^l_k \leqslant z^c_k \qquad \text{for all } k$$

$$z^c_k, z^l_k = 0 \text{ or } 1, \text{ for all } k \text{ and } x_\ell = 0 \text{ or } 1, \text{ for all } \ell,$$

where

a_ℓ = demand to be served at RN_ℓ,

$z_k^c = \begin{cases} 1 \text{ if an engine company is located in station } k \\ 0 \text{ otherwise,} \end{cases}$

$z_k^t = \begin{cases} 1 \text{ if a truck company is located in station } \ell \\ 0 \text{ otherwise,} \end{cases}$

$x_\ell = \begin{cases} 1 \text{ if } RN_\ell \text{ is covered by engine and truck companies} \\ 0 \text{ otherwise,} \end{cases}$

n^c = number of engine companies to be located,

n^t = number of truck companies to be located,

$K_\ell^c = \{k | d_{k\ell} \leq S^c\}$,

$K_\ell^t = \{k | d_{k\ell} \leq S^t\}$,

$d_{k\ell}$ = distance (time) from station k to RN_ℓ,

S^c = service standard for engine companies,

S^t = service standard for truck companies.

a. Explain the model.

b. Let the $c_{k\ell}$ data in Table 8.4 correspond to $d_{k\ell}$ (in *tenths* of minutes) here. Let a = (71, 62, 56, 39, 35, 21, 20, 19), $S^c = S^t = 15$ minutes, $n^c = 3$, and $n^t = 2$. Formulate the associated problem.

c. Explain how the model might be solved. Then use your suggested technique to solve the case developed in Exercise 8.4b. Comment on the result.

d. Criticize the model and suggest ways to overcome your criticisms.

e. Suppose the objective was changed to $\sum_\ell a_\ell^p x_\ell + w \sum_\ell a_\ell^v x_\ell$, where $w \geq$ 0, and a_ℓ^p, a_ℓ^v are population and property value weights, respectively. Explain how the new model could be used.

8.5 Consider the shortest distance matrix given in Table 8.2. Assume the table entries correspond to *tenths* of minutes of helicopter travel time between nodes. A hospital is located at node 8.

a. Use the Kolesar-Walker heuristic to find a minimum number of nodes to use as helicopter bases so that the response time to each node from the nearest base *plus* the trip time to the nearest hospital is less than 12 minutes. Indicate which sites are chosen as bases.

b. Use the cutting plane procedure to solve the problem in Exercise 8.5a.

c. Provide criticisms of the "solution." Rank the criticisms in importance, and then suggest means to overcome the criticisms.

8.6 Consider the shortest distance matrix given by Table 8.2. Let the entries correspond to round-trip time (for the route $k \to \ell \to k$) in minutes. Use linear programming to find a minimum number of sites to use as polling places for an upcoming election. Each node corresponds to a community, and it is required that residents of each community travel no more than 42 minutes round-trip to the nearest polling place. Indicate which sites are chosen and discuss criticisms as in Exercise 8.5c.

8.7 Use the context of Exercise 8.6, but apply the maximal covering model given by problem (8.7)-(8.11) with $m = 3$, $T = 30$, $T_\ell = 42$, $\ell = 1,...,12$.

Let all w_ℓ be equal. Solve the problem. Indicate which sites are chosen and discuss criticisms as in Exercise 8.5c.

8.8 Use the reduction rules R1, R2, and R3 of Section 8.1 to solve the covering problem with coefficients given in Table 8.3.

8.9 Cornuejols, Fisher, and Nemhauser (1977) It is economically advantageous for large organizations to maintain accounts in geographically dispersed banks so they can achieve lengthy check-clearing times. Let δ_k be the fixed cost of maintaining a bank account in city k; $\gamma_{k\ell}$ the average number of days to clear a check drawn on an account in city k when it is cashed in city ℓ; and ν_ℓ the dollar volume of checks to be cashed in city ℓ. Add any additional necessary information. Then formulate as problem (8.13)–(8.18) the problem of locating, at most, m bank accounts to take greatest economic advantage of check-clearing times. Describe the meaning of the objective function (including the units of measurement) and the constraints.

8.10 Nauss and Markland (1981) It is economically advantageous for large organizations to locate lock-boxes so that they will clear checks for funds due as quickly as possible. Lock-boxes are post office boxes operated by banks for corporations. They function as check-collection centers. Revise the terminology used in Exercise 8.9 to formulate the appropriate lock-box location problem as problem (8.13)-(8.18). Find a place in your model for $\bar{\gamma}_\ell$, the average number of days to clear a check cashed at the main corporate office that is drawn on a bank in city ℓ. Explain the objective function and the constraints.

8.11 a. Fill in the supporting detail for the use of DUALOC in Example 8.5a.
b. Fill in the supporting detail for the use of DUALOC in Example 8.5b.
c. Use DUALOC to solve Example 8.5a upon omitting site 4.

8.12 Erlenkotter (1977) Let $c_{k\ell} = -[R_\ell(D_{k\ell}) - t_{k\ell}D_{k\ell}]$ in the objective function (8.13). Here $D_{k\ell}$ is the demand quantity in demand zone ℓ if supplied from a facility at site k; $R_\ell(D)$ is the total revenue corresponding to demand D; and $t_{k\ell} > 0$ is the production and distribution cost per unit demand in demand zone ℓ if supplied from a facility at site k. The revenue function $R_\ell(\cdot)$ is assumed to be concave, differentiable, and bounded above, with $R_\ell(0) = 0$. The values for $D_{k\ell}$ are determined from the optimality conditions:

$$\text{if } dR_\ell(0)/dD \leq t_{k\ell}, \text{ then } D_{k\ell} = 0; \text{ and}$$

$$\text{if } dR_\ell(0)/dD > t_{k\ell}, \text{ then } dR_\ell(D_{k\ell})/dD = t_{k\ell}.$$

Add a site K for which $c_{K\ell} = 0$, $\ell = 1,...,L$, and $f_K = 0$. For reference, let $R_\ell(D) = p_\ell(D) \cdot D$, where $p_\ell(D)$ is price associated with demand D. Explain *and* justify the implied model.

8.13 Use Property 8.1 to show that $\epsilon_{\text{PIT/NY/BOS}}$ in Example 8.6 is indeed $500. Disaggregate the optimal flows indicated in Table 8.6. Then show that the disaggregated solution is feasible for the full problem and has the same cost as the optimal value of the aggregated problem.

8.14 Use Property 8.2 to find the a priori error bound for $H = 2$, using $L_1 = \{DAL,CHI,ATL\}$ and $L_2 = \{PIT,NY,BOS\}$. Solve the associated transportation problem. Disaggregate the flows and verify that the solution obtained is feasible for the full problem and has the same cost as $v[L_1,L_2$ aggregation]. Verify that the suboptimality of $v[L_1,L_2$ aggregation] satisfies the a priori bound.

8.15 a. Show that problem (CPLP) reduces to the classical transportation problem if the model doesn't involve facility location and all $\underline{V}_k = 0$.
  b. Explain why the method of aggregation used in Example 8.6 will honor the requirement of condition (8.27).

8.16 Geoffrion, Graves and Lee (1978)   The following exercises pertain to the distribution design problem (DD).
  a. Suppose a certain demand zone is to obtain some commodities directly from the plants, and others through a DC. Explain how this provision may be accommodated without changing the form of the model.
  b. Replace $D_{i\ell}$ by $D_{ik\ell}$. This allows demand in demand zone ℓ for commodity i to depend on the particular DC from which service is to be provided. Give the negative term that must be appended to the objective function (8.31) to ensure *net revenue maximization* when considering this feature of service elasticity of demand.
  c. Revise the design problem to include selection among alternative plant sites and plant expansion projects.
  d. Revise the design problem to include seasonal effects by letting plant capacities and customer demands be given on a monthly basis, thus requiring decisions concerning seasonal inventories.
  e. As demand zones are single-sourced [by constraints (8.34)], the annual flow on each outbound link $k \rightarrow \ell$ is known. The associated unit transportation rate is therefore determined primarily by the individual demand zones and is not significantly affected by the annual throughput at the DC. However, the larger the throughput of a DC, the lower the unit inbound transportation rates should be. Explain how to include economies-of-scale in inbound transportation costs that depend on each alternative size range for a DC from among "small," "medium," and "large."
  f. Consider an application characterized by diseconomies-of-scale in producing a given commodity at a given plant. In particular, marginal costs increase appreciably with volume over the relevant range of output. Give a *detailed* account of how to accommodate this feature within the model and explain your logic.
  g. Show the form of constraints (8.36) to accommodate: precedence relations relating to open DCs (eg, do not open DC A unless DC B is open); mandatory service constraints (eg, if DC A is open, it must serve demand zone B); and specification of a subset of DCs among which at least one is required to be opened.

h. More detailed capacity constraints than constraints (8.35) may be needed. First show how to weight the capacity consumption with a suitable weighting factor for each commodity and indicate how this affects units of measurement in the constraint. Then describe separate constraints for certain commodities.

i. Suppose the capacity limits $\bar{V}_k$ are not absolute, but may be augmented at a cost. The penalty (perhaps related to costs of leasing additional warehouse space) per unit overflow of $\bar{V}_k$ is $\bar{P}_k$. Show how to generalize the model to accommodate this feature.

8.17 a. Read Geoffrion (1976b) and Mairs et al. (1978) for perspective on distribution design modeling.

b. Read Geoffrion and Powers (1980, 1981) for perspective on facility location in the context of management support systems.

c. Read Economides and Fok (1984), Gelb and Khumawala (1984), and Davis, Kleindorfer, Kochenberger, Reutzel, and Brown (1986) for examples of actual applications of variants of models in this chapter. .

8.18 Let $S_{11} = S_{12} = 400$ in Example 8.7. Solve the revised problem with $\epsilon = 0$, letting all other data remain unaltered. Present the step-by-step results as was done in the example.

8.19 Dutton, Hinman and Millham (1974) It is required to find the optimal location of power plants in the Pacific Northwest with respect to capital-construction (f_k), operating (o_k), and transmission ($t_{k\ell}$) costs of providing peak ($y_{k\ell}$) and energy ($x_{k\ell}$) power. The following model is used:

$$\underset{x,y,z}{\text{minimize}} \sum_{k=1}^{13} \sum_{\ell=1}^{8} t_{k\ell} y_{k\ell} + \sum_{k=1}^{13} o_k \sum_{\ell=1}^{18} x_{k\ell} + \sum_{k=1}^{13} f_k z_k$$

subject to

$$\sum_{\ell=1}^{8} y_{k\ell} \leq (0.85 \, p_i) z_k \qquad \text{for all } \ell$$

$$\sum_{\ell=1}^{8} x_{k\ell} \leq (6130 \, p_i) z_k \qquad \text{for all } k$$

$$\sum_{k=1}^{13} y_{k\ell} \geq d_\ell \qquad \text{for all } \ell$$

$$\sum_{k=1}^{13} x_{k\ell} \geq e_\ell \qquad \text{for all } \ell$$

$$a y_{k\ell} \leq x_{k\ell} \leq b y_{k\ell} \qquad \text{for all } k,\ell$$

$$x_{k\ell}, y_{k\ell} \geq 0, \ z_k = 0 \text{ or } 1 \qquad \text{for all } k.$$

a. Give an account of how the Benders decomposition approach might be used here.

b. Schrage (1975)   Add the slack variable $s_{k\ell}$ to $ay_{k\ell} \leqslant x_{k\ell}$ to obtain $ay_{k\ell} + s_{k\ell} = x_{k\ell}$. Explain how this can be used to eliminate $x_{k\ell}$ from the problem as well as the constraint. Reformulate the problem after eliminating as many variables and constraints as possible. What was the reduction in the size of the problem?

8.20 After reading Fitzsimmons and Allen (1983), answer the following:
    a. Explain how the model can be cast in the form of the simple plant location problem (SPLP) given by problem (8.13)-(8.18), omitting constraint (8.16). Interpret the variables and parameters of problem (SPLP) in the context of the application.
    b. Is the model given by problem (8.22)-(8.26) appropriate for the case where there is a minimum and maximum number of auditors that can be assigned to any site? Explain.

8.21 Columbia Express, Inc.,* is a specialty forwarder whose business consists primarily of next-day delivery of perishable or urgent freight ranging from 10 to 50 pounds per item. Long-haul transportation is by the company's fleet of jet aircraft, with local pickup and delivery made through local contractors. Most of the freight is carried under long-term contracts with manufacturers who need fast service between dispersed manufacturing sites. Thus, the pickup and delivery sites are relatively small in number compared with, for example, mail forwarders or small-package operations.

Since its establishment five years ago, Columbia has used a single-hub dispatching system, under which all packages picked up are routed to the main Columbia base at Kansas City, and are forwarded from there to their eventual destinations. The continental U.S. is divided into districts, which are aggregated for supervisory purposes into multistate regions. Aircraft are assigned to make pickup rounds in each district, and the material picked up is then flown to Kansas City, where it is unloaded and sorted. Aircraft then return from Kansas City carrying the packages for unloading and delivery in the districts.

At first the number of districts was small, but it has expanded rapidly, along with the growth of Columbia's total shipping. However, this growth has not been without problems. The company has encountered control difficulties causing shipment delays. Since package forwarding is a highly competitive business, the market restrains the prices that can be charged, and Columbia has been only marginally profitable for the last year and a half. This marginal profitability has attracted attention in the business community. Recently, National Enterprises, a large holding company, announced its intent to make a hostile tender offer for Columbia.

You are director of the management science group on the corporate staff of US Communications, a company whose main business has been in pro-

---

*The Columbia Express, Inc., case was authored by Stephen M. Robinson, Department of Industrial Engineering, University of Wisconsin-Madison, and is used here with his permission.

viding telecommunications service to contracting businesses nationwide. You report to James Neesvig, Corporate Vice President and chief financial officer, who in turn reports to Harold Jensen, President and CEO. This morning, Neesvig stopped by your office and told you he had an urgent project for you to work on.

As you know, National Enterprises is tendering for Columbia Express. We're seriously considering fighting them with a competitive tender offer, and Harry Jensen has asked the board to be prepared for a special meeting if it looks as though we should go ahead. Columbia wants nothing to do with us, so it'll have to be a hostile offer.

We clearly don't want Columbia if it continues the way it's been going for the last year or so. Our interest is based on a gut feeling that we ought to be able to run it better than their current management is doing. They've been OK on day-to-day operations, but we don't think they've been doing the right kind of overall planning. The key question is whether doing things differently would get their profitability up enough to make the acquisition worthwhile.

We've asked Morgan Stanley to do an analysis of the acquisition, but they can only work with the figures we have on Columbia. I think we should try a parallel analysis based on how we'd operate Columbia if we had it. If we did that, we might be able to come up with a very different valuation of Columbia than would be made based on their current results. That's where your group comes in.

I think we have to focus on the way Columbia is running their shipments. We know they use a single-hub system because that's what Federal Express does. But Columbia is really a very different operation from Federal Express, and I'm not convinced that a single-hub system is the best way to go. I want you and your people to tell me what is the best way to operate, given the information we have ... and that's pretty sketchy at the moment.

We've had our liaison people dig out some information at the FAA that gives traffic averages for their regions, based on flights and weights reported. They also got some basic information about costs for the kind of aircraft Columbia is using. You may be able to get better information, and if you can, by all means do. But that's all we have at the moment.

What I need to know is the best way to run the Columbia operation, and how much we could get in cost savings if we did that instead of what they're doing. Once we have that, we'll work with Morgan Stanley to build a valuation based on the new operational concept, and we'll present that to the board along with the other valuation based on current operations. My guess is that there'll be quite a difference in the two.

The overriding need now is speed. We've got to decide what to do and, if we go ahead, organize the tender before National gets this thing wrapped up. I want you to give this top priority. Let me know daily how things are going on it. Any questions at this point?

Based on this narrative and the supporting information in Tables 8E.1 and 8E.2, and Exhibit 8E.1 below, prepare a report for presentation to Mr. Jensen. The report should be in the following format, with each section clearly headed and beginning on a separate sheet.

Table 8E.1 Regions for Columbia Express.

Region	States
1	Maine, New Hampshire, Vermont, Massachusetts, Rhode Island, Connecticut, New York, New Jersey
2	Pennsylvania, Delaware, Maryland, West Virginia, District of Columbia, Virginia
3	North Carolina, South Carolina, Florida, Georgia, Alabama, Tennessee
4	Mississippi, Louisiana, Arkansas, Oklahoma, Texas
5	Kentucky, Ohio, Indiana, Michigan, Illinois, Wisconsin
6	Missouri, Iowa, Minnesota, Kansas, Nebraska, North Dakota, South Dakota
7	New Mexico, Arizona, Colorado, Utah
8	Wyoming, Montana, Idaho, Oregon, Washington
9	Nevada, California

Table 8E.2. Regional Traffic Averages[a].

	To									
From	1	2	3	4	5	6	7	8	9	Total
1	71.2	5.1	2.3	17.8	21.6	1.4	3.6	6.9	50.5	180.4
2	10.5	38.1	7.9	2.1	19.2	5.2	6.1	3.3	8.9	101.3
3	6.4	2.1	32.1	8.4	11.6	2.2	3.1	3.7	15.6	85.2
4	12.1	13.8	6.3	62.8	18.9	13.7	7.4	4.7	25.1	164.8
5	14.6	10.2	4.9	16.7	49.2	3.1	4.8	6.2	11.6	121.3
6	7.1	5.4	2.4	8.2	7.8	27.6	3.1	4.0	6.5	72.1
7	9.2	5.8	2.9	10.2	12.4	1.8	38.2	2.1	12.2	94.8
8	5.1	3.8	1.9	6.4	7.3	2.0	3.5	28.1	9.3	67.4
9	18.7	12.4	4.8	13.1	11.8	17.6	8.2	5.8	59.8	152.2
	154.9	96.7	65.5	145.7	159.8	74.6	78.0	64.8	199.5	1039.5

[a]Traffic averages given are daily poundage (in thousands) in and out of the region, Monday through Friday (next-day service from Friday is Monday). These typically fluctuate by up to 30%.

Suggested Format for Solution Report

1. Executive summary: No more than one page, containing the main issues, conclusions, and recommendations.
2. Analysis and recommendations: Discussion of the analysis, emphasizing assumptions made, criteria applied, and conclusions drawn. Recommendations should follow, and they should be clearly supported by the analysis. DO NOT do mathematical modeling in this section.
3. Appendix containing mathematical models, computer results, and any other technical material needed.

Exhibit 8E.1   Fleet and Cost Data, Columbia Express.

Most of Columbia's present fleet is composed of AV-55 twin-jet transport aircraft. These are suitable for the mostly short-haul trips with frequent landings required in Columbia's operations. These craft have a payload of 31,250 pounds under normal operating conditions.

Estimated operating costs for the AV-55 are $9.92 per minute when on ground hold, and $14.59 per minute when airborne. These are marginal costs and they assume a normal cruising speed of 525 mph. A degradation factor of 75% to convert from cruising speed to average speed is normal for reasonably long flights, but this may require modification for very short flights. About half of the above costs are fuel and oil costs.

Based on the experience of other forwarders, if Columbia were to open additional hubs it would require an outlay of between $425,000 and $460,000 yearly for fixed expenses at each hub. To this would have to be added a variable cost for staffing and operations that would run between $22 and $24 per thousand pounds of freight processed through the center.

REFERENCE NOTES

SECTION 8.1 Set-covering models for facility location came into prominence with Toregas, Swain, ReVelle, and Bergman (1971), who suggested the cutting plane procedure. Toregas and ReVelle (1973) applied the reduction rules. Minieka (1970) treated the *m*-center problem. Church and ReVelle (1974) introduced the maximal covering location problem. Belardo, Harrald, Wallace, and Ward (1984) gave an application of the model to siting oil spill response equipment. Hogan and ReVelle (1986) discussed backup coverage.

SECTION 8.2 Baumol and Wolfe (1958), Kuehn and Hamburger (1963) and Manne (1964) contributed early formulations and (heuristic) solution procedures to the warehouse location literature. Balinski (1965) gave a counterexample due to Gomory to show that problem (SRS) would not automatically produce an integer optimal solution; Benders decomposition was suggested as a solution approach. Efroymson and Ray (1966) were the first to develop an efficient branch-and-bound procedure for solving problem (SPLP). They noted that the linear programming relaxation, problem (SRS), frequently produced integer optimal solutions. Khumawala (1972) improved the branching rules of their algorithm, and Spielberg (1969) developed an implicit enumeration method. ReVelle and Swain (1970) first suggested using linear programming directly to solve the problem in its *m*-median form; and in the "unlikely event of a non-integer solution," to use a branch-and-bound scheme. Morris (1978) discussed the linear programming approach applied to problem (SPLP). Schrage (1975) showed how the assignment constraints (8.15) can be handled implicitly in the simplex method. Erlenkotter (1978) developed DUALOC. The article by Bilde and Krarup (1977) contained a version with minor revisions of their earlier research report (in Danish), which introduced an approach similar to DUALOC. The discussion of surcharges applied to problem (SPLP) is from Mavrides (1979), who studied the problem of locating lock-boxes.

Cornuejols, Fisher, and Nemhauser (1977) gave a formal analysis of heuristics, whereas Geoffrion and Van Roy (1979) offered an informal analysis. A definitive account of the literature of problem (SPLP) was the survey and synthesis by Krarup and Pruzan (1983).

The demand point aggregation section is from Geoffrion (1976a), as is Section 8.4.

SECTION 8.3 This section is based on the work of Geoffrion and Graves (1974), which stands unique in its optimizing treatment of large-scale problems that contain most aspects of distribution design. The problem narrative follows Geoffrion (1976b). Aikens (1985) provided a review of location models for distribution planning.

APPENDIX–CHAPTER 8

Mathematical Notes

8.1 On Benders Decomposition. If the zero-one variables in problem (DD) are temporarily held fixed at feasible values, say z_k^H, $y_{k\ell}^H$, the reduced problem is given by:

$$\underset{x}{\text{minimize}} \sum_i \sum_j \sum_k \sum_\ell c_{ijk\ell} x_{ijk\ell}$$

subject to   (8.38)

$$\sum_k \sum_\ell x_{ijk\ell} \leqslant S_{ij} \qquad \text{for all } i,j$$

$$\sum_j x_{ijk\ell} = D_{i\ell} y_{k\ell}^H \qquad \text{for all } i,k,\ell$$

$$x_{ijk\ell} \geqslant 0 \qquad \text{for all } i,j,k,\ell.$$

Problem (8.38) is the partition of problem (DD) in terms of the transportation variables only and, as stated in the text, is assumed feasible for every choice of $y_{k\ell}^H$ satisfying constraint (8.34).

The dual of problem (8.38) can be written:

$$\underset{u,\pi}{\text{maximize}} \sum_i \sum_j (-S_{ij}) u_{ij} + \sum_i \sum_k \sum_\ell (-D_{i\ell} y_{k\ell}^H) \pi_{ik\ell}$$

subject to   (8.40)

$$-u_{ij} - \pi_{ik\ell} \leqslant c_{ijk\ell} \qquad \text{for all } i,j,k,\ell$$

$$u_{ij} \geqslant 0 \qquad \text{for all } i,j$$

and $\pi_{ik\ell}$ is unrestricted in sign for all i,k,ℓ.

The reason for considering problem (8.40) is that $y_{k\ell}^H$ appears only in the objective function. The set of feasible solutions for problem (8.40), say F, is therefore the same for *any* choice of values for $y_{k\ell}^H$. An optimal solution of problem (8.40) can be found by checking the extreme points of F, because problem (8.40) is a linear programming problem. Let F contain N extreme points denoted by (u^h, π^h), $h = 1,...,N$. In principle, then, problem (8.40) can be solved by finding:

$$\max \{\sum_i \sum_j (-S_{ij})u_{ij}^h + \sum_i \sum_k \sum_\ell (-D_{i\ell}y_{k\ell}^H)\pi_{ik\ell}^h, \; 1 \leqslant h \leqslant N\}. \quad (8.40')$$

Using this form to represent the dual of problem (8.38) and therefore the x-partition of problem (DD), for a given y-vector, problem (DD) can be solved by solving the following program, denoted problem (BDD):

minimize B (8.42)
$\quad B,y,z$

subject to

constraints (8.34) through (8.36) and:

$$B \geqslant \sum_k (f_k z_k + v_k \sum_i \sum_\ell D_{i\ell}y_{k\ell}) - \sum_i \sum_j u_{ij}^h S_{ij}$$

$$- \sum_i \sum_k \sum_\ell \pi_{ik\ell}^h D_{i\ell}y_{k\ell},$$

$$h = 1,...,N, \quad (8.43)$$

$$y_{k\ell}, z_k = 0 \text{ or } 1 \quad \text{for all } k,\ell. \quad (8.44)$$

This is because minimizing B is equivalent to minimizing:

$$\sum_k (f_k z_k + v_k \sum_i \sum_\ell D_{i\ell}y_{k\ell}) + \text{expression (8.40')},$$

which is equivalent to the objective function of problem (DD). Of course, N will be a prohibitively large number. The Benders decomposition procedure identifies only a small subset of the extreme points (u^h, π^h) of F. Let H be the number of extreme points identified so far and let problem (BDD^H) denote problem (BDD) with the associated $H \leqslant N$ constraints imposed on B, ie, the program in Step 1 of the procedure. As iterations proceed, H increases and upper and lower bounds (LB and UB) on the optimal value of B and therefore on v[DD] are calculated.

Determination of Upper and Lower Bounds   Consider an optimal solution of problem (BDD^H) when $H < N$. Denote the optimal solution by $(y^{H+1}, z^{H+1}, B^{H+1})$. Then $LB = B^{H+1}$, as problem (BDD^H) contains only a portion of the constraints of problem (BDD) when $H < N$. Using (y^{H+1}, z^{H+1}) and solving problem (8.38) produces x^{H+1}. Then, because $(x^{H+1}, y^{H+1}, z^{H+1})$ is feasible for problem (DD):

$$UB = \sum_i \sum_j \sum_k \sum_\ell c_{ijk\ell}x_{ijk\ell}^{H+1} + \sum_k (f_k z_k^{H+1} + v_k \sum_i \sum_\ell D_{i\ell}y_{k\ell}^{H+1}).$$

LB and *UB* converge as *H* increases; *LB* is monotonic increasing. When the procedure is terminated, a feasible solution to the distribution design problem (DD) that is within $UB-LB$ of v[DD] is thereby available.

8.2 Derivation of Equations (8.41). Consider problem (8.40) for a given *i*, again utilizing the $\bar{k}(\ell)$ notation. We have:

$$\text{maximize}_{u,\pi} \sum_j (-S_{ij})u_{ij} + \sum_\ell (-D_{i\ell})\pi_{i\bar{k}(\ell)\ell}$$

subject to   (8.40;*i*)

$$-u_{ij} - \pi_{i\bar{k}(\ell)\ell} \leqslant c_{ij\bar{k}(\ell)\ell} \qquad \text{for all } j$$

$$u_{ij} \geqslant 0 \qquad \text{for all } j$$

$$\text{and } \pi_{i\bar{k}(\ell)\ell} \text{ unrestricted} \quad \text{for all } \ell.$$

As $-D_{i\ell}y_{k\ell} = 0$ whenever $k \neq \bar{k}(\ell)$, the corresponding $\pi_{ik\ell}$ in problem (8.40) has no effect on the objective function value. Such variables have been omitted from problem (8.40) to produce problem (8.40;*i*) on the condition that these $\pi_{ik\ell} \geqslant \max_j\{-u_{ij} - c_{ijk\ell}\}$ in any synthesized dual solution to problem (8.38). Inspection of problem (8.40;*i*) reveals that this is the dual of the *i*th independent transportation problem given by problem (8.39). An immediate result is that $u_{ij}^* = \mu_{ij}^*$, where the μ_{ij}'s are the dual variables associated with the supply constraints in problem (8.39). Also, the $\pi_{i\bar{k}(\ell)\ell}$'s are the dual variables associated with the demand constraints in problem (8.39). Now $\pi_{i\bar{k}(\ell)\ell}$ in problem (8.40;*i*) must satisfy:

$$\pi_{i\bar{k}(\ell)\ell} \geqslant \max_j\{-u_{ij} - c_{ij\bar{k}(\ell)\ell}\},$$

and in view of the objective function coefficients $-D_{i\ell} \leqslant 0$, $\pi_{i\bar{k}(\ell)\ell}$ can be set equal to $\max_j\{-u_{ij} - c_{ij\bar{k}(\ell)\ell}\}$ in any optimal solution to problem (8.40;*i*). These conclusions underlie the synthesized dual solution to problem (8.38) given by equations (8.41).

Chapter 9

Floor Layout—
The Quadratic
Assignment Problem

The general nature of the quadratic assignment problem (QAP) is one wherein m facilities must be assigned to m different locations. Each location has available a certain amount of space that will be occupied by the facility assigned there. For each pair of facilities a nonnegative weight is associated with the activity between them. The problem is to place each facility in a location separate from all other facilities in such a way as to minimize the sum of weights times distances between pairs of facilities. An example is the placement of machines on a factory floor. The weights may represent trips that occur per unit time between each pair of machines. It is desirable to keep machines relatively close together in order to conserve space and minimize the weighted-distance costs. An example of a hospital layout problem is described by Elshafei (1977).

The following floor layout application was reported by Urquhart (1977). T and B Mechanical Contractors, Ltd., decided to rent a building to complete a heat exchanger fabrication contract. The job consisted of fabricating and assembling oil refinery radiant and convection heat exchanger sections. The tubes used were 8-inch-diameter steel pipe, about 50 feet long. The production manager sought a plant layout that minimized total material handling cost while completing the contract.

The layout problem was complicated by factors inherent to the plant structure and the work involved. Certain departments required areas of specific shape, rather than simply a certain number of square feet. Neither the shape nor the area requirements of the departments were uniform. Fitting the departments to the building structure was another consideration. Part of the shop was only 15 feet high and could not accommodate

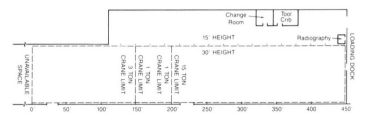

Figure 9.1   Floor Configuration.

convection coils. Certain departments had to be under the cranes. Figure 9.1 shows the configuration of the shop floor.

From the terms of the contract and a knowledge of the production processes involved, work flows (in tons) were determined. These are given in Table 9.1. Transportation costs were not as easily or as accurately found. Different transportation methods, operated at different costs, were to be used (towmotor, crane, and dolly). These costs were based on time and motion studies, maintenance records, and the experience of production personnel.

Table 9.1   Interfacility Work Flow.

FROM \ TO	LOADING/ UNLOADING	ROLL RACK	CONVECTION BOXES	CONV. TUBE STORAGE	RADIANT COIL ASSEMBLY	CROSSOVER	RADIANT HOOP ASSEMBLY	HOOP STORAGE	TUBE SHEET STORAGE	FITTINGS STORAGE	SAW	RADIOGRAPHY
LOADING/ UNLOADING		656				64		192	440	600		
ROLL RACK				1920	1480							6000
CONVECTION BOXES												3200
CONV. TUBE STORAGE			1920									
RADIANT COIL ASSEMBLY												1080
CROSSOVER											80	340
RADIANT HOOP ASSEMBLY								192				440
HOOP STORAGE							192					
TUBE SHEET STORAGE					880							
FITTINGS STORAGE		3400	1920		1440	440						
SAW						392						
RADIOGRAPHY		6000	3200		1080	340	440					

This sketch of an actual study indicates the typical complexity of floor layout problems and emphasizes the need to combine the methods of this chapter with judgment. The three elements of the typical layout problem are present: (1) a set of facilities to be located, with each requiring a certain amount of space; (2) interfacility weights, computed as work flow in tons times cost per ton per unit distance; and (3) a limited amount of space available in which to locate all the facilities.

The concept of locating space-consuming facilities is not limited to floor layout problems. The quadratic assignment model has been used to locate the instruments on helicopter control panels by Wyman and Callahan (1975). Each instrument corresponds to a facility, the control panel is the available space, and the weights correspond to the frequency of eye movement between each instrument pair during a sample of typical flight patterns. The study resulted in the discovery that helicopter instrument panels should have different configurations from those of fixed-wing aircraft.

In devising solution algorithms, some assumptions must be made concerning distances. A common assumption is that distances between spaces are rectangular and measured "center-to-center." This corresponds to the factory or warehouse floor application where movement takes place along a rectangular grid of aisles. In applications like the aircraft instrument panel, Euclidean distances may be more appropriate. If the effort involved in locating the proper gauge goes up more than linearly the farther away the pilot must look, squared Euclidean distances might be substituted for Euclidean distances to represent "costs."

A mathematical programming formulation of problem (QAP) for locating m facilities is:

$$\underset{x}{\text{minimize}} \sum_{i=1}^{m} \sum_{k=1}^{m} \sum_{j=1}^{m} \sum_{\ell=1}^{m} w_{ik} d_{j\ell} x_{ij} x_{k\ell}$$

subject to   (9.1)

$$\sum_{i=1}^{m} x_{ij} = 1 \qquad \text{for all } j$$

$$\sum_{j=1}^{m} x_{ij} = 1 \qquad \text{for all } i$$

$$x_{ij} = 0 \text{ or } 1, \text{ for all } i,j,$$

where w_{ik} is the non-negative weight that multiplies the distance between facilities i and k; $d_{j\ell}$ is the distance between locations j and ℓ; and

$$x_{ij} = \begin{cases} 1 \text{ if facility } i \text{ is assigned to location } j, \\ 0 \text{ otherwise.} \end{cases}$$

Each term of the quadruple summation considers the assignment of a pair of facilities to a pair of locations. The $w_{ik}d_{j\ell}$ product is the weight-times-distance component of the cost function resulting from the flow between facility i and facility k over the distance between locations j and ℓ. The first set of constraints requires each location to have a single facility located there. The second set of constraints ensures that each facility is assigned to a single location.

There may be more locations than facilities or the facilities may require different amounts of space. The former problem may be solved by using dummy facilities in the formulation, the latter by dividing facilities into subfacilities each requiring a standard amount of space and using large values for the interfacility weights between the component parts. The latter approach is not guaranteed to generate an optimal layout for the original problem however.

Problem (QAP) is not amenable to solution by standard linear and nonlinear programming algorithms. Some insight into the difficulty of formulating the problem as a well-behaved programming problem may be gained by examining a numerical example.

Example 9.1   Suppose we wish to locate three offices along a corridor, keeping a unit distance between them. Interoffice weights are given in Table 9.2. The available office locations along the x-axis are: $x = 1$, $x = 2$, and $x = 3$. Let the (unknown) locations of offices 1, 2, and 3 be x_1, x_2, and x_3, respectively. Then we may write this instance of problem (QAP) as:

$$\underset{x}{\text{minimize}} \; 3|x_1 - x_2| + |x_1 - x_3| + 4|x_2 - x_3|$$

subject to

$$|x_1 - x_2| \geqslant 1, \; |x_1 - x_3| \geqslant 1, \; |x_2 - x_3| \geqslant 1,$$

$$1 \leqslant x_1 \leqslant 3, \; 1 \leqslant x_2 \leqslant 3, \; 1 \leqslant x_3 \leqslant 3.$$

Table 9.2   Interoffice Weights w_{ik}.

Office i	Office k		
	1	2	3
1	0	3	1
2	0	0	4
3	0	0	0

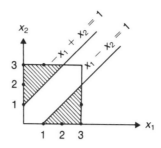

Figure 9.2   Feasible Region (Shaded Areas).

The objective function is convex and can be linearized as in Section 4.1. The main difficulty is with the constraints. Using the first constraint as an example, $|x_1 - x_2| \geq 1$ implies either $x_1 - x_2 \geq 1$ or $-x_1 + x_2 \geq 1$.

This either-or pair of constraints defines a disjointed feasible region as shown in Figure 9.2. Unfortunately, linear and nonlinear programming algorithms invariably require the feasible region to be connected.

9.1 SOLVING PROBLEM (QAP) BY A BRANCH-AND-BOUND TECHNIQUE

The combinatorial nature of problem (QAP) suggests the use of branch-and-bound techniques. Because of large computer storage space requirements and computation times these techniques are restricted to relatively small problems. However, it is instructive to consider one such approach. It is probably best to specify the method through a numerical example. To assist comprehension, we will provide complete detail. Should this begin to seem excessive, the reader may wish to skip to the "big picture" depicted in Figure 9.4.

Example 9.2   Table 9.3 gives the symmetric matrix of interfacility weights, and Figure 9.3 shows the required configuration of a problem with four facilities. Assuming unit square locations and rectangular distances, we obtain the symmetric distance matrix as given in Table 9.4. (For ease of exposition, locations will be denoted by the letters A, B, C, D.)

Table 9.3   Interfacility Weights for Example 9.2.

Facility	1	2	3	4
1	0	50	20	100
2	0	0	30	10
3	0	0	0	70
4	0	0	0	0

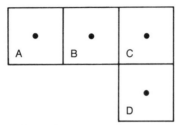

Figure 9.3 Required Configuration.

Table 9.4 Distance Matrix.

Location	A	B	C	D
A	0	1	2	3
B	1	0	1	2
C	2	1	0	1
D	3	2	1	0

The first step in the branch-and-bound procedure is to construct a matrix that shows the cost of assigning all possible facility pairs to each pair of locations. Let M be the number of different pairs of objects that may be chosen from m different objects. Then $M = (m^2 - m)/2$ and the cost matrix will be of dimension $M \times M$. Table 9.5 gives the assignment-to-location cost matrix C for the example.

We next cite a property [theorem 368 of Hardy, Littlewood, and Polya (1952)] of the inner product of two vectors to calculate a lower bound on the optimal solution value.

Table 9.5 Cost Matrix C of Assigning Each Pair of Facilities to Each Pair of Locations.

		Facility Pair					
		$1-2$	$1-3$	$1-4$	$2-3$	$2-4$	$3-4$
		Interfacility Weight					
		50	20	100	30	10	70
Location Pair	Distance	Cost Matrix					
$A-B$	1	50	20	100	30	10	70
$A-C$	2	100	40	200	60	20	140
$A-D$	3	150	60	300	90	30	210
$B-C$	1	50	20	100	30	10	70
$B-D$	2	100	40	200	60	20	140
$C-D$	1	50	20	100	30	10	70

Property 9.1 [*Minimizing the inner product of two vectors*]. *Given the vectors* $a = (a_1, a_2, ..., a_M)$, *and* $b = (b_1, b_2, ..., b_M)$, *the inner product* $ab = \sum_{i=1}^{m} a_i b_i$ *is minimized when the elements of either a or b are arranged in ascending order, and the elements of the other vector are arranged in descending order.*

Intuitively, this arrangement forces the angle between the two vectors to be as close to 90° as possible. The second step in the branch-and-bound method is to rank the distance and cost components so that the sum of the diagonal entries of cost matrix C becomes a lower bound on the cost of the optimal solution. Unfortunately, the diagonal assignment is usually not feasible. Table 9.6 shows this arrangement. The lower bound is $30 + 40 + 60 + 50 + 70 + 100 = 350$.

The next step is to "reduce" cost matrix C by successively subtracting constants from columns and rows. The object is to end up with all diagonal entries being zero, while keeping all other entries non-negative. Continued reference to the C matrix will be used as (an expedient) to mean the *latest* version of the cost matrix. First, subtract from each column the diagonal entry in that column as shown in Table 9.7. The sum, R, of the reducing constants is 350. The optimal assignment will remain unchanged because subtracting a constant from any row or column merely reduces the optimal cost by that amount. As we will need all entries of the cost matrix C to be non-negative, the next step is to subtract from each row the minimum entry in that row as shown in Table 9.8. The sum of the reducing constants now is $R = 240$. The process of subtracting diagonal entries and minimum

Table 9.6 Cost Matrix C with Ranked Distances and Flows.

		Facility Pair					
		2−4	1−3	2−3	1−2	3−4	1−4
		Interfacility Weight					
		10	20	30	50	70	100
Location Pair	Distance	Cost Matrix					
A−D	3	30	60	90	150	210	100
A−C	2	20	40	60	100	140	200
B−D	2	20	40	60	100	140	200
A−B	1	10	20	30	50	70	100
B−C	1	10	20	30	50	70	100
C−D	1	10	20	30	50	70	100

Table 9.7 Subtract from Each Column the Diagonal Entry in that Column: R = 30 + 40 + 60 + 50 + 70 + 100 = 350.

Location Pair	Facility Pair					
	2–4	1–3	2–3	1–2	3–4	1–4
A–D	0	20	30	100	140	200
A–C	−10	0	0	50	70	100
B–D	−10	0	0	50	70	100
A–B	−20	−20	−30	0	0	0
B–C	−20	−20	−30	0	0	0
C–D	−20	−20	−30	0	0	0

Table 9.8 Subtract from Each Row the Minimum Entry of that Row: R = 350 + 0 + (−10) + (−10) + (−30) + (−30) + (−30) = 240.

Location Pair	Facility Pair					
	2–4	1–3	2–3	1–2	3–4	1–4
A–D	0	20	30	100	140	200
A–C	0	10	10	60	80	110
B–D	0	10	10	60	80	110
A–B	10	10	0	30	30	30
B–C	10	10	0	30	30	30
C–D	10	10	0	30	30	30

row entries is continued, as shown in Tables 9.9, 9.10, and 9.11, at which point R = 350.

The beginning node of the branch-and-bound tree corresponds to being able to make any assignment, feasible or not. The minimum total cost has a lower bound of 350. This corresponds to the cost of the diagonal assignment. Let an entry in the ith row and j^{th} column of the cost matrix C be denoted by c_{ij}. In general, branching to the right from a node will imply the assignment of a particular pair of facilities to a particular pair

Table 9.9 Subtract Diagonal Entries from Each Column: R = 240 + 0 + 10 + 30 + 30 + 30 = 350.

Location Pair	Facility Pair					
	2–4	1–3	2–3	1–2	3–4	1–4
A–D	0	10	20	70	110	170
A–C	0	0	0	30	50	80
B–D	0	0	0	30	50	80
A–B	10	0	−10	0	0	0
B–C	10	0	−10	0	0	0
C–D	10	0	−10	0	0	0

Table 9.10 Subtract Minimum Entry from Each Row: R = 350 + 0 + 0 + 0 + (−10) + (10) + (−10) = 320.

Location Pair	Facility Pair					
Pair	2−4	1−3	2−3	1−2	3−4	1−4
A−D	0	10	20	70	110	170
A−C	0	0	0	30	50	80
B−D	0	0	0	30	50	80
A−B	20	10	0	10	10	10
B−C	20	10	0	10	10	10
C−D	20	10	0	10	10	10

Table 9.11 Subtract Diagonal Entries from Each Column: R = 320 + 0 + 0 + 0 + 10 + 10 + 10 = 350.

Location Pair	Facility Pair					
Pair	2−4	1−3	2−3	1−2	3−4	1−4
A−D	0	10	20	60	100	160
A−C	0	0	0	20	40	70
B−D	0	0	0	20	40	70
A−B	20	10	0	0	0	0
B−C	20	10	0	0	0	0
C−D	20	10	0	0	0	0

of locations. We will use the notation: A−D ← 1−3, for example, to denote the assignment of facilities 1 and 3 to the locations A and D. A branch to the left means the particular assignment is to be prohibited. We will denote this by: A−D → 1−3, for example. Each succeeding node to be chosen is decided by the following rule:

Selection of Next Node—Choose an entry c_{ke} in cost matrix C for the next node so that:

$$\theta_{ke} = \max \{\theta_{ij}\} \quad \text{where}$$

$$\theta_{ij} = \text{smallest entry in row } i, \text{ omitting } c_{ij} + \text{smallest entry in column } j, \text{ omitting } c_{ij}.$$

Table 9.12 indicates the θ_{ke} values in the upper right of each cell; max $\{\theta_{ij}\} = 10 = \theta_{11}$. Branching to the left is denoted on the tree by A−D. Branching to the right by A−D. The new lower bound of the left branch node is equal to the lower bound of the previous node plus θ_{ij}. The new lower bound of the right branch node is equal to the lower bound of the previous node plus the reducing constants obtained after cost matrix C is restricted. Restriction consists of an examination of remaining entries in cost matrix C to see if they correspond to acceptable assignments. If an entry

Table 9.12 $\theta_{k\ell}$ Values for Each Assignment.

Location Pair	Facility Pair					
	2−4	1−3	2−3	1−2	3−4	1−4
A−D	10	0	0	0	0	0
	0	10	20	60	100	160
A−C	0	0	0	0	0	0
	0	0	0	20	40	70
B−D	0	0	0	0	0	0
	0	0	0	20	40	70
A−B	0	0	0	0	0	0
	20	10	0	0	0	0
B−C	0	0	0	0	0	0
	20	10	0	0	0	0
C−D	0	0	0	0	0	0
	20	10	0	0	0	0

is not acceptable, the entry is deleted to remove it from further consideration. Consider a hypothetical example with five facilities as shown in Table 9.13. Suppose facility pair 3−4 has been assigned to location pair B−E (facility 3 is at location B or E, with facility 4 at the other location). The entries in the B−E row and the 3−4 column have been deleted except the intersection $c_{9,10}$, which is equated to zero. Then the location pairs not assigned are A−C, A−D, and C−D. In the rows with these labels, keep those entries whose column labels are facility pairs not assigned (in this case 1−2, 1−5, and 2−5); but delete entries from columns labeled 1−3, 1−4, 2−3, 2−4, 3−5, and 4−5, as they have a 3 or a 4 in their labels. In the remaining rows (labeled A−B, A−E, B−C, B−D, B−E, C−E, D−E), keep entries from columns 1−3, 1−4, 2−3, 2−4, 3−5, and 4−5, but delete entries with columns labeled 1−2, 1−5, and 2−5. Any reduction can now be made, ignoring deleted entries.

Using these rules, the branch-and-bound method is applied to the example in Tables 9.14 to 9.24.

Table 9.13 X's Indicate Entry Retained in the C Matrix (Partial Assignment, B−E ← 3−4).

Location Pair	Facility Pair									
	1−2	2−4	4−5	3−5	1−4	1−3	2−3	1−5	2−5	3−4
B−C		X	X	X	X	X	X			
A−D	X							X	X	
D−E		X	X	X	X	X	X			
C−E		X	X	X	X	X	X			
A−B		X	X	X	X	X	X			
C−D	X							X	X	
A−C	X							X	X	
A−B		X	X	X	X	X	X			
B−E										0
B−D		X	X	X	X	X	X			

Table 9.14 Restriction as Result of θ_{11} Assigning $2-4$ to $A-D$: Reduction Now Possible on Row 5.

Location Pair	Facility Pair					
	$2-4$	$1-3$	$2-3$	$1-2$	$3-4$	$1-4$
A–D	0					
A–C			0	20	40	70
B–D			0	20	40	70
A–B			0	0	0	0
B–C		10				
C–D			0	0	0	0

Table 9.15 Reducing Constant 10 Added to 350 for Lower Bound on Right Branch [branching will continue from left node ($\overline{A-D} \leftarrow 2-4$); this choice arbitrary as both lower bounds equal 360].

Location Pair	Facility Pair					
	$2-4$	$1-3$	$2-3$	$1-2$	$3-4$	$1-4$
A–D	0					
A–C			0	20	40	70
B–D			0	20	40	70
A–B			0	0	0	0
B–C		0				
C–D			0	0	0	0

Table 9.16 Branch on Node $\overline{A-D} \leftarrow 2-4$ (c_{11} is set equal to ∞ to block assignment of $2-4$ to $A-D$; row 1 reduced by 10; $\theta_{12} = 10$ selects node $A-D \leftarrow 1-3$).

Location Pair	Facility Pair					
	$2-4$	$1-3$	$2-3$	$1-2$	$3-4$	$1-4$
		10	0			
A–D	∞	0	10	50	90	150
A–C	0	0	0	20	40	70
B–D	0	0	0	20	40	70
A–B	20	10	0	0	0	0
B–C	20	10	0	0	0	0
C–D	20	10	0	0	0	0

Table 9.17 Restriction as a Result of θ_{12} Assigning $1-3$ to $A-D$ (the entries in $A-D$ row and $1-3$ column deleted; zero entered in c_{12}; reduction now possible on row 5).

Location Pair	Facility Pair					
	$2-4$	$1-3$	$2-3$	$1-2$	$3-4$	$1-4$
$A-D$	∞	0				
$A-C$			0	20	40	70
$B-D$			0	20	40	70
$A-B$			0	0	0	0
$B-C$	20					
$C-D$			0		0	0	0

Table 9.18 Reducing Constant 20 Added to 360 to Become the Lower Bound for Node $A-D \leftarrow 1-3$ (branching continues at node $A-D \leftarrow 2-4$, which now has the least lower bound of any of the active nodes).

Location Pair	Facility Pair					
	$2-4$	$1-3$	$2-3$	$1-2$	$3-4$	$1-4$
$A-D$	∞	0				
$A-C$			0	20	40	70
$B-D$			0	20	40	70
$A-B$			0	0	0	0
$B-C$	0					
$C-D$			0	0	0	0

Table 9.19 Branching on Node $A-D \leftarrow 2-4$ Where $\theta_{23} = 20 = \max \{\theta_{ij}\}$ (bound for node $A-C \leftarrow 2-3$ thus becomes $360 + 20 = 380$; Table 9.19 derives directly from Table 9.14).

Location Pair	Facility Pair					
	2-4	1-3	2-3	1-2	3-4	1-4
A-D	0					
A-C				20	0	0	0
A-C	0	0	0	20	40	70
B-D			0	0	0	0
B-D			0	20	40	70
A-B			0	0	0	0
A-B			0	0	0	0
B-C		0				
C-D			0	0	0	0
C-D			0	0	0	0

At this point the branch to the right from node $A-D \leftarrow 2-4$ to node $A-C \leftarrow 2-3$ specifies the complete assignment $\begin{vmatrix} A & B & C & D \\ 2 & 1 & 3 & 4 \end{vmatrix}$. This assignment has a total cost of 430. The next branch is thus from node $\overline{A-D} \leftarrow 1-3$, which has a lower bound of 370. The complete branch-and-bound tree appears in Figure 9.4 with the two optimal solutions.

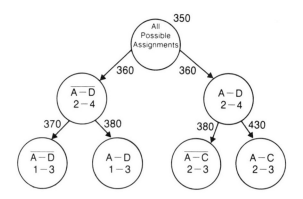

Table 9.20 Branching on Node $\overline{A-D} \leftarrow 1-3$ Where $\theta_{13} = 40 = \max \{\theta_{ij}\}$ (bound for node $\overline{A-D} \leftarrow 2-3$ becomes $370 + 40 = 410$).

Location Pair	Facility Pair					
	2-4	1-3	2-3	1-2	3-4	1-4
A-D			40	0	0	0
	∞	∞	0	40	80	140
A-C	0	0	0	0	0	0
	0	0	0	20	40	70
B-D	0	0	0	0	0	0
	0	0	0	20	40	70
A-B	0	0	0	0	0	0
	20	10	0	0	0	0
B-C	0	0	0	0	0	0
	20	10	0	0	0	0
C-D	0	0	0	0	0	0
	20	10	0	0	0	0

Figure 9.4 Branch-and-Bound Tree for Example 9.2.

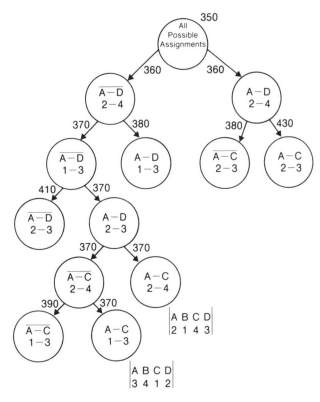

Table 9.21 Restriction as a Result of θ_{13} Assigning $2-3$ to $A-D$ (no reduction possible after restriction, so lower bound on node $A-D \leftarrow 2-3$ is 370; branching continues from node $A-D \leftarrow 2-3$ using the restricted cost matrix).

Location Pair	Facility Pair					
	$2-4$	$1-3$	$2-3$	$1-2$	$3-4$	$1-4$
A–D	∞	∞	0			
A–C	0	0		20	40	
B–D				20	40	
A–B	20	10		0	0	
B–C						0
C–D	20	10		0	0	

Table 9.22 All θ_{ij} Are Zero. (Arbitrarily consider node $\overline{A-C} \leftarrow 2-4$; the bound on node $\overline{A-C} \leftarrow 2-4$ is $370 + 0 = 370$; on node $A-C \leftarrow 2-4$ the bound is 370 and the procedure identifies the assignment $\begin{vmatrix} A & B & C & D \\ 2 & 1 & 4 & 3 \end{vmatrix}$. This is an optimal solution because no other active node has a lower bound.)

Location Pair	Facility Pair					
	$2-4$	$1-3$	$2-3$	$1-2$	$3-4$	$1-4$
A–D			0			
A–C	0					
B–D		0				
A–B				0	0	
B–C						0
C–D				0	0	

Branch-and-bound is a general method that gives optimal solutions. Any distances may be used. The implementation here is typical of several proposed methods. The maximum problem size that can be solved exactly on the largest generally available computers is about $m = 16$ facilities, whereas total enumeration of the set of all permutations of $\{1,2,...,m\}$ can solve problems up to about size $m = 11$.

Table 9.23 Branching on Node $\overline{A-C} \leftarrow 2-4$, Where $\theta_{22} = 20 = \max\{\theta_{ij}\}$ (the bound for node $\overline{A-C} \leftarrow 1-3$ thus becomes $370 + 20 = 390$).

Location Pair	Facility Pair					
	2−4	1−3	2−3	1−2	3−4	1−4
A−D	∞	∞	0			
		20		0	0	
A−C	∞	0		20	40	
B−D	0	0		20	40	
A−B	20	10		0	0	
B−C						0
C−D	20	10		0	0	

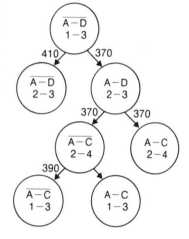

Table 9.24 No Reduction Possible After Restriction for Node $A-C \leftarrow 1-3$ (the lower bound on this node is 370; and the node defines the alternate optimal solution $\begin{vmatrix} A & B & C & D \\ 3 & 4 & 1 & 2 \end{vmatrix}$).

Location Pair	Facility Pair					
	2−4	1−3	2−3	1−2	3−4	1−4
A−D	∞	∞	0			
A−C	∞	0				
B−D	0					
A−B						
B−C						
C−D						

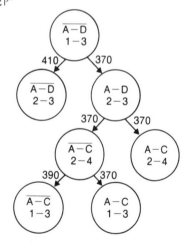

9.2 HEURISTIC PROCEDURES—CRAFT AND HC63-66

To "solve" large ($m > 16$) instances of problem (QAP) one must resort to heuristic procedures. Most of these methods are simplistic in nature and similar to each other. We briefly discuss two of them here. The first of these, CRAFT (computerized relative allocation of facilities technique) relies on the principle of pair-wise exchanges in order to improve a starting solution, which the analyst must specify. Pair-wise exchanging cannot be generally regarded as a "greedy" method because each variable is not changed optimally at each iteration of the solution method. A restriction is imposed at each move by specifying that if it is cost-attractive to move facility i, say, from location A to location B, the CRAFT procedure also moves the facility presently in location B to location A. This is done even when a better strategy may be to move this latter facility elsewhere. For this reason and others, CRAFT may not obtain optimal solutions. Of course, there are many ways to modify the basic approach of CRAFT to obtain improved versions. Our purpose here is to provide a description of two classical heuristic approaches to solving problem (QAP).

Example 9.3 We illustrate CRAFT using the problem data of Example 9.2, and the starting solution indicated in Figure 9.5.

A • 1 B • 3 C • 4	Exchange Pair	$1-2$	$1-3$	$1-4$	$2-3$	$2-4$	$3-4$
D • 2	Cost Change	-100	-50	-80	-60	90	-100

Figure 9.5 Starting Solution for CRAFT (Cost = 510).

Of the six possible pair-wise exchanges, either pair $1-2$ or pair $3-4$ could be exchanged to obtain a cost reduction of 100. We arbitrarily choose to exchange the locations of facilities 1 and 2. The second solution and the six possible pair-wise exchanges are shown in Figure 9.6.

A • 2 B • 3 C • 4	Exchange Pair	$1-2$	$1-3$	$1-4$	$2-3$	$2-4$	$3-4$
D • 1	Cost Change	100	-40	10	30	100	100

Figure 9.6 Second CRAFT Solution (Cost = 410).

Facilities 1 and 3 are now exchanged. This solution and the associated pair-wise exchange effects are given in Figure 9.7.

A • 2 B • 1 C • 4	Exchange Pair	$1-2$	$1-3$	$1-4$	$2-3$	$2-4$	$3-4$
D • 3	Cost Change	80	40	90	90	40	60

Figure 9.7 Final CRAFT Solution (Cost = 370).

The CRAFT procedure terminates owing to the positive cost changes for each exchange pair possibility. As this is one of the two optimal solutions, the heuristic has performed well.

The HC63-66 method employs the same basic algorithmic concept as CRAFT. In addition, it requires the floor layout to be a rectangular grid of unit squares. Rather than checking all pair-wise exchanges at each step, however, only pairs directly above, below, to either side, or on any of the four 45° diagonal lines emanating from the facility to be evaluated are checked for "move desirability." In addition, the user specifies a maximum number (say, K) of steps away that candidate pairs are tested. In a single pass the algorithm checks for pair exchanges K, $K-1$,...,1, steps away from each facility in the eight different directions. HC63-66 checks fewer candidate pairs at each step than does CRAFT and is therefore computationally faster.

Example 9.4   As an illustration of the limitations of pair-wise exchange methods, consider an $m = 6$ facility example with interfacility weights as given in Table 9.25. A candidate solution with a cost of 70 is shown in Figure 9.8.

A •4 B •3 C •2 D •1 E •5 F •6

Figure 9.8   Possible Solution for Example 9.4.

For this example, at each iteration there are 15 possible pair-wise exchanges. Starting with the solution in Figure 9.8, the effects for the first iteration are reported below.

Exchange Pair	1–2	1–3	1–4	1–5	1–6	2–3	2–4	2–5	2–6	3–4	3–5	3–6	4–5	4–6	5–6
Cost Change	10	30	10	25	30	30	20	40	45	5	70	110	90	60	5

As no pair-wise exchange will yield a cost improvement, a pair-wise exchange method would terminate with this solution. The optimum solution shown in Figure 9.9 has a cost of 55, which represents a 21.4% cost reduction.

A •1 B •2 C •3 D •4 E •5 F •6

Figure 9.9   Optimum Solution for Example 9.4.

Table 9.25   Interfacility Weights for Example 9.4.

Facility	1	2	3	4	5	6
1	0	15	0	0	0	0
2	0	0	10	0	0	0
3	0	0	0	10	0	0
4	0	0	0	0	5	0
5	0	0	0	0	0	15
6	0	0	0	0	0	0

9.3 THE HALL m-DIMENSIONAL QUADRATIC PLACEMENT ALGORITHM

We now describe the Hall method for generating optimal floor layout patterns where the assumption of minimizing weighted *squared* Euclidean distances can be made. The method is an optimizing technique that can solve large problems. The main advantage is that the facilities are not assigned to predetermined locations. The Hall method provides a layout pattern; the specific assignments or layouts are done by the analyst. In this regard, there is evidence that in some cases, an experienced practitioner can improve on the solution given by a heuristic algorithm.

One-Dimensional Problems

Let W be an $m \times m$ symmetric "connection" matrix in which the entry w_{ij} is the weight between points i and j; $w_{ij} = w_{ji}$, and $w_{ii} = 0$. Let the unknown vector of locations in one dimension be given by $X = (x_1, x_2, ..., x_m)$. Then the one-dimensional quadratic placement problem is stated as:

$$\underset{X}{\text{minimize}} \; Q(X) = \frac{1}{2} \sum_{i=1}^{m} \sum_{j=1}^{m} w_{ij}(x_i - x_j)^2$$

$$\text{subject to } XX = 1, \tag{9.2}$$

where XX denotes the inner product of X with itself, ie, $XX = x_1^2 + x_2^2 + ... + x_m^2$. The constraint is added to prevent the solution $x_1 = x_2 = ... = x_m = 0$. The solution method will be developed for one-dimensional problems and then generalized to two or more dimensions. It will be convenient to write $Q(X)$ in matrix form.

Let $w_{i.}$ and $w_{.j}$ be the ith row sum and the jth column sum, respectively, of the connection matrix W. Then let D be a diagonal matrix with $d_{ii} = w_{i.}$, and let matrix B be given by $B = D - W$. We can write $Q(X)$ in terms of the B matrix, as indicated by the following property.

Property 9.2 [*Quadratic equivalence using the matrix B*]. $Q(X) = XBX$.

PROOF:

$$Q(X) = \frac{1}{2} \sum_{i=1}^{m} \sum_{j=1}^{m} w_{ij}(x_i - x_j)^2 = \frac{1}{2} \sum_{i=1}^{m} \sum_{j=1}^{m} w_{ij}(x_i^2 - 2x_i x_j + x_j^2)$$

$$= \frac{1}{2} \left(\sum_{i=1}^{m} w_{i.} x_i^2 - 2 \sum_{i=1}^{m} \sum_{j=1}^{m} w_{ij} x_i x_j + \sum_{j=1}^{m} w_{.j} x_j^2 \right)$$

$$= \frac{1}{2} XDX - XWX + \frac{1}{2} XDX,$$

$$= XBX, \text{ since } w_{i.} = w_{.j} \text{ by symmetry.}$$

Because $Q(X)$ is a sum of convex functions, B must be a positive semidefinite matrix. To solve problem (9.2), introduce the Lagrange multiplier λ and form the Lagrangian function $L(X,\lambda) = XBX - \lambda(XX-1)$. Taking the first partial derivative of $L(X,\lambda)$ with respect to the vector X and equating to zero gives $2BX - 2\lambda X = \bar{0}$. Using the $m \times m$ identity matrix given by I, we may write:

$$(B - \lambda I)X = \bar{0}. \tag{9.3}$$

Solving this system of linear equations produces a nontrivial solution X if, and only if, λ is an eigenvalue of the matrix B, and X is the corresponding eigenvector. Premultiplying both sides of expression (9.3) by X and substituting $XX = 1$ gives:

$$\lambda = XBX = Q(X). \tag{9.4}$$

With the eigenvalues ranked in increasing order, the ith eigenvector gives the ith best solution, with the eigenvalue being its objective value. The least eigenvalue, $\lambda_0 = 0$, produces the solution $X = (1/\sqrt{m}, 1/\sqrt{m}, ..., 1/\sqrt{m})$, which is disregarded.

Example 9.5   We now apply the Hall method to the problem given in Table 9.3 and Figure 9.3. Because distances are rectangular, this layout problem is essentially one-dimensional with the equivalent required pattern as shown in Figure 9.10.

The W matrix is given by:

$$W = \begin{bmatrix} 0 & 50 & 20 & 100 \\ 50 & 0 & 30 & 10 \\ 20 & 30 & 0 & 70 \\ 100 & 10 & 70 & 0 \end{bmatrix}$$

The D and B matrices are as follows:

$$D = \begin{bmatrix} 170 & 0 & 0 & 0 \\ 0 & 90 & 0 & 0 \\ 0 & 0 & 120 & 0 \\ 0 & 0 & 0 & 180 \end{bmatrix} \quad B = \begin{bmatrix} 170 & -50 & -20 & -100 \\ -50 & 90 & -30 & -10 \\ -20 & -30 & 120 & -70 \\ -100 & -10 & -70 & 180 \end{bmatrix}$$

The four eigenvectors E_0, E_1, E_2, E_3 of matrix B and their associated eigenvalues λ_0, λ_1, λ_2, λ_3 are given in Table 9.26.

Using E_1 (because E_0 provides no information and is disregarded) the cost minimizing layout is the sequence 2,1,4,3 shown in Figure 9.11. This agrees with the branch-and-bound solution given earlier and is thus optimal.

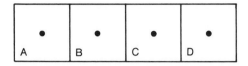

Figure 9.10 Layout Pattern Equivalent to Figure 9.3.

Table 9.26 Eigenvectors and Eigenvalues for Example 9.5.

Facility	E_0	E_1	E_2	E_3
		Eigenvectors		
1	.5	.07	.59	−.63
2	.5	−.84	−.16	.16
3	.5	.39	−.73	−.25
4	.5	.38	.30	.72
λ	0	112.55	158.05	289.40

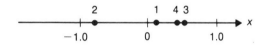

Figure 9.11 One-Dimensional Layout Using E_1.

Two-Dimensional Problems

Let $Y = (y_1, y_2, ..., y_m)$ be the vector of y-coordinates of the m points. Then the two-dimensional layout problem with weighted squared Euclidean distances can be written:

$$\text{minimize } Q(X,Y) = XBX + YBY$$
$$X,Y$$

$$\text{subject to} \qquad XX = 1 \text{ and } YY = 1. \qquad (9.5)$$

To solve problem (9.5), introduce two Lagrange multipliers α and β, and form the Lagrangian function

$$L(X,Y,\alpha,\beta) = XBX + YBY - \alpha(XX - 1) - \beta(YY - 1).$$

Taking first partial derivatives with respect to X and Y and equating to zero gives:

$$\partial L/\partial X = 2BX - 2\alpha X = \overline{0} \qquad (9.6)$$

$$\partial L/\partial Y = 2BY - 2\beta Y = \overline{0}. \qquad (9.7)$$

The solutions to these two systems of equations are provided by the eigenvectors of matrix B associated with the eigenvalues α and β, respectively. If both sides of expressions (9.6) and (9.7) are premultiplied by X and Y, respectively, and the constraints $XX = 1$ and $YY = 1$ are substituted, the result is that $Q(X,Y) = \alpha + \beta$. Let the m eigenvalues of B be given by $0 = \lambda_0 < \lambda_1 \leqslant \lambda_2 \leqslant ... \leqslant \lambda_{m-1}$. The cases for which $\alpha = \lambda_0$ and/or $\beta = \lambda_0$ correspond to the trivial solutions wherein all the x_i and/or all the y_i are equal. Such solutions are generally unsatisfactory. The most satisfactory choice in general is to let $\alpha = \lambda_1$ and $\beta = \lambda_2$. The vectors X and Y are the eigenvectors associated with α and β, respectively. With this choice the facilities are optimally located in the direction of the first coordinate axis and located "next-to-optimal" in the direction of the second coordinate axis.

The method can be extended to problems in three dimensions. In this case the eigenvalues used generally would be λ_1, λ_2, and λ_3, and $Q(X,Y,Z)$ is given by $Q(X,Y,Z) = \lambda_1 + \lambda_2 + \lambda_3$. The vectors of the coordinates of the points in three-dimensional space are given by the eigenvectors associated with λ_1, λ_2, and λ_3.

Example 9.6   To demonstrate the use of the Hall method in two dimensions, consider the following example with $m = 12$ facilities. The interfacility weights are given in Table 9.27, the first eight eigenvalues and eigenvectors in Table 9.28, and the plot of points with coordinates from E_1 and E_2 is given in Figure 9.12. The required layout pattern is 3 $\times$ 4, ie, unit square locations with three rows and four columns. The distance measure is rectangular. From Figure 9.12, several possible assignments of facilities to locations suggest themselves. Two of these are

Table 9.27   Interfacility Weights for Example 9.6.

Facility	1	2	3	4	5	6	7	8	9	10	11	12
1	0	5	2	4	1	0	0	6	2	1	1	1
2	5	0	3	0	2	2	2	0	4	5	0	0
3	2	3	0	0	0	0	0	5	5	2	2	2
4	4	0	0	0	5	2	2	10	0	0	5	5
5	1	2	0	5	0	10	0	0	0	5	1	1
6	0	2	0	2	10	0	5	1	1	5	4	0
7	0	2	0	2	0	5	0	10	5	2	3	3
8	6	0	5	10	0	1	10	0	0	0	5	0
9	2	4	5	0	0	1	5	0	0	0	10	10
10	1	5	2	5	5	2	0	0	0	0	5	0
11	1	0	2	5	1	4	3	5	10	5	0	2
12	1	0	2	5	1	0	3	0	10	0	2	0

Table 9.28 Eigenvectors and Eigenvalues for Example 9.6.

E_0	E_1	E_2	E_3	E_4	E_5	E_6	E_7
−.28867	−.16005	.34473	−.59992	.26253	.26205	.28205	−.40778
−.28867	.10995	.57340	.11717	.45403	−.18601	−.45069	.29537
−.28867	−.33526	.39847	.32322	−.63056	.31256	−.08582	.00580
−.28867	−.05577	−.25982	−.35224	−.06424	.10900	.00137	.55832
−.28867	.53305	−.17455	−.01189	−.03962	.51262	−.20459	.04993
−.28867	.41901	−.16926	.04645	−.10843	−.01365	−.21580	−.44567
−.28867	−.06845	−.20105	−.07629	−.08997	−.55242	−.24966	−.14494
−.28867	−.16645	−.07791	−.36893	−.28077	−.21821	−.06689	.19758
−.28867	−.25272	−.08623	.28277	.17122	−.06176	−.02018	−.30583
−.28867	.39380	.18960	.24365	−.03108	−.24346	.71057	.20714
−.28867	−.05245	−.14079	.06421	−.07551	−.18967	.19733	−.14108
−.28867	−.36467	−.39659	.33232	.43239	.26896	.10232	.13116
λ_0	λ_1	λ_2	λ_3	λ_4	λ_5	λ_6	λ_7
0.0000	14.6387	18.7578	21.0040	24.1576	26.6377	30.2883	34.1401

given in Figures 9.13 and 9.14. The associated costs using rectangular distances and assuming unit square locations are 302 and 310, respectively. Because these layouts are based on squared Euclidean distances and the shapes and sizes of the locations are not predetermined, they

Figure 9.12 Plot of Points for Example 9.6.

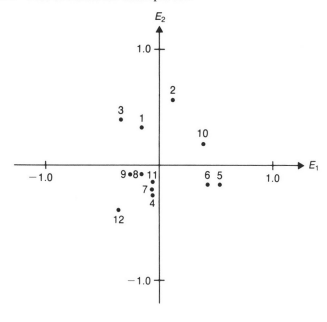

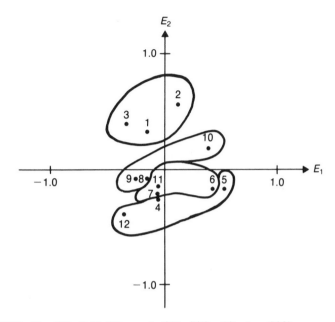

Figure 9.13 Possible 3 × 4 Layout of Facilities (Cost = 302).

Figure 9.14 Possible 3× 4 Layout of Facilities (Cost = 310).

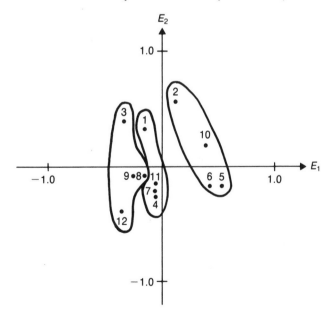

First initial solution (suggested layout from Figure 9.13)

3	1	2
9	8	10
7	11	6
12	4	5

Second initial solution (suggested layout from Figure 9.14)

3	1	2
8	11	10
9	7	6
12	4	5

should be tested for possible improvement. Using these two layouts as starting solutions for the HC63-66 algorithm, the following improved layouts were obtained:

From first initial solution (cost = 289)			From second initial solution (cost = 291)		
3	1	2	3	1	2
9	11	10	7	8	10
7	8	6	9	11	6
12	4	5	12	4	5

Bazaraa and Elshafei (1979) state that the least cost for this problem is 289.

Several points are worth emphasizing. Even when provided with a very good starting solution (as indicated in Figure 9.14), the pair-exchanging heuristic was unable to achieve the optimal solution. The first Hall solution (indicated in Figure 9.13) was only one pair-exchange away from the optimal solution. The Hall method is computationally feasible for large problems. It incorporates a great deal of flexibility because it is not restricted to predetermined location sizes or shapes. For problems having the requirement of unit square locations, a good procedure seems to be to use the Hall method to generate several initial layouts and then use a heuristic such as CRAFT or HC63-66 to improve upon these layouts.

EXERCISES

9.1 Six disk-shaped departments, each 20 feet in diameter, are to be located on a rectangular floor that is 40 feet by 60 feet. Assume that traffic flows occur along straight paths between the centers of the disks. The interfacility traffic flow matrix is given as follows:

Facility	1	2	3	4	5	6
1	0	5	7	3	2	4
2	0	0	6	4	9	5
3	0	0	0	7	1	3
4	0	0	0	0	6	3
5	0	0	0	0	0	8
6	0	0	0	0	0	0

a. Formulate the layout problem in a nonlinear programming format.
b. Analyze the objective function and constraints of the nonlinear program for their convexity and/or concavity properties.
c. What would happen if you attempted to solve this nonlinear problem using a nonlinear programming algorithm?

9.2 The following exercises refer to the data from Exercise 9.1.
    a. Display the W and D matrices of the Hall method. Then use the Hall method to develop a layout of the departments. Calculate the associated cost.
    b. Use a pair-wise exchange method to obtain a final layout of the departments and its associated cost using the layout developed in Exercise 9.2a as an initial layout.

9.3 Solve the following four-facility layout problem using the branch-and-bound technique.

Interfacility Traffic Flow

Facility	1	2	3	4
1	0	10	20	5
2	18	0	9	4
3	5	6	0	8
4	8	0	15	0

Interlocation Distances

Location	A	B	C	D
A	0	1	2	3
B		0	4	5
C			0	6
D				0

9.4 Four machines are to be located on an aisle on a plant floor. The average number of fork-lift trips made each week between the machines is given below.

Machine	1	2	3	4
1	0	12	7	18
2	0	0	9	14
3	0	0	0	6
4	0	0	0	0

Starting with the machines in the order 1-2-3-4, use pair-exchanging to improve the solution as much as possible.

9.5 A company that does job machining and assembly would like to re-layout its production facilities in order to reduce its materials handling costs (see Figure 9E.1). The required floor space, interfacility activity flows, and present layout are given below. Develop a new floor layout using the Hall method followed by an improvement method such as pair-exchanging.

Facility	Name	Required Area (Square Meters)
1	Receiving & Raw Material Storage	400
2	Cleaning & Grinding	300
3	Automatic Screw Machines	200
4	X-Ray Inspection	100
5	Drilling	100
6	Hobbing	100
7	Broaching	100
8	Milling	100
9	Turning (Lathes)	100
10	Assembly	400
11	Plating	200
12	Finished Goods & Shipping	300

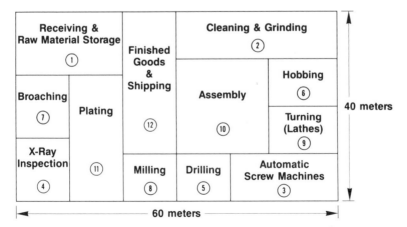

Figure 9E.1 Present Floor Layout.

Part Type	Unit Sales Per Year	Activity 1	2	3	4	5	6	7	8	9	10	11	12
1	200	X	X	X	X	X	X	X	X	X	X		X
2	1200	X			X	X			X				X
3	1950	X	X	X	X			X	X				X
4	700	X	X	X	X			X	X				X
5	400	X			X	X		X		X			X
6	1800	X	X	X	X	X						X	X
7	650	X				X	X				X		X
8	250	X			X					X		X	X

Note: As an aid to reading the preceding table, consider part type 8. It has a total volume of 250 per year. Each part starts in department 1, then moves successively through departments 4, 9, 11, and 12.

REFERENCE NOTES

SECTION 9.1 The branch-and-bound example is based on the approach suggested by Gavett and Plyter (1966). Branch-and-bound methods were also given by Bazaraa and Elshafei (1979), Elshafei (1977), Gilmore (1962), Graves and Whinston (1970), Lawler (1963), Bazaraa and Kirca (1983), Burkard and Stratmann (1978), Pierce and Crowston (1971), and Land (1963). Through suitable transformations the problem can be formulated as a mixed-integer programming problem. Transformation of this type was given by Love and Wong (1976a, 1976b), Bazaraa and Sherali (1980), and Kaufman and Broeckx (1978). Comparisons of the efficiencies of various algorithms were given by Nugent, Vollmann, and Ruml (1968) and Ritzman (1972). An early discussion of the floor layout problem was given by Wimmert (1958).

Burkard (1984) and Kusiak and Heragu (1987) surveyed applications, formulations, and exact and heuristic solution methods.

SECTION 9.2 The CRAFT procedure was developed by Armour and Buffa (1963). HC63-66 was given by Hillier and Connors (1966).

SECTION 9.3 It was shown by Scriabin and Vergin (1975) that in some cases experienced practitioners using computer graphics can improve layouts given by heuristic algorithms. The example problem given in Table 9.27 was given by Nugent, Vollmann, and Ruml (1968). An important background article for this section is that by Steinberg (1961). Hall (1970) proposed the eigenvector approach to quadratic placement.

Chapter 10

Mathematical Models of Travel Distances

In this chapter we discuss mathematical models for estimating travel distances from point references. Consider the ℓ_p metric* given by $\ell_p(q,r) = [|q_1 - r_1|^p + |q_2 - r_2|^p]^{1/p}$, $p \geq 1$, where q and r are points in the plane. Clearly if p is tailored to actual travel distances in a study area, the resultant metric must be at least as accurate as the special cases of $p = 1$ and $p = 2$. Experimental evidence presented here indicates that it is inappropriate to simply assume a convenient value for p in a location study. This suggests the general strategy of using such empirical distance functions in facilities location studies, and motivates the attention we have paid to ℓ_p models.

Of course, greater accuracy can be expected from methods that calculate inter-site distances using actual road network data bases. Kleindorfer, Kochenberger, and Reutzel (1981) described such a method. However, it is difficult to incorporate actual distances in the iterative location algorithms described in previous chapters. Those algorithms depend on an explicit functional relationship between location coordinates and distances. Looking up actual distances would be impractical because source locations are changed continuously as iterations proceed. In a reverse sense, Ginsburgh and Hansen (1974) suggested the use of empirical distance functions to verify arc lengths between nodes in road network data bases. Screening road network data is advisable because these data often contain errors.

---

*A metric, $d(q,r)$, is a measure of distance between points q and r and is defined by the following properties: *symmetry*: $d(q,r) = d(r,q)$; *positivity*: $d(q,r) \geq 0$; *identity*: $d(q,r) = 0$ if, and only if, $q = r$; and *triangle inequality*: $d(q,r) \leq d(q,t) + d(t,r)$.

Empirical distance functions are useful in initial stages of distribution studies. Rough estimates of unit transportation costs can be efficiently determined by weighting the distance estimates that are computed from point coordinates. This avoids measuring actual unit costs between myriads of potential source-demand *point* links and supports a demand point aggregation analysis. Thereafter, more accurate cost data can be obtained by actually looking up best transportation rates for the source-demand *zone* links chosen for inclusion in the model.

In their distribution study, Mairs et al. (1978) reported that transportation costs to small demand zones had to be approximated because shipments were made by a truck delivering to several zones on a delivery tour. As thousands of such transportation costs were involved, a quick, reasonably accurate approach was needed. The cost-estimating relationship used (see Section 8.3) was based on the Euclidean metric.

In another study, Westwood (1977) used an empirical distance function to compare trunking versus tramping modes of bulk transfer of finished product linked with backloading of raw materials. In Section 8.1 we cited the following model of Kolesar et al. (1975) for predicting fire engine travel time, where d is travel distance:

$$T(d) = \begin{cases} 2(d/a)^{1/2} & \text{, if } d \leq 2d_c \\ v_c/a + d/v_c, & \text{if } d > 2d_c. \end{cases} \tag{10.1}$$

This model or a variation of it should be useful for other types of vehicle travel times. Using the empirical methods suggested here, given the coordinates of any point in the area to be served and the coordinates of the service center, the travel distance may be generated within the model. When large numbers of points are to be considered or the points are not known in advance, there is great advantage to using an empirical distance function. These benefits motivate the use of the continuous location models of Chapters 2 through 7 to generate candidate sites for more detailed study. Furthermore, when the planning horizon is quite distant, transportation cost estimates based on distances may be more accurate than using current freight rates.

10.1 EMPIRICAL DISTANCE FUNCTIONS

To study the relative merits of empirical distance functions, Love and Morris (1972, 1979) fit a variety of mathematical forms to samples of intercity, urban, and rural road distances. Let us discuss these five forms initially:

$$d_1(q,r; k,\theta) = k \sum_{i=1}^{2} |q_i(\theta) - r_i(\theta)| = k\ell_1(q(\theta), r(\theta)), \ k > 0,$$

where $q_1(\theta) = q_1 \cos \theta + q_2 \sin \theta$,

$$q_2(\theta) = -q_1 \sin \theta + q_2 \cos \theta$$

and similarly for $r(\theta)$,

$$d_2(q,r; k) = k[\sum_{i=1}^{2} (q_i - r_i)^2]^{1/2}$$

$$= k\ell_2(q,r), \ k > 0,$$

$$d_3(q,r; k,p) = k[\sum_{i=1}^{2} |q_i - r_i|^p]^{1/p}$$

$$= k\ell_p(q,r), \ k > 0, \ p \geqslant 1,$$

$$d_4(q,r; k,p,s) = k[\sum_{i=1}^{2} |q_i - r_i|^p]^{1/s}$$

$$= k[\ell_p(q,r)]^{p/s}, \ k > 0, \ p \geqslant 1, \ p/s \geqslant 1,$$

$$d_5(q,r; m_1,m_2,m_3) = [m_1(q_1-r_1)^2 + m_2(q_1-r_1)(q_2-r_2) + m_3(q_2-r_2)^2]^{1/2},$$

$$\text{where } m_1 > 0 \text{ and } m_2^2 < 4m_1m_3.$$

Discussion

The indicated parameter restrictions are required for convexity of the functions. The parameters are to be evaluated empirically. The mathematical forms might be considered variations on the theme of the Euclidean metric, scaled by a constant k. d_1 is the rectangular metric with axes rotated through an angle θ from the original coordinate axes. d_3 and d_4 replace the square root and square of the Euclidean metric by 1 and 2 parameters, respectively. d_5 provides for weighted squared coordinate differences. A multiplicative constant k can be considered to have been factored into the values of m_1, m_2, and m_3. d_5 chooses the best direction of axes through the parameter m_2 in accordance with a best-fit criterion. Except for the special case of $p = 2$, the analyst's choice of axes affects the ability of d_3 and d_4 to predict distances accurately. The inclusion of θ in d_1 allows for a properly oriented coordinate system to study the accuracy of the weighted rectangular metric. For all but d_5, sets of points equidistant from the origin $\bar{0} = (0,0)$ are symmetric with respect to orthogonal coordinate axes. To illustrate this symmetry, Figure 10.1 plots unit distance contours for the ℓ_p metric. The contours bulge from being diamond shaped for $p = 1$, to being circular when $p = 2$, and ultimately toward the shape of a square as p is increased still further. For $0 < p < 1$, the contours bend inward indicating the triangle inequality is actually reversed, and so ℓ_p is no longer a metric in this range. The unit distance contour for d_5 is an ellipse. This is because $d_5(q,\bar{0}; m_1,m_2,m_3) = 1$ implies $m_1q_1^2 + m_2q_1q_2 + m_3q_2^2 = 1$, which is the equation for an ellipse when $m_2^2 < 4m_1m_3$. The directional bias inherent in d_5 is such that the travel direction of greatest ease is perpendicular to that of greatest difficulty. Figure 10.1 shows that for d_3, with $p \neq 2$, these directions are at 45° angles to one another.

Indeed, the best-fit parameters characterize road networks. Consider d_3. If k and $p \simeq 1$, the network is basically a rectangular grid. The ratio of travel distance to straight-line distance increases from 1 when travel is parallel to an axis, to $\sqrt{2}$ when travel is at a 45° angle to an axis. As k increases while $p \simeq 1$, the form and degree of directional bias remain the same, but there is an increasing nonlinearity in the roadway. The degree of rectangular bias reduces as p increases to 2. If $p \simeq 2$, the road network is highly developed and relatively free of directional bias. If $p > 2$ the directional bias is inverted because travel is most efficient at 45° angles to the axes and least efficient parallel to the axes.

10.2 EMPIRICAL STUDIES

Two goodness-of-fit criteria were used to determine the distance function parameters. The first is the minimization of a sum of absolute deviations given by:

$$AD_f = \sum_{j=1}^{v-1} \sum_{t=j+1}^{v} |d_f(a_j, a_t) - A_{jt}|,$$

Figure 10.1 Contours for $\ell_p(q,\overline{0}) = [|q_1|^p + |q_2|^p]^{1/p} = 1$.
(Reprinted by permission, "Mathematical Models of Road Travel Distances," Love and Morris, *Management Science,* Vol. 25, No. 2, February, 1979. Copyright (1979), The Institute of Management Sciences, 290 Westminster Road, Providence, RI 02903.)

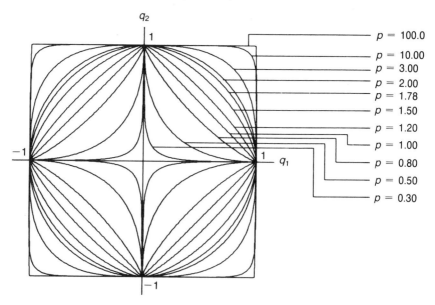

where A_{jt} is the actual travel distance between points a_j and a_t, and v is the number of points chosen for consideration. The implication of using this criterion is that the distance function whose parameters are being determined will estimate the greater actual distances more accurately than the shorter distances in the sample. The second criterion is the minimization of a sum of squares given by:

$$SD_f = \sum_{j=1}^{v-1} \sum_{t=j+1}^{v} [d_f(a_j,a_t) - A_{jt}]^2/A_{jt}.$$

Division by A_{jt} normalizes the squared deviation and makes this criterion more sensitive than the first to large errors in relation to A_{jt}.

The parameters of the functions were chosen as those best fitting the given criterion. This was done by performing exhaustive searches over intervals, as described in the Appendix, mathematical note 10.1. The differing estimating accuracy of the functions was associated with statistical significance using the t-test for matched pairs. The test is unaffected by the lack of independence of the error in the distance functions.

Urban and Rural Road Distances

Results of fitting the functions to urban and rural road distances are given in Tables 10.1 to 10.5. Ohio distances (in miles) were supplied by the Ohio Department of Transportation. Wisconsin road distances were measured directly from published road maps (in inches). Each sample set

Table 10.1 Minimizing Parameters of d_1.

Sample	AD_1	k	θ	SD_1	k	θ
Canton	123.05	1.04	21	14.11	1.03	20
	(136.71)[a]	(0.95)		(17.86)	(0.96)	
Columbus	86.097	1.02	5	10.53	1.01	5
	(88.35)	(0.99)		(10.91)	(1.00)	
Madison	1015.96	0.98	4	157.49	0.98	3
	(1057.83)	(0.97)		(163.42)	(0.98)	
Milwaukee	628.95	0.95	5	66.86	0.94	6
	(727.10)	(0.95)		(87.88)	(0.94)	
Rural Wis.	508.42	1.05	3	94.95	1.04	3
	(515.81)	(1.05)		(96.38)	(1.04)	
Toledo	99.73	0.97	15	14.47	0.98	12
	(114.83)	(0.99)		(18.30)	(0.98)	
Toledo Sub.	69.60	0.97	15	11.42	0.97	20
	(76.12)	(0.94)		(13.98)	(0.94)	

[a]Values in parentheses correspond to the original axes.

Table 10.2 Minimizing Parameters of d_2.

Sample	AD_2	k	SD_2	k
Canton	78.39	1.20	7.42	1.22
Columbus	80.20	1.27	8.78	1.28
Madison	869.40	1.25	125.73	1.25
Milwaukee	714.83	1.16	72.17	1.18
Rural Wis.	480.19	1.35	72.90	1.34
Toledo	74.13	1.21	8.70	1.24
Toledo Sub.	49.17	1.21	7.18	1.23

Table 10.3 Minimizing Parameters of d_3.

Sample	AD_3	k,p	SD_3	k,p
Canton	65.62[a]	1.16,1.49	6.03[a]	1.18,1.56
Columbus	68.54	1.18,1.47	6.86	1.18,1.45
Madison	830.34	1.16,1.48	113.24	1.18,1.56
Milwaukee	508.81[a]	1.03,1.30	46.31[a]	1.07,1.35
Rural Wis.	452.74[a]	1.24,1.45	70.45	1.29,1.68
Toledo	71.69	1.18,1.74	8.41[a]	1.20,1.73
Toledo Sub.	48.13[a]	1.18,1.78	7.07[a]	1.21,1.81

[a]Result is for axes rotated through the angle given in Table 10.1; unmarked results correspond to the original axes.

Table 10.4 Minimizing Parameters of d_4.

Sample	AD_4	k,p,s	SD_4	k,p,s
Canton	60.34[a]	1.43,1.66,1.78	4.10	1.53,1.81,1.99
Columbus	53.76	1.45,1.38,1.52	4.39	1.49,1.41,1.57
Madison	824.20	1.01,1.56,1.51	113.20	1.14,1.54,1.53
Milwaukee	508.81[a]	1.06,1.30,1.30	46.29[a]	1.03,1.34,1.33
Rural Wis.	447.10	1.56,1.50,1.59	70.24	1.37,1.65,1.68
Toledo	54.90	1.56,1.68,1.90	4.95	1.56,1.70,1.92
Toledo Sub.	34.08*	1.55,1.88,2.12	2.69	1.64,2.35,2.70

[a]Same as for Table 10.3.

Table 10.5 Minimizing Parameters of d_5.

Sample	AD_5	m_1,m_2,m_3	SD_5	m_1,m_2,m_3
Canton	63.37	1.47, - 0.41,2.02	5.17	1.47, - 0.29,1.92
Columbus	70.99	1.46, - 0.09,1.78	7.52	1.50, - 0.04,1.81
Madison	855.30	1.65, - 0.01,1.46	120.00	1.64, - 0.00,1.44
Milwaukee	657.70	1.64, - 0.09,1.27	62.05	1.56, - 0.11,1.31
Rural Wis.	430.60	1.82, - 0.48,1.90	66.80	1.81, - 0.36,1.85
Toledo	67.90	1.52, - 0.23,1.37	8.01	1.57, - 0.21,1.47
Toledo Sub.	47.54	1.58, - 0.09,1.43	6.77	1.70, - 0.08,1.44

consisted of 105 road distances corresponding to distances between all pairs of 15 randomly selected points. To explore the effects of a natural barrier, a Toledo subarea sample (Toledo Sub.) was established. This consisted of 15 randomly chosen points west of the Maumee River, which divides the city of Toledo. The other Toledo sample set included points on both sides of the river. The cities were chosen to provide a spectrum of road network regularity and varying degrees of accommodations to physical obstructions.

The goodness-of-fit of d_4 to the actual road distances was superior to that of d_5, the other three-parameter function, except for the rural Wisconsin data. Statistical significance (at the 1% level) accompanied this superiority in the Columbus, Milwaukee, Toledo, and Toledo Sub. samples. d_4 includes d_1, d_2, and d_3 as special cases and therefore estimates distance at least as accurately.

This structural superiority led to statistical significance at every opportunity except for d_2 and d_3 in the Madison and rural Wisconsin samples. The fitted parameters of d_4 do not satisfy convexity conditions for any but the Madison and Milwaukee data sets. This would complicate the use of d_4 in facilities location objective functions that are part of urban location models. The fitted parameter values for d_3 and d_5 satisfy the respective convexity conditions in every case.

The rectangular distance function d_1 does not fare well compared to the alternatives. This inferiority was usually supported by clear statistical significance. Only for the Milwaukee sample did the accuracy of d_1 surpass even that for the Euclidean function d_2, and this was not statistically significant. d_2, which models road systems as having no directional bias, emerges as preferable to d_1 on the basis of accuracy and convenience. Only the inflation factor k must be estimated. If an optimal coordinate system were not incorporated into d_1 via the angle θ, the dominance of d_2 over d_1 would be complete. A travel network must have a particularly strong rectangular bias for d_1 to come to the fore. Then why has so much of the analysis in previous chapters addressed this metric? Settings such as plant floors where travel is along aisles laid out in a rectangular grid surely satisfy the rectangular bias requirement (see below). Many central sections of city street networks approximate a rectangular grid. Moreover, d_1 possesses structure that often leads to efficient solution algorithms for solving location problems. The median weight property of Section 2.2 is an example.

The two-parameter function d_3 is not decidedly inferior to either d_4 or d_5, each of which requires the estimation of three parameters. Values of p do not appear to be consistently close to unity, further substantiating the lack of a strong rectangular bias in the road networks of the chosen study areas.

The "elliptical" function d_5 proves to be relatively accurate. The absolute value of m_2 is typically close to zero, but because $m_1 \neq m_3$, the locus of points satisfying $d_5(q,\bar{0}) = 1$ is indeed an ellipse. The rural sample produces a unique parameter pattern. For this sample, $m_1 \simeq m_3$ and the magnitude of m_2 exceeds that found in other samples. And d_5 best estimates the rural distances under both criteria.

The rural distances sample leads to the greatest value of k in d_1, d_2, and d_3. Values of p show no tendency toward 1 or 2 in d_3, whereas the values of p and s that are similar for d_4 also fall almost midway between 1 and 2.

Intercity Road Distances

Two additional data sets were constructed to study the effect of length of trip on the parameters and on relative estimating accuracy. The points were 12 cities from the mileage panels of a Wisconsin road map and a *Rand McNally Road Atlas*. Results are reported in Tables 10.6 and 10.7.

Perhaps not surprisingly, d_1 proves to be relatively inaccurate. This is most pronounced in the U.S. sample. d_3 is relatively accurate, even outperforming d_5 for the Wisconsin sample. The values of p and s in d_4 were approximately equal for each sample and according to each fit criterion. This adds to the appeal of d_3, which sets p and s equal. The convexity condition $p/s \geqslant 1$ of d_4 is satisfied for the U.S. sample and p/s is just slightly less than unity for the Wisconsin sample. This is in opposition to the typical result found above.

We observe that parameters differ substantially over the various data sets. Analysts should therefore determine their own "fudge factors" and not generalize from the problem-specific experience reported here.

Table 10.6 Minimizing Parameters Under AD_f.

f	Values of AD_f		Minimizing Parameters	
	Wis.	U.S.	Wis.	U.S.
1	625.3	5192.4	$k=0.86,\ \theta=3$	$k=0.90,\ \theta=17$
1[a]	638.7	5574.7	$k=0.87$	$k=0.91$
2	416.5	2172.2	$k=1.16$	$k=1.18$
3	370.3	1943.0	$k=1.11,\ p=1.69$	$k=1.15,\ p=1.78$
4	354.0	1633.2	$k=1.18,\ p=1.50$ $s=1.53$	$k=0.92,\ p=1.73$ $s=1.68$
5	398.1	1825.5	$m_1=1.28,\ m_2=-0.09,$ $m_3=1.35$	$m_1=1.36,\ m_2=-0.15,$ $m_3=1.50$

[a]These results are for the original axes, ie, $\theta = 0$.

Table 10.7 Minimizing Parameters Under SD_f.

f	Values of AD_f Wis.	U.S.	Minimizing Parameters Wis.	U.S.
1	54.6	525.0	$k=0.88, \theta=0$	$k=0.92, \theta=19$
1[a]	54.6	607.4	$k=0.88$	$k=0.92$
2	29.3	110.0	$k=1.16$	$k=1.18$
3	19.8	95.7	$k=1.09, p=1.57$	$k=1.15, p=1.78$
4	19.2	73.5	$k=1.16, p=1.55$ $s=1.57$	$k=0.93, p=1.75$ $s=1.70$
5	27.0	79.0	$m_1=1.30, m_2=-0.11,$ $m_3=1.35$	$m_1=1.35, m_2=-0.13,$ $m_3=1.48$

[a]These results are for the original axes, ie, $\theta = 0$.

Rectangular Distances with "Doubling Back"

The distances that are inherent in many industrial office or street grids are often rectangular in nature. In practice, however, the distances between point pairs are, on average, greater than would be indicated by the ℓ_1 metric. This extra travel distance is caused by the necessity to "double back." Doubling back may occur due to the existence of blocks or bays into which a floor area is divided, or the necessity to travel between closed areas. For example, a closed area might be a walled-off production cell with an entrance on one side. Such areas may necessitate travel in directions that are different from those which would be traveled if the assumption of perfect rectangular distances prevailed. Doubling back may also occur on street grids due to one-way streets or other restrictive traffic rules.

In order to examine the effect of doubling back on rectangular distances, Love and Dowling (1985) fitted d_3 to a sample of layout patterns which were basically rectangular. However, actual travel in each distance sample was greater than rectangular due to factors which caused doubling back. The results of this study showed that the increased travel distance arising from doubling back on rectangular grids will be accounted for by the k value in d_3 rather than the value of p. As the amount of doubling back increased in successive layouts, the value of k also increased while the value of p tended to stay close to unity.

Several conclusions were drawn from the study. In situations of this type, practitioners can assume $p = 1$ with no cause for concern that they are using an invalid model. Furthermore, if the metric is being used in a location model and the only result that is important is that of obtaining optimal facility location(s), it is not necessary to know the correct value of k for that particular situation (ie, set $k = 1$). However, if the objective is to model *distances* rather than obtain *locations*, the unweighted ℓ_1 metric will likely be inappropriate. Arbitrarily setting $k = 1$ in d_3 could result in a serious understatement of total distance.

10.3 THE WEIGHTED ONE-INFINITY NORM

A norm in R^2 is a function, $\|\cdot\| : R^2 \to R^1$, having the following properties: *positivity*: $\|v\| > 0$ for $v \neq 0$; *identity*: $\|v\| = 0$ if and only if $v = \overline{0}$; *triangle inequality*: $\|u + v\| \leqslant \|u\| + \|v\|$; *homogeneity*: $\|\alpha v\| = |\alpha|\|v\|$ for every real number α. We observe that $\ell_p(q,r)$ is actually $\|v\|_p$ where $v = q - r$ and $\|v\|_p$ is defined as $[|v_1|^p + |v_2|^p]^{1/p}$, $p \geqslant 1$.

A hybrid norm based on the extreme norms given by $p = 1$ and $p = \infty$ has interesting properties. In particular, letting $p \to \infty$, $\|v\|_p$ becomes max $\{|v_1|,|v_2|\}$, denoted by $\|v\|_\infty$. This limiting process is portrayed in Figure 10.1 for the case $p = 100$. Letting k_1 and k_2 be non-negative numbers, not both of which are zero, the hybrid distance predicting function to be studied is:

$$d_6(q,r; k_1,k_2) = k_1\ell_1(q,r) + k_2\sqrt{2}\,\ell_\infty(q,r).$$

The function d_6 is convex because it is a non-negative linear combination of convex functions. The reason for the $\sqrt{2}$ factor is that $\sqrt{2}\,\ell_\infty$ can be viewed as a rectangular metric defined on a 45° rotated coordinate system (see Exercise 10.9). This can be motivated using Figure 10.1. The unit distance contour for $\sqrt{2}\,\ell_\infty$ would be a contraction of the ℓ_∞ contour. The contracted contour is simply a 45° rotation of the ℓ_1 contour.

Figure 10.2 shows unit distance contours of d_6, which are piecewise-linear approximations of ℓ_p contours when $1 < p < \infty$. The function d_6 can be viewed as characterizing distance in the following way. Let $v = q - r$. Then the vector v can be considered as representing a *trip* between the points q and r. Write d_6 as:

$$(k_1 + k_2)[\|(k_1/(k_1 + k_2))v\|_1 + \sqrt{2}\,\|(k_2/(k_1 + k_2))v\|_\infty]. \qquad (10.2)$$

As $\sqrt{2}\,\ell_\infty(q,r)$ measures ℓ_1 distances in a 45° rotated coordinate system, these are distances for rectangular paths in the rotated system. Back in the original system these are *diagonal* paths, ie, 45° rotations of rectangular paths. Therefore, expression (10.2) views $k_1/(k_1 + k_2)$ of the trip between points q and r as being along rectangular roads, and $k_2/(k_1 + k_2)$ of the trip as being along diagonal roads. The factor $(k_1 + k_2)$ outside the bracket is analogous to the inflation factor k in functions d_1 through d_4. The ratio k_1/k_2 can be idealized as the relative proportion of a trip using rectangular roads to the relative proportion using diagonal roads.

To test d_6 as an empirical distance function the parameters k_1 and k_2 were determined by Ward and Wendell (1980) as those minimizing SD_6 for the intercity data sets. The SD values and (k_1,k_2) values are 24.225

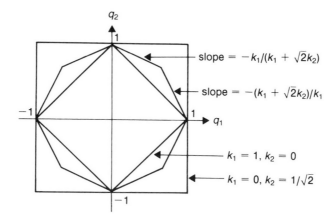

Figure 10.2 Contours for d_6 $(q,\bar{0}; k_1,k_2) = 1$.
(Reprinted with permission from OPERATIONS RESEARCH, 28, 3, 1980, part II, Copyright (1980), Operations Research Society of America. No further reproduction permitted without the consent of the copyright owner.)

for (0.62884,0.27320) and 125.249 for (0.53316,0.39251), respectively, for the Wisconsin and U.S. samples. We see that d_6 outperforms d_2, the Euclidean distance function for the Wisconsin sample. There is a clear advantage over d_1, which is a special case of d_6.

For the Wisconsin sample, $k_1/k_2 = 2.30$, implying a dominant use of rectangular paths. This is borne out by the relatively low value of p (1.57 versus 1.78) for d_3, indicating more rectangular bias than in the U.S. sample. Not unexpectedly then, d_6 fares better in the Wisconsin sample.

A practical benefit of d_6 is that location problems have linear forms. To see this, consider the minimum sum problem:

$$\text{minimize } \underset{X}{W(X)} = \sum_{j=1}^{n} w_j d_6(X,a_j; k_1,k_2) \qquad (10.3)$$

which is:

$$\text{minimize } \sum_{j=1}^{n} w_j[k_1(|x_1-a_{j1}| + |x_2-a_{j2}|) + k_2\sqrt{2} \max\{|x_1-a_{j1}|, |x_2-a_{j2}|\}].$$

Using the fact that max $\{|\alpha|, |\beta|\} = \frac{1}{2}(|\alpha + \beta| + |\alpha - \beta|)$ we can write max $\{|x_1-a_{j1}|, |x_2-a_{j2}|\}$ as

$$\frac{1}{2}(|x_1 + x_2 - a_{j1} - a_{j2}| + |x_1 - x_2 - a_{j1} + a_{j2}|)$$

and using the approach of Section 4.1 for removing absolute values, problem (10.3) can be written as the linear program:

$$\text{minimize } \sum_{X,d^+,d^-}^{n} \sum_{j=1}^{n} w_j[k_1(d_{j1}^+ + d_{j1}^- + d_{j2}^+ + d_{j2}^-) + \frac{k_2}{\sqrt{2}}(d_{j3}^+ + d_{j3}^- + d_{j4}^+ + d_{j4}^-)]$$

subject to   (10.4)

$$x_1 - d_{j1}^+ + d_{j1}^- = a_{j1}$$

$$x_2 - d_{j2}^+ + d_{j2}^- = a_{j2}$$

$$x_1 + x_2 - d_{j3}^+ + d_{j3}^- = a_{j1} + a_{j2}$$

$$x_1 - x_2 - d_{j4}^+ + d_{j4}^- = a_{j1} - a_{j2} \quad j = 1,...,n,$$

$$x_1, x_2, d_{jk}^+, d_{jk}^- \geqslant 0 \qquad j = 1,...,n; \ k = 1,2,3,4.$$

The analogous minimax problem is to:

$$\text{minimize } M(X) = \max\{w_j d_6(X, a_j; k_1, k_2); j = 1,...,n\} \quad (10.5)$$
$$X$$

which can be written as the linear program:

minimize x_0
x_0, d^+, d^-

subject to   (10.6)

$$x_0 \geqslant w_j[k_1(d_{j1}^+ + d_{j1}^- + d_{j2}^+ + d_{j2}^-) + \frac{k_2}{\sqrt{2}}(d_{j3}^+ + d_{j3}^- + d_{j4}^+ + d_{j4}^-)] \quad j = 1,...,n,$$

together with the constraints of problem (10.4).

Clearly $x_0 \geqslant 0$, and so this condition can be added to the non-negativity conditions. The problems are assumed to be posed in the first quadrant in order that the conditions $x_1, x_2 \geqslant 0$ included in problems (10.4) and (10.6) will not affect the optimal solution. Linear constraints on the co-ordinates x_1 and x_2 can be added to restrict location. Extension to the multi-facility cases is straightforward.

It is useful to summarize the trade-offs between using d_6 and using d_3. Both d_6 and d_3 are two-parameter functions. In comparative studies reported thus far, d_3 has given more accurate fits to geographical data than d_6. Yet d_6 allows for linear formulations of location problems (with a considerable number of variables and constraints), whereas d_3 for $1 < p < \infty$ yields intrinsically nonlinear location problems.

10.4 EMPIRICAL "METRICS," CONVEXITY, AND OPTIMAL LOCATION

All of the empirical functions except d_4 are metrics; d_4 is not guaranteed to satisfy the triangle inequality. To see this, let $d_4(q,r)$ be written $k[\ell_p(q,r)]^K$, where $K = p/s \geqslant 1$, and let $k = 1$. Consider the points $a_1 = (-1,0)$, $a_2 = (0,0)$, and $a_3 = (1,0)$. Then $d_4(a_1,a_3) = 2^K$, whereas $d_4(a_1,a_2) +$

$d_4(a_2,a_3) = 1^K + 1^K = 2$. This means the triangle inequality $d_4(a_1,a_2) + d_4(a_2,a_3) \geqslant d_4(a_1,a_3)$ is violated for $K > 1$. However, for $0 < K \leqslant 1$, the triangle inequality is preserved (see the Appendix, mathematical note 10.2). For $K = 1$, d_4 reverts to d_3, which is a metric.

Define:

$$d_4'(q,r; \, k,p,K) = k[\ell_p(q,r)]^K = k[|q_1-r_1|^p + |q_2-r_2|^p]^{K/p},$$

where $k > 0$, $p \geqslant 1$, $0 < K < 1$. d_4' is a metric. Perhaps not surprisingly, the empirical studies described above typically produced d_4' rather than d_4. This is because $p/s(= K)$ was typically less than unity.

In application using cost terms given by $w[d(X,a_j)]^K$, $K > 0$, rather than $wd(X,a_j)$, provides for more general forms of proportionality. Example cost structures are portrayed in Figure 10.3, where $w = 1$. Evidently, d_4 models diseconomies-of-scale and d_4' models a cost function characterized by economies-of-scale. In the case of expression (10.1) travel time may be modeled by d_4' (as $K = \frac{1}{2}$) for short distances.

Minimum sum and minimax problems involving d_1 through d_5 are convex minimization problems. The standard myopic strategy of finding a local optimum, when successful, finds a global optimum. However, typical nonlinear minimization techniques use derivatives to guide the search for optimality. Because $d(x,a_j)$ is not differentiable at $X = a_j$, $j = 1,...,n$, when given by d_1, d_2, d_3, d_5 or d_4', something must be done. As described in Chapter 2, distance functions can be smoothed by introducing a constant $\epsilon > 0$. While $d_4(X,a_j)$ is differentiable at $X = a_j$ when $K > 1$ (see the Appendix, mathematical note 10.3), the *formula* for the derivative yields an indeterminate form there. A computational expedient is to introduce $\epsilon > 0$ and use problem (2.19) to yield:

$$WH(X) = \sum_{j=1}^{n} w_j[((x_1-a_{j1})^2+\epsilon)^{p/2}+((x_2-a_{j2})^2 + \epsilon)^{p/2}]^{K/p}.$$

Figure 10.3 Cost Terms as Powers of the Distance Variable.

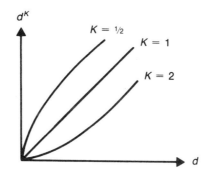

$WH(X)$ approximates $W(X)$ when distance is estimated either by d_4 or by d_4'. For $1 \leqslant p \leqslant 2$ and $0 < K \leqslant p$, $\Delta(\epsilon)$ of equation (2.20) becomes:

$$\Delta(\epsilon) = 2^{K/p} \epsilon^{K/2} \sum_{j=1}^{n} w_j.$$

Modeling with d_4' is computationally inconvenient. The following results indicate why, in the context of minimizing $W(X)$.

Property 10.1   [*Inconvenience of d_4'*]. *$W(X)$ is neither convex nor concave when d_4' models distance.*

Property 10.1 can be justified graphically. Let $n = 1$ and $w_1 = 1/k$. Then $W(X)$ reduces to $d_4'(X,a_1; 1,p,K)$ and in the one-dimensional case this becomes $|x_1|^K$, $0 < K < 1$, after shifting the origin to the point a_1. The graph of this function would have the shape of the $K = \frac{1}{2}$ curve in Figure 10.3 for positive values of x_1 together with the mirror image of this curve (with respect to the vertical axis) for negative values of x_1.

Property 10.2   [*Local minima at existing facility locations using d_4'*]. *When d_4' models distance, $W(X)$ has local minima at a_j, $j = 1,...,n$.*

The Weiszfeld algorithm has been proved to converge to a stationary point for $W(X)$ using d_4 or d_4' when $1 \leqslant p \leqslant 2$ and $0 < K \leqslant p$. Limited computational experience with d_4' suggests the convergence point is usually a global minimizer of $W(X)$, although this tendency appears to weaken as $K \rightarrow 0$. Nonetheless, it is prudent to use the algorithm with more than one starting point. Of course, if d_4 is used, a stationary point must be a global minimizer.

A question naturally arises from this discussion: Can differing parameter values lead to significantly different optimal locations? To see that this can happen, let $a_1 = (0,0)$, $a_2 = (1,0)$, and $a_3 = (0,1)$ with $w_1 = w_2$ $= w_3 = 1$. The minimizer of $W(X) = \sum_{j=1}^{3} [(x_1 - a_{j1})^2 + (x_2 - a_{j2})^2]^{K/2}$ is $(0,0)$ when $K = \frac{1}{2}$, $(0.2113,0.2113)$ when $K = 1$, and $(1/3,1/3)$ when $K = 2$.

10.5 LARGE REGION METRICS

Large region location problems arise when the difference between the Euclidean and great circle metrics is considerable. Location of international headquarters, distribution centers, or military bases are examples. As an illustration consider the plight of Jack Smooth (introduced in Exercise 2.10) who is in charge of planning a sales meeting for sales representatives of Globetrotter Business Machines. The company wants Jack to concentrate on minimizing total round-trip airfare costs for 100 representatives. Departure cities are given in Table 10.8. To generate candidate sites, Jack assumes airfares are proportional to distance and independent of destination. The objective then is to find a point that minimizes the weighted sum of flight distances from the cities. As discussed in Section 3.1, if the point falls in an ocean, some form of sensitivity analysis using objective function contour curves can be used to guide location. This section treats metrics pertinent to such large regional locational analysis.

We will approximate great circle distances by converting latitude and longitude to coordinates on a Mercator projection, and then compute rhumb line* map distances. Specifically, conjure up a Mercator map whose width is 21,600 miles at the equator. Let $q = (q_1, q_2)$, where q_1 is stated in degrees of latitude (north positive, south negative) and q_2 is stated in degrees of longitude (west positive, east negative). Then q_1 is converted to the Mercator coordinate $\hat{q}_1$ using:

$$\hat{q}_1 = 7915.704468 \log_{10}\cot (45° - 0.5q_1).$$

The map coordinate corresponding to q_2 is:

$$\hat{q}_2 = 60q_2.$$

The rhumb line map distance between points q and r is calculated according to the Euclidean formula:

$$d^M(q,r) = [(\hat{q}_1 - \hat{r}_1)^2 + (\hat{q}_2 - \hat{r}_2)^2]^{1/2}.$$

Table 10.8 Departure Cities for Sales Representatives.

City	Latitude (degrees)	Longitude (degrees)	Number of Representatives
London	51.5	− 0.4	12
Paris	48.9	− 2.3	7
Zurich	47.4	− 8.5	8
Rome	41.9	− 12.5	5
Copenhagen	55.7	− 12.6	8
Berlin	52.5	− 13.4	7
Stockholm	59.3	− 18.9	6
Athens	38.0	− 23.7	7
Ankara	39.9	− 32.8	5
Tel Aviv	32.1	− 34.8	5
Moscow	55.7	− 37.7	5
Teheran	35.4	− 51.4	7
Bombay	18.9	− 72.8	3
Manila	14.6	−121.0	5
Tokyo	35.6	−139.7	10

*Rhumb lines are straight lines on a Mercator projection.

Map distances are converted to nautical miles using:

$$d^N(q,r) = d^M(q,r) \cdot \cos ((q_1 + r_1)/2), \qquad (10.7)$$

and this may be converted to rhumb line statute miles by multiplying by 1.1515. The factor $\cos ((q_1 + r_1)/2)$ corrects for distortions of the Mercator projection as either polar region is approached. This implies as a seventh empirical distance function an inflated rhumb line distance given by:

$$d_7(q,r; k) = k(1.1515) \, d^N(q,r), \, k > 0.$$

A rhumb line between two points (with different longitudes) on the earth's surface intersects intervening longitudinal meridians at a constant angle. Other than at the equator, the great circle route will not do so. Thus $d_7(q,r; 1)$ only approximates great circle distance. As an example, consider the distance from Seattle, Washington, $q = (47° \, 36' \, N, 122° \, 20' \, W)$, to Miami, Florida, $r = (25° \, 45' \, N, 80° \, 11' \, W)$. The respective Mercator map coordinates are $(3255.8, 7340)$ and $(1599.8, 4811)$. Then $d^M(q,r) = 3022.9$ and $d^N(q,r) = 2424.5$ nautical miles. We find $d_7(q,r; 1.18) = 3294.3$ miles, using $k = 1.18$ which is the intercity route factor for U.S. distances from Table 10.6 and 10.7. A road map indicates that the road travel distance is 3273 miles. The estimate is off by less than 1%.

But how well does $d_7(q,r; 1) = 2791.8$ miles approximate the great circle distance between the two cities? Using equation (3.2), the great circle arc between points q and r is defined by α such that:

$$\cos \alpha = \cos q_1 \cos r_1 \cos (q_2 - r_2) + \sin q_1 \sin r_1. \qquad (10.8)$$

Expression (10.8) defines the great circle metric, ie, the shortest arc length between points q and r is α. We find $\alpha = 39.55°$, which is 11% of a great circle. The great circle distance between Seattle and Miami is 0.11(24,902 miles) = 2739.2 miles, using the circumference of the earth at the equator. $d_7(q,r; 1)$ is off by less than 2%.

Large region metrics are convenient to use even in studies of not-so-large regions because the latitude and longitude of points of interest are often readily accessible. This obviates the need to define an original co-ordinate system. Furthermore, certain large region location problems can be solved approximately via $d^M(q,r)$ which relies on the convenient Euclidean formula. The location problem is thereby translated to the Mercator map. For instance, the Globetrotter sales meeting problem is approximated by:

$$\underset{X}{\text{minimize}} \; W(X) = \sum_{j=1}^{15} w_j d_7(X, a_j; k). \qquad (10.9)$$

Replacing d_7 by d^M, problem (10.9) is approximated by:

$$\underset{X}{\text{minimize}} \;\; W(X) = \sum_{j=1}^{n} w_j[(x_1 - \hat{a}_{j1})^2 + (x_2 - \hat{a}_{j2})^2]^{1/2}, \qquad (10.9a)$$

which can be solved by the Weiszfeld iterative procedure (2.6). Indeed, approximating d_7 by d^M gains access to the wealth of techniques for handling a variety of Euclidean distance location problems. However, reliance on d^M ignores the correction term in equation (10.7). This leads to significant distortions of distances near a polar region, or when considering a region larger than a hemisphere.

10.6 MODELING VEHICLE TOUR-DISTANCES

Suppose distribution to customers is by a fleet of vehicles. The much-studied model for locating a facility to minimize the average cost of distribution is:

$$\underset{X}{\text{minimize}} \;\; W(X) = \sum_{j=1}^{n} w_j \ell_p(X, a_j). \qquad (10.10)$$

To be valid this objective must somehow account for the actual delivery operations from the facility, operations that involve optimal vehicle *tours* with deliveries to several customers at a time. But $\ell_p(X, a_j)$ estimates the "direct" distance to customer j. Treating a sum of weighted direct-distances must somehow account for the sum of vehicle tour-distance costs. Let N be the estimated average of the maximum number of customers that can be supplied on one vehicle route; N is determined by such factors as vehicle capacity and maximum duration for a route. If the number of customers, n, greatly exceeds N, then problem (10.10) may well be a reasonable approximation of the underlying location-routing problem. Otherwise, problem (10.10) is inappropriate; vehicle routing and facility location become inextricably connected. Model formulation becomes considerably more complex than heretofore. This problem area has only recently begun to attract efforts to construct solution procedures.

EXERCISES

10.1 a. Use the selection process described in Exercise 1.1 to choose 10 pairs of cities randomly. Construct a coordinate system and then use intuition to estimate appropriate values of k and p for d_3. Using the randomly generated trips, calculate AD_3. Then calculate AD_2 using $k = 1.15$ in d_2, and comment on the results.

b. Describe applications wherein SD would be preferable to AD as a goodness-of-fit criterion, and conversely. Justify your answer.

c. Suggest an alternative fitting criterion that reflects an asymmetric loss for distance estimation error.

10.2 Suppose outbound transportation costs $t_{ik\ell}$ are to be approximated using the cost-estimation relationship given in Section 8.3.
   a. What method would you recommend for calculating $d_{k\ell}$, the distance from site k to demand zone ℓ? Why?
   b. If an empirical function is used, how would barriers such as large lakes, river segments between bridges, or mountain ranges with no crossings enter into the analysis? What about multiple barriers?

10.3 Show that the rectangular and Euclidean distances are equal if the line segment between $q = (q_1, q_2)$ and $r = (r_1, r_2)$ is parallel to one of the coordinate axes, whereas the rectangular distance exceeds the Euclidean distance by a factor of $\sqrt{2}$ when the line segment is at a 45° angle to an axis.

10.4 Explain why the choice of coordinate axes affects the ability of the rectangular distance function to accurately predict actual distances on a rectangular grid.

10.5 Show that: $\ell_1(q,r)/\sqrt{2} \leqslant \ell_2(q,r) \leqslant \ell_1(q,r)$ and that $\ell_\infty(q,r) \leqslant \ell_2(q,r) \leqslant \sqrt{2} \ell_\infty(q,r)$.

10.6 Graph the unit "circle" for d_5 using the parameters determined from the rural Wisconsin sample according to AD_5. Describe and then try to justify the directional bias found.

10.7 a. Using the data from Example 2.2, formulate problem (10.4) using $k_1 = 0.6$ and $k_2 = 0.3$.
   b. Solve the problem formulated in Exercise 10.7a using linear programming.
   c. Compare the solution found in Exercise 10.7b with that found in Example 2.2.

10.8 Formulate the multi-facility version of problem (10.6), and tell how many variables and constraints there are.

10.9 a. Show that d_6 is a metric.
   b. Using an original orthogonal coordinate system based on the vectors $(1,0)$ and $(0,1)$, we can write $q = q_1(1,0) + q_2(0,1)$ and $r = r_1(1,0) + r_2(0,1)$. Show $\sqrt{2}\,\ell_\infty(q,r)$ equals the rectangular distance defined on the 45° rotated coordinate system based on the orthonormal vectors:

$$(1/\sqrt{2})[(1,0) + (0,1)] = (1/\sqrt{2}, 1/\sqrt{2})$$

and

$$1/\sqrt{2}\,[(1,0) - (0,1)] = (1/\sqrt{2},\ -1/\sqrt{2}).$$

10.10 a. Use d_7 with $k = 1.18$ to estimate the road travel distance (approximately 1281 miles) between Chicago, Illinois, (41° 49'N, 87° 37'W) and Albuquerque, New Mexico (35° 05'N, 106° 40'W).

    b. Use d_7 (with $k = 1$) to estimate the great circle distance from London, England, to Bombay, India (see Table 10.8). Then calculate the great circle distance according to expression (10.8).

    c. Find a reference on spherical trigonometry; then trace the derivation of expression (10.8).

10.11 a. Solve the Globetrotter Business Machines location problem (Table 10.8) using formulation (10.9a).

    b. Evaluate the solution found in Exercise 10.11a according to the objective function in problem (10.9), and then according to that in problem (3.1).

    c. Evaluate the solution (49° N, 19° E) according to the objective function in problem (3.1).

    d. Solve the problem of Example 3.1 using formulation (10.9a).

    e. How would winds aloft or restricted regions affect the validity of using the great circle metric to model airline flight distances?

10.12 Radio transmissions follow a great circle arc. Suppose a radio station is to be located to minimize the greatest distance to intended listeners in the 15 cities of Table 10.8. Use d^M as an approximation to d_7 and one of the techniques of Chapter 6 for Euclidean distances to solve this minimax location problem. Comment on this process and on the result.

10.13 Suppose you have been hired as a consultant. Give a detailed account of an approach you would use to locate a distribution point from which customer demand will be met using a fleet of vehicles.

REFERENCE NOTES

SECTION 10.1 This and the succeeding section draw on the studies reported in Love and Morris (1972, 1979). Perreur and Thisse (1974) proved location properties for metrics approximating travel distance on star-shaped networks and networks with circumferential transport systems.

SECTION 10.3 The work of Ward and Wendell (1980) is closely followed here. Witzgall (1964) appears to have been the first to recognize the application of polyhedral norms to facility location.

SECTION 10.4 Cooper (1968) extended the minimum sum problem to consider distances raised to the power K and proved Property 10.2 for Euclidean distances. Morris (1981) studied the problem for the case of ℓ_p distances. If the cost functions are only assumed to be continuous and increasing in distance, a global minimizer for the minimum sum problem can be obtained using the big square-small square method described in Hansen, Peeters, and Thisse (1983).

SECTION 10.5 Translating the location problem to a Mercator map was suggested by Kuenne and Soland (1972).

SECTION 10.6 Christofides and Eilon (1969) did early work on estimating the sum of tour lengths in a location-routing problem. Dohrn and Watson-Gandy (1973) and Burness and White (1976) provided early discussions of the problem. Laporte, Nobert, and Pelletier (1983) developed exact algorithms for selected location-routing problems and surveyed related efforts.

APPENDIX–CHAPTER 10

Mathematical Notes

10.1 Determination of Parameter Values. For d_3 the "confidence" intervals searched exhaustively were $k\epsilon[0.80, 2.29]$ and $p\epsilon[0.90, 2.29]$ using a grid width of 0.01. For d_1 the intervals of search were $k\epsilon[0.8, 1.25]$ and $\theta\epsilon[0°, 90°]$, whereas for d_2 the search interval was $k\epsilon[0.8, 2.29]$. Searches were conducted in the following way for the three-parameter distance models.

First, the criterion function was evaluated at every grid point in a unit cube in the parameter space, using a grid width of 0.1. In almost all cases the minimum value of the criterion function was obtained at an interior point of the cube. Where this did not happen, the process was repeated after shifting the cube in the appropriate direction until an interior minimum was obtained.

Then a search was conducted on the grid points in a cube with a side length of 0.2 centered on the best point in the coarse grid, using a grid width of 0.01. When the minimum value of the criterion function was obtained at an interior point of the cube, the parameter search was terminated. This happened in all instances when d_5 was employed. In many cases with d_4 the search over the fine grid had to be repeated, each time shifting the cube in an appropriate direction until an interior minimum was found. A sensitivity analysis showed that for a fixed value of k, SD_4 gives rise to a surface like a flat-bottomed valley with steep sides. This accounts for the relative difficulty in estimating the parameters of d_4. Parameter values in an extended region may give a near-optimal fit, as long as the proper balance is maintained between p and s.

The search procedure employed does not ensure that a global optimum (to two decimal places) was found. However, since several of the parameter values were verified by doing a total enumeration using a grid width of 0.1, the reported parameter values are in most cases optimal or at least near-optimal with respect to the value of the criterion function.

10.2 *Prove d_4' satisfies the triangle inequality*

PROOF: We must prove $[\ell_p(q,r)]^K \leqslant [\ell_p(q,t)]^K + [\ell_p(t,r)]^K$, for $0 < K < 1$. The triangle inequality $\ell_p(q,r) \leqslant \ell_p(q,t) + \ell_p(t,r)$ holds since ℓ_p is a metric. Thus $[\ell_p(q,r)]^K \leqslant [\ell_p(q,t) + \ell_p(t,r)]^K$, for $K > 0$. From Hardy, Littlewood and Polya (1952, p. 32), $[a + b]^K \leqslant a^K + b^K$ for $0 < K < 1$ and $a,b \geqslant 0$. Letting $a = \ell_p(q,t)$ and $b = \ell_p(t,r)$ yields the required result.

10.3 *Prove d_4 is differentiable at a_j when $p/s > 1$*

PROOF: Write $d_4(X,a_j; 1,p,s)$ as $f_j(X) = [|x_1 - a_{j1}|^p + |x_2 - a_{j2}|^p]^{K/p}$, $K > 1$. A direction in R^2 is determined by the vector $\mu = (\mu_1,\mu_2)$ where $\|\mu\| = 1$. Let the first directional derivative of f_j at any point a_j in the plane be given by:

$$D_\mu f_j(a_j) = \lim_{\lambda \to 0} \frac{f_j(a_j + \lambda\mu) - f_j(a_j)}{\lambda}$$

$$= \lim_{\lambda \to 0} \frac{[|\lambda\mu_1|^p + |\lambda\mu_2|^p]^{K/p}}{\lambda}$$

$$= \lim_{\lambda \to 0} \frac{|\lambda|^K [|\mu_1|^p + |\mu_2|^p]^{K/p}}{\lambda}$$

$$= \lim_{\lambda \to 0} \text{sign} (\lambda)|\lambda|^{K-1}[|\mu_1|^p + |\mu_2|^p]^{K/p}$$

$$= 0, \text{ since } K > 1.$$

Bibliography

Adcock, R. J. 1878. A problem in least squares. *Analyst* 53.

Aikens, C. H. 1985. Facility location models for distribution planning. *European Journal of Operational Research* 22:263–279.

Armour, G. C., and E. S. Buffa. 1963. A heuristic algorithm and simulation approach to relative location of facilities. *Management Science* 9:294–309.

Balas, E. 1983. A class of location, distribution and scheduling problems: Modeling and solution methods. In *Proceedings of the Chinese-U.S. symposium on systems analysis,* eds. P. Gray and L. Yuanzhang. New York: Wiley.

Balinski, M. L. 1965. Integer programming: Methods, uses, computation. *Management Science* 12:253–313.

Balinski, M. L., and W. J. Baumol. 1968. The dual in nonlinear programming and its economic interpretation. *Review of Economic Studies* 35:237–256.

Bazaraa, M. S., and A. N. Elshafei. 1979. An exact branch and bound procedure for the quadratic assignment problem. *Naval Research Logistics Quarterly* 26:109–121.

Bazaraa, M. S., and O. Kirca. 1983. A branch-and-bound-based heuristic for solving the quadratic assignment problem. *Naval Research Logistics Quarterly* 30:287–304.

Bazaraa, M. S., and H. D. Sherali. 1980. Benders' partitioning scheme applied to a new formulation of the quadratic assignment problem. *Naval Research Logistics Quarterly* 25:29–41.

Baumol, W. J., and P. Wolfe. 1958. A warehouse-location problem. *Operations Research* 6:252–263.

Beckenbach, E. F., and R. Bellman. 1965. *Inequalities.* Berlin: Springer-Verlag.

Belardo, S., J. Harrald, W. A. Wallace, and J. A. Ward. 1984. A partial covering approach to siting response resources for major maritime oil spills. *Management Science* 30:1184–1196.

Bellman, R. 1965. An application of dynamic programming to location-allocation problems. *SIAM Review* 7:126–128.

Bilde, O., and J. Krarup. 1977. Sharp lower bounds and efficient algorithms for the simple plant location problem. *Annals of Discrete Mathematics* 1:79–97.

Bindschedler, A. E., and J. M. Moore. 1961. Optimal location of new machines in existing plant layouts. *The Journal of Industrial Engineering* 12:41–48.

Bos, H. D. 1965. *Spatial dispersion of economic activity.* Rotterdam: University Press.

Brady, S. D., and R. E. Rosenthal. 1980. Interactive computer graphical solutions of constrained minimax location problems. *AIIE Transactions* 12:241–248.

Brady, S. D., R. E. Rosenthal, and D. Young. 1983. Interactive graphical minimax location of multiple facilities with general constraints. *IIE Transactions* 15:242–254.

Burkard, R. E. 1984. Quadratic assignment problems. *European Journal of Operational Research* 15:283–289.

Burkard, R. E., and K. H. Stratmann. 1978. Numerical investigations on the quadratic assignment problem. *Naval Research Logistics Quarterly* 25:129–148.

Burness, R. C., and J. A. White. 1976. The traveling salesman location problem. *Transportation Science* 10:348–360.

Cabot, A. V., R. L. Francis, and M. A. Stary. 1970. A network flow solution to a rectilinear distance facility location problem. *AIIE Transactions* 2:132–141.

Calamai, P. H., and A. R. Conn. 1987. A projected Newton method for ℓ_p norm location problems. *Mathematical Programming* 38:75–109.

Chalmet, L. G., R. L. Francis, and A. Kolen. 1981. Finding efficient solutions for rectilinear distance location problems efficiently. *European Journal of Operational Research* 6:117–124.

Charalambous, C. 1981. An iterative algorithm for the multifacility minimax location problem with Euclidean distances. *Naval Research Logistics Quarterly* 28:325–337.

———. 1985. Acceleration of the HAP approach for the multifacility location problem. *Naval Research Logistics Quarterly* 32:373–389.

Chatelon, J. A., D. W. Hearn, and T. J. Lowe. 1978. A subgradient algorithm for certain minimax and minisum problems. *Mathematical Programming* 15:130–145.

Chen, R., and G. Y. Handler. 1987. Relaxation method for the solution of the minimax location-allocation problem in Euclidean space. *Naval Research Logistics* 34:775–788.

Christofides, N., and S. Eilon. 1969. Expected distances in distribution problems. *Operational Research Quarterly* 20:437–443.

Church, R. L., and C. S. ReVelle. 1974. The maximal covering location problem. *Papers of the Regional Science Association* 32:101–118.

———. 1976. Theoretical and computational links between the *p*-median, location set covering and the maximal covering location problem. *Geographical Analysis* 8:406–415.

Converse, A. O. 1972. Optimum number and location of treatment plants. *Journal of Water Pollution Control Federation* 44:1629–1636.

Cooper, L. 1963. Location-allocation problems. *Operations Research* 11:331–343.

———. 1964. Heuristic methods for location-allocation problems. *SIAM Review* 6:37–53.

———. 1968. An extension of the generalized Weber problem. *Journal of Regional Science* 8:181–198.

———. 1972. The transportation-location problem. *Operations Research* 20:94–108.

Cornuejols, G., M. L. Fisher, and G. L. Nemhauser. 1977. Location of bank accounts to optimize float. *Management Science* 23:789–810.

Dahlquist, G., and Å. Björck. 1974. *Numerical methods.* Translated by N. Anderson. Englewood Cliffs, NJ: Prentice-Hall.

Daskin, M. S., and E. H. Stern. 1981. A hierarchical objective set covering model for emergency medical service vehicle deployment. *Transportation Science* 15:137–152.

Davis, S. G., G. B. Kleindorfer, G. A. Kochenberger, E. T. Reutzel, and E.W.Brown. 1986. Strategic planning for bank operations with multiple check-processing locations. *Interfaces* 16/6:1–12.

Dearing, P. M., and R. L. Francis. 1974. A network flow solution to a multifacility minimax location problem involving rectilinear distances. *Transportation Science* 8:126–141.

Dohrn, P. J., and C. D. T. Watson-Gandy. 1973. Depot location with van salesmen-A practical approach. *OMEGA* 1:321–329.

Domschke, W., and A. Drexl. 1985. *Location and Layout Planning: An International Bibliography* Vol. 238. In: Lecture Notes in Economics and Mathematical Systems. Berlin: Springer-Verlag.

Donnay, J. D. H. 1945. *Spherical trigonometry.* New York: Interscience.

Drezner, Z. 1984. The planar two-center and two-median problems. *Transportation Science* 18:351–361.

Drezner, Z., and G. O. Wesolowsky. 1978a. Facility location on a sphere. *Journal of the Operational Research Society* 29:997–1004.

———. 1978b. A new method for the multifacility minimax location problem. *Journal of the Operational Research Society* 29:1095–1101.

———. 1980a. Single facility ℓ_p-distance minimax location. *SIAM Journal on Algebraic and Discrete Methods* 1:315–321.

———. 1980b. Optimal location of a facility relative to area demands. *Naval Research Logistics Quarterly* 27:199–206.

———. 1980c. A maximin location problem with maximum distance constraints. *AIIE Transactions* 12:249–252.

———. 1981. Optimum location probabilities in the ℓ_p distance Weber problem. *Transportation Science* 12:85–97.

Dutton, R., G. Hinman, and C. B. Millham. 1974. The optimal location of nuclear-power facilities in the Pacific Northwest. *Operations Research* 22:478–487.

Economides, S., and E. Fok. 1984. Warehouse relocation or modernization: Modeling the managerial dilemma. *Interfaces* 14/3:62–67.

Efroymson, M. A., and T. L. Ray. 1966. A branch-and-bound algorithm for plant location. *Operations Research* 14:361–368.

Eilon, S., C. D. T. Watson-Gandy, and N. Christofides. 1971. *Distribution management.* New York: Hafner.

Elshafei, A. N. 1977. Hospital layout as a quadratic assignment problem. *Operational Research Quarterly* 28:167–179.

El-Shaieb, A. M. 1973. A new algorithm for locating sources among destinations. *Management Science* 20:221–231.

Elzinga, J., and D. W. Hearn. 1972a. The minimum covering sphere problem. *Management Science* 19:96–104.

———. 1972b. Geometrical solutions for some minimax location problems. *Transportation Science* 4:379–394.

———. 1973. A note on a minimax location problem. *Transportation Science* 7:100–103.

———. 1983. On stopping rules for facilities location algorithms. *IIE Transactions* 15:81–83.

Elzinga, J., D. W. Hearn, and W. D. Randolph. 1976. Minimax multifacility location with Euclidean distances. *Transportation Science* 10:321–336.

Erlenkotter, D. 1977. Facility location with price-sensitive demands: Private, public, and quasi-public. *Management Science* 24:378–386.

———. 1978. A dual-based procedure for uncapacitated facility location. *Operations Research* 26:992–1009.

———. 1981. A comparative study of approaches to dynamic location problems. *European Journal of Operational Research* 6:133–143.

Eyster, J. W., J. A. White, and W. W. Wierwille. 1973. On solving multifacility location problems using a hyperboloid approximation procedure. *AIIE Transactions* 5:1–6.

Fitzsimmons, J. A., and L. A. Allen. 1983. A warehouse location model helps Texas comptroller select out-of-state audit offices. *Interfaces* 13/5:40–46.

Francis, R. L. 1963. A note on the optimum location of new machines in existing plant layouts. *The Journal of Industrial Engineering* 14:57–59.

———. 1964. On the location of multiple new facilities with respect to existing facilities. *The Journal of Industrial Engineering* 15:106–107.

———. 1967. Some aspects of a minimax location problem. *Operations Research* 15:1163–1168.

———. 1972. A geometrical solution procedure for a rectilinear distance minimax location problem. *AIIE Transactions* 4:328–332.

Francis, R. L., and A. V. Cabot. 1972. Properties of a multifacility location problem involving Euclidean distances. *Naval Research Logistics Quarterly* 19:335–353.

Francis, R. L., and J. M. Goldstein. 1974. Location theory: A selective bibliography. *Operations Research* 22:400–410.

Francis, R. L., L. F. McGinnis, and J. A. White. 1983. Locational analysis. *European Journal of Operational Research* 12:220–252.

Francis, R. L., and J. A. White. 1974. *Facility layout and location: An analytical approach.* Englewood Cliffs, NJ: Prentice-Hall.

Gavett, J. W., and N. V. Plyter. 1966. The optimal assignment of facilities to locations by branch and bound. *Operations Research* 14:210–232.

Gelb, B. D., and B. M. Khumawala. 1984. Reconfiguration of an insurance company's sales regions. *Interfaces* 14/6:87–94.

Gelders, L. F., L. M. Pintelon, and L. N. Van Wassenhove. 1987. A location-allocation problem in a large Belgian brewery. *European Journal of Operational Research* 28:196–206.

Geoffrion, A. M. 1971. Duality in nonlinear programming: A simplified applications-oriented development. *SIAM Review* 13:1–37.

———. 1975. A guide to computer-assisted methods for distribution systems planning. *Sloan Management Review* 16/2:17–41.

———. 1976a. Customer aggregation in distribution modeling. Western Management Science Institute Working Paper No. 259, UCLA, October.

———. 1976b. Better distribution planning with computer models. *Harvard Business Review* 54:92–99.

———. 1976c. The purpose of mathematical programming is insight, not numbers. *Interfaces* 7/1:81–92.

———. 1977a. Objective function approximations in mathematical programming. *Mathematical Programming* 13:23–37.

———. 1977b. A priori error bounds for procurement commodity aggregation in logistics planning models. *Naval Research Logistics Quarterly* 24:201–212.

Geoffrion, A. M., and G. W. Graves. 1974. Multicommodity distribution design by Benders decomposition. *Management Science* 20:822–844.

Geoffrion, A. M., G. W. Graves, and S. Lee. 1978. Strategic distribution system planning: A status report. In *Studies in operations management,* ed. A.Hax. New York: North Holland/American Elsevier.

———. 1983. A management support system for distribution planning. *INFOR* 20:287–314.

Geoffrion, A. M., and R. F. Powers. 1980. Facility location analysis is just the beginning (if you do it right). *Interfaces* 10/2:22–30.

———. 1981. Management support systems. *The Wharton Magazine* 5/3:26–35.

Geoffrion, A. M., and T. J. Van Roy. 1979. Caution: Common sense planning methods can be hazardous to your corporate health. *Sloan Management Review* 20/4:31–42.

Gilmore, P. C. 1962. Optimal and suboptimal algorithms for the quadratic assignment problem. *SIAM Journal on Applied Mathematics* 10:305–313.

Ginsburgh, V., and P. Hansen. 1974. Procedures for the reduction of errors in road network data. *Operational Research Quarterly* 25:321–322.

Graves, G. W., and A. B. Whinston. 1970. An algorithm for the quadratic assignment problem. *Management Science* 16:453–471.

Hall, Kenneth M. 1970. An *r*-dimensional quadratic placement algorithm. *Management Science* 17:219–229.

Handler, G. Y., and P. B. Mirchandani. 1979. *Location on networks: Theory and algorithms.* Cambridge, MA: MIT Press.

Hansen, P., D. Peeters, and J. F. Thisse. 1983. Public facility location models: A selective survey. In *Location analysis of public facilities,* eds. J. F. Thisse and H. G. Zoller. Amsterdam: North Holland.

Hansen, P., J. Perreur, and J. F. Thisse. 1980. Location theory, dominance and convexity: Some further results. *Operations Research* 28:1241–1250.

Hansen, P., and J. F. Thisse. 1983. Recent advances in continuous location theory. *Sistemi Urbani* 1:33–54.

Hardy, G. H., J. E. Littlewood, and G. Polya. 1952. *Inequalities.* London: Cambridge University Press.

Harvey, M. E., M. S. Hung, and J. R. Brown. 1973. The application of a p-median algorithm to the identification of nodal hierarchies and growth centers. *Economic Geography* 50:187–202.

Hearn, D. H., and J. Vijay. 1982. Efficient algorithms for the (weighted) minimum circle problem. *Operations Research* 30:777–795.

Hertz, D. B., and R. T. Eddison, (eds.). 1964. *Progress in operations research, vol.II,* 110–113. New York: Wiley.

Hillier, F. S., and M. Connors. 1966. Quadratic assignment algorithms and the location of indivisible facilities. *Management Science* 13:42–57.

Hogan, K., and C. ReVelle. 1986. Concepts and applications of backup coverage. *Management Science* 11:1434–1444.

Juel, H. 1975. Properties of location models. Ph.D. Dissertation, University of Wisconsin-Madison.

―――. 1984. On a rational stopping rule for facilities location algorithms. *Naval Research Logistics Quarterly* 31:9–11.

Juel, H., and R. F. Love. 1976. An efficient computational procedure for solving multi-facility rectilinear facilities location problems. *Operational Research Quarterly* 27:697–703.

―――. 1980. Sufficient conditions for optimal facility locations to coincide. *Transportation Science* 14:125–129.

―――. 1981a. On the dual of the linearly constrained multi-facility location problem with arbitrary norms. *Transportation Science* 15:329–337.

―――. 1981b. Fixed point optimality criteria for the location problem with arbitrary norms. *Journal of the Operational Research Society* 32:891–897.

―――. 1983a. The solution of location problems with certain existing facility structures. *INFOR* 21:145–150.

―――. 1983b. Hull properties in location problems. *European Journal of Operational Research* 12:262–265.

Katz, I. N. 1969. On the convergence of a numerical scheme for solving some locational equilibrium problems. *SIAM Journal of Applied Mathematics* 17:1224–1231.

———. 1974. Local convergence in Fermat's problem. *Mathematical Programming* 6:89–104.

Katz, I. N., and L. Cooper. 1974. An always-convergent numerical scheme for a random locational equilibrium problem. *SIAM Journal of Numerical Analysis* 17:683–693.

———. 1976. Normally and exponentially distributed locational equilibrium problems. *Journal of Research of the National Bureau of Standards* 80B:53–73.

———. 1980. Optimal location on a sphere. *Computers and Mathematics with Applications* 6:175–196.

Kaufman, L., and F. Broeckx. 1978. An algorithm for the quadratic assignment problem using Benders decomposition. *European Journal of Operational Research,* 2:204–211.

Keeney, R. L. 1980. *Siting energy facilities.* New York: Academic Press.

Kermack, K. A., and J. B. S. Haldane. 1950. Organic correlation and allometry. *Biometrika* 37:30–41.

Khumawala, B. M. 1972. An efficient branch and bound algorithm for the warehouse location problem. *Management Science* 18:718–731.

Kleindorfer, G. B., G. A. Kochenberger, and E. T. Reutzel. 1981. Computing inter-site distances for routing and scheduling problems. *Operations Research Letters* 1:31–33.

Kolen, A. J. W. 1986. Tree network and planar rectilinear location theory. Amsterdam: CWI Tract 25, CWI.

Kolesar, P., and W. E. Walker. 1974. An algorithm for the dynamic relocation of fire companies. *Operations Research* 22:249–274.

Kolesar, P., W. E. Walker, and J. Hausner. 1975. Determining the relation between fire engine travel times and travel distances in New York City. *Operations Research* 23:614–627.

Krarup, J., and P. M. Pruzan. 1983. The simple plant location problem: Survey and synthesis. *European Journal of Operational Research* 12:36–81.

Kuehn, A. A., and M. J. Hamburger. 1963. A heuristic program for locating warehouses. *Management Science* 10:643–666.

Kuenne, R. E., and R. M. Soland. 1972. Exact and approximate solution to the multisource Weber problem. *Mathematical Programming* 3:193–209.

Kuhn, H. W. 1967. On a pair of dual nonlinear problems. In *Nonlinear programming,* chapter 3, ed. J. Abadie. New York: Wiley.

———. 1973. A note on Fermat's problem. *Mathematical Programming* 4:98–107.

———. 1976. Nonlinear programming: An historical view. *SIAM-AMS Proceedings* 9:1–26.

Kusiak, A., and S. S. Heragu. 1987. The facility layout problem. *European Journal of Operational Research* 29:229–251.

Land, A. H. 1963. A problem of assignment with interrelated costs. *Operational Research Quarterly* 14:185–198.

Laporte, G., Y. Nobert, and P. Pelletier. 1983. Hamiltonian location problems. *European Journal of Operational Research* 12:82–89.

Larson, R. C. 1974. A hypercube queuing model for facility location and redistricting in urban emergency services. *Computers and Operations Research* 1:67–95.

Larson, R. C., and A. R. Odoni. 1981. *Urban operations research.* Englewood Cliffs, NJ: Prentice-Hall.

Lawler, E. L. 1963. The quadratic assignment problem. *Management Science* 9:586–599.

Lawson, C. L. 1965. The smallest covering cone or sphere. *SIAM Review* 7:415–417.

Leamer, E. E. 1968. Locational equilibria. *Journal of Regional Science* 8:229–242.

Litwhiler, D. W. 1977. Large region location problems. Ph.D. Dissertation, The University of Oklahoma.

Litwhiler, D. W., and A. A. Aly. 1979. Large region location problems. *Computers and Operations Research* 6:1–12.

Love, R. F. 1967a. The location of single facilities in three-dimensional space by nonlinear programming. *Journal of the Canadian Operational Research Society* 5:136–143.

———. 1967b. A note on the convexity of siting depots. *The International Journal of Production Research* 6:153–154.

———. 1969. Locating facilities in three-dimensional space by convex programming. *Naval Research Logistics Quarterly* 16:503–516.

———. 1972. A computational procedure for optimally locating a facility with respect to several rectangular regions. *Journal of Regional Science* 12:233–242.

———. 1974. The dual of a hyperbolic approximation to the generalized constrained multifacility location problem with ℓ_p distances. *Management Science* 21:22–33.

———. 1976. One-dimensional facility location-allocation using dynamic programming. *Management Science* 22:614–617.

Love, R. F., and P. D. Dowling. 1985. Optimal weighted ℓ_p norm parameters for facilities layout distance characteristics. *Management Science* 31:200–206.

———. 1986. A generalized bounding method for facilities location models. *Research and Working Paper Series No. 250,* Faculty of Business, McMaster University.

Love, R. F., and H. Juel. 1982. Properties and solution methods for large location-allocation problems. *Journal of the Operational Research Society* 33:443–452.

———. 1983. Hull properties in location problems. *European Journal of Operational Research* 12:262–265.

Love, R. F., and S. A. Kraemer. 1973. A dual decomposition method for minimizing transportation costs in multifacility location problems. *Transportation Science* 7:297–316.

Love, R. F., and J. G. Morris. 1972. Modelling inter-city road distances by mathematical functions. *Operational Research Quarterly* 23:61–71.

———. 1975a. A computational procedure for the exact solution of location-allocation problems with rectangular distances. *Naval Research Logistics Quarterly* 22:441–453.

———. 1975b. Solving constrained multi-facility location problems involving ℓ_p distances using convex programming. *Operations Research* 23:581–587.

———. 1979. Mathematical models of road travel distances. *Management Science* 25:130–139.

Love, R. F., W. G. Truscott, and J. H. Walker. 1985. Terminal location problem: A case study supporting the *status quo*. *Journal of the Operational Research Society* 36:131–136.

Love, R. F., G. O. Wesolowsky, and S. A. Kraemer. 1973. A multi-facility minimax location method for Euclidean distances. *International Journal of Production Research* 11:37–45.

Love, R. F., and J. Y. Wong. 1976a. Solving quadratic assignment problems with rectangular distances and integer programming. *Naval Research Logistics Quarterly* 23:623–627.

———. 1976b. On solving a one-dimensional space allocation problem with integer programming. *INFOR* 14:139–143.

Love, R. F., and W. Y. Yeong. 1981. A stopping rule for facilities location algorithms. *AIIE Transactions* 13:357–362.

Love, R. F., and L. Yerex. 1976. Application of a facilities location model in the prestressed concrete industry. *Interfaces* 6/4:45–49.

MacKinnon, R. D., and G. M. Barber. 1972. A new approach to network generation and map representation: The linear case of the location-allocation problem. *Geographical Analysis* 4:156–168.

Mairs, T. G., G. W. Wakefield, E. L. Johnson, and K. Spielberg. 1978. On a production allocation and distribution problem. *Management Science* 24:1622–1630.

Manne, A. S. 1964. Plant location under economies of scale—decentralization and computation. *Management Science* 11:213–235.

Marucheck, A. S., and A. A. Aly. 1981. An efficient algorithm for the location-allocation problem with rectangular regions. *Naval Research Logistics Quarterly* 28:309–323.

Mavrides, L. P. 1979. An indirect method for the generalized *k*-median problem applied to lock-box location. *Management Science* 25:990–996.

Miehle, W. 1958. Link-length minimization in networks. *Operations Research* 6:232–243.

Minieka, E. 1970. The *m*-center problem. *SIAM Review* 12:138–139.

Morris, J. G. 1973. A linear programming approach to the solution of constrained multi-facility minimax location problems where distances are rectangular. *Operational Research Quarterly* 24:419–435.

———. 1978. On the extent to which certain fixed-charge depot location problems can be solved by LP. *Journal of the Operational Research Society* 29:71–76.

———. 1981. Convergence of the Weiszfeld algorithm for Weber problems using a generalized "distance" function. *Operations Research* 29:37–48.

————. 1982. Lawson's algorithm for p-norm minimax facility problems. Paper presented at the Joint National Meeting of ORSA/TIMS, San Diego.

Morris, J. G., and J. P. Norback. 1980. A simple approach to linear facility location. *Transportation Science* 14:1–8.

Morris, J. G., and W. A. Verdini. 1979. A simple iterative scheme for solving minisum facility location problems involving ℓ_p distances. *Operations Research* 27:1180–1188.

Nair, K. P. K., and R. Chandrasekaran. 1971. Optimal location of a single service center of certain types. *Naval Research Logistics Quarterly* 18:503–510.

Nauss, R. M., and R. E. Markland. 1981. Optimizing procedure for lock-box analysis. *Management Science* 27:855–865.

Nugent, C. E., T. E. Vollmann, and J. Ruml. 1968. An experimental comparison of techniques for the assignment of facilities to locations. *Operations Research* 16:150–173.

O'Kelly, M. E. 1986. The location of interacting hub facilities. *Transportation Science* 20:92–106.

Ostresh, L. M., Jr. 1973. TWAIN-Exact solution to the two-source location-allocation problem. In *Computer programs for location-allocation problems*, eds. G. Rushton, M. F. Goodchild, and L. M. Ostresh, Jr. Iowa City: Monograph No. 6, Department of Geography, University of Iowa.

————. 1975. An efficient algorithm for solving the two center location-allocation problem. *Journal of Regional Science* 15:209–216.

————. 1977. The multifacility location problem: Applications and descent theorems. *Journal of Regional Science* 17:409–419.

————. 1978. On the convergence of a class of iterative methods for solving the Weber location problem. *Operations Research* 26:597–609.

Pardalos, P. M., and J. B. Rosen. 1986. Methods for concave minimization: A bibliographic survey. *SIAM Review* 28:367–379.

Pearson, K. 1901. On lines and planes of closest fit to systems of points in space. *Philosophical Magazine and Journal of Science*, Sixth Series 2:559–572.

Perreur, J., and J. Thisse. 1974. Central metrics and optimal location. *Journal of Regional Science* 14:411–421.

Pierce, J. F., and W. B. Crowston. 1971. Tree search algorithms in quadratic assignment problems. *Naval Research Logistics Quarterly* 18:1–36.

Planchart, A., and A. Hurter, Jr. 1975. An efficient algorithm for the solution of the Weber problem with mixed norms. *SIAM Journal of Control* 13:650–665.

Plane, D. R., and T. E. Hendrick. 1977. Mathematical programming and the location of fire companies for the Denver Fire Department. *Operations Research* 25:563–578.

Pritsker, A. A. B., and P. M. Ghare. 1970. Locating new facilities with respect to existing facilities. *AIIE Transactions* 2:290–297. Errata and revisions in *AIIE Transactions* 1971; 3:158–159.

Rao, M. R. 1973. On the direct search approach to the rectilinear facilities location problem. *AIIE Transactions* 5:256–264.

ReVelle, C., and R. Swain. 1970. Central facilities location. *Geographical Analysis* 2:30–42.

Ritzman, L. P. 1972. The efficiency of computer algorithms for plant layout. *Management Science* 18:240–248.

Roodman, G. M., and L. B. Schwarz. 1977. Extensions of the multi-period facility phase-out model: New procedures and applications to a phase-in/phase-out problem. *AIIE Transactions* 9:103–107.

Schilling, D., D. J. Elzinga, J. Cohon, R. Church, and C. ReVelle. 1979. The team/fleet models for simultaneous facility and equipment siting. *Transportation Science* 13:163–175.

Schrage, L. 1975. Implicit representation of variable upper bounds in linear programming. *Mathematical Programming Study* 4:118–132.

Scott, A. J. 1971. *Combinatorial programming, spatial analysis and planning.* London: Methuen.

Scriabin, M., and R. C. Vergin. 1975. Comparison of computer algorithms and visual based methods for plant layout. *Management Science* 22:172–181.

Sherali, A. D., and C. M. Shetty. 1977. The rectilinear distance location-allocation problem. *AIIE Transactions* 9:136–143.

Späth, H. 1978. Explizite losung des dreidimensonalen minimax-standortproblems in der city-block-distanz. *Zeitschrift fur Operations Research* 22:229–237.

Spielberg, K. 1969. An algorithm for the simple plant location problem with some side conditions. *Operations Research* 17:85–111.

Steinberg, L. 1961. The backboard wiring problem: A placement algorithm. *SIAM Review* 3:37–50.

Sylvester, J. J. 1857. A question in the geometry of the situation. *Quarterly Journal of Pure and Applied Mathematics* 1:79.

———. 1860. On Poncelet's approximate linear valuation of surd forms. *Philosophical Magazine* 20/Fourth Series:203–222.

Thisse, J. F., J. E. Ward, and R. E. Wendell. 1984. Some properties of location problems with block and round norms. *Operations Research* 32:1309–1327.

Toregas, C., and C. ReVelle. 1973. Binary logic solutions to a class of location problems. *Geographical Analysis* 5:145–155.

Toregas, C., R. Swain, C. ReVelle, and L. Bergman. 1971. The location of emergency service facilities. *Operations Research* 19:1363–1373.

Urquhart, M. 1977. Pipe fabrication shop layout. Undergraduate Thesis, Department of Mechanical Engineering, University of Waterloo, Spring Semester.

Van Roy, T. J., and D. Erlenkotter. 1982. Dual-based procedure for dynamic facility location. *Management Science* 28:1091–1105.

Vergin, R. C., and J. D. Rogers. 1967. An algorithm and computational procedure for locating economic facilities. *Management Science* 13:256–264.

Walker, W. 1974. Using the set-covering problem to assign fire companies to fire houses. *Operations Research* 22:275–277.

Walker, W., J. M. Chaiken, and E. J. Ignall, eds. 1980. *Fire department deployment analysis: A public policy analysis case study.* New York: Elsevier/North-Holland.

Ward, J. E., and R. E. Wendell. 1980. A new norm for measuring distance which yields linear location problems. *Operations Research* 28:836–844.

Weber, A. 1909. *Ueber den standort der industrien.* Tübingen (English translation: Friedrich, C. J. (translator) 1929. Theory of the location of industries. Chicago: University of Chicago Press).

Weiszfeld, E. 1936. Sur un problème de minimum dans l'espace. *Tôhoku Mathematical Journal* 42:274–280.

———. 1937. Sur le point lequel la somme des distances de *n* points donnés est minimum. *Tôhoku Mathematical Journal* 43:355–386.

Wendell, R. E., and A. P. Hurter. 1973. Location theory, dominance, and convexity. *Operations Research* 21:314–320.

Wendell, R. E., A. P. Hurter, and T. J. Lowe. 1977. Efficient points in location problems. *AIIE Transactions* 9:338–346.

Wersan, S. J., J. E. Quon, and A. Charnes. 1962. Systems analysis of refuse collection and disposable practices. *American Public Works Association, Yearbook*:195–211.

Wesolowsky, G. O. 1970. Facilities location using rectangular distances. Ph.D. Dissertation, University of Wisconsin-Madison.

———. 1972. Rectangular distance location under the minimax optimality criterion. *Transportation Science* 6:103–113.

———. 1973. Dynamic facility location. *Management Science* 19:1241–1247.

———. 1974. Location of the median line for weighted points. *Environment and Planning A* 7:163–170.

———. 1977. The Weber problem with rectangular distances and randomly distributed destinations. *Journal of Regional Science* 17:53–60.

———. 1982. Location problems on a sphere. *Regional Science and Urban Economics* 12:495–508.

Wesolowsky, G. O., and R. F. Love. 1971a. Location of facilities with rectangular distances among point and area destinations. *Naval Research Logistics Quarterly* 18:83–90.

———. 1971b. The optimal location of new facilities using rectangular distances. *Operations Research* 19:124–130.

———. 1972. A nonlinear approximation method for solving a generalized rectangular distances Weber problem. *Management Science* 18:656–663.

Wesolowsky, G. O., and W. G. Truscott. 1975. The multiperiod location-allocation problem with relocation of facilities. *Management Science* 22:57–65.

Westwood, J. B. 1977. A transport planning model for primary distribution. *Interfaces* 8/1:1–10.

White, J. A. 1971. A note on the quadratic facility location problem. *AIIE Transactions* 3:156–157.

Wimmert, R. J. 1958. A mathematical model of equipment location. *The Journal of Industrial Engineering* 9:498–505.

Witzgall, C. 1964. Optimal location of a central facility: Mathematical models and concepts. *National Bureau of Standards Report 8388,* Gaithersberg, Maryland.

Wolfe, P. 1961. A duality theorem for non-linear programming. *Quarterly Journal of Applied Mathematics* 19:239–244.

Woolsey, R. E. D. 1986. The fifth column: On the minimization of need for new facilities, or space wars, lack of presence, and Delphi. *Interfaces* 16/5:53–55.

Wyman, Samuel D. III, and L. G. Callahan. 1975. Evaluation of computerized layout algorithms for use in design of control panel layouts. In *Proceedings, Fourteenth Annual U.S. Army Operations Research Symposium,* Fort Lee, Virginia, November, Vol. 2, 993–1002, Maryland: Director, U.S. Army Material Systems Analysis Activity, Aberdeen Proving Ground.

Index